IN PURSUIT OF HONOR AND POWER

IN PURSUIT OF HONOR

AND POWER

NOBLEMEN OF

THE SOUTHERN CROSS

IN NINETEENTH-CENTURY

BRAZIL

EUL-SOO PANG

The University of Alabama Press

Tuscaloosa and London

Copyright © 1988 by
The University of Alabama Press
Tuscaloosa, Alabama 35487
All rights reserved
Manufactured in the United States of America

Library of Congress Cataloging-in-Publication Data
Pang, Eul-Soo
In pursuit of honor and power.
Bibliography: p.
Includes index.
1. Brazil—Nobility—History—19th century.
2. Brazil—Economic conditions—19th century. I. Title.
HT653.B65P36   1988   305.5′223′0981   86-7081
ISBN 0-8173-0317-0

British Library Cataloguing-in-Publication Data is available.

TO LAURA

Contents

Preface

A few words are in order on the designation of nobiliary titles and the evolution of Portuguese orthography.

The most common error in identifying several nobles with the same names, such as Rio Branco, São Francisco, Rio das Contas, and so forth, has been assigning the order of First, Second, and Third in front of the title-name. The recent rectification by the research personnel of the National Archives, in Rio de Janeiro, headed by José Gabriel da Costa Pinto and Rui Vieira da Cunha, both accomplished heraldic genealogists, calls for the numerical designation *only* when both titles and names are identical. Thus, it is justified to refer to the "First Barão do Rio das Contas" and the "Second Barão do Rio das Contas," but, according to the archival research staff, not the "First Visconde do Rio Branco" and the "Second Barão do Rio Branco." Because I have chosen to follow this new rule adopted by the National Archives of Brazil, the reader will find that my designation of titles and names by number differs from that in Carlos G. Rheingantz's *Titulares do império* (Rio, 1960), the standard listing of Brazilian imperial titles. That work also suffers from some omissions as well as errors in the birthplaces of some of the nobles. The Barão do Rio Branco, the renowned diplomat and patron of the Brazilian foreign service during the first half of the Old Republic, does not even appear in the book.

Unlike Spanish orthography, that of Brazilian Portuguese has gone through several changes. The modern spelling mode has been pre-

served in the text and tables, but in the Notes and Bibliography the original forms have been retained in deference to scholarly accuracy. To say
the least, this is confusing. Afonso de E. Taunay, the noted historian of
São Paulo, spelled his name four different ways: Affonso de Escragnolle
Taunay, Affonso de E. Taunay, Afonso de E. Taunay, and Affonso d'E.
Taunay. As a rule, I have modernized Luso-Brazilian names, including
both given and surnames, in accordance with Lei 5705 of 18 December
1971: for example, "Luís," not "Luiz" and "Vasconcelos," not "Vasconcellos," and likewise with baronesa/baroneza, Iguaçu/Iguassu, açúcar/
assucar, and so forth. In the case of non-Luso-Brazilian proper names,
however, I have retained their original spellings; hence, "Ottoni," not
"Otoni."

Acknowledgments

Various Brazilian and North American scholars, genealogists, and archivists were of invaluable assistance to me while I was writing this book. José Gabriel da Costa Pinto, Rui Vieira da Cunha, Jaime Antunes da Silva, and Hamilton de Mattos Monteiro, all of the Arquivo Nacional, in Rio de Janeiro (and the latter a professor of history at the Universidade de Brasília since 1979), provided special guidance in archival materials and in tracking down descendants of old families. Staff members of the Instituto Histórico e Geográfico Brasileiro, the Biblioteca Nacional, and the Itamarati Library, in Rio, were of considerable help as well. Maria Amélia dos Miguéis, formerly of the Museu Imperial and now with Casa Rui Barbosa, granted me access to numerous personal archives of the imperial household in Petrópolis.

My research was also conducted in São Paulo, Minas Gerais, Brasília, Bahia, Pernambuco, and Goiás, all of which contained many of the vital materials that went into this book. It was a particular pleasure to research outside such metropolises as Rio and São Paulo. My fondest memories of good "hunts" occurred not in the well organized archives and historical institutes of the large cities, but in courthouses in Valença, Santo Amaro, Leopoldina, Itu, Goiás Velho, and Goiânia. Many of the archival staffs of these places were walking deposits of local history, myths, and oral traditions that they were willing to share with me. Although I cannot possibly name them all, I extend my deep appreciation for their assistance.

My original field trip to Brazil for this project was financed by a National Endowment for the Humanities Research Fellowship in 1977.

The American Philosophical Society (1978), the Universidade Federal de Goiás (1979, a visiting professorship), and the Faculty Research Council of the Graduate School of the University of Alabama at Birmingham (1980) provided funds that enabled me to travel back to Brazil for additional research. In addition to these field trips, the deans of the Graduate School and my own School of Social and Behavioral Sciences furnished me funds to visit Washington, D.C., and Salt Lake City to check out additional secondary materials as well as parish birth, baptism, marriage, and death registries. Chapters 6 and 9 were based on both probate court records in Brazil and parish vital statistics of various counties and cities of Brazil that are contained in the Mormon archives in Utah.

My thanks are also expressed to the two unnamed outside evaluators for The University of Alabama Press. Their constructive comments helped me immensely in the final reorganization and revision of this book.

I owe a special debt to my wife, Laura Jarnagin Pang, who first researched and wrote a master's thesis as Laura Jarnagin on "The Role and Structure of the Brazilian Imperial Nobility in Society and Politics," for the Latin American Studies Program at Vanderbilt University. This work is now a lengthy article of the same title (also by Laura Jarnagin) in the *Anais do Museu Paulista* 29 (1979). She has not only enthusiastically supported my book project but has also been a rich fount of information. Her doctoral dissertation on the Brazilian agricultural societies of the nineteenth century has further enlightened me in the areas of planter and merchant interests in the export agriculture of Brazil. Her field work in 1977–78 overlapped with my own, and we were able to collaborate on our projects in Brazil.

The manuscript was typed by Jeanne Holloway, who demonstrated a considerable amount of Oriental patience through the various revisions. Particularly appreciated was her enthusiastic support throughout the final phases of manuscript preparation. Finally, I thank former Dean George Passey and current Dean Blaine A. Brownell, of the School of Social and Behavioral Sciences, the University of Alabama at Birmingham, who generously funded the preparation and revision of this work.

Eul-Soo Pang
Evergreen, Colorado

IN PURSUIT OF HONOR AND POWER

Introduction

The Brazilian nobility was a unique institution in several respects. First, it was not a formal corporation of elite as in the feudal monarchies and their successors in the Old World, but its members were readily identifiable and occupied prominent positions of power and wealth in a capitalist society. Their titles were in essence badges of an officially selected elite. Second, Brazilian titles were for *one life only* and could be passed on to subsequent generations only if the emperor explicitly rechartered them. They carried no stipend, afforded no public office, and granted no special juridical privileges. Yet, tens of thousands of Brazilians sought nobiliary honors.[1] Third, the total universe of the "noblemen of the Southern Cross" was quite small: a total of 980 men and women held 1,278 titles, according to the most reliable source. Out of a nation of 14 million (as of 1889), these few played crucial roles as the empire's leading landowners, merchants, politicians, generals and admirals, diplomats, intellectuals, and high priests of the Catholic church.

Fourth, the importance of the institution did not lie in its corporate status, but rather in its institutional impact on society and polity. Titleholders came from all walks of life, but the ennobled tended to represent the elite segment of each profession, class, and region. Being a noble in the empire indicated that the titleholder possessed either money or influence or both in a rigidly stratified society. A title constituted a special honor to the holders in that it represented *ab extra* recognition from the patrimonial Crown that was not easily available to other members of their own class and profession. Fifth, in spite of the closed nature of Brazilian society, the nobility was a remarkably open institution, contrary to the original intent of the founder, Dom João VI. This can be attributed to the inability of Brazilian nobles to lay any legitimate claims to being descendants of Portuguese *fidalgos* or nobles, as well as their desire to erase the parvenu past by ennobling acquired wealth and social station. Also, society and economy were in the midst of transformation, as Atlantic world-capitalism began to stimulate broad changes in all levels. In brief, a title represented the ultimate, formal recognition of the transformed family, professional, and class status that social convention had neglected to bestow. The inherent contradiction was that such feudal distinctions came about during the throes of Brazil's capitalist transformation.

This book is divided into three principal sections, each consisting of three chapters, plus Introduction and Conclusion. Chapters 1 and 2 provide the setting in which this New World nobility came into being by examining the forces and circumstances that shaped Brazil from late colonial times through independence and into the 1840s. The founders and shapers of the nobility were three Braganza monarchs: João VI, Pedro I, and Pedro II. Their life-styles, thoughts, and actions left indelible marks on the institution, and often served as both desirable and undesirable role models for future nobles. João led an urbane but self-indulgent life. He ate too much, spent too much, and gave too little. His son, Pedro I, was almost the exact opposite. He pursued an ostentatious, imperious way of living that was peppered with casual "Don Juan-like" conquests. By contrast, his son, Pedro II, the American Braganza, graced the court with a simple, austere but respectable life. Chapter 3 probes the varied origins of the "noblemen of the Southern Cross" by analyzing the class distinctions of the candidates, the rationale for the creation and rejection of titles by the Braganza monarchs, and the regional distribution of the honors throughout the empire.

Chapters 4 and 5 analyze the formation of the regional economic elites, principally capitalist landed and mercantile groups, that succeeded in obtaining titles and honors from the five demographically and economically important provinces of the two major regions: the sugar-growing northern (today's northeastern) provinces of Pernambuco and Bahia; and the coffee-producing south-central provinces of Rio (plus the court), Minas Gerais, and São Paulo. Together, these five contained more than 80 percent of the nation's population and accounted for an equal portion of titles throughout the nineteenth century; they were also the economic epicenter of the country. These two chapters also depict the differences in the elite's mentalities: the capital-risking, profit-seeking entrepreneurial capitalists as opposed to the status-quo-conscious, tradition-bound landowners. The former group was comprised of "gentry" landowners, merchants, and urban professionals; the latter, of aristocratic planters and their purveyors. These two types were found throughout Brazil, but evidence is strong that coffee planters in the south-central provinces tended to be more gentry-minded and therefore more entrepreneurial in their use of capital, labor, and land than the northern sugar planters.

Chapter 6 measures the wealth of noble families by examining their marriage strategies, clan patronages, and godparent bonding systems in baptism and marriage rituals. These ritual bonds were often an important means for families to protect and preserve as well as to diversify and expand their bases of wealth. Significant regional differences also help to distinguish gentry from aristocrat.

Chapter 7 reveals how imperial honors were debased through politicization and commercialization (the sale of titles, or "vanity financing," a major source for supporting favorite imperial charities). As capitalism began to pervade Brazil, a peripheral economy of the Atlantic world-system, wealth replaced inherited social position as a major yardstick for determining class status. These practices contributed to diluting the principal intent of the nobiliary system, which originally purported to recognize the meritorious who rendered "service to the State and Humanity." Titles and other imperial honors were also increasingly used by politicians to reward their supporters, a tendency that became more pronounced during the second half of the nineteenth century. For personal and political reasons, many rejected such offers.

Chapter 8 is a study of "Who ruled the empire?" As a single group, the nobility of both agrarian and mercantile origins failed to dominate the monarchy, a fact challenging the historiographical assumption that the economic elite always ruled politically. Perhaps this is a distinction that makes monarchical Brazil different from republican Chile or Mexico. Instead, the empire devised a system of career political servants, or mandarins, who were often detached from their economic base and made dependent on imperial favors for their livelihood and career advancement. This system worked well initially, but began to show signs of aging and faltering as Brazil evolved economically, thus sharpening class and regional distinctions toward the end of the century. Concurrently, the political power of the centripetal monarchy expanded by fortifying the state apparatus, as the economy became more capitalistic, therefore specialized and diversified. The monoclass domination of politics practically ceased to exist at the close of the Paraguayan War in 1870. Thus, political mandarins were often well rewarded with nobiliary titles and honors.

Chapter 9 examines the vagaries of the nobiliary families of the rich and poor by demonstrating that the noblemen of the Southern Cross were no more immune to the rapid capitalistic changes of Brazilian society and economy than was the rest of the nation. Therefore, this study is also a microcosm of the Brazilian imperial elite as a whole.

What is unique about this work is its analysis of a situation where a feudal institution (nobility) was implanted during the age of capitalism (the nineteenth century) in a New World state that was rapidly experiencing transformation from an imperial colony to a peripheral dependent economy of the Atlantic world-system. During that century, Brazil created a premier coffee and sugar export economy. Its social and political systems were subject to persistent changes. The weak state system introduced in the early part of the century gave way to a centripetalist apparatus based on a growing but still partially differentiated bureaucracy; the monocultural economies of coffee in the Center-South and sugar in the North first fragmented the nation, but by 1870 began to precipitate integration. The state intervened in railroad building, importing technology and immigrant labor for commercial agriculture, and promoting related modernization projects. By the last two decades of the century, the rhythm of industrialization had begun to accelerate: in São Paulo, the number of industrial enterprises increased threefold in ten years (1885–95), from 150 to 452. Such economic diversification, accompanied by urbanization, further undermined feudal values, now much eroded but strong enough to support the nobiliary institution. In brief, the failure of the imperial nobility as a system can be attributed to the inherent contradictions of the time and place: when and where it was seeded. The nobility was introduced at the wrong time and in the wrong place.

This profile of the Brazilian elite has been reconstructed from both archival data and secondary sources. It reveals that landowners constituted the single richest group in the country during the nineteenth century, particularly the titled nobiliary landowners. But the richest *individuals* were merchants. The Mesquita clan of Rio was the wealthiest: one of its members left a staggering 9.919:903$. The richest merchant in northern Brazil was from the Marinho clan of Bahia. One heiress in the family left an estate of 5.862:000$. Coffee planters in the south-central provinces often invested portions of their wealth in non-agrarian activities, such as urban transportation; textile, shoe, and food-processing factories; banks; and even trade.[2] Such wealth diversification was virtually unknown among and unpracticed by the plantocracy of the North. A stepped-up transfer of wealth in the coffee-growing region during the 1870s and 1880s became a major source of industrialization in the south-central region.

My research also shows that, though it was true that the agrarian class controlled most of the nation's wealth, the society devised ways to impose a considerably more "democratic" distribution of wealth than historians have so far believed. After 1842 the empire allowed both legitimate and legitimized as well as natural children to hold shares of their parents' wealth. In spite of the persistent age-old Latin custom of marrying "inward"—family endogamy as opposed to class endogamy—the abolition of mortmain in 1835 and the adoption of new inheritance legislation made it difficult for traditional families to retain their wealth and power. Among the landowners, the tendency to marry cousins and close relatives continued as a means of preventing the unwarranted dissipation of wealth. However, this negatively affected estate management and hence wealth diversification over the long run. Such a family strategy reinforced the stagnant mentality of status quoism and discouraged the capitalistic use of resources. A close examination of the parish records of baptism, marriage, and god-parenting in the city of São Paulo shows that in the 1870s marrying "outward" was widely practiced among urban merchants and professionals as well as among the landed gentry of the interior. This reinforced the emerging class bonds, built new ties with different classes, and even created a new integrated class that had linkages with merchants, landowners, bankers, and politicians, of both Brazilian and immigrant origins.

In addition to discussing the two contrasting patterns of wealth management and family strategies, I argue that agriculture as a whole began to show signs of becoming "capitalistic" in the nineteenth century, especially after 1830, when the country was fully incorporated into the Atlantic world-economy as the principal supplier of coffee and reemerged as a major producer of sugar. I am well aware of the early 1960s Marxist debate over the "transition from feudalism to capitalism" as well as the impact of its inconclusive outcome on Latin American scholarship. Historians of Brazil have traditionally accepted the Marxist notion that capitalism and slavery (by extension, a slave economy) did not mix; they were mutually antagonistic and exclusive. But such a view has been challenged by more empirical research. Now, it is fair to say that the tide has been slowly turning in favor of the view that Brazilian export agriculture in the nineteenth century was a "capitalistic" institution.[3]

By "capitalist agriculture"—a concept used throughout this book—I mean an economic system that not only allows private ownership of production factors, such as land, capital, labor, and ancillary means of production, but which also institutionalizes the process of maximizing profit by risking production factors. My contention is that Brazil had such a system during the period under study. The backbone of the nation's economy in the nineteenth century was slavery—involuntary, coerced labor. According to one Marxist test, an economy based on coerced labor cannot pass as capitalistic. I disagree with that. My contention, shared with Wallerstein, is that a mixed form of labor regimes was a fundamental characteristic of world capitalism. It was more likely for the "periphery" to have coerced labor, while the "core" utilized free labor. Perhaps "semiperipheries," such as Brazil or the antebellum United States, were conducive to both systems prevailing simultaneously, albeit only temporarily during the transitional period.[4] By the late 1870s and the early 1880s, evidence abounds that on the coffee plantations in northern and western São Paulo province and the sugar refineries (engenhos centrais) of northern Brazil, free laborers often worked side by side with slaves. This is an unchallengeable fact.

Therefore, the concept of capitalist agriculture used herein emphasizes the extent of the use of production factors by the elite—how decisions to use capital, free and servile labor, land, and other production factors were made—instead of the labor system. In this context, the agrarian nobility in the North exhibited less of a tendency to apply capital, labor, land, and means of production to maximize economic gains than the south-central coffee planters. Naturally, there were exceptions. Those slavocratic sugar planters who founded refineries in the 1870s and 1880s were one such group. Therefore, if the primary purpose of holding land, capital, and labor served to reinforce the social status of the elite, it is argued that the elite exhibited an "aristocratic mentality" in wealth management. Conversely, if the use of these elements was devoted to profit, it is argued that the user reflected "gentry mentality."

The terms "bourgeois" and "bourgeoisie" are eschewed in this book both for ideological and etymological reasons. "Bourgeois" is most often used to describe societies that transformed economies and polities from feudalism to capitalism, such as the nations of Western Europe, as well as in societies where considerable urban development took place. Such a process did not take place in Brazil during the period under study. When talking about a rural and agrarian society like that in Brazil, "bourgeois" is hardly an appropriate concept because it literally means an urban dweller who exhibits the characteristics of an urban economic being. The distinction between aristocratic and gentry behavior will be discussed further throughout this book and will be one of the several analytical elements that distinguishes the complex nature of the Brazilian imperial nobility.

PART I

ESTABLISHMENT OF THE BRAGANZA MONARCHY IN BRAZIL

Brazil

1

The Luso-Brazilian Court in Rio de Janeiro

In this land, I was happy and was king. JOÃO VI
Brazil is the land of negroes and lice. CARLOTA JOAQUINA

The House of Braganza, one of the principal agrarian dynasties of Portugal, came to power in 1640. The head of the ducal house, Dom João, led a popular revolt against the Spanish overlords in Portugal and attained independence, thus ending six decades of Babylonian captivity. Proclaimed as King João IV, he launched a restoration movement that lasted until 1668, when Spain reluctantly recognized Portugal's independence.[1] Between the proclamation of independence in 1640 and the transfer of the Braganza court to the New World in 1808, the principal concerns of Portugal's kings were to consolidate the restored empire in the "three continents and five seas" and to rebuild the bankrupt imperial economy.

In this restoration of the kingdom and the recovery of the overseas empire, Brazilians became legitimate partners. A combined force of Lusitanians and Brazilians dislodged the Dutch from the Brazilian Northeast and Angola. By the second half of the seventeenth century, the empire had been transformed into a Luso-Brazilian seaborne system. Because Portuguese Asia was lost to the Dutch and the economic structure of the overseas colonies was virtually destroyed by the decadent imperial finance system under the aegis of the three Philips of Spain,[2] Portuguese hopes settled on America. By establishing the Brazil Company in 1649, retrieving the sugar-growing Northeast in 1654, and founding the southernmost trading outpost of Colônia do Sacramento in the Banda Oriental in 1680, the Braganza kings made a concerted attempt to consolidate American interests.

The consolidation of Portugal's empire in the Atlantic, however, was hampered by lack of revenues. The kings, even during the prosperous times of Manuel of Aviz (1495–1521) and João V of Braganza (1706–50), did not pay well royal officials who were serving overseas. Often, these officials were forced to engage in "private trade" to augment their incomes, thus spurring pernicious corruption and contraband.[3] During this period, Portuguese administrators in Brazil became dependent on the colonial social and economic elite; on many occasions, Coimbra-trained bureaucrats were absorbed by colonial society through marriage. This was only one aspect of the complex process of Brazilianization of overseas civil, military, and religious servants. Between 1609 and 1758, some 168 *desembargadores* (judges) served at the Bahian High Court (Relação da Bahia), in the colonial capital. No fewer than thirty-five (counting only those identifiable) of them married Brazilians, and were thus effectively drawn into the local society as its nascent allies.[4] This number (20.8 percent) is rather high considering that the advanced status of desembargador was usually awarded only to persons possessing mature experience.

Although the retreat of the Dutch from the Brazilian Northeast in the mid-seventeenth century represented a military victory for Portugal, it signaled an economic defeat for its empire. Western European colonial powers established sugar colonies in the Caribbean; and, by the second half of the century, Portugal's monopoly had been truncated. The zealous protective policies of France, England, and the Netherlands kept Brazilian sugar out of the market. Thus, by the 1670s, Portuguese America was experiencing a dire economic depression.[5] The flagrant abuse of office by colonial officials to supplement income became widespread throughout the empire. The king's councillors deplored the pervasive corruption, but in the 1660s were able to point to only one honest governor, who was assumed to be so because of the lack of complaints lodged against him.[6]

The discovery of gold in the 1690s and diamonds during the first decade of the eighteenth century in Brazil not only injected new vitality into the abiotic empire system, but also marked a new phase in the Brazilianization of colonial society. The eighteenth century constituted a significant watershed in colonial history, for Brazil emerged both as an integrated society and as an economy ready to surpass those in Portugal. In Boxer's words, the country was a "milche cow" that offered rejuvenating drinks to Europe. Brazilian gold stimulated the industrial capitalism of England and Western Europe, while Portugal lapsed further into dependence on England. The signing of the Methuen Treaty in 1703 sealed this dependency relationship: Crown officials agreed to prohibit industrialism at home and in overseas colonies in return for a concession granting Portuguese wine entry into the English market. The victory for the small agrarian elite of Portugal was to be modified some half-century later when the Marquês de Pombal sought to nationalize Portuguese domestic and overseas economies. This brinkmanship of the anti-English policies persisted even after the removal of the dynamic minister from office in 1777.[7] In power for twenty-seven years, he had instilled in the Portuguese a measure of national pride that ended the once pervasive adulation of England among the ruling elite.

The internal changes in Brazil, in contrast to those in Portugal, were seismic. The burgeoning economic activities of the gold- and diamond-mining districts in Minas Gerais, Goiás, and Mato Grosso provided the first major impetus to integrate colonial society from within. Pressures *ab extra*, such as French military designs on Rio de Janeiro and Maranhão, were contained. Internal trade from Pará and Maranhão, Pernambuco and Bahia, Rio de Janeiro and São Paulo, and Rio Grande do Sul to the mining highlands fostered fluvial navigation and the building of new backcountry roads that crisscrossed half the South American continent. The transfer of the colonial capital from Salvador, the once opulent heartland of the sugar economy, to the equally old but underdeveloped port of Rio kindled a new spirit in colonial society. The multiplication of captaincies, the rise of urban centers and economies, and the demographic shift and growth affected the internal migration of plantation slaves from the Northeast and accelerated the import of Africans across the Atlantic.[8]

In addition to spurring the growth of cities such as Rio, Salvador, Recife, and Belém, the gold boom aided the rise of several major interior towns as centers of commerce and industry. Guaratinguetá, in São Paulo, originated as a stopping place for the mule train that connected Minas Gerais and the littoral; Angra dos Reis, Parati, and Campos, all in the Rio de Janeiro captaincy, emerged as the principal suppliers of foodstuffs to the mines.⁹ The cities' role would be reversed in the 1780s, when the gold mines played out and Minas Gerais turned to a new activity: production of agricultural crops. By 1800 rice, beans, *farinha de mandioca*, and dairy products consumed in the city of Rio were imported from Minas, which remained a key agricultural province throughout the nineteenth century under the Braganza American empire.

The so-called "agricultural renaissance" in the country by the 1790s was a simultaneous response to both internal and external stimuli. The chattel labor force left idle by a declining mining economy was diverted to the middle Paraíba Valley, where coffee plantations were established. Because of an unlimited land supply and the easily available slave labor, the colony entered another phase of its economic career as a producer of coffee. First cultivated on an experimental basis in Maranhão in the 1720s (reportedly smuggled in from French Guiana), coffee was planted in the city of Rio and its adjacent region by the 1770s. However, not until the 1790s did this crop become popular among landowners. In 1800 the port of Rio exported only 10 sacks of coffee; in 1817 the figure jumped to the astronomical total of 63,986, and, in 1821, to 105,386.¹⁰

Paralleling the expansion of the coffee economy was the reviving sugar industry. Its long record as the principal money-maker for Portugal and its colony began in the 1530s, matured by the end of the sixteenth century into the world's major producer, and languished in the face of still challenges from the Caribbean by the 1660s. The collapse of the Haitian colony in 1794 renewed Brazil's dream of recapturing the lost world market, and, through the next two decades, the expansion of sugar plantations in the Northeast as well as in the South (Rio, São Paulo, and Minas Gerais, principally) marched hand in hand with the growth of the coffee economy.¹¹ The renewed role of Brazil as an agrarian colony became a fait accompli in the 1790s. As economic exigencies changed, the colonial bureaucracy completed its metamorphosis by 1800 and emerged as a parasite on society.

Historians have often maintained that the marching armies of Napoleon Bonaparte in 1807 marked the major turning point for the colonial role of Latin America; some even go so far as to argue that the region's independence began with his invasion of Iberia.¹² Although such a thesis is easy to accept, it is clear that ongoing structural changes in colonial Brazil during the eighteenth century created the proper internal conditions for independence. The transatlantic transfer of the members of the House of Braganza and its courtiers, numbering some 15,000, simply reinforces the view that colonial society had grown sufficiently attractive to the Portuguese rulers to make such a voyage worthwhile.

The transfer of the ruling house to the New World offered both historic and practical significance in terms of completing the process of Brazilianization. As early as the 1730s, Portuguese politicians entertained the possibility of moving the imperial center from Lisbon to Rio, where the new capital of Portugal's Atlantic empire would be located.[13] The lure of Brazilian gold was not the only factor in such a consideration. Although Lisbon was an emporium for the Asian spice trade, African slaves, and American sugar, as well as the seat of the central government, it had never been the economic epicenter of the empire. Non-Portuguese and non-Iberian traders, bankers, shippers, and industrialists had always held sway over colonial commerce. João III (1521–57) was said to have been so disturbed by the extent of non-Portuguese control of overseas trade and finance that he attempted to end the first three decades of "neglect" by introducing a privately financed *capitania* system in 1532. During the sixteenth century, somewhere upward of 66 percent of Brazil's trade was carried by Dutch bottoms; Brazilian sugar was refined in Dutch-owned mills in Rotterdam and Amsterdam.

Spanish rule, in spite of Philip II's lip service to Portuguese autonomy in overseas administration and trade, further weakened Lisbon's position as the center of the colonial system. The Braganza kings after 1640 found it prudent to exchange economic concessions with various European powers for diplomatic and military alliances to attain Portuguese independence from Spain. Ironically, because of the discovery of mineral wealth in Brazil and the fact that it produced about 40 percent of the world's gold in the eighteenth century, Portugal grew more dependent on England; Lisbon became the center of government in name only. Thus, the idea of transferring the Portuguese court to the New World was broached to thwart the European hegemony of the nation and to revitalize a veritable seaborne empire.

Under these circumstances, the House of Braganza would quit Portugal in November 1807 under the escort of a British naval fleet. By July of that year, it had become clear that Napoleon was striving to disrupt Anglo-Portuguese relations, forcing Portugal to deny Britain access to its ports and to expel British diplomats and merchants. By mid-October, the idea of transferring the royal family was openly espoused.[14] Finally, the deteriorating military situation in Iberia forced the House of Braganza to depart. On 24 November 1807, in a meeting of the Council of State, Prince Regent João accepted the British offer to transfer the court to Brazil, and left a council of regents to administer Portugal in the name of the absent queen.[15] Clarence H. Haring described the situation: "When Junot the Commander of the French invading army approached the city gates, the royal flight had the appearance of a panic, but . . . treasure, archives, and all the apparatus of administration were on board the fleet."[16]

The question of moving the royal family to the New World had in fact been under deliberation since July. The Treaty of Tilsit, between Alexander of Russia and Napoleon of France, made the *grande armée* invincible, and the dictator was consumed by his insatiable desire to conquer the whole continent. In light of this situation, the Portuguese Council of State was forced to consider various options for keeping the kingdom out of the engulfing war and for saving the overseas colony. Portugal was in dire diplomatic and economic difficulty. Its traditional amity toward England naturally caused Napoleon to suspect its neutrality. Conversely, the continental blockade had provoked Britain to retaliate against the collaborators with the French and to destroy Denmark's capital by a naval bombardment. Worse, the Portuguese court feared the loss of Brazil to Britain in the wake of a war that had already deprived the latter of markets on the continent.[17] But it was the September demand by Napoleon and his subject kingdom, Spain, that Portugal close its ports to the British naval and mercantile fleet that prompted the Crown and the Council of State to begin exploring alternatives to save the kingdom and the colony.

The councillors and Prince Regent João reviewed various options. The fear of an English takeover of Brazil as a potentially lucrative market was clearly foremost in the minds of the Portuguese. To preserve the empire under the Braganza rule, the council raised the possibility of sending the Prince of Beira, the future Pedro I of Brazil, to the New World as a Braganza ruler. He could be accompanied by one of the princesses or Infante Dom Miguel, his brother. Spain, presumably speaking for France, adamantly opposed such a plan.[18] Because Napoleon stood firm, the prospect of a diplomatic solution dissipated rapidly. By mid-October, George Canning, British foreign secretary, had managed to negotiate a secret treaty with Portugal, under which its military and mercantile fleet would be moved out of Napoleon's reach and England would offer a naval escort for the royal family to set sail for Brazil. In late November, a total of twenty ships (sixteen being the Portuguese Royal Armada plus four British escort ships) left Lisbon. Fearful of Napoleon's spies in his court, the prince regent withheld the existence of the secret accord with England from his councillors.[19] Thus, the departure of the Braganzas and their corporate nobles was neither reluctant nor sudden, as some historians have believed.

When Dom João and his entourage, astray from the fleet, arrived at Bahia in 1808, the captaincy was one of the major centers of colonial economic activity. In 1807 it produced 20,000 boxes of sugar; the three captaincies of Rio, São Paulo, and Pernambuco together produced 24,000. That same year, Bahia exported 10,000 bales of cotton.[20] Such statistics underscored the increasing economic significance of Brazil's agriculture to Portugal since the demise of mining activities. Between 1796 and 1806 three-quarters of the Portuguese traders were Brazilian-born; about 80 percent of Portuguese exports to Europe and elsewhere, or 11,472 *contos* of the total 13,413, originated from Brazil. In 1806 Portugal sold 9,885 contos worth of goods to Brazil, which constituted 70 percent of the exports, totaling 14,086 contos. In the face of opposition from Lisbon merchants, the Portuguese government even considered establishing a bank in colonial Brazil to facilitate the expanding trade, which was accompanied by demographic and therefore market growth.[21] Between 1775 and 1819 the population of Bahia almost doubled, and in 1820 that of the city of Salvador was 150,000 people; the figure for Rio de Janeiro was 110,000. The populations of New York and Philadelphia were about 200,000 and 150,000, respectively.[22]

A scant five days after his royal hegira to the New World, the prince regent decided to establish an "open door" policy in Brazilian trade. Historians have attributed his liberal economic stance to British pressure; thus, the opening of Brazilian ports in 1808 and the Treaty of 1810 have often been viewed as the price that Britain extracted from Portugal for naval protection during the transatlantic voyage. A more realistic view is that the decision to open doors was prompted by a combination of Luso-Brazilian economic realities, nationalism, and an enlightened reform movement. Keeping Brazilian ports closed would mean the eventual loss of the essential Portuguese trade because Lisbon was under French control. Limited opening of the ports, another option, or granting an exclusive concession to British merchants to trade in Brazil, would lead to a complete takeover by British mercantile interests that in effect would transfer the Portuguese trade to British hands. Opening the Brazilian ports to all friendly nations, therefore, remained the only viable option that would guarantee both Luso-Brazilian commercial hegemony and trade activities worldwide.

That the Crown and Council of State decided to include leading merchants in the exodus plan some months before the November voyage supports the claim that Portuguese economic nationalism played a key role in the "open door" decision. From one perspective, the primary reason for moving the government to Brazil was to ward off British forays into the Portuguese treasure chest. Under an open-port policy, British mercantile houses, a limited number of which had been granted access to Brazil after the 1660s, could not successfully monopolize its trade.

During the first decade of João's rule, Rio de Janeiro grew from a sleepy town of 50,000 to a bustling commercial port of 110,000. Some 25,000 European residents, among them British, French, Italian, and German merchants, shippers, artisans, and military advisers, constituted a vigorous adjunct to Braganza court life.[23] Some 280 sugar mills were to be found in the Paraíba delta region alone, where Campos is located. Serving as the region's principal market, Rio boasted seventy-five public parks, forty-six streets, four *travessas* (cross streets), six alleys, and nineteen public squares.[24] Besides the commercialized downtown area, the docks, and the customhouses, the major sections of the city were Engenho Novo, Catete, São Cristóvão, Glória, and Botafogo. Once the home of a Portuguese merchant, the small but adequate palace of São Cristóvão, at the Boa Vista estate, was purchased by the royal government to house Dom João, who continued to reside there as king until his return to Lisbon in 1821. His wife, the Spanish consort Carlota Joaquina, lived in another palace in Botafogo with their daughters. By 1819 new wings were being added to the existing buildings of the São Cristóvão palace to make it befit the home for the king and later emperors.[25]

Life in Rio de Janeiro after 1808 was strongly influenced by the burgeoning costs of government and free trade. Governmental receipts in
1808, João's first year in Rio, amounted to 2,297,904$099; expenses ex-
ceeded receipts by 2,234,985$204. The royal household expenses alone
were larger than the budget for the army; the figures were 456,724$059
and 454,638$515, respectively.[26] Although the coming of the court to
Rio added a welcome dimension to the Brazilian economy as a whole,
it brought disaster to colonial finances. By 1820, burdened by the expenses of João's two imperialistic wars (in French Guiana in 1808 and
the Banda Oriental in 1815), the military budget climbed to an all-time
high of 2,000 contos, 44 percent of the total governmental revenue of
4,500 contos. In addition to the military spending, royal financial obligations included the colonial bureaucracy and military expenditures
earmarked for the defense of Portugal.[27]

Under the open-port system, Brazilian exports declined from
34,819,000 *cruzados* in 1807 to 1,368,000 the following year, climbing to
12,048,000 in 1809 but falling in 1810 to 9,280,000. Almost totally dependent on foreign trade for manufactured goods, Brazil under João had
little choice but to offer trade incentives. To encourage trade with Britain, facilitated by sixty British merchant houses in Rio alone, João
signed the Treaty of 1810, under which British imports were taxed 15
percent; Portuguese, 16 percent; and others, 24 percent. Such a treaty
offered both advantages and disadvantages. Politically unpopular because it guaranteed express advantages only to the most industrialized
nation of the world, not to Portugal and Brazil, the treaty was further
maligned for undermining Brazilian manufacturing and factory activities, which Dom João had encouraged in 1808 by revoking the historic
1785 ban on home industry and manufacture. Furthermore, one provision in the treaty called for the regular monthly dispatch of a ship
from England to Brazil, thereby guaranteeing Brazil's communication
with Europe.[28]

Trade with the United States also increased after 1800, when the first
North American ship arrived at Rio. In 1802 U.S. exports to Brazil totaled only $1,041; the year after the opening of ports, they climbed to
$540,653, peaked in 1810 at $721,899, but fell in 1811 to $671,417 and
again in 1812 to $426,982. U.S. exports consisted of foodstuffs, some
iron, and textiles; Brazilian exports to the United States were principally coffee and sugar. Boston, New York, Philadelphia, and Baltimore

became Brazil's major U.S. trading partners. In 1810 and 1811 the Yankee traders sent fleets of fifty-seven and fifty-four ships, respectively. By 1812 no fewer than twenty-four North American firms were actively trading with Brazil.[29]

If Prince Regent João showed considerable daring and acumen in his progressive economic policies, he was a political conservative and kept a tight rein on the four ministries of his government: Kingdom (*Reino*), Navy and Overseas Affairs (*Marinha e Ultramar*), War and Foreign Affairs (*Guerra e Estrangeiros*), and the Royal Treasury (*Real Erário*).[30] During his thirteen-year rule (1808–21), João relied on a group of Portuguese-born politicians, men who had been ministers and councillors of state in Portugal and possessed expertise in statecraft. No Brazilian was given a ministry and only ten Portuguese were so honored. Of these, only three ministers—the Marquês de Aguiar (Fernando José de Portugal), the Conde da Barca (Antônio de Araújo de Azevedo), and Tomás Antônio de Vilanova Portugal—held all four portfolios.[31]

Once Dom João organized his government, the court took on the semblance of being the seat of a kingdom. By 1815 João had elevated Brazil to the status of cokingdom, equal to Portugal, by revamping the administration. Rio de Janeiro now became the capital of the United Kingdom of Portugal, Brazil, and the Algarve. The following year, the demented queen died and the prince assumed the title of King João VI. The Joanine court was eager to Europeanize its style and did so by selectively bestowing royal honors and nobiliary titles on Portuguese and Brazilians. Life in Rio was almost idyllic for King João, who swore he would never risk the arduous transatlantic voyage back to Portugal.

But the Liberal Revolution of 1820 in Portugal drew him back. The country was engulfed in a radical revolt that began in Oporto and threatened to undo the monarchy. Britain could not afford to have Portugal become a republic, which would make the Iberian Peninsula hostile to its commercial and military interests in the Mediterranean. Once again, João—this time as king—was pressured by Britain to return home. Reluctantly, he decided to depart from his beloved Brazil, leaving Prince Pedro as his regent.

2

The American Braganzas and Court Life

Portuguese colonization in Brazil was marked by the almost exclusive domination of the rural or semi-rural family. GILBERTO FREYRE

Rapidly unfolding events in Portugal in 1820 and 1821 moved Brazilian independence toward reality. Before João's return to Portugal, the junta in Lisbon had begun to organize a new system of government. With João's blessing, Brazil dispatched representatives to the Portuguese Cortes, a unicameral institution under mandate to write a new constitution. Meeting in January 1821, some eight months before the first Brazilian contingent arrived, the constituent assembly drew up a liberal constitution that alienated loyalists, the church, the Holy Alliance, and Brazilians. Sovereignty belonged to the nation, not to the king, it proclaimed, and the Holy Inquisition and other religious offices were not granted sanctimonious recognition by the new magna carta.

Jacobin radicals pushed for more liberal measures internally and sought a recolonization of Brazil for the sake of public sentiment and Portugal-based economic reasons. The abolition of the courts of appeals and other administrative offices in Brazil, the existence of which symbolized the equality between the two cokingdoms, was much debated. Thus, the threat existed that Portuguese America would be reduced to colonial status. The demands and counterdemands by Brazilian and Portuguese deputies between October 1821 and June 1822 became so explosive that reconciliation between the two factions was impossible. Even the most conservative Brazilians could not accept the

Portuguese demands. In May 1822 the Brazilians granted an additional title to their regent, proclaiming Dom Pedro their "perpetual defender and protector," a mark of popular approval tantamount to electing him as their national leader. The Brazilian deputies in Lisbon proposed the establishment of three separate yet coordinated legislatures: one each for Portugal and Brazil, and another for the two combined. The Portuguese arrogantly rejected the idea. When the Brazilian deputies were impeded from leaving Lisbon through confiscation of their passports by the Portuguese government, British consular and diplomatic agents practically smuggled them out of the country.

The Portuguese government chose to react forcibly to the boycott of the constituent assembly by the Brazilian deputation. In July and August 1822 the Cortes voted to dispatch troops to Brazil. A contingent of Portuguese soldiers arrived in Rio, where Dom Pedro forbade their landing; no violent clash took place, and they returned home. The irate Cortes ordered the prince regent to return to Lisbon for further "education" befitting the "First Citizen" and a tour of various European courts. The Brazilian reaction to this frivolous demand was to bolt the kingdom. On 7 September 1822 Pedro formally proclaimed the independence of his adopted country. By October the First Citizen had been crowned the constitutional emperor of Brazil as Pedro I. Impotent to enforce its demand, the Portuguese Cortes met in December without the Brazilian deputies. Barred from the assembly were the nobility, the clergy, and other privileged classes. Those who failed to render an oath to the new constitution were stripped of their citizenship and banished from the kingdom. The defiant Spanish queen, Carlota Joaquina, true to her upbringing, tore up a copy of the constitution and refused to swear to it, though her husband João VI meekly pledged his allegiance. The physicians' proclamation that she was ill and unfit to travel saved Carlota Joaquina from banishment. She was removed from Lisbon and housed at one of the Braganza palaces outside the capital.[1]

The strongest opposition to Brazilian independence did not emanate from João VI, the king of Portugal, but from his court politicians, members of the Braganza family, and the public in general. The radical regime in power since 1820 collapsed by mid-1823, having alienated the king, the nobility, the church, and even Lisbon's powerful mercantile community. João regained his powers—but at a price. Carlota Joaquina, now supported by Spain and indirectly by the commitment of the Holy Alliance (which stood against the constitutional government in Portugal), again began mobilizing factions supporting her son Infante Miguel as the restorer of royal absolutism and eventual king of Portugal. The Madrid court championed Miguel's right, and Carlota Joaquina accused her own son, Pedro I, of having reneged on his obligation to Portugal. By September 1823 her opposition to Brazil's independence prompted João VI to seek British mediation in the negotiations between Portugal and Brazil. His letter to Pedro had been returned unopened the previous month, and João was convinced that Britain held the key for his own survival in the face of his wife's treachery. The king, as in 1807, once more ordered his minister in London to solicit British Foreign Secretary Canning's help.[2]

Not until 1824, when João recovered his powers from the liberal regime, did negotiations for Brazil's independence become possible. The task of obtaining recognition from Portugal was deftly delegated to the British minister in Lisbon. From the British standpoint, there were four main preoccupations: (1) formal recognition of Brazil by Portugal; (2) Britain's desire to enforce the ban on the slave trade; (3) renewing the Treaty of 1810, in similar terms, with an independent Brazil; and (4) defining the British role in Pedro's war with his Spanish-American neighbors in the Río de la Plata region. Britain's interests were to serve as the overriding considerations in the forthcoming negotiations between Portugal and Brazil.

For the next two years, until the treaty of recognition was signed in August 1825 by Brazilian and Portuguese negotiators, Canning, Charles Stuart (the British minister in Lisbon and later in Rio), and Henry Chamberlain (the British consul general in Rio) played key roles in both the outcome of the treaty as well as shaping the future geopolitical position of Britain in the South Atlantic world. Part of the delay in negotiations was the personality clash between Pedro I and the British minister. Impatient and somewhat haughty, Stuart was not one of Pedro's favorite foreign diplomats resident in Rio. Once, when the British minister followed Pedro all the way to Bahia to discuss a minor matter, the irate emperor granted him an audience, but refused to hear him out and dismissed him.[3] Chamberlain, on the other hand, had been in Brazil longer, spoke Portuguese, and knew his way around the court. It was obvious that, for the betterment of diplomatic relations between the Court of St. James and São Cristóvão, the consul general would in time replace Stuart.

On 14 March 1825 Secretary of State for Foreign Affairs George Canning instructed Charles Stuart on how to conduct the recognition negotiations.[4] First, Canning stressed, Brazilian independence should be separated *from that of Spanish America*. No public statement, either from the British Parliament or from the Crown, sought to mix these two issues. Canning added emphatically that "our conduct in respect to each is necessarily guided by distinct principles and controlled by peculiar considerations." Britain had concluded a series of treaties with Portugal in the past, he continued, that bound the two kingdoms against common enemies; furthermore, Britain was obligated under the treaties to defend Portugal from "all external hostility." Therefore, Britain was in dire difficulty so long as Portugal deemed Brazilian independence an act of hostility toward its sovereignty. Both the Cortes and the king sought to interpret the Anglo-Portuguese treaties as "extending to the internal institutions of the Portuguese monarchy and as binding us [Britain] to preserve the several territories of the House of Braganza, in both hemispheres, in their existing connection with each other."

Canning saw illogic in the Portuguese interpretation. The treaties signed under Charles I, Protector Oliver Cromwell, and Charles II were confined to "external interests" of the two countries. Britain had neither obligation nor interest in maintaining the constitutional regime (the radical Cortes) in power; neither was Britain interested in restoring absolutism in Portugal under João. What Britain sought was "to reconcile the two parts of the dominions of the Portuguese crown with each other and to preserve in both hemispheres the interest of the family of Braganza." Canning could have added that so long as the British objective was the renewal of the "most favored nation" status in the Treaty of 1810 with an independent Brazil, the separation of the two realms of the Braganzas was actually desirable. The future of British economic interests lay in Brazil, not in Portugal, whose importance was diplomatic and strategic in terms of British relations with continental and Iberian powers.

Meanwhile, the Brazilian envoys in London had been imposing their own stringent conditions. To their way of thinking, the recognition treaty should come before the Anglo-Brazilian commercial treaty. Canning conveyed his personal analysis of the situation to Charles Stuart in the following terms: "It is true that the Brazilian government may permit the stipulations of that Treaty to remain unquestioned, but is equally true that Portugal has set to Brazil the example of questioning them." In fact, the Portuguese government had informed Britain of the suspension of certain articles in the 1810 treaty. Canning was preoccupied with French interests in Brazil and anxious to preserve the British "pre-eminence" that it gained. To the foreign secretary, "a new commercial [treaty] arrangement with Brazil is a matter of more indispensable necessity to us than was the formation of one with the States of Spanish America." From the outset, monarchical Brazil received special attention from him.

The problem that prevented the speedy conclusion of the negotiations, however, was that Britain and Portugal had their priorities reversed. Portugal pressed for a redefinition of its relationship with Brazil, and Britain viewed the independence of Brazil to be an indisputable reality, ipso facto beyond negotiation. What should be negotiated was the future relationship among the three countries. Canning's principal objective was to sign a commercial treaty with Brazil, where the lucrative market lay. In July 1824 the Brazilian proposal was countered by the Portuguese representative (the Conde da Vila Leal) with a new proposal, whose terms were highly acceptable to Canning. João VI was prepared to confirm the title of "emperor" for Pedro I and to transfer all his claims and rights in Brazil to his son, provided that His Most Faithful Majesty the King of Portugal would be addressed as "Emperor," a rank equal to his son's, and that Pedro I would accept the additional title of "regent." João's proposal, in reality, on its face constituted a moderate attempt to retain colonial rights over Brazil. It was no more than a face-saving measure, however, because the Brazilian Constitution of 1824 prohibited Pedro I from reuniting the empire with Portugal. Such a renunciation of the Portuguese Crown was conspicuously absent from the recognition treaty, which satisfied Canning but neither the majority of Portuguese politicians nor Brazilians. Revised, the treaty of 29 August 1825 granted Brazil full independence from the mother country, and Britain succeeded in preserving the monarchical institutions in "both hemispheres."[5]

Between 1808 and 1831 the House of Braganza had weathered the arduous transatlantic move, division of the ruling dynasty, independence, internal and external wars, time-consuming diplomatic negotiations, and abdication of the first emperor, but the consolidation of the American Braganza monarchy itself took an additional two decades. Not until 1849 was the empire completely free of civil wars, rebellions, and external threats. The three principal rulers of the house have been variously described, with some basis, in fact, as "a prince with bourgeois tastes" (João VI), "a medieval king" (Pedro I), and "the most perfect public functionary of the empire" (Pedro II).[6]

Their contributions to the monarchy and the making of the nobility were as distinct as their character. Born in 1767, King João VI, founder of the American House of Braganza and the United Kingdom of Portugal, Brazil, and the Algarve in 1815, was introverted and at times indecisive. His marriage to the power-hungry Carlota Joaquina, daughter of Charles IV of Spain, was a mismatch carried out against his will. Between 1793 and 1806, according to one biographer, the unhappily married couple "brilliantly fulfilled their reproductive functions" by producing nine children; the third-born, Maria Isabel, became the queen of Spain, marrying her uncle King Ferdinand VII; and the fourth-born, Pedro, became the first emperor of independent Brazil.[7]

The legendary incompatibility of João and Carlota Joaquina was not only confined to their personalities. Politically, João was somewhat liberal, judged by the standards of fellow European monarchs, and Carlota Joaquina was a staunch champion of royal absolutism whose zeal easily surpassed that of her equally strong-willed brother, Ferdinand VII of Spain. Suffering from the gout inherited from his forebears, João, a devout Catholic, was fond of spending time in the quiet of his chapel. In 1792 he was made regent of Portugal, governing the kingdom and empire in the name of his demented mother Queen Maria during the period following the French Revolution when European politics swung pendulum-like between liberalism and absolutism. Portugal was caught in mid-swing between Britain and France. After 1803 the prince regent's declaration of neutrality, even with the explicit consent of Britain, did not satisfy Napoleon Bonaparte. Increasingly, it became clear to the regent and the Council of State in Lisbon that Portugal could not remain neutral in the wake of the Franco-Spanish alliance in Iberia and that the wrong political move could prompt Britain to take over Brazil in retaliation. The prince regent chose to save Brazil and leave Portugal to its fate. By September 1807 the court was making arrangements for the royal flight to the New World.

The "prince with bourgeois tastes" loved Brazil. In fact, João encouraged many of his ministers and counselors to dispose of their holdings in Europe and settle permanently in the New World.[8] He divided his days between the court in Rio and the Real Fazenda de Santa Cruz, confiscated from the Society of Jesus in 1759. In addition, the royal family had three principal residences: the São Cristóvão Palace, at the Boa Vista estate; the City Palace (today a post office at Rua 1 de Março); and a house at Botafogo. João lived at São Cristóvão with two sons (Pedro and Miguel), his mother, and daughter Maria Teresa, the widow of Infante Carlos of Spain. Carlota Joaquina resided with the other daughters at Botafogo. During the early years, the City Palace was reserved for official functions and receiving dignitaries. As facilities were expanded at São Cristóvão, João gradually moved both his official and his unofficial activities to the Boa Vista estate.

The best-known ritual of Joanine times was the daily beija-mão ceremony, usually held at São Cristóvão. The ancient custom of granting audiences and allowing subjects to "kiss the hand" of the sovereign provided João opportunities to know the leading citizens of the realm, the clergy, nobles, foreign residents, and diplomats. The bulk of the Portuguese elite, transplanted with their king to Brazil, paid homage to their leader. João's key ministers as well as his purveyors were Portuguese-born. The Portuguese Carneiro, Viúva e Filhos Company, for instance, financed a munitions factory near Lagoa Rodrigo Freitas with 100,000 cruzados of its own capital, three and one-half times the annual income of the royal plantation of Santa Cruz. Dowager of the mercantile dynasty and widow of the Carneiro furtune, Ana Francisca Maciel da Costa (the future Baronesa de São Salvador de Campos) was to become a key courtier during the times of Dom João and Pedro I. Also active in the court's social life was another Portuguese merchant, the future Marquês de Jundiaí, formerly the Barão and Visconde do Rio Seco. One foreign visitor, impressed by the splendor of Rio Seco's wealth, commented on his opulent Chinese-style mansion and the jewels that the women of the Rio Seco house displayed. Because of the economic boom after 1808, Brazilian society rose from moderate wealth to near-opulence, a splendor the colony had never known. The same foreign visitor observed, "The clergy and nobility in this country en-joy[ed] privileges that no class in Europe can."[9]

Although the Brazilian subjects adored their prince regent, later king, they despised his consort. Carlota Joaquina was often described as "vulgar, badtempered, unscrupulous, and malicious."[10] Forced into marriage by long-standing dynastic ties and by all accounts neither a faithful wife nor model mother, she hated her husband with as much passion as he despised her. The stronger and more forceful of the two, she was a born conspirator. Back in Lisbon in 1806, the Spanish prin-cess had attempted to overthrow her husband; as punishment, João de-cided the couple would live separately, a custom that endured after they moved to the New World. Carlota also had a series of men in her life, and on one occasion the wife of the French ambassador was led to ob-serve that "the interesting thing about the royal family of Portugal is that one child never resembles a brother or sister."[11] Allegedly, Carlota Joaquina was responsible for the death of the wife of her Brazilian lover, the future Conde de Vila Nova de São José. The Rio police produced evidence that the queen hired an assassin to murder the woman on ac-count of jealousy, but João VI suppressed the charge.

After the transfer of the court to Brazil, Carlota was approached by Spanish-American creoles from the Río de la Plata to serve as regent for her brother, Ferdinand VII, then a captive guest of Napoleon. Sens-ing yet another conspiracy to get rid of him, João scuttled the plan by removing Carlota's favorite Spanish secretary, who had wielded an evil influence over her.[12] Until João's dying days, Carlota Joaquina never gave up plotting against him, even involving her son Miguel. To the Spanish queen, Brazil was "the land of negroes and lice" where "noth-ing can resist, nothing lasts, but everything rots."[13] Since the day she had arrived in Salvador in 1808 with her head cleanly shaven to fight off the vermin, Portuguese and Brazilians held the queen in contempt. In fact, other members of the House of Braganza were equally known for unhealthy habits. Gilberto Freyre commented that João, though put on a strict diet to control hereditary gout and overweight, loved to indulge in eating, and was described as "slovenly, flabby, his fingers sticky with chicken gravy."[14]

Dom Pedro, the crown prince and fourth-born of the royal couple, fortunately did not inherit degenerative traits from his grandmother or his father. Brought to the New World at the age of nine, the epileptic youth was practically Brazilian. The "prince royal," as the British liked to call him, was a high-spirited, rough-and-tumble boy, more physical and sports-minded than his younger brother, Miguel. Pedro would grow up to be a liberal monarch by old European standards. His major tutors were Frei Antônio de Arrabida (later a member of the Brazilian Second Council of State) and Coronel João Rademaker, former Portuguese minister to Amsterdam. The first doubled as Pedro's confessor as well as teacher of letters, and the second managed the overall coordination of the prince's education until his death in 1814. Also cooperating to educate the heir apparent were Padre Guilherme Paulo Tilbury, chaplain of the imperial guards, and Roberto João Damby, former instructor at the College of Nobles, in Lisbon. The padre was Pedro's English teacher and Damby his equestrian instructor.[13] Pedro's English was passable, his French excellent, and his Latin "tolerable." His artistic forte was music. He organized a choir of black and mulatto servants, played the organ and other instruments well, and wrote a composition that was later presented in a Paris opera theater. One biographer judged Pedro's appreciation of literature "parsimonious" and of natural science "still less."[16]

The future emperor was more soldier than scholar. A superb horseman, he thought nothing of riding forty to fifty miles a day. The forty-mile distance from São Cristóvão to Fazenda de Santa Cruz was a short hop. Once Pedro rode three days from São João d'El Rey to Rio with few rests, and his escorts were the ones who were tired. Furthermore, the prince relished danger, often riding during the night with a minimum of bodyguards. Although both Pedro and Miguel were mischievous and at times violent in their play, the elder preferred military games; the younger was fond of pranks, such as stampeding cattle.[17] Those foreign residents who knew Pedro often remarked that he looked much like a dashing French officer.

The most careful attention paid Pedro by his biographers and contemporaries concerns his role as a womanizer. One historian called him a "tropical Don Juan." Born macho, the prince, later the emperor, tirelessly chased women of all breeds and social classes, both foreign and Brazilian. He procreated sixteen children, half illegitimate. In 1817 the prince married Maria Leopoldina of Austria, daughter of Franz I and sister of Napoleon's second wife. A science buff and something of a bookworm (mineralogy being her favorite subject), Leopoldina was far more intellectual and intelligent than her husband. The marriage was, however, not the result of a fairy-tale princess finding her prince charming. João's foreign policy exigencies called for such a union. Wary of ever-expanding British influence and its meddlesome role in internal politics, the king resolved to widen Portugal's links with other European powers. The House of Hapsburg was an attractive candidate; Emperor Franz I of Austria was a staunch advocate of the Holy Alliance, whose objectives were in consonance with João's thinking. An embassy was dispatched to Vienna to contract a double marriage: Isabel Maria of Braganza for the crown prince of Austria and Pedro for Leopoldina. The first overture never materialized, in the face of open opposition by Prince Metternich, but the second offer was accepted. The marriage not only brought about close ties with the Austrian government, but also led to visits by Austrian scientific and cultural missions to Brazil, and later to Austrian immigration.[18]

Pedro I, emperor of Brazil and twenty-eighth king of Portugal (Pedro IV there), and Empress Leopoldina had seven children: four daughters and three sons. The first-born, Maria da Glória, became the twenty-ninth monarch of Portugal; the second- and third-born (Miguel and João Carlos) died in infancy; the next three were princesses: Januária, Paula, and Francisca. The seventh and last-born was Pedro Alcântara Brasileiro, the second emperor of Brazil. Princess Paula died at the age of ten in 1833, and only three of the seven siblings survived the American monarchy: Pedro II died in 1891, Francisca in 1898, and Januária in 1901.[19]

Some years before his marriage to Leopoldina, Pedro began to sire bastards. Of the innumerable women and girls with whom he had affairs, three stood out as his favorite consorts: Madame Saisset, the Baronesa de Sorocaba, and the Marquesa de Santos, the last two being sisters. Pedro's women ranged from slave girls in the *senzala* of Fazenda de Santa Cruz to dancers, seamstresses, working-class women, wives of foreign diplomats and generals, and daughters of courtier nobles. In the aftermath of his affairs, he was known to be generous to his discarded mistresses. One married his general; another the paymaster of the imperial house. His first son was born to a French dancer, Moemi, a scant three months before the arrival of Leopoldina in Brazil. At the order of João VI, Moemi was packed off to Recife, where she was married to a government official; the husband was given a well-paying sinecure. When the bastard son died, the provincial government of Pernambuco conducted a lavish funeral; and the members of the Braganza house, including Leopoldina, contributed to the aggrieved mother's pension fund.[20]

Among Pedro's favorite mistresses was Clemence Saisset, wife of a French shopkeeper at Rua do Ouvidor in Rio. Saisset's boutique, which sold the latest fashions, was temporarily salvaged when the married crown prince arranged for the use of the royal coat of arms for the store, a symbol of patronage and mark of approval. (Such a custom was to endure throughout the nineteenth century, when eager merchants and manufacturers sought to label their products "imperial," the sign of acceptance and use by the highest potentate of the empire.) Clemence, or Clemência, as she was known to Brazilians, had two sons, one of whom was officially recognized as Pedro Alcântara Brasileiro. The House of Braganza paid 79,000 *francs* (6,000 of which were in gold) to buy the Saissets off. Enriched by the pension, the couple left Brazil quietly with the young Pedro in his mother's arms.[21]

The sensual side of monarch Pedro, described as "absolutist, prodigal, barbaric, despotic, and tyrannical," surfaced most strikingly in his magnetic attraction to the "unhappily married" wife of an army lieutenant in September 1822. During a visit to São Paulo, he performed gallantly for the country by declaring independence and by bringing his mistress and her family to Rio. It remains unclear if his desire to remain in Brazil was romantically linked to his acquisition of the most celebrated, and perhaps most notorious, lover in Brazilian history. For whatever reasons, his personal and political life between 1822 and 1831 was intertwined with that of this mistress.

Domitila de Castro Canto e Melo was a year older than Pedro. She was twenty-four when they first laid eyes on each other. That the two met by chance, as so romantically described by one of Pedro's biographers, should not be taken seriously. Her brother Francisco, an aide to Pedro, was probably responsible for bringing the couple together. Domitila, or Domitília, had a fair complexion and blue eyes, a rare combination among Portuguese women. In fact, her physical beauty was so striking that her hand was asked in marriage at the age of fourteen. Her first husband, Felício Pinto Coelho de Mendonça, was a scion of an important Mineiro family and an officer in the Portuguese regular army. His father, member of a seventeenth-century family that was established in Brazil, was a man of considerable wealth. Settling in the city of Vila Rica do Ouro Preto, Domitila and Felício had two sons, born in 1815 and 1816. As she continued to attract attention from lascivious men, her husband grew intensely jealous, often throwing violent temper tantrums. One biographer claimed that, during her third pregnancy, the jealous Felício stabbed her in a fit of anger. After the birth of the third child, she returned to her parents' home in São Paulo. By then somewhat deranged, her husband sought custody of the children.[22] About this time, Domitila met Pedro.

"Titília," as Pedro fondly called her, came from a family that had a history of seducing Iberian kings. Pedro I of Castile became the victim of the "inspiring love" of a Castro woman. Another Castro, Inês, Domitila's ancestor, was a favorite mistress of Pedro II, king of Portugal. (One story has it that when jealous nobles had Inês killed, the aggrieved king personally tracked down the killer, tore him apart with his bare hands, drank his blood, and ate the torn flesh of the body. In a bizarre coronation ceremony conducted by himself, Pedro then proclaimed Inês his queen.)[23] Between 1822 and 1831 four children were born of the love affair between the descendant of the Pedro of Portugal and of his Inês. Isabel Maria, born on 23 May 1824, was legitimized in July 1826; ennobled as the Duquesa de Goiás; and married a German prince, the Second Count of Treuberg, in 1843. The first son of the *liaison imperiale* was born only five days after the birth of the future emperor Pedro II; he died at three weeks. The third-born, Maria Isabel, Duquesa do Ceará, died at fourteen months in October 1828. The fourth, also named Maria Isabel, was born in 1830, and in 1848 married a Brazilian noble, the Conde de Iguaçu.[24] Excepting only the Condes de Iguaçu, all the Braganzas born in America married Europeans, thus inadvertently failing to build dynastic linkages with leading Brazilian latifundiary and mercantile clans.

Alberto Rangel, who wrote the definitive biography of Pedro and Domitila, also collected and published their existing letters. The names and nicknames they both used in their intimate letters reveal much about their relationship. One letter, dated November 1822, two months after they first made love, was signed by Pedro as the "big devil" (*demonão*). Although he customarily signed as "Imperador," he was fond of ending letters with such affectionate phrases as "teu filho," "amigo," or "teu amante," and of calling his Titília "minha querida

filha," "querida Marqueza," "amiga do coração," and simply "filha."
Domitila usually addressed her master as "senhor," often signing her
name with the title of nobility, the Viscondessa de Santos and later the
Marquesa de Santos. In one letter, she called Pedro "meo pai." To modern readers, this appellation seems puzzling. "Pai," often meaning
"lord" in the vein of father, conveyed respect; "filho" carried a sense of
the filial love of a vassal.[25]

The letters clearly show the impetuous side of the emperor, who was
dominated by his mistress and was more infatuated with her than she
with him. The relationship was a stormy one, conducted amidst not
only wagging tongues, but also powerful opposition from such established Brazilian politicians as the Andrada brothers: José Bonifácio,
Martim Francisco, and Antônio Carlos. The empress was also opposed. By one account, Pedro beat her when she demanded that he for-
sake Domitila and died as a result of the injuries. By another account,
Leopoldina in her eighth pregnancy was disheartened by Pedro's re-
fusal to get rid of his mistress and attempted an abortion, which
caused her death.[26] Late in 1826 Leopoldina died of a "puerperal infec-
tion." Although Pedro did not love the woman, her death saddened him.
The court nobles, political advisers, and diplomatic corps urged him to
send Domitila off to São Paulo and sever the relationship. Such an action would facilitate a marriage contract for him in Europe. Although
he often called Domitila "my empress," her unpopularity prevented
her from becoming his second wife. Writing her on his birthday in
1827, Pedro was moody and lonesome:

> I wrote you as the emperor. Now I am writing you as your vassal,
> friend, and lover to show you that I miss you. My vassal, I cannot
> tear my heart away but send you two whiskers of my mustache
> that I have just pulled for you. Today, I am in a sad mood and mel-
> ancholy, much missing you. . . . This your disgraced, but always
> true, grateful, and zealous vassal, friend, and lover.
>   (signed) The Emperor[27]

A scant nine days before his second marriage, this time to Amélia of
Leuchtenberg in 1829, Pedro attempted to rekindle his rapidly deteriorating relationship with Domitila by sending lilies as a gesture of
peace—"from this your vassal, lover, and friend, true and faithful till
death."[28]

Aside from passionate letters and gifts that the emperor bestowed generously on Titília, her social and political positions were much enhanced during their courtship. The "fire" or "little fire," as Pedro liked to call himself during the early years of the dalliance, appointed her as the first lady-in-waiting for Empress Leopoldina in 1825. The three-year-old relationship had been hidden from the empress until that time. That honor was followed by a title of nobility, the Viscondessa de Santos, in October 1825. The choice of the "Santos" nomenclature carried a significant political implication, intended to annoy and even embarrass the Andradas of the city of Santos, who were persistent critics of Domitila. José Bonifácio, by then ousted from power, reportedly said, "Who dreamed Domitila the little ant-eater would be the viscondessa of the home of the Andradas? What a hare-brained insult!"[29] Later, all the Andradas refused titles of nobility, including José's daughter, the widow of Martim Francisco, when she was offered the title of the Viscondessa de Ipiranga by Pedro II. A year after Domitila bore Pedro a son in December 1825, the grateful emperor elevated her to the rank of marquesa, the second highest title in the hierarchy of the Brazilian nobility. The scroll that ennobled her reads in part: ". . . for distinguished merits and services rendered as the First Lady in Waiting to the Empress, my much loved and dear wife."[30]

The "merits and services" of Titília brought other honors and material benefits to her family, though Rangel states that her influence on affairs of state was virtually nil. All her brothers were serving in the army, as her father had before them, and they were rewarded with titles, promotions, and commendations. Her father, the old colonel, was given the title of the Visconde de Castro and made an imperial chamberlain; her older brother, João, was honored with the title of visconde a year after the death of the father in 1827. Her sister, Maria Benedita, and her husband, Boaventura Delfim Pereira, were given titles of the Barões de Sorocaba in October 1826, three years after the Baronesa de Sorocaba gave birth to a son, Rodrigo, whose paternity was attributed to the emperor.[31] Aside from immediate siblings and relatives, Domitila also arranged several minor political appointments for her protégés.

It is highly doubtful that the imperial mistress exercised as much influence on major state decisions as many people alleged.[32] Yet, José Bonifácio, the patriarch of independence, blamed the Marquesa de Santos for his fall from power, including his bitter relationship with Pedro

I after 1823. In fact, most contemporaries believed that her role in the dismissal of the Andrada brothers was minor. The turbulent Constituent Assembly of 1823, the repressive policies of José Bonifácio toward the "government's foes" (read José Bonifácio's), and the patriarch's condescending attitude toward the young, imperious sovereign contributed first to acrimony and later to enmity between Pedro I and his first minister. If Pedro chose "Santos" for his mistress's title to irk the patrician politician from Santos, Domitila openly despised José Bonifácio; her attitude was a matter of public record. Considering the political differences between the Andradas and Pedro I, independent of Domitila's personal feelings, the downfall of the brothers would have come sooner or later. The Marquesa de Santos probably accelerated the process during her bedtime chats with Pedro.

Another example in support of Domitila's purported Madame Pompadour role was her rumored intervention in the selection of two senators of the empire. Both were clergymen: José Caetano de Aguiar and Nuno Eugênio de Lóssio e Seiblits. Although she had influenced the nomination of parish priests in São Paulo and Rio, the selection of senators was an imperial prerogative exercised by the emperor and guaranteed by the Constitution of 1824 that was beyond her domain. Furthermore, from a political standpoint, Pedro would himself choose such conservative politicians for the life-tenure senatorial offices in view of rising anti-Portuguese sentiment in the country and of growing opposition from such liberals as the Andradas.[33]

In Rio's diplomatic community, however, the ministers and consuls of Europe and the United States continued to believe in the political power of the imperial mistress. Based on countless cases in European court politics, this was a reasonable assumption. British Minister Charles Stuart openly curried favors from Domitila, who in fact was a partisan to the early ratification of the Anglo-Brazilian Treaty of 1825. The minister of the United States in Rio reported to the secretary of state that she was the ruler of the country; another diplomat related to his government that she was in fact the "empress of Brazil and supreme dispenser of honors and official favors."[34] Her power over political and diplomatic matters was probably exaggerated. Furthermore, although friendship with her provided any aspiring politician or diplomat easy access to the emperor, judged by existing public and private records, her patronage power was also vastly exaggerated, in reality being confined to her immediate family and relatives. She was by no means a power-hungry éminence grise.

When anti-Portuguese feelings exploded in various parts of the empire in 1831, the emperor was forced in early April to abdicate in favor of his five-year-old son. This April 1831 event constituted not a change of command, but the end of Portuguese domination and the beginning of Brazilian. The last of the seven children of Pedro I and Leopoldina, Pedro II, was not coronated until 1841; the constitution prohibited a minor from assuming that power. Pedro was to be the first and last American-born emperor in Brazil as well as in the New World.

Pedro II was uniquely a child of the New World in several ways. He took after his mother in both his physical and intellectual makeup. Blond, blue-eyed, and tall for his age, the Braganza-Hapsburg prince was reared by his affectionate sisters, a string of doting courtiers, and a coterie of distinguished tutors. Pedro I, though bitter about the popular opposition from Brazilians, chose José Bonifácio, the savant of the empire, to be the imperial tutor. Repentant and mellowed by age, the patriarch from Santos assumed the responsibility of training an emperor for the American empire. Among the corps of the prince's pedagogues was the future Duque de Caxias, Pedro's equestrian teacher. The young boy was, however, more a bookworm than the rough-and-tumble buck his father had been. Like his mother Leopoldina, young Pedro enjoyed natural science, foreign languages, and philosophical treatises. His tutors' attempts to arouse interest in girls and later women never seemed to succeed. Of the three sisters who lived with him, Januária, only three years older, became his surrogate mother.[35]

By the time Pedro II reached adolescence, discussions of suitable marriage partners had begun. In 1838 there was even talk of a collective sibling marriage proposal between the American Braganza house and the Spanish royal family. Infanta Luisa Fernanda or one of the daughters of Infante Francisco de Paula would be matched with Dom Pedro II; Januária would marry one of the infante's sons. Court politics and diplomatic difficulties in Rio and Madrid prevented pursuing such plans further, however. By 1841, when Pedro was crowned, the Brazilian government had turned elsewhere for a prospective bride for the young emperor. Consideration was still being given to a collective marriage of the three Braganzas, this time with the offspring of the House of Hapsburg. Wary of potential opposition from Britain, the government dispatched a former minister of foreign affairs to Austria to carry out a discrete negotiation. The Hapsburgs were related to the American Braganzas, and the father of Leopoldina, Franz I of Austria, continued to show sympathy to both emperors after the death of his daughter. In view of the historical and emotional ties, Brazil made a firm offer to the current emperor, one of Leopoldina's brothers. The Brazilian envoy was astonished to find the Austrian court and Prince Metternich unreceptive. As in 1829, the power behind the throne was against such an alliance-marriage between Austria and a second-rate power—and an American monarchy at that. Instead, Metternich proposed an alternate plan, a union between the Italian branch of the Hapsburgs and the American Braganzas.[36]

Princess Teresa Cristina was the youngest child of the Duque de Calabria and his second wife Princess Maria Isabel, sister of Carlota Joaquina and the great-aunt of the Brazilian emperor. The duke, who later became King Francesco I of Two Sicilies, was of Hapsburg blood. Thus, Teresa Cristina, the future empress of Brazil, was related to Pedro II on both sides. Such a marriage of close blood relatives required papal dispensation. In this case, the Pope agreed not only to bless the marriage proposal but to perform the ceremony.

Once the marriage contract was duly signed and approved by both parties, the betrothed exchanged portraits. The marriage, which took place at Naples in 1843, was conducted by proxies. In September of that year, the entire city of Rio turned out to greet their empress on her arrival. To the public's consternation and Pedro's shock, she did not measure up to her official portrait; clearly her real beauty was anything but physical. The young emperor wept in disappointment, saying to his governess, "They deceived me!"[37] In pathetic contrast to the tall, blond, blue-eyed, almost Aryan American Braganza, the empress was squat, brunette, dark-eyed, and slightly lame, a physical defect that became more pronounced as years went by. Although the marriage was to be among the emperor's personal tragedies, his upbringing and forbearance outweighed his young impulses, and he accepted the consequences. What Teresa Cristina lacked in physical beauty she made up for in her devotion as wife and mother. She came to be adored by her imperial subjects—one of the two European additions to the American house (the other being Leopoldina) whom the Brazilians came to accept as their own. Of this loveless but respectful marriage, four children were born: two sons and two daughters. The male heirs died in infancy. Princess Isabel, the heiress to the throne and, like her mother, no physical beauty, was to marry a Frenchman; Leopoldina, the younger of the two, married the Fifth Duque of Saxe-Corburg-Gotha.[38] Like their American-born aunts, neither Isabel nor Leopoldina was ever considered for a morganatic marriage with a Brazilian.

Like that of their brother Pedro II, the marriages of Januária and Francisca were full of travail. The original plan had been a double marriage of Teresa Cristina to Pedro and her brother, the Conde de Lecce, to Januária, but upon Lecce's sudden death another brother, Luís (the Conde de Aquila), came on the scene.[39] Accompanying his sister, the empress, to Brazil, he was easily persuaded to make such a marriage. The ceremony took place in 1844. As her dowry, Januária brought twelve cattle ranches in Piauí, all formerly Jesuit and state property after 1759, four square leagues of land in Santa Catarina, and six more in Curitiba, Paraná. Because at the time of the marriage the emperor had no heir, Januária and Aquila were next in line to the Brazilian succession and by contract were required to reside in Brazil. Aquila was given citizenship and the rank of admiral in the imperial navy. Should the couple choose to live outside the empire, they could exchange the landed properties for a cache of 750 contos, roughly 1 million francs. It was a veritable fortune. (Teresa Cristina brought to Brazil a dowry of 2 million francs.) Januária and her husband, however, were not to live in Brazil after their marriage. Aquila was involved in a political conspiracy that sought to replace Dom Pedro with Januária. In mid-October 1844 the disgraced couple was forced to leave for Europe.[40] The following February, the imperial couple had their first child, Prince Afonso, whose birth resolved any doubts about the succession and preempted Januária's role as an immediate pretenderess.

Princess Francisca, Pedro's favorite sister, had been the first of the three remaining Braganzas to marry, her betrothal to a Frenchman, being hurried along by French diplomatic concern over Pedro's betrothal to a Neopolitan princess, according to one historian. The possibility of Francisca marrying an Italian was swiftly dealt with by the nomination of a French candidate, Joinville, a son of King Louis Philippe. Joinville was no stranger to Brazil. In 1840, visiting Bahia, he had been mistaken for the leader of an invading army and was almost shot to death by a firing squad. The timely intervention of a local noble who recognized him prevented disaster. Only three years later, Joinville returned to Brazil to marry an imperial princess. Francisca brought a dowry of 1 million francs (750 contos), twenty-five square leagues of land in Santa Catarina, and other personal properties that produced an annual income of 26,000 francs. Later, her Italian brother-in-law would complain of his relatively small income, and the Brazilian government was called upon to rectify the situation by equalizing the dowries of the two princesses. Even in her marriage, Francisca remained the emperor's favorite sister. She and her husband moved to Paris to live at the court.[41]

The second emperor of Brazil had rather simple habits, as those of monarchs went. He lacked the imperial affectation in which his father excelled, but was physically fit and enjoyed robust health until his fifties, in marked contrast to his grandfather, who overate himself to death. Pedro II drank moderately, mostly wine, and did not smoke. Late in life, as irony would have it, the emperor of the land that produced the finest sugar in the world suffered from diabetes. He liked fruits of all kinds; ate his dinner, it was said, at the unusual hour of four in the afternoon; went to bed early; and arose early. He relished early morning promenades in Rio and Petrópolis.

The São Cristóvão Palace continued to be the principal residence. State business was first conducted at the City Palace and later at São Cristóvão, where for instance the Council of State regularly met. Not attracted by the Imperial Fazenda de Santa Cruz, where his grandfather and father loved to retreat, Pedro chose the imperial city of Petrópolis, named after him, as the summer capital in 1847. There, the imperial government, the entire diplomatic corps, and court hangers-on escaped the muggy, humid summer of Rio between November and May each year. During the summer, the emperor commuted between the two capitals, usually holding his cabinet and Council of State meetings on Saturdays either at the City Palace or São Cristóvão and returning to Petrópolis on Sundays.

Pedro preferred to answer his own mail, held regular weekly audiences, and, after his first visit to Europe in 1871, abandoned the ceremonial beija-mão custom that his grandfather had so thoroughly enjoyed. In defiance of tradition, the imperial couple remained on their feet when receiving guests. His father had preferred to sit on a high chair; his grandfather, suffering from gout, had propped his ulcerous foot on a hassock, forcing the bent head of a hand-kissing guest uncomfortably near the sore.[42]

Pedro's political role as the ruler will be discussed in later chapters. He viewed himself as a liberal in the nineteenth-century mold, dreamed of becoming a teacher, and appreciated both philosophical and scientific subjects. Inheriting his mother's intellect, he was a natural-science buff, ever curious about gadgets and machines. One of his favorite pastimes was to watch trains arrive at the Petrópolis station from Rio. His linguistic ability was better than his father's—English, French, Italian, and Latin being his favorite languages—and he even studied Sanskrit and Hebrew. He corresponded with leading intellectuals of his time: Gobineau, Longfellow, Agassiz, Emerson, James, and Holmes.[43] To these distinguished minds, Pedro later added Pasteur, Quatrefages, and Victor Hugo. The last called Pedro II "the grandson of Marcus Aurelius."[44] Actually, Hugo erred; Pedro was the American Marcus Aurelius, a true philosopher-king in the New World.

The history of the Brazilian monarchy in many ways was that of Pedro II—not of his grandfather, who brought the House of Braganza to the tropics, or of his father, who gained independence for Brazil. João VI helped lay the foundations for the American monarchy; Pedro I molded the Brazilian character, which was built upon the colonial heritage and the New World boldness and foresight that his ancestors lacked. The vicissitudes of the Brazilian monarchy after 1831 were really the growing pains of the young emperor, and this book is a history of the empire that matured along with its natural prince: Pedro Alcântara Brasileiro, the American Marcus Aurelius, the noblest of all Brazilian nobles.

3

Noblemen of the Southern Cross

The new nobility is but the act of power,
but ancient nobility is the act of time. FRANCIS BACON

In the virtues of the nobles . . . lies the remedy
for the evils of the time; the weal of the kingdom, the peace of
the church, the rule of justice depended on them. GEORGES CHASTELLAIN

The Braganza monarchy in America (1808–89) was not the first to create a nobility in the New World. Titled *conquistadores, adelantados,* and civil-military administrators had begun to appear in continental Spanish America as early as the 1520s. Although small in number, this cadre of Spanish nobles firmly ensconced themselves in the highest niches of colonial society. In Spanish Peru, one prominent historian reports, "the interrelated class of dons, nobles, and hidalgos" provided the first stitching of the colonial sociopolitical fabric by becoming the elite in the viceregal court.[1] In New Spain, eight captains-general were ennobled for valiant service during the age of conquest, and between 1535 and 1821 thirty-seven of the sixty-three viceroys of New Spain, or 58.7 percent, were nobles. Of the thirty-seven, only three were *criollos* (two Cubans and one Peruvian), and no Mexican-born noble ever served either as the viceroy in his homeland or in Peru.[2]

In Portuguese Brazil, no titled nobles were ever reported as having served as conquistadores and *donatários.* Such well-known fidalgo-entrepreneurs and soldier-statesmen as Martim Afonso de Sousa, his brother Pero Lopes de Sousa, and Duarte Coelho were not titled nobles, in spite of their distinguished military service to the House of Aviz. Although colonial historians seldom mentioned the creation of a nobility in Brazil, a few salient designations were made. At least two grandsons of Duarte Coelho, the donatário of Pernambuco, one of whom was born in Brazil, were made nobles; Judge João Antônio Salter de Mendonça, born in Pernambuco (1746), was ennobled as the Visconde de Azurara in 1820 after half a century of judicial service to the Braganza state; and a descendant of General Salvador Correia de Sá e Benevides, the governor-general of Rio who had won back Angola from the Dutch, was ennobled as the Visconde de Asseca. At least seven of the visconde's heirs held nobiliary titles and became leading latifundiary clansmen in Campos, Rio, where they figured prominently as a local elite until the mid-nineteenth century. Much like the descendants of Duarte Coelho, the Assecas amassed their fortune in land and agriculture.

No Brazilian ever held the highest offices of colonial governors and later viceroys under Portuguese rule; no prominent planters, miners, or merchants in colonial Brazil were honored with titles of nobility. In Bourbon Spanish America, the contrary was the case. Affluent miners, merchants, and landowners often sought and obtained titles. Actually, in eighteenth-century Mexico, the richest class was made up of the nobility and *peninsulares*.[3] Nobles were politically, socially, and economically without peers in colonial society.

In contrast to that in Europe, the Brazilian nobility performed a different function in society and polity. Unlike the older nobilities of Europe, it consisted of affluent and pauperized landed aristocrats and gentry, town merchants, rural and urban bourgeois intellectuals, leading military and naval officials, major ecclesiastical leaders, and political loyalists. The crucial distinction between the Brazilian and the older European nobilities lies in the former's corporate status as well as its socioeconomic origins. Constraints on social mobility were imposed during colonial times through the royal practices of the Luso-Brazilian administration. Unlike Bourbon France, Portugal under Aviz, Hapsburg, and Braganza rule did not allow key officeholders to enjoy the nobiliary titles customarily automatic to office.[4] The builder of a far-flung seaborne empire, the country tightly supervised its civil, military, and religious servants. The facile concession of privileges and titles could have resulted in the emergence of a rival overseas power elite. Consequently, the Crown made certain that its overseas administrators were periodically rotated from post to post, and the kingdom even came to maintain two separate branches of foreign service, one in the Atlantic (Brazil and West Africa) and another in the Indian zone (East Africa, India, and the Orient).[5] Such a division of labor within the bureaucratic structure discouraged the rise of important colonial economic and political clans closely tied to Portugal. In short, marriage with the overseas rich could terminate the career of an ambitious Portuguese *letrado* or military officer if he chose to remain abroad; if he preferred to continue in the foreign service, the rotation system weakened his ties with his overseas in-laws.

Despite such official discouragement, a few colonial families in Brazil succeeded in winning the privileges of fidalguia, but not of nobility. The House of Torre, in the Northeast, for instance, had all the outward trappings of any European feudal noble family, lacking only formal titles. In 1699 the dowager of the house actually bought the *foro* of fidalguia, or privileges, from the Braganza Crown for 60,000 cruzados, a veritable fortune, payable in nine annual installments. Only a quarter of a century earlier, the Portuguese king had sold the entire captaincy of Espírito Santo for only 40,000.[6] Obviously, wealth alone could not qualify the Torres for a noble title, but Mexicans or Peruvians of similar stature would easily have succeeded in becoming nobles. João Antonil, an Italian Jesuit who lived in colonial Brazil during the last quarter of the seventeenth century, reported that no titled nobility existed there, but added that the *senhor de engenho* class in the Recôncavo of Bahia rivaled rich nobles of the Old World in wealth. In fact, the planter class of sixteenth-century origin constituted the closest thing to a bastard aristocracy within the empire.[7] As in the cases of the Torres of Bahia and the Coelhos of Pernambuco—but not the Assecas of Rio—the Portuguese New World colony possessed an agrarian aristocracy, but lacked titled nobiliary clans. A French traveler observed in the nineteenth century that being a sugar planter in Rio province assured the status of a noble. Such late colonial savants as Rocha Pita, Caldas, and Vilhena made no mention of a *mazombo* nobility in Bahia, though they dwelled on the opulence of the agrarian and mercantile classes during the second half of the eighteenth century.[8] Colonial Brazil could claim an aristocracy, but not a nobility. The absence of nobility as an incorporated class remained true for nineteenth-century Brazil.

The transfer of the ruling House of Braganza from Portugal to Brazil in early 1808 formally introduced the nobiliary system and other honorific commendations to the New World. After arriving in Brazil, Dom João, then the prince regent ruling the empire in the name of his demented mother, Queen Maria I, bestowed a number of titles and honors on Brazilians and Portuguese in the colony. Significantly, the recipients of titles during the first years of the Joanine rule were urban merchants of humble origin. No major agrarian aristocrat of Brazilian birth was ennobled until 1822, a few months after independence. The tradition of a nonaristocratic Brazilian nobility, therefore, was finally established when the prince regent ennobled court politicians and leading merchants of Rio. The first group of bourgeois merchants and gentry included his closest advisers and courtiers. In December 1808 six condes and one marquês were created; among the condes were João's three "prime ministers." The only marquês (Vila do Olhão) was formerly a conde.⁹ All were Portuguese.

The first title of nobility for a Brazilian in the nineteenth century was awarded to the widow of a wealthy Portuguese merchant in Rio. In 1813 "the prince with bourgeois taste," in the words of Gilberto Freyre, created three titles of baron, of which one was bestowed on a Brazilian: the merchant's widow, the Baronesa de São Salvador de Campos (Ana Francisca Maciel da Costa).¹⁰ All came from the ranks of the *novos ricos* and demonstrated strong gentry-bourgeois characteristics: an enterprising desire to diversify wealth and the maintenance of major interests in trade and commerce. These appointments set the pattern for the nonaristocratic character of the Brazilian nobility.

The fame and wealth of the Baronesa de São Salvador de Campos was based on the Carneiro fortune, which facilitated her rise in court society during Joanine and Pedro I's times. The founder of the largest mercantile fortune in Brazil was Portuguese merchant Brás Carneiro Leão. Born in Portugal in 1732, he migrated to the colony, where he made money as a trader in the mining region of Minas. Wisely investing in land in and around the city of Rio, he soon became wealthy; the principal commercial activity of the family was located in Candelária, the heart of Rio's business district. Soon after the arrival of the Braganza court in 1808, Brás died, leaving the entire fortune to his widow and children. The first-born, Fernando, took over the family business, rechristening it Carneiro, Viúva e Filhos. Partner in or correspondent for several major commercial houses in Europe, the firm easily expanded its business. When Brazil was elevated to the status of coking-dom with Portugal, the city of Rio had a dozen major mercantile clans; the Carneiro Leão interests were intimately tied to those of Geraldo Carneiro Belens and Eduardo de Faria, both major merchants in the court and sons-in-law of the founder. Brother José Alexandre, educated in England, was a sometime financier and diplomat; years later, he be-came an envoy extraordinary in the embassy to Naples that contracted for the imperial marriage of Pedro II and Teresa. The first-born Fer-nando became the Barão de Vila Nova de São José in 1825 and conde the following year; the youngest of the siblings, José, became the Visconde de São Salvador de Campos, the dowager's title, in 1846. One of Fernan-do's daughters married José.[11]

Not all the children of Brás and Ana Francisca married gentry and bourgeois merchants. One daughter wed Manuel Jacinto Nogueira da Gama (the future Marquês de Baependi), a high-ranking treasury of-ficial during Joanine times and a cabinet minister for Pedro I. Baependi was a holder of thirteen *sesmarias* in Valença, Rio, and the adjacent re-gion; the wedding dowry of his wife was Fazenda Santa Mônica, the jewel of the Nogueira da Gama landed properties. Another daughter married the future Visconde de Cachoeira; still another wed Paulo Fer-nandes Viana, the Intendente de Polícia of Rio, and their daughter Ana Luisa became a Duquesa de Caxias. All in all, the children of Brás and Ana Francisca married wealthy Portuguese merchants and Brazil-ian politicians. Grandchildren of the founders intermarried within the clan. A son of Baependi, Francisco Nicolau Carneiro Nogueira da Gama (the future Barão de Santa Mônica), married his cousin, a daugh-ter of Caxias. By the third generation, the transition from merchant to gentry to aristocracy was complete.[12]

Equal in wealth to the Carneiro Leãos, the Barão do Rio Seco played a less prominent role in establishing ties with Brazilian gentry and ar-istocracy. Little is known about his background. A Portuguese mer-chant, Joaquim José de Azevedo made his fortune in import and export trade. Proud owner of two palaces, Rio Seco epitomized the "grotesque figure of Brazilian" novo rico: overdressed; consumed by the avarice to be still richer; eager to be decorated with medals, patents, and titles; and finally an inveterate social climber. When the Braganzas moved to the New World, there were one duque, seven marquêses, six condes, and numerous viscondes and barões. In the new Rio of court, nobles, and fast-rising urban bourgeois fortunes, Rio Seco was an archetype. He was looked on as an ambitious upstart, ready to lend money to the royal house and its counselors; although his wealth earned him an entrée to the world of high society, he was never completely accepted. One foreign visitor observed that Rio Seco—from the ostentation of the Chinese-red front door of his palatial residence to the overly made up and grandly bejeweled womenfolk—manifested an excessive desire to overcome the inferiority complex of a bourgeois gentilhomme. When he loaned the royal house 500 contos without interest, five carriages and eleven slaves were needed to cart the money. Still another foreign visitor pointedly mentioned the humble origins of Rio Seco's Irish wife, whose mother was said to have been a washwoman. The equally bourgeois prince regent ennobled Joaquim José de Azevedo and *that* underscored the rising importance of the mercantile influence in the Braganza court in Brazil. That the Carneiro Leãos succeeded in diversifying their social and economic capital by becoming in-laws of Brazilian aristocracy, and that Rio Seco reinforced his ties with the Portuguese elements, tells much about the diversity of the commercial, urban elite of Rio, especially the different avenues open for social mobility.[13]

Because the transformation of social values, economic patterns, and political alliances in nineteenth-century Brazil was conditioned by rural-urban contacts, precise definitions of gentry and aristocracy as they applied to the society are important. The distinction in the concept of aristocracy in Brazilian history can be made in the following way. To a certain extent, the aristocracy there resembled that of Old Europe: a rural latifundiary class, whose members at times were holders of entail (*morgado*); established lineages dating back at least to the seventeenth century, preferably before the discovery of gold at the end of that century; a strong proclivity for endogamy; and property owners whose land, the principal source of family or clan wealth, guaranteed social prestige and political power rather than social and economic mobility. In this connection, the Albuquerques of Pernambuco and Bahia were aristocrats by birthright, but failed to mobilize their wealth by modernizing family-clan economic holdings during the decades of the 1870s and 1880s, which marked the advent of sugar-refinery technology. In contrast, the eighteenth-century family of Carneiro da Silva of Macaé, Rio, was a risk-taking planter clan that had built the first modern refinery in imperial Brazil by 1877. In addition to entailed property, lineage, and their accompanying social and political status, the aristocracy was known for its universal ineptness in managing estates and wealth. Even in England, where the aristocracy joined the gentry in diversifying its interests in commerce and industry, the majority remained rentiers, not direct participants in business; on the Continent, their more conservative counterparts continued to collect dues in kind, not rents.[14]

The gentry concept, though peculiarly English in origin, is analytically useful for nineteenth-century Brazil. Combining *gentry* with the more Continental term *bourgeoisie* adds flexibility, for the former carries rural connotations, the latter, urban. In England, the aristocracy and gentry were joined politically and economically; the Industrial Revolution allowed them to reap profits without becoming completely urbanized;[15] parliaments and cabinets were dominated by these two classes. Hence, England never became a bourgeois state. Political and economic changes led to the rise of a court gentry in London as well as to the decline of the court aristocracy. What set the gentry apart from the aristocracy was a class mentality: a willingness to be transformed into bourgeois capitalist agriculturists, as well as an eagerness to accept bourgeois values.[16]

Similar characteristics were observed in Brazil as well. Rio Seco was a court bourgeois; Brás Carneiro Leão was a court bourgeois; his wife, the Baronesa de São Salvador de Campos, a court gentry; and her children and grandchildren, such as the Marquesa de Baependi, the Duquesa de Caxias, and the Baronesa de Santa Mônica, court aristocrats by marriage. It was time, however short it might have been, and wealth, coupled with titles that transformed them into aristocracy. In geographical terms, the sugar-growing Northeast tended to have more families belonging to the aristocratic lineages, and the coffee-growing Center-South was home to the gentry.

In the analytical framework of Blum and Sombart, Brazilian society in the nineteenth century was in a twilight era, a transitional phase from a society of "order" to a society of "class," or from a "traditional" to a "modern" phase. To argue that Brazil during the nineteenth century, when the slave regime was at the bottom and the centripetal Braganzas at the top, was solely a precapitalist society of caste is to deny the dynamics of the empire, where individual, not collective, political power and social status were often based on the ability to accumulate wealth. In such a transitional society, birthright and privilege did not automatically accord power and wealth. The social history of Brazil during the nineteenth century evolves, to some extent, around the story of the rise of the gentry elite in the coffee-growing Center-South and the decline of aristocratic rulers in the sugarcane-cultivating Northeast as well as the consequent struggle of the two rivals for social and political hegemony. In this emerging "modern" and "class" society, the imperial nobility was recruited from all walks of life, including the old and new twin rivals (aristocracy and gentry) of the agrarian interests.[17] It is in this context of social history of the mutation from a society of order to a society of class that the historical role of the Brazilian nobility should be understood.

Nobility is a juridical term. In Portugal, it included both titled and untitled personages who held concessions of privileges (*foro*) from the king. Although such a concept is useful, it hardly renders a neatly drawn analytical framework. *Fidalgo Cavaleiro* and *Fidalgo Moço* of the Portuguese royal house and later the Brazilian imperial house, for instance, considered themselves to be part of the nobility, entitled to such perquisites as the right to take out a coat of arms when requested and approved. For the purpose of identifying the holders of nobiliary titles as social achievers, however, whether of the aristocracy, gentry, or bourgeoisie, the fidalgos must be placed in a separate category of honors.

The Brazilian imperial nobility was structured in five principal grades: *duque, marquês, conde, visconde,* and *barão,* in descending order. All the titles were *for one life only,* but could be renewed for heirs with imperial consent. The two lowest grades carried categories of either *com honras de grandeza* or *sem honras de grandeza*—with or without the honors of grandee. The three remaining ranks automatically bore the distinction of grandeza.[18] Thus, in theory, a grandee of the empire held at least the rank of conde.

In addition to these titles, the empire bestowed other honorific commendations on the deserving. Below the nobiliary titles came a series of imperial orders that were organized in a hierarchy of importance and prestige:

  1. *The Ordem Imperial do Cruzeiro.* Established in 1822, this

commendation was designed to honor the supporters of independence. This order had a number of awards to be made in several categories: *Grande Cruzeiro* (8 *efetivos* and 8 *honorários*), *Dignitário* (15 efetivos and 30 honorários), *Oficial* (200 efetivos and 120 honorários), and *Cavaleiro* (no limit). Prestigious politicians, military officers, diplomats, and some leading merchants and planters were the primary recipients of this order.

2. *The Ordem de Nosso Senhor Jesus Cristo.* This order, established in Portugal in 1316, was adopted in Brazil in 1823. It was principally designed to recognize ecclesiastical elite as well as laymen who performed a substantial service for the Religion. It was not uncommon for a town priest to hold this honor after a successful career. The breakdown was the same as the Rosa (see 4 below), but Grão Cruz recipients could number 12 and the ranks below had no limit.

3. *The Ordem Imperial de D. Pedro I.* Created in 1826, this honor was held by the Marquês de Barbacena, Pedro's confidant and personal emissary to various courts in Europe, and the Duque de Caxias, the empire's soldier-statesman of the Second Reign.

4. *The Ordem da Rosa.* This order, created in 1829, consisted of a fixed number of honors, including Grão Cruz (8 efetivos and 8 honorários), Grande Dignitário (16), Dignitario (32), Comendador, Oficial, and Cavaleiro, the last three without limit. Rosa was most coveted by regional and local elites who had little or no connections at the court. Often, this order served as a stepping-stone for a higher one and even for a title.

5. *The Ordem de São Bento de Avis.* Also a Portuguese order, this one had originated in 1162 and been adopted in Brazil the same year the Cristo was introduced. Cristo was the most fitting honor for regalist ecclesiastics, and Avis was reserved for loyal military officers. Its internal structure was the same as those of the Rosa and Cristo. Often the empire granted Avis to a wounded officer as well as to one who was to retire after decades of imperial service. This honor was the sine qua non for any military man who aspired to a title.

6. *The Ordem de São Tiago.* Established in 1174 in Portugal, this honor was introduced in Brazil in 1843, but was never granted to anyone.[19]

On a par with these imperial honors were other kinds of *graças honoríficas*: Fidalgo Cavaleiro and Moço Fidalgo da Casa Imperial, Grande do Império, Gentil-Homem da Casa Imperial, and Conselheiro. The holders of the first two honors were usually imperial elect, the majority being children of the titular nobility; the Fidalgo Cavaleiro was reserved for adults, the Moço Fidalgo for minors. The award of this honor, or imperial recognition, simply established or strengthened the pedigree of a particular family. Gentil-Homem always went to adults who enjoyed close personal friendships with the emperors and their immediate family members. The title of Conselheiro was automatic for those middle- and upper-echelon functionaries of the imperial civil and military service who had served for twenty or more years. The claim was made by a supplicant toward the end of his term of service.

Grande do Império was a separate title. Although this honor was automatically granted to those ennobled above the grade of conde, it could be awarded separately to stress the importance of an occasion or personage. Isabel Maria Brasileira, the Duquesa de Goiás and a love child of Pedro I and the Marquesa de Santos, was awarded a separate grant of Grande do Império as an infant in 1829. She lost the honors accruing to the title of duquesa when she married a Brazilian conde, but was permitted to retain the honors of a grandee. Other elites of the empire were also honored. All Brazilian bishops were made ex officio Grandes do Império, a tradition that predated national independence. Also customary was the award of the honor to all the councillors of state. In November 1823 Pedro I made his councillors grandees; likewise, his son Pedro II in February 1842 made the first members of the Second Council of State grandees of the empire.[20] Not all the councillors in the Second Reign were titled nobles, however, and those possessing titles were not always condes or above (see chapter 8).

All imperial honors and titles were required to be registered and proper fees were to be paid at the Imperial Chancellery, where custom also called for taking out patents and coats of arms. Only military officers granted titles after 1850 were exempt from paying fees. Not every titleholder observed the custom, however. In a strict sense, unregistered titles and honors were invalid. Furthermore, nobles, fidalgos, and other recipients of imperial commendations were obliged to solicit imperial sanction for marriage. This rule was especially observed for marriages between "noble persons" as well as for unions between a noble

and a commoner.[21] The surviving records of title registration and so-
licitation for the imperial authorization of marriage reveal a fascinating aspect of the life-styles of the Brazilian upper class, especially the
nobiliary elite. The empire created between December 1822 and November 1889 a total of 1,278 titles that were distributed to 980 men and
women.[22]

Comparing that number with the population of Brazil (4 million in
1822 and 14 million in 1889) provides insight into the structure of the
nobility. Titles went to deserving citizens of all twenty provinces, Uruguay (the Província Cisplatina until 1828), and six foreign countries,
including the United States. However, the five demographic and economic centers of the realm succeeded in holding the lion's share (see
table 1). Pernambuco and Bahia, in the Northeast, and Rio (including
the court), São Paulo, and Minas Gerais in the Center-South contained
690 nobles, or 70.4 percent of the total. Between 1822 and 1889, when
the population more than tripled, the five provinces consistently maintained more than 60 percent of the total, with 63.7 percent in 1822 and
62.2 percent in 1889. The coincidence of nearly synchronized distribution of titles and demographic figures reveals that no particular region or province claimed a disproportionately higher number. At least
on paper, the organization of the imperial nobility reflected a well-bal-
anced social and economic representation; and its geographical distribution, a solid nationwide composition. Hence, a social analysis of the
nobility can be a significant means of shedding new light on a phase of
national history: a history of the elite.

The nobility system, first introduced in Brazil by the prince regent
(later King João VI) changed little after independence in September
1822. In the constituent assembly of 1823 and within the intimate cir-
cle of the imperial advisers, much discussion occurred about the re-
structuring of the nobility. The definition of nobility, which included
the twin pillars of titulars and fidalgos as in Portugal, was widely accepted in Brazil. A title in Portugal was for one life only, but fidalguia
was hereditary for three generations, and the fourth must request its
renewal.[23] During the draft stage of the Brazilian Constitution of 1823,
Pedro I and his closest adviser, Chalaça (Francisco Gomes da Silva),
considered establishing a class of formalized hereditary nobility, thus
extending transmissibility to titles as was the practice with fidalguia.
The imperial philosophy was that a hereditary nobility would serve as

Table 1 Title Distribution in Five Provinces of Brazil, 1822–1889

Province	Number of individuals	Percent of five provinces (total number of titleholders: 690)	Percent of total number of titleholders in Brazil (980)
Bahia	115	16.7	11.7
Pernambuco	90	13.0	9.2
Rio and Court	224	32.5	22.9
Minas Gerais	155	22.5	15.8
São Paulo	106	15.4	10.8
Total	690	100	70.4

Sources: Laura Jarnagin, "The Role and Structure of the Brazilian Imperial Nobility in Society and Politics," M.A. thesis, Vanderbilt University (1977), p. 8; Carlos G. Rheingantz, *Titulares do império* (Rio, 1960).

a stronger foundation for the empire. Pedro went one step further, proposing the establishment of a special nobiliary tribunal, like those in Europe, to govern the corporation and protect its interests. At the outset of forging an empire in the 1820s, such a notion strongly appealed to the emperor and Brazilians who were prone to centripetalism. But not all shared this view. A political impasse immediately arose between the Crown and the constituent assembly on the issue. The deputies could not agree on the size of the nobility, the conditions for titular awards, or even the amount of compulsory fees to be levied on them. The uncertain political and social milieu of the court and of the rest of the country also contributed to the lack of consensus. When the liberal-dominated assembly voted down any bill to create a cadre of hereditary titleholders and fidalgos, the nobility became a creature of the imperial household, not of the nation. The Crown eventually reacted by dissolving the assembly.

Subsequently, Pedro's hand-picked counselors modified the original plans in the Constitution of 1824, making the final structure of the nobility a variation of the Portuguese model. The nobiliary titles remained under the purview of the imperial House of Braganza and their award became the prerogative of emperors. Brazil had no parliament-enacted nobility to grant stipends, land, or offices.[24] Until the end of the monarchy, the nobility was a collective social elite, many of whom amassed fortunes as landowners and merchants or held high political offices.

The selection of prospective candidates for titles and honorific commendations rested on several factors. Pedro I and Pedro II relied on the broadly defined doctrine of "service to the State" and "service to Humanity." The first category was decidedly political and military in nature, and the second concerned social, cultural, and religious causes that the Crown upheld as its declared and charitable objectives. Pecuniary contributions to such causes were the most decisive factors in selection. A candidate could directly solicit the emperor to grant him a title; or he could hire a recognized figure in the court as his intermediary, one generally familiar with court manners; or the government could recommend a meritorious candidate for a title or honor in public recognition of worthy service rendered. Titles and honors were traditionally issued on the birthdays of the imperial couples, and on such joyful occasions as the births of imperial princes and marriages. Once titles and honors were granted, recipients were required (a requirement not always honored) to register with the Scribe of the Nobility and Fidalguia of the Empire. Dom João VI created this office in 1811 as prince regent and seven people eventually served as scribe, their principal duty being to maintain the Book of Registry for titles and coats of arms as well as perform other bureaucratic chores, which included designing heraldic symbols. The Nobiliary Record Office (cartório da nobreza) was part of the imperial household.[25]

The founder of the "national nobility" was Pedro I, whose father, João VI, had conspicuously failed to ennoble leading landowners of Brazilian birth. The record of Pedro I was not much superior, but the 146 titles he created between 1822 and 1831 did include a few landholding nobles. The majority of the ennobled came from the ranks of court aristocrats and the military-civil service elite of the realm, plus a scattering of social notables from among the landowners, merchants, and miners.[26] From the landowning elite, Pedro I made a few but significant choices. The morgado do Cabo in Pernambuco, Francisco Pais Barreto, already a visconde in 1824, was made the Marquês do Recife; others were the Barão de Valença (Estêvão Ribeiro de Resende), a major planter in Valença; the Barão de Pirajá (Joaquim Pires de Carvalho e Albuquerque), brother of the morgado da Torre (the Visconde da Torre de Garcia d'Ávila); and the Barão de Pedra Branca (Domingos Borges de

Barros)—each a major landowner in his respective bailiwick.[27] A large group of landowners would not be ennobled until after 1850, in the coffee-growing region of the Paraíba Valley of São Paulo and Rio province and in the Zona de Mata of Minas Gerais.

On 10 December 1822, a few months after independence, the grateful emperor ennobled Antônio Joaquim Pires de Carvalho e Albuquerque, the morgado of the House of Torre in Bahia and the soldier-planter who consolidated independence for Pedro in that province. The title of the Barão da Torre de Garcia d'Ávila was bestowed on the Bahian sugar planter, a descendant of a sixteenth-century latifundiary family, whose economic wealth and social prestige were legendary and qualified him as a true aristocrat. After the proclamation of independence in São Paulo (September 1822), the Portuguese garrison in Bahia chose to defend the status quo, and many Bahian planters raised armies to defend their patriotic interests. In this war, Antônio was responsible for defeating the Portuguese reactionary forces, thus consolidating the northern half of the territory for the newly born empire. The citation of the concession decree reads in part as follows: ". . . for the relevant services that he has rendered with the greatest honor, patriotism, and determined enthusiasm to the well-being of the State and the glorious cause of Independence and centralization of This Empire."[28] On the same day, three other titles were honored with the status of grandee. The Barão de São João Marcos (Pedro Dias Pais Leme) was a Portuguese-born landowner in Rio province; his title, created in 1818, was reconfirmed as Brazilian. Similarly, the Barão de Itanhaém (Manuel Inácio de Andrade Souto Maior), first ennobled in 1819, was reconfirmed; and the Visconde do Rio Seco (promoted to that rank in 1818) was additionally honored with the title of grandee, thus transforming the Portuguese title into Brazilian.[29]

On 10 December 1826, the first birthday of Crown Prince Pedro, the same four were elevated to still higher titles: Torre de Garcia d'Ávila to visconde with the honors of grandee and the other three to marquêses. Rio Seco was given a new name for his title—the Marquês de Jundiaí—and was made a Grand Doorman (Porteiro Maior) of the imperial houses.[30] Significantly, those honored in December 1822 represented the hegemonic class of latifundiary landowners and the empire's major mercantile fortune. All had made either pecuniary or military contributions to the empire's founding and consolidation.

In accordance with his concept of nobility as a corporate class that would buttress the empire, the emperor created sixty titles in 1824 and 1826, some 61 percent of those created between 1822 and 1831, which served as the foundation of the Brazilian imperial nobility. Powerful politicians ennobled included the Visconde de Cachoeira (Luís José de Carvalho e Melo), the Visconde de Santo Amaro (José Egídio Álvares de Almeida), the Visconde de Baependi (Manuel Jacinto Nogueira da Gama), the Visconde de Barbacena (Felisberto Caldeira Brant Pontes), the Visconde de Queluz (João Severiano Maciel da Costa)—to name only the well-known individuals of the early years of the empire. By the end of the 1820s, these politicians were promoted, except for Cachoeira, to the marquisate. The title of visconde became a popular grade bestowed by both Pedro I and Pedro II on leading civilian and military officials of the monarchy.

Leading merchants and imperial siblings were also ennobled and honored with commendations. In addition to the elevation of Rio Seco to marquês, the heir of the Carneiro Leão fortune in Rio was first made the Barão de Vila Nova de São José, then conde. Isabel Maria Alcântara Brasileira, born in 1826 and the third child of Pedro and the marquesa, was made the Duquesa de Goiás. Courtiers were also made nobles. The Viscondessa de Santos was promoted to the marquisate, and Ana Romana de Aragão Calmon, a Bahian-born tutoress of Pedro I's children, was made the Condessa de Itapagipe.[31] To institutionalize the nobility, Pedro I did his best to lay a firm foundation for the corporation by personally selecting his acquaintances from various walks of life.

The second half of the twenties was a stormy era in Pedro I's personal and political life. The death of his first, unhappy empress (Leopoldina) and his uncontainable dalliance with Santos made him unpopular; the empire was in the midst of an international war; and he was preoccupied with a crescendo of anti-Portuguese sentiment in society and politics. The Andrada brothers of Santos, São Paulo, emerged as his leading detractors in imperial politics. Partly inspired by his desire to regain popularity with his Brazilian subjects and partly to pursue his notion of a new imperial ruling class, Pedro resorted to bestowing titles with largesse, unfortunately politicizing concession criteria as well as circumstances for selection. José Bonifácio was offered a title of marquês, which the patriarch of independence haughtily turned down; his daughter and his brother Martim Francisco were also offered titles by Pedro I and Pedro II repeatedly, but they too chose to honor the family tradition of refusing imperial titles.[32] The Andradas would not be the last to reject such titles for political reasons.

Peace with the regional agrarian aristocracy and gentry became the principal concern of the empire in the late twenties, and Pedro I, as did Philip II of Spain with the nobles of Aragon and Andalusia, chose to coopt the peripheral potentates. In 1828 and 1829 the children of the imperial nobility were given titles: Frutuoso Vicente Viana, the twenty-two-year-old first-born of the First Barão do Rio das Contas, was made the Second Barão do Rio das Contas. The elder barão was the first provincial president of Bahia after independence. The first-born male heirs of Baependi, Cachoeira, Queluz, Santo Amaro, Lages, and a few other notables were all given titles for their fathers' services to the state.[33] Pedro accomplished his political objective: to suborn powerful Brazilian aristocratic and gentry clans in exchange for loyalty and imperial harmony. It was a fitting move to bolster his power base and expand support for the House of Braganza at the periphery. If Pedro I succeeded in ennobling the heirs of the leading latifundiary and regional political clans on the empire's periphery, he conspicuously failed to reward the fast-rising young court mandarins in the center. Pedro de Araújo Lima, Antônio Francisco de Paula e Holanda Cavalcanti de Albuquerque, both of Pernambuco and prominent politicians, and Miguel Calmon du Pin e Almeida, of Bahia, were not to be titled until the early years of Pedro II's rule.

Pedro I's political troubles steadily worsened after the end of the Cisplatine War in 1828, and the impetuous, short-tempered emperor began to drift away from his Brazilian counselors and move closer to his father's loyal and proven servants of Portuguese origin. His final cabinet, the tenth since independence, was made up entirely of nobles and senators: five marquêses and one visconde. Commonly known as the "cabinet of marquêses," it lasted only two days. On 7 April 1831 the first emperor renounced his throne in favor of his five-year-old son, Pedro Alcântara Brasileiro, the only surviving male American Braganza. During the turbulent years of the Regency (1831–40), a law (Lei of 14 June 1831) specifically prohibited the government from "granting titles, honors, military orders, and distinctions."[34]

The first to receive titles of nobility after the ascent of Pedro II was a group of loyalist mandarins in July 1841 who had defended the political supremacy of the Crown and the integrity of the empire. Pedro de Araújo Lima, the last imperial regent and centripetal loyalist, was made the Visconde de Olinda (and later marquês in 1854) and was probably the longest-serving imperial politician of the century. Other titles were issued the same day (July 18). Miguel Calmon was made the Visconde de Abrantes (later likewise made marquês) for "relevant services rendered."[35] Two other former imperial regents and a general were ennobled along with Olinda and Abrantes: the Barão de Monte Alegre (José da Costa Carvalho), a transplanted Bahian in São Paulo and a nemesis of Regent Diogo Feijó in provincial politics; the Barão da Barra Grande (Francisco de Lima e Silva), father of Caxias and general in the imperial army; and his son Luís, the Barão de Caxias, for his role in the pacification of Maranhão in the mid-1830s. Caxias was destined to become the only duque in the Second Reign, outranking even a son-in-law of the emperor, the Conde d'Eu. Of the four ducal grades the Braganza House created in the New World, three belonged to the offspring of the imperial family: the Duquesa de Goiás and the Duquesa do Ceará, both daughters of Pedro I and Santos, and the Duque de Santa Cruz, Prince Auguste Charles Eugene Napoleon de Beauharnais, the first husband of Princess Maria, sister of Pedro I. It has been alleged that the Duquesa do Ceará died in infancy, a few days after the title was created, and therefore her title was never properly registered and thus was not legitimate.[36]

Caxias was the only Brazilian not a blood relation of the Braganzas to earn the highest grade in the nobiliary hierarchy. Because a teenaged emperor was on the throne, the early years of the Second Reign (1840–89) were difficult times. The monarchy was torn apart by partisan strife, multiple regional loyalties, and the Crown's attempt to regain the authority lost to its provinces—all legacies of the "democratic experiments" during the Regency years. The threat to imperial stability was real, requiring the constant services of the military and of political loyalists in restoring law and order. Caxias stood at the forefront of the imperial cadre of civil-military servants who upheld the unity of the monarchy. The empire's top soldier and troubleshooter, he put down revolts in Maranhão in the 1830s, in Minas Gerais and São Paulo in the early 1840s, and in Rio Grande do Sul in the mid-1840s. His service as military commander, provincial president, senator of the empire, cabinet minister, and finally prime minister stretched for almost a half century and well qualified him for the highest title. The young emperor made his former equestrian instructor barão in 1841, conde in 1845, marquês in 1852, and duque in 1869, when Caxias was commander in chief of the Brazilian forces in Paraguay. Others who served the cause of the monarchy were also generously rewarded with titles: the Barão de Sabará (Manuel Antônio Pacheco) received a title in 1843 for the military service he rendered in quelling the Liberal Revolt in Minas Gerais.[37]

If the two emperors granted titles and honors as part of their imperial prerogative, the practice also proved to be both a political asset and a liability. Court favorites and powerful politicians sought to usurp the prerogatives, thus first politicizing and then partisanizing award practices (see chapter 7). Not everyone who sought titles and honors was granted them; at the same time, not all who were offered them accepted them. The Crown interpreted titles and honors as just rewards to personal and public servants of the Braganza House and monarchy (state), and the eager supplicants presented themselves as legitimate members of the bastion of the monarchy. The proper balance between supply and demand was tricky to maintain; more often than not, the political mood of the time, the popularity of the ruling house, and the economic conditions of society at large influenced the flow of titles. Those who accepted or rejected titles and other honors did not represent any particular sector of society or walk of life: among them were aristocrats; wealthy gentry; urban patricians; civil and military officials; high functionaries of the imperial bureaucracy, including the diplomatic and consular corps; religious prelates; and household servants of the Braganzas.

Politicians acquired more than their share of titles. The three most powerful offices of the monarchy that a person could aspire to hold were a ministerial portfolio (including prime minister), councillor of state, and senator of the empire. The first category served at the pleasure of the emperor; the second and third offices, once appointed and elected, were for life. Of the 219 men who served as ministers, 84 (38.4 percent) were nobles before or during their tenures in the office. Of the 23 men who held the highest appointive office in the realm, that of president of the council of ministers, or prime minister, 15 (65.2 percent) held titles. The empire had two Councils of State—the first, 1823–34, and the second, 1842–89. A total of 88 men were appointed to and held this privileged post: 16 for the First Council and 72 for the Second Council. Of the 88, some 57 (64.8 percent) were nobles: the First Council had 16 nobles (100 percent) and the Second Council 41 (56.9 percent). Of the 235 life-tenure senators, 93 (39.6 percent) were titled.[38] It should be noted that the minister and senator pool had fewer nobles than the more elitist prime minister and councillor of state category. The latter two groups exercised political power as chief mandarins and advisers to the emperor. Hence, the reason that the higher proportion of nobiliary honors was bestowed upon these groups can readily be understood.

From a political perspective, telling facts emerge from the distribution of the three key imperial offices among the nobility on an empire-wide basis: (1) 39 men (46.4 percent) held all three offices—minister/councillor/senator—concurrently; (2) 11 (13.1 percent) served as minister/councillor; (3) 12 (14.3 percent) served as minister/senator; and (4) 20 (23.8 percent) were cabinet officers only. Bahia, for instance, claimed 14 (35.9 percent) in the first category; in the second, only 1 (0.9 percent); in the third, 2 (16.7 percent); and in the fourth, 5 (25 percent). Thus, a total of 22 (26.2 percent) of the 84 titled cabinet ministers came from Bahia.[39] If different combinations of imperial offices, using, for example, the senator as a common base, are computed, the figure will vary slightly. But, because the key to the analysis of power distribution lay in the office of imperial minister, the above computation based on cabinet offices is a more valid way to show the nexus of political power and patronage held by the nobility and by province. A full 66 percent of the Bahian *political nobles* fell in the category of cabinet level or higher. Together with titled mandarins from other provinces, the Bahian titles constituted the core of the imperial power elite, a point difficult to dispute.

Particularly for Pedro I, cronyism played a role in ennobling politicians, albeit the decrees cited "service to the State." Neither the Andrada brothers, his arch-nemesis in politics, nor the powerful senator Nicolau Pereira de Campos Vergueiro, another critic, received titles. Of the seven provisional and permanent regents (1831–40), only one was a noble (the Marquês de Caravelas) during his tenure in office. General Francisco de Lima e Silva, José da Costa Carvalho, and Pedro de Araújo Lima were ennobled later by a grateful Pedro II. The single-regent government was installed in 1833 under Padre Diogo Antônio

Feijó, who was replaced by the last of the regents, Pedro de Araújo Lima, in 1837. In spite of his brilliant but somewhat erratic career as a state minister, Feijó, a diehard liberal of the nineteenth century in the mold of the French intellectuals, was denied the title and other honors by Pedro II. In 1842 Feijó was the leading conspirator in the Liberal Revolt in São Paulo. Former regent José Carvalho (the Barão de Monte Alegre) was the president of São Paulo, the defender of the constitutional authority of the empire. Caxias, the son of still another regent and himself a former aide to Feijó, became the military commander in charge of suppressing the Liberal Revolt. The disgraced priest died the following year (1843) at the age of forty-nine.[40]

Several distinguished ministers and senators also refused titles on various grounds. Francisco Gê Acaiaba de Montezuma, of Bahia, was an accomplished parliamentarian in the First Reign. He refused the title of Barão de Cachoeira in 1822; later, he was persuaded to accept the higher title of Visconde de Jequitinhonha. Fewer politicians turned down titles and honors under the First Reign than under the Second Reign, however. Upon the successful conclusion of a diplomatic mission to Río de la Plata, the Barão de Cotegipe was offered the title of visconde in 1872, but turned it down on the ground that he could not financially afford the appropriate life-style. The Visconde de Abaeté (Antônio Paulino Limpo de Abreu), one of the political caciques of Rio province, turned down the marquês honor, and the Visconde de Camaragibe (Pedro Francisco de Paula Cavalcanti de Albuquerque), of Pernambuco, likewise refused the honor of conde. Afonso Celso de Assis Figueiredo, the last Liberal prime minister of the empire, first refused the honor, but, six days after he became president of the council of ministers, accepted the title of the Visconde de Ouro Preto.[41]

Of the fifty-nine noble-ministers whose partisan affiliation can be readily identified, the Conservatives represented a higher percentage than the Liberals, using the five demographic and economic centers of the realm: 80 percent and 69.6 percent, respectively. (The Conservative and Liberal parties did not exist during the First Reign except as ideological hues, but the party system, as such, definitely took shape after the death of Pedro I in 1834.) By regional origin, the Northeast (Pernambuco and Bahia) claimed sixteen Conservative and seven Liberal titles; in the Center-South (Rio province and the court, Minas Gerais, and São Paulo), the Conservatives claimed twelve and the Liberals nine.[42]

In rejecting titles, political reasons outweighed the personal among both Liberals and Conservatives. José Tomás Nabuco de Araújo, a brilliant legal mind and prominent senator of the Liberal party during the decades of the 1850s through 1870s, turned down a title; his son, Joaquim Nabuco, a fire-breathing abolitionist Liberal, upheld his father's precedent. The Liberal chieftains of Bahia, Manuel Pinto de Sousa Dantas and José Antônio Saraiva, both prime ministers in the 1880s, were offered the titles of visconde and marquês, respectively. Dantas was an abolitionist, increasingly opposing the reactionary wing of his party, led by Saraiva, a champion of electoral reforms but a defender of slavery. Probably the inferior title of visconde offended Dantas, for the partisan power struggle in Bahia had just begun raging between his followers and Saraiva's. Personal relations between the emperor and Saraiva deteriorated during the second half of the eighties; on one occasion, the Bahian Liberal chief tartly suggested that the monarch return the crown to the people instead of passing it to Crown Princess Isabel. Conservative Paulino José Soares de Sousa, son of the Visconde do Uruguai and an important slavocratic coffee planter in Cantagalo, twice refused a title. Conservative and Liberal prime ministers during the last decade of the empire sought to suborn a disgruntled General Manuel Deodoro da Fonseca with a title. His candidacy for the imperial senate from Rio province resulted in a humiliating defeat, and he increasingly embraced the cause of rebellious officers; Cotegipe, João Alfredo, and Ouro Preto all offered him a title. Deodoro da Fonseca turned it down. His brother, also a general, who accepted the title of the Barão de Alagoas (Severino Martins da Fonseca), was probably one of the shortest-lived titleholders in the empire: fifteen days.[43] These were salient examples of crown co-optation that backfired.

If political considerations were a factor in turning down titles among dissident mandarins and generals, the imperial appointment prerogatives could become a liability. It was the first emperor who recognized this risk, choosing to strengthen his power base among the Brazilian territorial aristocracy and gentry by co-opting them. Aware of the potential pitfalls of an aristocracy and a gentry wielding political clout, Pedro I granted titles and honors, but seldom any accompanying power and authority that might threaten him on the periphery. The practice of appointing Portuguese and Brazilian politicians who had no significant clan connections was a key feature of his rule. Conversely, the ennoblement of a territorial aristocracy of time-honored lineage on the periphery became important in consolidating the monarchy by creating an elite corps to counterbalance the political mandarins. With few exceptions, the peripheral aristocracy throughout the nineteenth century failed to make its regional power felt at the court and remained instead a regionalized social and economic nobility. The transformation from economic to political nobility never occurred.

Although the foundation of the Brazilian nobility came from the ranks of the mercantile and agrarian elite, outstanding persons from other professions also won titles. The leading noble banker-financier of the empire was the Visconde de Mauá (Irineu Evangelista de Sousa). A man of humble origin from Rio Grande do Sul, he had worked as an office boy in an English firm in Rio, and then steadily rose to the position of a Brazilian Baring. At the height of his career, Mauá held interests in banks, import-export firms, railroads, and shipping lines from Amazonas to Rio de Janeiro to Montevideo to London.[44] The Visconde de Porto Seguro (Francisco Adolfo de Varnhagen), the Barão do Rio Branco (José Maria da Silva Paranhos, le fils), and the Barão de Penedo (Francisco Inácio de Carvalho Moreira) were outstanding diplomats. Porto Seguro served in various European posts, including Lisbon and Vienna, where his pioneering research on the colonial history of Brazil was conducted; Rio Branco, consul in Liverpool at the time of the fall of the Braganza monarchy, eventually became foreign minister under four presidents of the First Brazilian Republic; and, during the critical years of the Paraguayan War, Penedo was the imperial plenipotentiary in London and negotiated numerous financial deals with British bankers.[45] Such military and naval officers as General Manuel Luís Osório (the Marquês de Erval) and Admiral Joaquim Marques Lisboa (the Marquês de Tamandaré) were made nobles for their service in the Paraguayan War. At least three mine owners were also ennobled.[46]

By one count, fifty physicians and surgeons were similarly recognized: two condes, nine viscondes, and the rest barões. The Conde de Prados (Camilo Maria Ferreira Armond), a Paris-trained physician, became a full-time politician by the 1860s; similarly, the physician Visconde de Lima Duarte (José Rodrigues de Lima Duarte) practiced politics, serving as deputy from Minas, senator, and Cabinet officer during the later years of his life. Both Prados and Lima Duarte were Liberals of national stature from Minas. The Visconde de Inhomirim

(Francisco de Sales Torres Homem), also a physician, was a strong proponent of fiscal conservatism, a stand that elevated him in the late 1850s and 1860s to the post of minister of finance. The other conde was a personal physician of Pedro II: Conde de Mota Maia (Claúdio Velho da Mota Maia), a native of Itaguaí, Rio, who was trained in the faculty of medicine at the court and who faithfully followed the emperor into exile in France after 1889.[47] Numerically a minority, physicians nevertheless played a significant role in imperial politics. Intellectual and lawyer José Antônio Pimenta Bueno, a future prime minister, was made a noble for "his relevant services that he has rendered in science and letters." He was made the Visconde de São Vicente, who later became a marquês, and was considered to be one of the most erudite minds in and out of the political arena, "modest as Thiers" and brilliant enough "to enter the Pantheon through the front doors."[48] Many, but not all, acquired their titles through individual virtues, accomplishment, and "services to the State and Humanity."

Although the foundation for the Brazilian nobility was laid by Dom João, the sage king and founder of the American monarchy, the two emperors, Pedro I and Pedro II, nurtured the growth and guided the evolution of the corporation. Unlike the older nobilities of continental Europe, the Brazilian institution lacked juridical status. This is in part accounted for by the time of its creation. The nineteenth century was a capitalist era and hardly propitious for "refeudalization"; the Braganza monarchy was in spirit the continuum of the Portuguese kingdom. Therefore, the Brazilian imperial nobility was a personal institution, a key adjunct to the Crown. It was not a social institution that had grown out of the economy. Its status as a corporation did not derive from juridical principles, but rather from imperial prerogatives.

Pedro I attempted to incorporate the nobility as a status class, but the recalcitrant Constituent Assembly refused to go along. The liberal-controlled assembly even attempted to impose stiff taxes on title bearers. It should be noted that João VI made no attempt to use nobiliary titles as a political means to strengthen his power base because his favorite courtiers were the most frequent recipients of his royal largesse. His son, Pedro I, politicized the nobility by selectively rewarding those loyal to his perception of the empire as well as those who could reinforce his power on the periphery. Pedro II, the American Marcus Aurelius, made valiant efforts to bring integrity into the nobility by maintaining high standards for imperial grants of titles, but by the 1850s was persuaded by his advisers to open the door to the nobiliary corporation by liberally inducting men and women of influence, money, and power in an imperial gesture recognizing their social status ipso facto. Thus, for the better part of a century, the distinctive policies of three monarchs played the propitious role in producing a nobility that represented the broad spectrum of Brazilian society.

PART II

SOCIAL AND ECONOMIC ORIGINS
OF THE NOBILITY

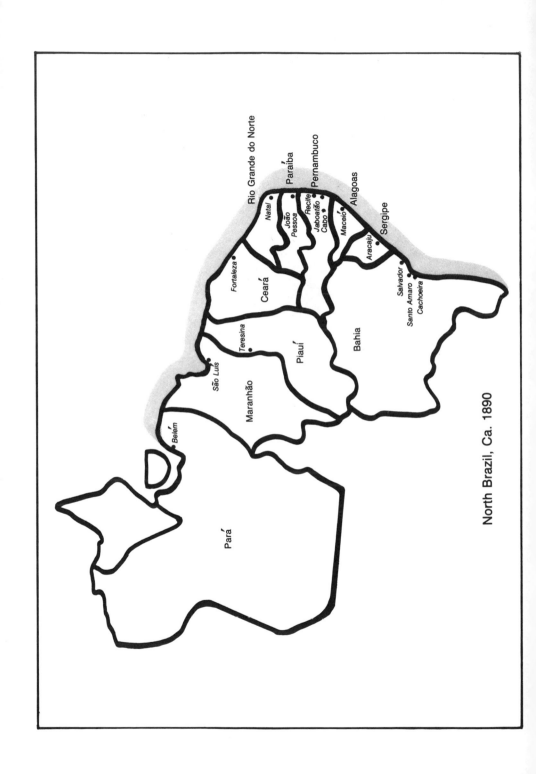

North Brazil, Ca. 1890

Rio Grande do Norte

Paraíba

Pernambuco

Alagoas

Sergipe

Natal

João Pessoa

Recife

Jaboatão

Cabo

Maceió

Aracaju

Fortaleza

Ceará

Salvador

Santo Amaro

Cachoeira

Teresina

Piauí

Bahia

São Luís

Maranhão

Belém

Pará

4

Aristocratic Clans of Brazil

There is not a Wanderley who is not a drunkard,
an Albuquerque who is not a liar, a Cavalcanti who is not
in debt. Nor a Souza Leão or a Carneiro da Cunha
who is not fond of a Negro woman. GILBERTO FREYRE

The mainstay of the nineteenth-century Brazilian economy was capitalist agriculture, and the twin export pillars were sugar in the Northeast and coffee in the Center-South. Dynastic landowners and merchants who played a key role in sustaining the export agriculture came from the ranks of the nobility, but not all titled landowners were aristocrats. Many were gentry in mentality and some were practicing businessmen. Significant regional variations existed. In the Northeast (principally Pernambuco and Bahia), class lines held firm in the nineteenth century: no merchant became an operator of a large-scale export agricultural establishment, nor did any planter diversify his activities to include banking, *comissário* activities, or transportation. Although the norm was for the agrarian and mercantile sectors to remain intricately interdependent, few families completely abandoned one activity for the other or, more importantly, held an interest in both. By contrast, in the provinces of the Center-South (Rio, São Paulo, and Minas especially), a high degree of social mobility prevailed. Many merchants, comissários, and *tropeiros* (muleteers) invested in land and soon became the agrarian elite. Equally often, landowners and their descendants went into banking, brokerage, transportation, and other commercial activities, thereby strengthening their original economic stake. These changes, both across class lines and over generations, were the trademark of an expanding coffee economy. No such transformation took place in the staid sugar industry of the Northeast, where the major changes were a declining slave population and a structural transformation of low-technology engenhos into refineries by the 1880s—a movement principally sponsored by the incipient capitalist slavocracy, involving limited foreign and Brazilian mercantile or state participation.

The two major custodians of the export economies were landowners and merchants. As many as 200 nobiliary titles were given out to the Center-South coffee planters alone, and fewer than 30 leading merchants were awarded titles during the nineteenth century. Among the outstanding mercantile fortunes in Minas, Rio, and São Paulo, several families gained imperial titles, honors, and offices. The structure of Brazil's landowning and mercantile elites, in particular of that titled segment to which the Braganza Crown wanted to appease, sheds light on the role of capitalist agriculture. This group of the imperial agrarian and mercantile elite did not participate in toto in political decision making; a few held offices above the rank of provincial president or cabinet officer, but the key offices held were local or regional, with an occasional sprinkling of provincial deputies, vice-presidents, and presidents. On the whole, the elite of the export economies confined their activities to agriculture, banking, commodity brokerage, import-export, and the transportation industries.

This economic elite came from established dynastic families of the agrarian aristocracy (in the Northeast), of its ancillary mercantile purveyors, and of the aspiring, mobile gentry (in the Center-South)— all attempting to reach or retain that social apex. Titled dynasties in the Brazilian empire were rare. In this context, "dynasty" refers to a family that had successfully maintained elite hegemonic status for three generations or longer in commercial agriculture, that is, as planters, merchants, comissários, and/or bankers. Furthermore, in the absence of entail, dynastic status relied heavily on a family's ability to retain and expand its wealth; hence, another characteristic of a successful dynasty was engagement in clan-borne endogamy (mostly cousin and cross-cousin marriages) as well as occasional conjugal unions with elite political families. The Brazilian dynasty, therefore, was not an inherited status, but one acquired in the existing mold of the prevailing elite system of the empire and established by both aristocratic and gentry families. In a New World setting, whether a family was aristocratic or gentry should be determined by lineage, duration of residence in Brazil, and the types of economic activities in which it was involved. Thus, a dynasty was a dynamic or acquired social distinction. A family's ability to retain or expand wealth and fame for generations was therefore a significant factor in perpetuating the statuses of both aristocratic and gentry dynasties.

Bahia and Pernambuco, the two economic centers of the Northeast since colonial times, were the homes of the Brazilian agrarian aristocracy. The export economies of sugar, tobacco, cotton, and hides were built there, and Portugal placed its first colonial capital in Salvador, which remained the administrative and commercial center of Brazil until the middle of the eighteenth century. Pernambuco, which was occupied by the Dutch for a quarter of a century (1630–54), built a unique social structure. When the colonial society was disrupted by the intrusion of new elements—Dutch administrators and mercantile burghers, the religious hierarchy of the Reformed church, Jewish slave traders, and other non-Lusitanian settlers—the regional elite was reshaped to reflect the fine mix of the old and new groups. Unlike that in Bahia, the Pernambucan elite rejuvenated its established aristocracy by drawing members from the Dutch, in the process modifying its mentality: the Pernambucans, though equally as closed and endogamous as the Bahians, were less xenophobic.

Only after the discovery of gold in the 1690s were the social and economic systems in the Northeast restructured; the population shifted to the Center-South, especially to Minas Gerais, and Rio by 1763, which compounded the ongoing economic decadence of the region. Before 1690 the aristocracy was small and compact. Its core characteristics were ancient lineage of European origin, newly amassed wealth in the New World, careful grooming of descendants through marriages and mergers with other monied families, ability to transmit clan wealth to succeeding generations with or without entails, and inherent claim to high political and social positions. Defined in the hallowed tradition of blood, money, status, and longevity, only a score or so of families could legitimately call themselves aristocrats. Appropriately, the first two aristocratic landowners in Bahia and Pernambuco to acquire titles were the Visconde da Torre de Garcia d'Ávila, the morgado of the

House of Torre of Bahia, and the Visconde do Recife, the morgado do Cabo of Pernambuco. Designating these titles, the empire began to honor and recruit the agrarian aristocracy at the periphery as a foundation for the Braganza's New World political system.

By the nineteenth century, fewer than a dozen clans in Bahia could claim the status of agrarian aristocracy based on origins dating to the seventeenth century. The two oldest families were the House of Torre and the House of Ponte, of whose humble origins in the sixteenth century as minor conquistadores and holders of *sesmarias* much has been written. Both houses dominated the regional economy as powerful cattle barons (*poderosos do sertão*) and held seats in the municipal council of Salvador by 1591. By the middle of the seventeenth century, they had acquired the privileges of fidalguia. Descendants of these houses continued to hold the posts of aldermen throughout the next century.[1] Marriage among the founding families of the colony's first century was frequent, firmly rooting the tradition of endogamy among cousins in the Bahian agrarian aristocracy.

In addition to these two distinguished houses, sixteenth-century Bahia had been settled by lesser aristocrats: the Monizes and the Araújos. Moniz de Barreto, born in Ilha Terceira, came to Bahia with the first colonial governor, Tomé de Sousa. Also among the first colonial settlers in the captaincy was João de Araújo, the founder of the Araújo clan. By the end of the century, the Monizes and Araújos held political and economic positions of command, as city aldermen and sugar planters.[2] By the seventeenth century, more founders of the Bahian aristocracy had settled in the region: The Bulcãos, the Calmons, the Carvalho e Albuquerques, and the Góises, to cite the most eligible. Gaspar de Faria Bulcão, who arrived in Bahia in 1650, was a descendant of an Azorian fidalgo, whose origins dated back to the middle of the fifteenth century. João Calmon (du Pin) was born in Portugal in 1620, a naval officer whose offspring carried both patronym and matronym, Calmon du Pin e Almeida. The clan diversified its activities: part of the family began a new career in sugar planting, and the other part continued in the traditional naval military service. The Calmons would marry the Góises by the end of the eighteenth century. Of the Albuquerques who had settled in Pernambuco during the colony's first century, one Albuquerque (a judge) had moved to Bahia by the third decade of the seventeenth century and soon married into a local family, thus eventually establishing the dynasty of Carvalho e Albuquerque.[3] Toward the end of the eighteenth century, the Albuquerques settled in most of the major northern provinces.

The agrarian pattern in colonial Bahia changed considerably after 1690, when the economy experienced both depression and expansion in tandem. By the mid-eighteenth century, however, Bahian sugar was firmly restored as the mainstay of the captaincy's economy. During the first decade of the seventeenth century, Bahia possessed 63 sugar mills, in addition to numerous cane farms; by 1711, the number had increased to 146; by 1759, 172; by 1803, 260; and by 1881, 511.[4] This kind of expansion over the years presumes a considerable amount of social and economic mobility; consequently, some new families began to appear among the roster of the traditional agrarian elite. Often, but not always, the descendants of the families of the colony's first and second centuries dominated the agrarian economy as the richest clans until technology reshaped the capitalist agriculture by the 1880s. The names of Calmon, Rocha Pita, Araújo, Bulcão, and Góis appeared as sugar-mill owners; and the richest clan, the Rocha Pitas (brothers Lourenço and Luís together), held three mills, producing some 6,500 arrobas of white (branco) and 3,600 of brown (mascovado) sugar.[5] The absence of the Guedes de Britoses (the House of Ponte) and the Garcia d'Ávilas (the House of Torre), however, would seem to indicate that owning sesmarias alone did not guarantee success in agrarian capitalism, especially in the competitive sugar trade after 1650, when the Caribbean emerged as the major producer. Furthermore, the two elite houses of Torre and Ponte failed to enter the sugar business, confining their economic activities to the less competitive cattle raising. The productivity of gentry-owned sugar mills was not inferior to that of the mills held by the aristocrat planters. The Rocha Pitas, who by the beginning of the nineteenth century would be leading aristocrats of the province, had begun as gentry planters. By the middle of the eighteenth century, this clan was Bahia's biggest sugar producer.

Aside from the traditional characteristics of ancient lineage, tenure in power, entail, and accumulated wealth, the landed gentry could be distinguished from the aristocracy by its relative role in the diversification of economic activities. The raison d'être of a sugar planter (and mill owner) was to export, a motive that did not require an aristocrat to enter into a business partnership through a marriage or similar social merger. The gentry, on the other hand, was distinguished by its diversified social and economic involvement outside its class, especially with merchants. Such future Bahian gentry-nobility as the Borges de Barroses, the Araújo Pinhos, and others were solid members of the well-to-do rural gentry as of 1750.[6] Interestingly enough, considerably more gentry planters were active in the *cachaça*-making business than were aristocratic landowners, a phenomenon suggesting that the gentry as a whole was more interested in quick turnaround on an investment, thus directing their resources to internally marketable items, such as rum. This venture also involved close dealings with merchants in towns and cities, with whom many of the gentry established marital and business ties. Such nineteenth-century gentry-nobility as the Vianas, the Ferreira Bandeiras, and the Gonçalves Martins had been urban merchant families in the middle of the eighteenth century. The father of the First Barão do Rio das Contas (Frutuoso Vicente Viana) was a prominent merchant in Salvador; the father-in-law of the future Marquês de Barbacena was also a wealthy merchant, probably a shareholder in a slave-trading firm; the father-in-law of the Visconde do Rio Branco was also a merchant. Intermarriage between wealthy merchants and pauperized aristocracy and gentry families not only became commonplace, but was also a necessity for the survival of the elite.[7]

By the middle of the eighteenth century, therefore, the agrarian aristocracy of Bahia, and by extension of Brazil, was no longer a monolithic hegemonic elite; it faced both internal and external class rivals. When the agrarian aristocracy of the sugar economy was revamped during the first two decades of the nineteenth century, it had been penetrated by gentry and mercantile families; this restructured aristocracy served as the basis for the Brazilian imperial nobility at the periphery. Such major landed aristocratic families of Bahia as the Monizes (de Aragão), the Calmons, the Góises, the Bulcãos, the Rocha Pitas, the Araújos, and the Carvalho e Albuquerques were among the leading survivors of the reformed agrarian elite. These groups were all ennobled during the last two reigns of Braganza rule, thus constituting the Bahian titled aristocracy.[8]

Rivalry between the rural gentry and aristocracy, however, was not widespread and intense before the mid-nineteenth century, when the Brazilian sugar economies in the Northeast and Center-South began to experience a series of structural modernizations, such as an intense use of technology to build refineries and railroads, and land enclosures to expand cane cultivation. In many regions of Brazil, it was the gentry who possessed good connections at the court and with urban merchants who led the modernization of capitalist agriculture. By the end of the nineteenth century, new entrepreneurial agribusiness corporations had been established either from earlier ventures jointly financed by gentry and merchants, or by Brazilian and foreign investors speculating for quick profit. With the possible exception of those in Pernambuco, few aristocratic families survived this economic transformation without serious consequences for their dynastic status.

Trade with Portugal, Africa, and Asia expanded throughout the first half of the eighteenth century. The mid-century was a decisive turning point for the agrarian elite in colonial Brazil, which had begun to erode long before. The growth of trade stimulated capitalist agriculture, where anticipated production increased the demand for African slaves. By 1759 the city of Salvador had some 130 merchants, commission agents, moneylenders, and direct retailers. Bahia traded with Lisbon and Oporto in Portugal, the Costa da Mina of West Africa, Angola and Alma Coast, and other parts of the world, including the Orient. Mercantile houses exported tobacco, sugar, rum, hides, and cotton; they imported ten to twelve thousand African slaves per annum.[9] By the dawn of the nineteenth century, Bahia had acquired a considerable number of foreign commercial houses, principally English, French, Danish, and German.

Of the fourteen major Bahian capitalists in 1759, two were the direct ancestors of Bahian nobles: Frutuoso Vicente Viana for the two Rio das Contas and the Barão de Viana; and Tomás da Silva for the Barão de Uruguaiana, future prime minister of the empire.[10] In addition, two Costa Bragas (João and Domingues) were listed as important merchants of the captaincy in the league of Viana and Ferraz, but no Costa Braga in Bahia ever received a title under the empire. An ancestor of the Marquês de Caravelas, a prominent politician during the First Reign, was a commission agent in the trade with Oporto.[11] Such major nineteenth-century merchants in Bahia as the Pereira Marinhos and the Novises had not begun their businesses at mid-century.

Of the 115 titles of nobility that the province of Bahia netted during the empire, ten families amassed a total of 36; this came down to more than 3 titles per family, not counting those gained through marriage (see table 2). The Moniz family garnered 6; the Carvalho e Albuquerques 5; the Bulcão clan 4; and the families of Araújo Góis, Borges de Barros, Calmon, Costa Pinto, Oliveira Mendes, Tosta, and Viana 3 each.[12] Such aristocratic clans as the Rocha Pitas and the Araújos failed to acquire multiple titles. Among the unique honors, the family of Pereira Marinho was the only Bahian mercantile clan holding a Brazilian title; the Tostas were the only multiple-titled family with a marquês; and the merchant-turned-gentry family of Viana produced the first provincial president of Bahia after independence. Only the Tostas, the Vianas, and the Bulcãos were represented by politicians of national stature, in the categories of provincial president, senator, and cabinet minister. The Marquês de Muritiba (Manuel Vieira Tosta) was senator from Bahia, a member of the Second Council of State, a three-time cabinet minister, and provincial president of Pernambuco, Sergipe, and Rio Grande do Sul. The First Barão do Rio das Contas was Bahia's first provincial president, and the Third Barão de São Francisco (Antônio de Araújo de Aragão Bulcão) was also provincial chief executive of Bahia from 1879 to 1881.

A significant generalization that can be drawn from this is that, though one aristocratic family among the multiple-titled produced a famous politician, no politician of national reputation came from the ranks of the Bahian aristocracy. Such stalwarts of the aristocracy as the Carvalho e Albuquerques and the Monizes contributed no politician of national stature. A hypothesis this book will test on other provinces is that not only was the Brazilian agrarian nobility organized in two

Table 2   Single-Family Multiple Titleholders in Five Provinces of Brazil, 1822–1889

Province	Number of families	Number of titles
Bahia	10	36
Pernambuco	3	16
Rio and Court	5	22
Minas Gerais	4	15
São Paulo	3	11
Total	25	100

Source: Carlos G. Rheingantz, *Titulares do império* (Rio, 1960).

major segments of aristocracy and gentry, but also that gentry-nobles, not aristocratic nobles, generally monopolized political offices; this state of affairs suggests that the monarchy was a semiopen political system that permitted some class- and status-group participation. Furthermore, such clans as the Monizes and the Albuquerques, and, to a certain extent, the Calmons devoted their energy to the economic enterprise of sugarcane cultivation instead of politics.

A comparison with another northeastern province, Pernambuco, is apt and illuminating. The leading agrarian aristocracy of that province was far more closed, practiced a higher degree of endogamy than did its Bahian counterpart, and was thereby successful in consolidating its power base on all fronts. Only three single-unit patronymic families holding three or more titles existed in the province: the Cavalcanti de Albuquerques, the Sousa Leaõs, and the Lins.

Interestingly enough, the descendants of Duarte Coelho, the donatário of Pernambuco, did not constitute a major power group in the nineteenth century. The first Albuquerque came to the captaincy with its proprietary lord in the 1530s. Married to the Cavalcanti family, allegedly Florentine nobility, the Cavalcanti de Albuquerques became the original aristocracy of Pernambuco. Jerônimo de Albuquerque, "the Pernambucan Adam," was a brother-in-law of Duarte Coelho. The Conde de Pernambuco (the Marquês de Bastos being his second title) was a grandson of the founder of the captaincy and of Jerônimo. Hence, the full name of the conde-marquês was Duarte de Albuquerque Coelho or Coello.[13] Filippo Cavalcanti was similarly the founder of the noted Pernambucan clan. The Florentine founder was part of the triumvirate of the colonial aristocracy of the captaincy, along with the Coelhos and the Albuquerques. The descendants of these clans settled throughout northeastern Brazil from Ceará to Bahia, with Pernambuco, Alagoas, and Paraíba as the clans' principal home territory. One historian observed that the Cavalcanti de Albuquerques were the "most aristocratic of the aristocracy."[14] Had the Braganzas considered a marital union with the Brazilian landed class, the Albuquerques of Pernambuco would have been the logical choice, and the course of Brazilian history could have been significantly altered.

There were other distinguished aristocratic families in Pernambuco. The Wanderleys were a Dutch-Pernambucan family whose forebear was Gaspar van der Lei, a Dutch noble and "gentleman-in-waiting" for the governor of New Holland, Johan Moritz van Nassau. Gaspar was known for his weakness for money as well as for hard liquor and bequeathed to his family the popular saying that "a sober Wanderley is an illegitimate one." Betraying his overlord, Gaspar changed his allegiance by taking up with Pernambucans and married a daughter of a rich planter in the captaincy's southern districts. Freyre considered the clan entirely inbred, calling them "the blondest and pinkest of the lot of the aristocracy."[15] This clan is a good example of the aristocracy-gentry merger that eventually evolved into nobility. The origins of the Sousa Leãos are obscure, but they were probably a seventeenth-century family. This clan was also an agrarian dynasty, much in the mold of the Cavalcanti de Albuquerques. The Linses, settling in the captaincy in the eighteenth century and later expanding south to Alagoas, intermarried with landed families of both provinces. One of the Liberal prime ministers, the Visconde de Sinimbu (João Lins Vieira Cansanção de Sinimbu), was a brother-in-law of one Cavalcanti de Albuquerque of Pernambuco—the Barão de Atalaia (Lourenço Cavalcanti de Albuquerque Maranhão).[16]

Inbreeding among cousins shocked Maria Graham, an English lady in the service of the House of Braganza in the 1820s; others condemned the consanguineous unions so prevalent among the Pernambucan and Bahian aristocracy as incestuous marriages whose bio-psychological effects were often linked to degeneracy. Popular adages ridiculed aristocratic foibles: "There is not a Wanderley who is not a drunkard, an Albuquerque who is not a liar, a Cavalcanti who is not in debt. Nor a Sousa Leão or a Carneiro da Cunha who is not fond of a Negro woman."[17] The aristocracy in the Old and New Worlds was no paragon of virtue. Nor was the Pernambucan aristocracy immune from mythomania, dowry-hunting, erotomania, and other worldly sins.

Gilberto Freyre warns that the surname is a "precarious means" of identifying the origins of a Brazilian pedigree for a number of reasons. Many individuals simply chose the better known of the matronym or patronym. The Barão de Moribeca, a brother of three other dynastic politicians of a Cavalcanti de Albuquerque family, never used the patronym and was simply known as Manuel Francisco de Paula Cavalcanti. The Barão do Buique was Francisco Alves Cavalcanti Camboim, but preferred to sign Cavalcanti de Albuquerque as his surname. His father was Francisco Alves da Silva and his mother Leonarda Arcoverde

Cavalcanti de Albuquerque. The three political brothers of the Calmons of Bahia in the First Republic—Francisco, Antônio, and Miguel—had two different last names: Francisco, governor of Bahia
(1924–28), was Góis Calmon; Antônio and Miguel used du Pin e Almeida. In the fast-moving and fluid society of Minas Gerais, it was customary as early as the eighteenth century for children to use their
mother's name, not their father's.[18] The vast dependent population, including slaves and their descendants, often used the surname of the
master, a practice in many cases fully justified by the master's sexual
monopoly of female slaves and dependents outside formal marriage
that often resulted in the procreation of "natural" offspring. In other
cases, members of the aristocracy as well as the gentry, especially poor
members, had African or Indian forebears. These descendants of mixed
races who received titles of nobility and other honorific commendations under the monarchy were maliciously called "chocolate barons"
by title bearers of more European descent.[19]

The ruling gentry in Pernambuco offers an interesting contrast to
that in Bahia as well as, to a small extent, that of the Center-South. In
Pernambuco, the commercial hub of Alagoas and Paraíba, both ecolog-
ical and economic factors played a powerful galvanizing role in forming
a closely knit elite. An example is the Pais Barretos, a seventeenth-century family like the Wanderleys. Ensconced in Cabo county, their economic interests expanded over the centuries. By the time of Pedro I, the
clan fortune was large enough to warrant imperial attention and the
morgado, Francisco Pais Barreto, was ennobled as the Visconde (and
later marquês) do Recife in 1824, the first from Pernambuco after independence.[20] Although Cabo was one of the richest sugar-growing
municípios in the province, by the 1870s the Pais Barretos were no
longer the region's ruling house. The abolition of entail in 1835 had
simply dispersed the family wealth, and in all probability the clan
lacked the gentry spirit to marshal and diversify its interests. It ended
in bankruptcy.[21]

The Linses in Escada, the Sousa Leãos in Jaboatão, and the Sá Albuquerques in Cabo were among the wealthiest gentry in the province
and were extensively linked by marriage and business to the older aristocratic families of the Cavalcantis, the Albuquerques, and the Wanderleys. Furthermore, these gentry families also created an economic
counterweight by establishing themselves in Alagoas. Thus, the Wan-

derleys, who had settled in Serinhaém, a southern county in Pernambuco, crossed the border into Alagoas, marrying the Barros Pimentels and the Mendonças; the Linses married into the Aciólis and the Vieiras. Although Alagoas lacked the aristocracy of indigenous origin as in Pernambuco and Bahia, its gentry built strong connections with outside aristocratic families.[22]

Pernambuco had only three single-family holders of multiple titles (three or more): the Cavalcanti de Albuquerques, the Sousa Leãos, and the Linses. As is frequent in the Northeast, the perimeters of patriarchical clans must be extended to absorb those of in-laws in the case of the closely grouped Pernambucan aristocracy and gentry. Capitão-Mor Francisco de Paula de Holanda Cavalcanti de Albuquerque, of Jaboatão, near Recife, could claim among his noble ancestry four of the most distinguished sixteenth-century families established in the province: the Coelhos, the Cavalcantis, the Albuquerques, and the Holandas. (Arnau de Holanda, also a gentleman in the service of the donatário Duarte Coelho, was a founder of the captaincy's "first family.") Capitão-Mor Francisco had four sons, all ennobled during the Second Reign. As the lord of Engenho Suassuna, hence the nickname Coronel Suassuna, Francisco was an innovator in agriculture and a colonial savant, a role common in the New World, which was infatuated with eighteenth-century revolutionary ideas. His plantation served as the home of the Academia Suassuna, a school and debating society that was the first of its kind in northeastern Brazil. Francisco married a cousin, also an Albuquerque, and was counted among the leaders of the Revolution of 1817, in which the father and mother of Prime Minister Sinimbu, of Alagoas, were also involved.[23] (Another outstanding leader in the revolution was Francisco Pais Barreto, the Marquês do Recife; in fact, the revolutionary movement was pandemic among the leading aristocratic and gentry families of the province and its adjacent neighbors, such as Alagoas and Paraíba.)

For readily understandable reasons, neither Francisco nor Manuel Vieira Dantas (Sinimbu's father) was ennobled by the first two rulers of Brazil in the nineteenth century. Francisco's four sons and a grandson were ennobled, however: three viscondes (Albuquerque, Suassuna, and Camaragibe) and one baron (Moribeca). The only other Brazilian family that received four titles for siblings was the Carneiro da Silva family, of Quissamã, Rio, one of the wealthiest sugarocrats in the Center-South.

All four titled sons of Capitão-Mor Francisco were politicians of regional and national prestige. Albuquerque was chieftain of Pernambuco's Liberal party, senator (appointed in 1838), councillor of state (nominated in 1850), and eleven-time cabinet minister between 1830 and 1862, when he died.[24] On the opposite side politically from their brother Albuquerque were two Conservative chiefs, Camaragibe and Suassuna. Camaragibe, the third of the four brothers, was the most intellectual, studying in Coimbra and Göttingen as would his young brother, Moribeca. Camaragibe was professor of law in São Paulo in 1829 and taught in Olinda between 1830 and 1875, when he retired. He served as the president of the province of Pernambuco (1859); president of the chamber of deputies on two different occasions (1861–63 and 1869); and was appointed to the senate in 1869, still serving in the lower chamber.[25] More militant and far more radical in thought and action than his brother, Suassuna was the first-born (*primogenitor*), thus occupying a special place in the family. He was a career military officer during the time of João VI, retiring from active service as a general in 1829. He was appointed to the presidency of Pernambuco (in 1826 and again in 1835–38) and was named as a senator in 1839, the year after brother Albuquerque entered the upper chamber. Like Albuquerque, Suassuna served as a cabinet minister in 1840. He died in 1880, his political career outshone only by those of his two younger siblings.[26] The youngest of the four, Moribeca, was the least political. Trained in law at Göttingen, he devoted his life to agriculture, only briefly interrupting it to serve as a provincial deputy in 1835–37.[27]

All four brothers married well. Moribeca was a son-in-law of the Conde de Boa Vista (Francisco do Rego Barros), a coleader of the Rego Barros-Cavalcanti (Albuquerque) oligarchy that dominated the province during the 1830s and 1840s. Albuquerque was a son-in-law of Manuel Caetano de Almeida e Albuquerque, a relative and senator from Pernambuco (1828–44); between 1838 and 1844, the Visconde de Albuquerque had as colleagues in the senate both his brother and his father-in-law, a distinction only a handful of Brazilians could claim. Both Suassuna and Camaragibe married into wealthy gentry families of the province, and the capitão-mor's offspring constituted a veritable aristocracy-nobility of the empire. The clan and its cousins claimed fifteen titles under the empire, making it the realm's most decorated dynasty.[28]

The Sousa Leãos were hardly less pervasive in their control of wealth and power.[29] The clan held eight titles, spread among five families of the same patronym. Two sons of Domingos Sousa Leão—the Barão de Vila Bela (the namesake) and the Barão de Caiará (Augusto)—were trained in law at the Olinda academy. Jaboatão county was their home, where other noble families also held plantations; two Sousa Leãos, the Visconde de Tabatinga (Domingos Francisco) and the Barão de Jaboatão, were landowners in Cabo; and the third, Caiará, had an engenho in São Lourenço da Mata. Moreno was the largest planter, owning eight sugar mills, and his brother Campos Alegre held seven. Only one titled Sousa Leão, Vila Bela, reached the post of cabinet minister; three titled clansmen occupied the office of the provincial president: Sousa Leão (Barão), Vila Bela, and Caiará.[30] Although no titled Sousa Leão held the post of senator or councillor of state, Luís Felipe, Vila Bela's son, was the unchallenged "lion" (leão) of the Liberal party of Pernambuco in the 1880s. Deputy in 1858 and senator in 1880, he became the minister of navy in Saraiva's second ministry of May–August 1885.

In Escada county, the most productive sugar-growing zone in the province, where fewer than ten families ruled with absolute control, the elite family was the Linses. The Visconde de Utinga (Henrique Marques Lins) came to possess some thirty sugar mills and plantations in Escada. His grandfather had begun the clan's agrarian holdings in 1813, and by mid-century the sugar business had brought wealth to the family. By the 1870s and 1880s the Linses had pioneered the construction of mechanized mills and, by 1895, had opened a third refinery. That landed interests were concentrated in the hands of a few was glaringly apparent. One historian of Pernambuco has claimed that nine families in Escada controlled 114 engenhos, suggesting the hegemony of a tight-knit familiocratic oligarchy. Local political power was virtually monopolized by the Linses and their in-laws, though, unlike the Albuquerques and the Sousa Leãos, this Escada-based clan did not attain power posts at the national level.[31] In this sense, the Lins clan fit more in the mold of typical Brazilian gentry. The Linses and similar cases of gentry control of local offices directly aided the expansion of their economic activities.

The Bahian and Pernambucan patterns of nobility make a few generalizations possible. First, the dominance of an agrarian aristocracy-nobility in national politics was far less pervasive than historians have imagined.[32] Even a superficial look at the distribution of officeholders of the presidency of the council of ministers (1847–89) reinforces this assertion. Twenty-three men held the highest appointed post in the empire; fourteen came from the four northern provinces, eight from the three southern provinces, and one from Portugal. Bahia led all other provinces, claiming nine prime ministers; Pernambuco and Piauí, two each; and Alagoas, one. Only one Bahian prime minister could claim a tie to aristocratic roots and none belonged to a major agrarian dynasty by birthright. Cotegipe (prime minister, 1885–88) owned four plantations at one point, but had inherited them from his wife; in spite of the ancient lineage of the Wanderleys of Pernambuco, Cotegipe's father was known as "the poorest of the Wanderleys," who had to migrate to the interior of Bahia to seek a fortune.[33] Monte Alegre (1848) was a landowner in São Paulo through his wife's family; Sousa Dantas (1884–85) came from a moderately rich landowning family in the northeastern corner of Bahia, but definitely did not belong to the mainstream sugarocracy; and Saraiva (1880–82; 1885) was a sugar planter by marriage, but was hardly in the league of the agrarian aristocracy. Uruguaiana (1859–60), Rio Branco (1871–75), and Macaé (1848), all from Bahia, were from mercantile families or married into them. Zacarias (1862; 1864; 1866–68) and the First Visconde de Caravelas (1847–48), the first man to hold the office of the president of the council, were of moderately well-off gentry origin.[34] Cotegipe was the only one who could claim aristocratic beginnings on his father's side and his wife's side, but his family was poor, from the *sertão*, and had married blacks. When Cotegipe was growing up in the middle São Francisco River Valley, his father was a country gentleman rather than an aristocrat in terms of wealth and social prestige. Thus, except Cotegipe, all the Bahian-born prime ministers came from mercantile or modest gentry families, whose economic stakes in capitalist agriculture were either minor or marginal.

The two Pernambucan prime ministers were the Marquês de Olinda (Pedro de Araújo Lima) and João Alfredo Correia de Oliveira. The staunchest loyalist mandarin in the empire, Olinda began his political career in 1822; it ended only upon his death at the age of seventy-six in 1866. He was a senator, councillor of state, minister (ten times), imperial regent (1837–40), and prime minister (four times). His father was a nonaristocratic landowner, but his mother was a Cavalcanti; the family wealth was at most modest.[35] João Alfredo, whose most laudable political decision was the abolition of slavery in 1888, was also the son of rural gentry. Neither Olinda nor João Alfredo had strong connections with the landed aristocracy or any direct stake in agrarian interests. Sinimbu, the only Alagoan to become prime minister, was the son of a rich gentry family. His father, Manuel Vieira Dantas, was a senhor de engenho; his mother, Ana Lins, was of the better known family. Sinimbu did not use the surname of his father and added Cansanção de Sinimbu to his name.[36] Besides the three Cavalcanti de Albuquerque brothers (Suassuna, Camaragipe, and Albuquerque), the Conde de Boa Vista, and the Second Barão de Vila Bela, Pernambuco produced no aristocratic politicians of national reputation. In Bahia, even by a considerable stretch of the imagination, Cotegipe was the only "aristocratic" politician.

What this finding suggests is the strengthening of the hypothesis that the empire came to generate two sets of nobilities—economic and political—separated by function. Politics had more appeal for elites of moderately rich to humble origins—therefore from gentry and mercantile families. In contrast, members of the planter nobility confined themselves to local and regional politics that did not remove them from plantations for extended periods of time because, though commercial agriculture such as cane and coffee cultivation offered a lucrative future, it required the plantocracy's constant attention. The practice of absentee landlordship under the slavocratic regime simply was not realistic in the Bahian and Pernambucan cases and perhaps, in a larger context, for nineteenth-century Brazilian capitalist agriculture as a whole. Supervision in loco, in the days of difficult communications and transportation, was an absolute necessity to turn a profit. This hypothesis concerning the existence of separate economic and political nobilities can be further tested by looking at the southern case, a major coffee economy in the nineteenth century, that of Rio.

The province of Rio de Janeiro was created in 1834 from parts of the old captaincies of Paraíba do Sul, São Paulo, and Espírito Santo. Rio had been a port city of moderate prosperity, a principal outlet for the gold and diamonds of Minas Gerais as well as an emporium for slave trades until 1763, when the Crown government of Portugal transferred the colonial capital from Bahia to Rio as the economic epicenter moved from the North to South-Central Brazil. The expanding commercial agriculture in the Paraíba Valley, the Campos Basin, and the Zona da Mata during the late eighteenth and early nineteenth centuries owed its prosperity to the interior mining activities and the bustling trade in Rio. The oldest families of agrarian origin resided in the Campos Basin, through which the Paraíba River drains. Sugar and small cattle grazing were the mainstay of the local economy, whose expansion was closely tied to the general cycles of "boom and bust" of Brazilian history.

Coffee growing, which began in the Paraíba Valley in the 1780s, produced a host of new plantocrats concentrated north, northwest, and southwest of Rio. Although a few aristocratic planters of other regions settled in this area, the majority of the Fluminense agrarian elite constituted Brazil's premier gentry, measured in terms of their entrepreneurial endeavors and political power at regional and national levels. Successful planter families in the valley, as opposed to the agrarian clans in Campos and its adjacent region, were of mercantile and gentry origin, or in some cases of even humbler backgrounds. Despite the pervasive claims to noble and aristocratic ancestry, few in the valley could document them because many of the nineteenth-century gentry-nobility in Minas Gerais, São Paulo, and Rio were interprovincial migrants; the founder of a clan from one province often settled in another and prospered there. Sons and grandsons became the leading agrarian and mercantile elite of nineteenth-century society. Hence, unlike the situation in the more static Northeast, two kinds of gentry and aristocracy emerged in the triprovince area: transplanted and native.

Rio de Janeiro was court, political capital, and business hub of the empire. Although they were separate administrative units, province and city functioned as one. Together, they accounted for 226 titles. For the first century of the coffee boom (1830–1930), Rio was the harbinger of Brazil's "miracle" of the nineteenth century. A total of eighteen families won more than three titles each. Of these, only the Neto Cruz and Neto dos Reis clan, of Campos, and the Carneiro da Silvas, of Quissamã, were in the sugar business, and eleven families were in coffee, all in the Paraíba Valley. The established "native" aristocracy, such as the Azeredo Coutinhos and the Assecas in Campos, failed to attain imperial titles; they had been pauperized by 1830. Therefore, the Lima e Silvas were the sole native aristocracy-nobility in Rio province, netting five titles; they were also Brazil's foremost titled military, not agrarian, clan. The transplanted aristocratic clan of Nogueira da Gama (from Minas Gerais) acquired six titles. The most-titled clans, however, each with nine, were the Wernecks and the Avelars, both gentry-nobility. The Carneiro Leãos and the Mesquitas were mercantile nobility, and the Clemente Pintos and the Faros had interests in both capitalist agriculture and commerce.

The Lima e Silva clan was unique among the aristocracy of Brazil. The only non-Braganza duque was Luís Alves de Lima e Silva, better known as Caxias. His paternal forebears were soldiers in the thirteenth-century war against the Moors in Portugal, his grandfather and father were both marshals in the Portuguese and Brazilian armies, and his mother was also a descendant of a military family and related to the Assecas, of Campos. Although the family owned rural propertics, none of the clansmen was a career planter; every one of them was a professional soldier. The three sons of Marechal José Joaquim de Lima e Silva, Caxias's grandfather, became generals in the imperial army and nobles: Francisco (the Barão da Barra Grande), José Joaquim (the Visconde de Magé), and Manuel Fonseca (the Barão de Suruí); two grandsons became titled generals, Caxias and his brother José Joaquim Sobrinho (the Conde de Tocantins). Three times prime minister (1856–57; 1861–62; 1875–78), Caxias was an unrivaled political and military leader in the empire, a staunch defender of imperial authority, a champion of centripetalism, the empire's foremost troubleshooter in the nation-dividing regional revolts of the 1830s and 1840s, and the supreme commander of the allied forces in the Paraguayan War. Caxias enjoyed another distinction: he was the only son to receive his first title of nobility on the same day as his father.[37] This clan was a service, not an agrarian, aristocracy of the empire.

The Rio case further strengthens the hypothesis derived from the Pernambucan and Bahian patterns of nobility. The majority of Rio's provincial nobility was of gentry stock and humble origin. Furthermore, of the twelve gentry-noble clans, none produced politicians of national importance; aside from Caxias, Rio's sole politician of note came from the Nogueira da Gamas, a transplanted aristocratic family of Minas. The absence of political participation among the province's noble families can be explained in terms of the structure of Rio's export agriculture as well as its social and economic value system. The province consisted of four major geoeconomic zones: the oldest, the sugar-growing northeast (the São Fidelis-Campos-Macaé axis); the second, Vassouras-Valença-Paraíba do Sul, the northern perimeter of the coffee zone near Minas; the third, also a coffee zone, Piraí-Mangaratiba-Barra Mansa-Resende, the western part of the valley closest to São Paulo; and the fourth, the province's newest coffee frontier, Nova Friburgo-Cantagalo-Santa Maria Madalena, between the first and second zones. These four agricultural zones constituted the home of the Fluminense gentry-nobility.

Campos, or São Salvador de Campos dos Goitacazes, was unique as an agricultural town: its export economy accommodated both big commercial sugar plantations and small farms. The port of São João da Barra, in spite of its sandbars and constant dredging needs, was Campos's contact with outside markets until a series of canals and railroads provided an inland contact between the province's sugar capital and Rio de Janeiro. Campos's "Seven Captains" of 1627, original sesmaria-holding families, were regrouped and their lands were divided among the two surviving captains, the numerous heirs of the other original holders of land grants, including General Salvador Correia de Sá e Benevides (the Assecas), the local Jesuit chapter, and the convent of São Bento.[38] On these lands, where both commercial and subsistence agriculture were organized, sugarcane did particularly well. In 1734 Campos had 34 working engenhos; in 1778, 168; in 1816, 360; and in 1828, some 700.[39]

By the mid-nineteenth century, none of the 1,627 land grantees had survived as a major capitalist agriculturalist. Instead, the three largest landowners in Campos were relative newcomers: the Ribeiro de Castros, the Neto Cruzes, and the Neto dos Reises, the last two sharing a common ancestry. All three acquired nobiliary titles. The Barão de Santa Rita (Manuel Antônio Ribeiro de Castro) accumulated several fazendas. When he died in the 1840s, his four sons succeeded him as his heirs, together owning seven fazendas and three islands in the Muriaé River.[40] One of the sons, José, later became the Visconde de Santa Rita. In addition to being one of the biggest landholding clans in Campos, the Ribeiro de Castros were also in-laws of other planter families in the Campista Basin.

Equally prominent and wealthy was the family of Manuel Pinto Neto

Cruz (the Barão de Muriaé). Jerônimo, the founder of the clan and Manuel's father, was also a recipient of sesmarias; much like his in-law, the Barão de Santa Rita, he cultivated sugarcane as the principal economic activity. The Barão de Muriaé was more productive as a planter-landowner than was Santa Rita. He diversified more. Also a descendant of the colonial dynasty of the Azeredo Coutinhos of Campos, Muriaé was a cousin-in-law of the Visconde de Araruama (José Carneiro da Silva), an opulent landowner and entrepreneur in the neighboring county of Macaé and uncle to the Barão de Carapebus (see below). When the Barão de Muriaé died in 1855, his fortunes passed to his widow and two legitimate children. The Baronesa de Muriaé (the future viscondessa) declared in the parish land registry that she owned seven properties, including one island in the Muriaé River. Her Fazenda São Francisco de Paula was one of the best sugar plantations in Campos in its time. Son Jerônimo Pinto Neto Cruz and daughter Antônia Carolina de Castro Neto declared the ownership of three properties in the land registry. In addition to these properties, Antônia Carolina also registered more "lands and islands" (*terras e ilhas*) whose ownership she claimed.[41]

The founder of the third major landowning clan in Campos, the Neto dos Reis, was Bernardo Pinto Neto da Silva, a Portuguese merchant who made money in trade and invested in land. His brother Jerônimo became the founder of the Neto Cruz clan, of which the Barão de Muriaé became a part. The children of the two brothers intermarried. The Barão de Carapebus, son of Bernardo, was named Joaquim Pinto Neto dos Reis and married Antônia Joaquina da Cruz Neto, daughter of the Barão de Muriaé. Carapebus and his wife-niece owned one fazenda in Campos and "terras" of at least three leagues by 500 braças. His son, Antônio Dias Coelho Neto dos Reis (the future Conde de Carapebus) was a Coimbra-educated planter and became a prominent courtier noble in the 1880s. His marriage to the Nogueira da Gamas, of Valença, won him membership in a small coterie of the major agrarian noble families of Rio province, the court, and São Paulo. In the absence of a juridical status of the noble corporation to advance their economic and social interests, business partnerships (particularly jointly inherited and held properties and stocks) and marriages played a key role in fostering a corporate solidarity among Brazilian nobles. The future conde, like his cousins, was a large landowner in Campos, owning at least one fazenda and more "terras."[42] In the 1880s the clan incorporated itself as a business firm, pioneering the construction of sugar refineries in the Campos region.

That the agrarian families in the Campos Basin were tightly knit by marriages and business investments reinforces the hypothesis that a strong undertone of social and economic corporatism existed in the empire, especially among the nobility. Joint ownership (therefore joint ventures) of fazendas and lands by several clans related by blood ties appeared in the parish registries. Sítio N. S. dos Prazeres (one-half *legua* by 2,500 braças) was registered by the Visconde de Santa Rita and Conêgo Manuel do Brito Coutinho as a property that they had *bought*. Fazenda N. S. do Desterro was a gargantuan property built on three sesmarias of half a league each, formerly held by the Neto dos Reis; at the time of the registries, this fazenda was owned by three cousins; later, it was passed on to the Conde de Carapebus.[43] And the Conde's father owned two properties with his cousin, formerly their respective fathers.[44] This trend of joint ownership and therefore joint business alliance by mid-century in Rio province was a logical phenomenon. After 1830 coffee became a profitable business, which in turn helped the rise and consolidation of capitalist agriculture, including sugar. Marriages as well as business partnerships were frequently employed by the heirs of late colonial landowners as a means of maximizing their economic gain.

The triple marital linkage of the families of Muriaé, Santa Rita, and Araruama resulted in the corporate ownership of at least several other properties. The Visconde de Araruama, the Baronesa de Muriaé, and five other relatives collectively claimed "terras" as well as cane from a sesmaria once owned by the Barão de Santa Rita. Another group of six clansmen that included a son of Araruama, the future Conde de Araruama, together owned "terras" and "outras terras" inherited from the Barão de Muriaé.[45]

Probably the largest single landowner in Campos was the widow of the Barão de Abadia (Gregório Francisco de Miranda). The baronesa, Maria Isabel de Gusmão Miranda, was also the sister-in-law of the Barão da Lagoa Dourada (José Martins Pinheiro), another Campos landowner. When Abadia died in 1850, he left an immense fortune to his widow and heirs. The baronesa registered a total of nineteen times for scores of fazendas, sítios, and "terras" scattered in the three *fre-*

guesias of Santo Antônio dos Guarulhos, São Sebastião, and São Gonçalo. Thirteen holdings were at São Gonçalo, almost all rented out to tenants; two properties at São Sebastião; and four at Santo Antônio dos Guarulhos. One property was held in partnership with her brother-in-law, the future Barão da Lagoa Dourada. Abadia's other heirs, in an unspecified number, registered seven landholdings in the parish registry, of which two were located in São Gonçalo.[46]

Two other landowning clans in Campos are worth mentioning. One is the successors of the Visconde de Asseca; the other is the São Bento Order, the Benedictine college and monastery. At the time of the registration, the heirs of Asseca declared ownership of nine properties in São Gonçalo and four in São Sebastião that were in the process of being sold.[47] The Mosteiro de São Bento clearly held the most properties in Campos: it rented out seventy-five sítios in São Gonçalo and owned two properties in São Sebastião. The parish land registry did not reveal the terms of the rental agreements, but the majority of renters, but not all, were small subsistence farmers, judging from the location of the properties. One renter, Justiniano Manhães Barreto, was an important planter, who utilized the leased land for cane growing. Barreto was one of the major agrarian modernizers of Campos, a founder of a refinery in the 1880s.

In the sugar-growing region of Rio province, one more county is noteworthy: Macaé. Adjacent to Campos, São João de Macaé was made up of two districts, Macaé and N. S. de Desterro de Quissamã, which accounted for a total of 124 entries in the land registry. (Campos, the largest county in Rio, boasted more than 3,000 entries; Santo Antônio dos Guarulhos Parish led with 1,248, followed by São Sebastião with 842 and São Gonçalo with 769, these three being the core agricultural area.) The registry figures do not represent the exact number of plantations and farms because some entries recorded multiple holdings. Thus, Macaé's 93 and Quissamã's 31 registered holdings were fewer than the total number of fazendas.

The undisputed landowning clan in the county was the Carneiro da Silva family. At the time of the parish registration, the founder, "the capitão-mor," was already dead, having amassed a fortune in trade. When the Braganza court moved to the New World, his son José (the future Visconde de Araruama) became the titular of the clan. Dabbling both in sugarcane growing and trade, Araruama turned out to be an innovative planter.[48] Together with his sons, he became the first Brazilian slavocratic entrepreneur to found a refinery, the Engenho Central de Quissamã, in 1877. In the urban Macaé district, where trade, retail, and fishing were mainstay economies, the family owned one "casa grande" built on 1,150 braças, in addition to 7,500 braças of urban properties. The registry clearly reveals that the process of urbanizing Carneiro da Silva's agrarian wealth was complete by mid-century. The entry mentions that some of the urban properties were part of the family heritage: they came from "meu mano o Barão de Muriaé" and "minha quinta avo D. Catarina de Azeredo Coutinho e Mello."[49] In the district of Quissamã, the clan listed at least thirteen holdings, including eight fazendas. The pride of the family, Fazenda Quissamã, belonged to the visconde and is still in the hands of his descendants. In addition to the developed landholdings, the family acquired a series of tracts of land (*datas de terras*) throughout the district. Paulista sociologist Maria Isaura Pereira de Queirós has advanced the thesis that, in colonial Brazil, the município was often a de facto fief of a dominant family. Quissamã was certainly a single family-held domain.[50]

The four major landowning families in the Campos Basin were related: the Ribeiro de Castros, the Neto Cruzes, the Neto dos Reises, and the Carneiro da Silvas. A Castro female married the Barão de Muriaé, who was in turn father-in-law to the Conde de Araruama (a son of the visconde) and cousin to the Barão de Carapebus. The Carneiro da Silvas were related to the families of the Duque de Caxias and Eusébio de Queirós. Such a corporatist pattern of linkage will be seen also in the western part of the Paraíba Valley, where the Barão de Piraí was related to the Sousa Breveses, the Teixeira Leites, and the Oliveira Roxos, all premier coffee plantocracies of Rio province. This pattern of "marrying outward" as opposed to the pattern in the Northeast of "marrying inward" significantly prolonged the groups' corporate influence in the social, economic, and political spheres. Furthermore, the Northeastern pattern fits the classic oligarchic model of single-clan or vertical familiocratic dominance, and the Campos Basin and Paraíba Valley cases suggest a different structure: multiclan horizontal roles. The importance of these structural differences for the political arena as well as for economic modernization efforts was to become too apparent by the 1880s.

Such family-connected landholding was not a norm in the more urban Município Neutro, as the court and its adjacent region of Rio were known. At least six districts in that region—Campo Grande, Guaratiba, Inhauma, Irajá, Santa Cruz, and Jacarepaguá—contained coffee and sugar plantations, and several subsistence farms. In 1864 a total of 367 plantations and farms were registered. The outstanding planter in Jacarepaguá, where 181 agricultural establishments existed, was an imperial household staff member. Within Campo Grande Parish for instance, another owned Fazenda do Bangu. The future Visconde de Mauá owned Sítio Sapopemba, in Irajá, where he cultivated coffee, presumably as a hobby.[51] Leading merchants, bankers, and permanent courtiers held land in the município and its neighboring districts, but little commercial use was made of the properties. Most landowners in the court region cultivated foodstuffs to be consumed by the local denizens.

The agricultural activities of the House of Braganza were concentrated at Imperial Fazenda de Santa Cruz, in the district of the same name. Located about eleven leagues, or five and a half hours by horse-drawn coach, from Rio, this fazenda was a Jesuit property that had been founded in the late seventeenth century. As in the cases of numerous staple-growing sítios and fazendas in the valley, it prospered during the mineral age, supplying foodstuffs to mines and the city of Rio. Toward the end of the last years of Jesuit rule, the fazenda produced an impressive annual income of 30,000 cruzados.[52] After the expulsion of the Black Robes from the New World, a nearby secular clergy ran Santa Cruz until the state took over its operation in 1761. By Joanine times, the plantation had become a favorite retreat for the royal family, its courtiers, foreign diplomats, and state ministers, and in 1817 João VI established a coach line that carried passengers and goods between Santa Cruz and Rio. Among the Braganza monarchs, Pedro I showed the most interest in improving and developing Santa Cruz, raising cattle and horses; planting sugarcane, coffee, and corn; and even building a crude home factory (fábrica) that produced farm tools and other utensils for the fazenda.[53] Pedro liked to receive state dignitaries in Santa Cruz's rustic, relaxed ambience, and also used the retreat for his frequent amorous encounters; on one occasion at least, he took both his wife, Leopoldina, and his mistress, the Marquesa de Santos, to the fazenda. The emperor was also said to have bedded down with slaves there.[54]

Although the boundary of the fazenda had been demarcated in 1731, the loss of the *Livro do Tombo*, which contained that valuable information, prompted a new cadastre in 1827. Because this entire valley had been consumed by coffee-growing fever, some of the Crown land had been appropriated by local potentates. Thus, the findings of the new survey were vociferously disputed by some 600 local landowners from Vassouras, Valença, Piraí, São João Marcos, and Barra Mansa— their outcry justified by the knowledge that restoring the cultivated land to the Crown would destroy the basis for the new coffee boom. (Late in the 1820s, coffee surpassed all other crops as a money-maker: in 1828 coffee produced revenues of 5.121:244$ for the province, and sugar netted 3.466:800$.)[55] Among the protesters were the future Barão de Piraí and the Barão do Rio Bonito, who owned 540 and 400 slaves each in the disputed region alone. In the three districts of Piraí, São João Marcos, and Barra Mansa, 172 planters threatened with eviction by the Crown together produced 175,000 arrobas of coffee and employed 6,309 slaves. The imperial attempt to appropriate this vast rich region was aborted by the resistance, and the plan was eventually shelved.[56] No economic interaction occurred between Santa Cruz and its surrounding region; the income from the plantation went directly to the Braganza household coffers in the court, and nothing was spent to stimulate the local economy. Therefore, the largest fazenda in the Paraíba Valley did not play a crucial role in the growth of the coffee economy throughout the nineteenth century.

The Braganzas, then, were landlords without local ties; and their fazenda, a symbol of imperial and feudal landownership, contributed little to the region. The Barão de Sorocaba, a brother-in-law of the Marquesa de Santos, was the imperial factor of the fazenda. The Baronesa de Sorocaba, the sister of Santos, was also Pedro's mistress at one time and produced a son from their liaison. When the emperor's slaves were manumitted, they were allowed to till land on the imperial fazenda as peons, a practice more of humanitarian than economic importance. In terms of the agrarian history of the empire, the anomaly was that the American House of Braganza neglected to tie its interests to those of the Brazilian planters, and thus failed to establish a legitimate role in the dominant economy. A joint partnership with and/or a leasing of land to planters could have turned Santa Cruz into an enterprising capitalist venture. The Braganza's right to rule Brazil certainly could have been reinforced, further legitimizing their status, which had only served as a facile transition from Portuguese to Luso-Brazilian to Brazilian emperorship. In a peculiar way, the absence of common agrarian identification with other dominant clans in Rio and the valley considerably weakened the future position of the House of Braganza, especially the right to the throne by the heiress Princess Isabel and her French consort. This fatal flaw was further compounded by the absolute lack of intermarriage with the Brazilian aristocracy or gentry. In short, the establishment of a corporate class of nobility drawn from the landholding, mercantile, religious, and civil-military groups was the only bond between the ruling house and the people. The linchpin of the Brazilian empire and its capitalist agriculture should have been a joint economic partnership reinforced by kinship linkages between the House of Braganza and the leading agrarian clans, a structure that would have made the imperial system more sensitive to the major economic groups and the exigencies of the realpolitik of the empire. Such a morganatic or other entrepreneurial bonding process never took place.

5

Gentry Planter and Merchant Families

*The capitalist era in the countryside is ushered
in by a period of large-scale agriculture on the basis
of serf labor services.* KARL MARX

The epicenter of Brazilian capitalist agriculture through the nineteenth century was first located in the Paraíba Valley and then shifted to the Paulista north and west. The valley gained its economic importance when gold and diamonds were discovered in Minas Gerais, Goiás, and Mato Grosso, first as a provider of subsistence foodstuffs and after 1830 as the producer of coffee for European and North American markets. The second region, São Paulo's north and west, did not emerge as an economic center until the 1870s. One historian, describing the economic growth of the valley during the late eighteenth and early nineteenth centuries, aptly traced the rise of the towns from the "bandeirante" incursions to the "mining" economies to the "fazenda" cycle.[1] The vigorous intercolonial trade between Rio and Minas, between São Paulo and Rio, and between São Paulo and Minas Gerais sparked the growth of the valley economy. Elite families in the three captaincies mingled, intermarried, and formed partnerships in trade and agriculture. By the early nineteenth century, the major patterns of development had been permanently established by the pioneering families. It was they who had acquired sesmarias when João was prince regent and king, they who had built trade outposts, organized mule-train companies, built Brazil's first railroads, and financed the expansion of coffee plantations. These agrarian families of the valley, and of the Paulista north and west after the 1870s, constituted the bedrock of the new emerging gentry elite of the empire and later of the First Brazilian Republic (1889–1930).

Rio's Paraíba Valley

By the 1740s the colonial structure of agricultural exploitation had begun to change. Various towns that had sprouted in the Paraíba Valley evolved from humble way stations for mule trains into food-growing colonies. Parati, a port and a major producer of sugarcane and rum, was among the several littoral embarkation points that tied the interior mines to the port of Rio. Along with Parati, the ports of Mangaratiba, Angra dos Reis, and Itaguaí (through a canal) were the principal coastal settlements, exclusively devoted to trade, subsistence farming, and fishing. São João do Príncipe (also known as São João Marcos), Rio Claro, Resende, Vassouras, Valença, Paraíba do Sul, and Barra Mansa were notable food-producing towns and mule-train outposts for the mines and the city of Rio in the late eighteenth century, before they converted to coffee cultivation by the 1780s. By the early nineteenth century, these towns had acquired the status of *vilas* or even *cidades*, and capitalist agriculture based on seemingly inexhaustible supplies of virgin land and chattel slavery was firmly established.

The importance of this economic transformation was duly recognized by colonial governors; the citizens of São João Marcos, for instance, were exempt from military service, for the drain of labor would impede the rapid expansion of the coffee culture. Angra dos Reis and Mangaratiba served as ports for transshipping this crop from Rio Claro, Resende, and São João Marcos; the shipments went to Rio, where international carriers took over. The road linking these interior coffee towns and the ports was so critical that in 1855 alone the provincial government spent 632:000$ on its maintenance.[2] Until the railroad came through the western part of the valley linking Rio and São Paulo in 1877, these coastal towns continued to remain as significant to export agriculture as they had to the mining economy of the previous century.

The formation of the Paraíba Valley coffee economy was a concerted effort by Fluminense and migrant families from Minas and São Paulo. The migration from Minas Gerais and São Paulo had continued through the first half of the nineteenth century, as had the arrival of foreign immigrants. In 1808 one law (Lei de November 25) permitted foreigners to receive land grants in accordance with João VI's policy of expanding European colonization in the empire. By 1818 the Colônia de Leopoldina, in Nova Friburgo, Rio province, was founded by Swiss immigrants from the Canton of Friburg.[3] In 1835 one of Napoleon's generals (the Conde de Hogendrop) reportedly started coffee cultivation at his farm in the Tijuca forest in the city of Rio; one José Maria Correia de Sá e Benevides, *veador* of the imperial household, was the first planter of coffee bushes in Engenho d'Água, in Jacarepaguá, a few miles south of the city of Rio.[4] By 1860 the Rio side of the Paraíba Valley contained some 600 coffee fazendas that produced 52.811:000$ worth of exports, or three times the Bahian exports (18.029:000$), more than four times the Pernambucan (12.472:000$), and more than six times the Paulista (8.413:000$).

Vassouras-Valença-Paraíba do Sul

Alberto Lamego, a noted historian-geographer of Rio province, calls Valença "the old city of the Marquêses" and Vassouras "the biggest lair of rural aristocracy [sic] of Brazil after Campos." Another historian observed that Valença was by far the more democratic, in spite of its haughty name and noble population, and that Vassouras (literally, "a broom") became the more "oligarchical."[5] Arch-rivals in social fashion, economic modernization, and political power, the two cities were the province of Rio's bastions of liberalism and staunch bases for the Liberal party. An important adjunct to their plantocracy was Paraíba do Sul, founded on private land given by the Pais Leme family (the Marquês de São João Marcos). Many of the founding families in the Vassoura-Valença area branched out to the town of Paraíba. Intermarriages among the premier clans were common, and business ties were strong.

Of some ten major families in Valença, all transplanted from Minas, the Resendes and the Nogueira da Gamas stood out as the cream of the local agrarian elite. The founder of the Resende family, Severino Ribeiro, was probably a miner in the Rio das Mortes region. By the 1760s he had married Josefa Maria de Resende; two sons became the principal founders of the distinguished gentry clan: Estêvão and Geraldo. Estêvão studied in Coimbra; held judgeships in both Juiz de Fora, Minas, and Palmeal, Portugal; and at the time of the Napoleonic invasion of Portugal left there with the royal family. A key functionary during the time of King João VI, Estêvão acquired sesmarias in Valença and married Ilídia Malfada de Sousa Queirós, daughter of "the richest man in São Paulo," Brigadier Luís Antônio de Sousa Queirós; the couple had sixteen children.

Estêvão steadily rose in the government during the early years of Pedro I's rule, and in 1825 was ennobled as the Barão de Valença with honras de grandeza, in 1826 as the conde, and in 1848 as the marquês. Between 1824 and 1827 he served as minister of justice and minister of the empire. In 1826 he was named as senator from his home province, Minas Gerais, and became president of the upper chamber in 1841. The Marquês de Valença was therefore a classic example of a good mandarin who became a wealthy landowner by the right mix of marriage and politics. His settling in Valença, in the coffee zone, was probably precipitated by rapidly declining mining activities, his desire to hold offices in the nearby court, and his economic ties with the Sousa Queiróses, of São Paulo.

As the marquês exemplified the transfer of wealth from one economic activity to another (from mining to agriculture), the dispersal of his children also represented a prudent form of economic diversification. Four sons and a daughter became nobles: the Second Barão de Valença (Pedro Ribeiro de Sousa Resende), the Barão de Resende (Estêvão Ribeiro de Sousa Resende), the Barão de Geraldo de Resende (Geraldo Ribeiro de Sousa Resende), and an illegitimate son, later legitimized, the Barão de Lorena (Estêvão Ribeiro de Resende). A daughter married a French titleholder, the Marquis de Palarimi. The Barão de Resende and the Barão de Geraldo de Resende were born in the court while their father was still in the service of the government. Resende eventually settled in Piracicaba, São Paulo, where he became a wealthy coffee planter. Brother Geraldo also moved to São Paulo, where he was a leading coffee fazendeiro in Campinas. The Second Barão de Valença took over the family business of coffee cultivation at home. Lorena settled down in Piraí, marrying into a rich family, and became a major coffee planter.[6]

Coronel Geraldo Ribeiro de Resende, brother of the Marquês de Valença, remained in Minas. Having left the decaying Rio das Mortes, once a thriving gold-mining district, he settled in Juiz de Fora, founded a coffee plantation, and prospered. A son, José, became the Barão de Juiz de Fora and continued the coffee farming. Two of José's sons, also coffee planters in Minas—Juiz de Fora and Rio Novo—became nobles: the Third Barão do Rio Novo (José Augusto) and the Barão de Retiro (Geraldo Augusto). In addition to these, a sister of the two founders of the fabulous coffee fortunes in Minas and Rio, Leonarda Maria, married into the Avelar dynasty, in Vassouras, an equally rich coffee planter family. In all, the two founding families held eight titles, not counting foreign and Brazilian honors that female members acquired through marriage. Except the Marquês de Valença, none of the heirs became a politician; all devoted their lives to capitalist agriculture. The clan became a triprovincial gentry of new money.[7]

South of Valença, also known as the "Princess of Coffee," was the most imperious town in the empire, Vassouras, which did not become a freguesia until 1801 or a city until 1857. Part of Valença *comarca* in its early years, Vassouras was better situated than Valença as the center of the Fluminense coffee boom. By mid-century, Vassouras was producing 1.5 million arrobas of coffee per annum, yet Valença was still larger in size and contained the second largest number of slaves in the province. Stanley J. Stein identified nine major families in Vassouras who together controlled eighty-two fazendas.[8] The four major clans were the Wernecks (and Rocha Wernecks), the Avelars, the Ribeiro Leites, and the Teixeira Leites, the last two being related. Much like Valença, Vassouras began when the mining economy declined; many miner families and merchants of Minas Gerais settled in the valley when the coffee boom began. Settlers also came from Valença, and some moved to Paraíba do Sul and Valença from Vassouras. During the early years of the coffee boom, intraprovincial, or even intrazonal, migration was frequent.

The Ribeiro Leite and Teixeira Leite clans were descendants of two eighteenth-century migrants from Rio das Mortes. Sargento-Mór José Leite Ribeiro (1723–1801), born in Minas Gerais, was a well-off miner wise enough to invest some of the profits in land. As the mining cycle came to a close, he and his son-in-law Francisco José Teixeira moved to Vassouras, where coffee cultivation was just beginning. These two families were among the pioneers of the local coffee economy by the 1780s. The real consolidators of the family fortune were, however, sons of the two pioneers. Of the fourteen children born to José Leite and his wife, the sixth son, Custódio, became the Barão de Aiuruoca. Demonstrating the pioneer spirit, Aiuruoca also established coffee plantations in Barra Mansa, of western Rio province, and in Mar de Espanha, a county in the Zona da Mata, Minas. In all three places, his children and brothers married into local landholding families. With brother Francisco, Custódio built the Estrada Magé, which tied Mar de Espanha to Rio city via Sapucaia. Landholding by his clan was very extensive, and a total of ten direct male descendants held Brazilian titles. Among their in-laws were the Avelars, the Almeidas, the Teixeiras Leites, all of Vassouras, and the Gomes de Carvalhos, of Barra Mansa.[9]

The Teixeira Leites, less numerous in titled offspring, were equally opulent and enterprising. Francisco José Teixeira (the second) was Aiuruoca's nephew and himself a coffee planter. He was ennobled as the Barão de Itambé, and his son, Francisco José (the third), became the first generation Teixeira Leite who held a title, the Barão de Vassouras. The archetype of the gentry planter, whose tendency to overdecorate, overspend, and outdo others was frequently reported by both foreign and Brazilian visitors to Vassouras, the Barão de Vassouras was one of Itambé's seven sons. The brothers, led by Francisco José, advocated railroad construction by the 1840s. Rallying their in-laws—such as Caetano Furquim de Almeida, another rich planter, comissário, and Francisco José's son-in-law—the clan valiantly attempted to change the course of the Dom Pedro II Railroad, which would link Rio and São Paulo by 1877. The imperial government finally turned down their proposal, and the line passed south of Vassouras. When another line was eventually laid along the right bank of the Paraíba River just north of Vassouras, the local planters raised enough money to run a trunk line to Juparanã. Politically, the clan was Liberal, though Itambé was a staunch Conservative; none was a big name in imperial politics, however. At least four female members of the clan married Brazilian nobles, among them the Viscondessa de Taunay, grandmother of the renowned Paulista historian.[10] This illustrious clan was gentry to the core, based on its economic actions as well as its tenure as a plantocracy.

The Wernecks and Avelars were as numerous as the Ribeiro Leites. The founder of the Werneck clan in Vassouras was Inácio de Sousa Werneck, a transplanted miner-turned-planter in Valença. The patriarch of the clan, Inácio settled in Vassouras in the early nineteenth century and was a Mineiro like the majority of the settlers in this part of the valley. Inácio and his children grew coffee. The Brazilian saying "The father a miner, the son a gentleman, and the grandson a shoemaker" is especially apt for the Werneck clan. Through marriages, the family acquired additional surnames, such as Sousa, Santos, Lacerda, Chagas, Furquim, and Rocha, and male Wernecks acquired nobiliary titles directly. If female Wernecks with titled children were counted, the clan had a total of nine titles, including two América Pinheiros and two Almeida Ramoses.[11] All were rich planters, but the Second Barão de Pati do Alferes (Francisco Peixoto de Lacerda Werneck) was considered to be one of the ten major fazendeiros in Vassouras.

The Avelar family had two principal branches: Avelar e Almeida and Ribeiro de Avelar. Much like other pioneer planters in Vassouras, this family settled in the early nineteenth century. Together, the clan produced nine titles: five for Ribeiro de Avelar and four for Avelar e Almeida. The Barão de Ribeirão (José de Avelar e Almeida) and his three sons were rich fazendeiros. Ribeirão and son, the Visconde de Cananéia (Bernardino Rodrigues de Avelar), were objects of popular respect and envy as the owners of the best palaces in Vassouras. The other branch of the family—Ribeiro de Avelar—consisted of equally rich gentry, whose titular was the First Barão de Capivari (Joaquim Ribeiro de Avelar), a cousin of the Barão de Ribeirão. Three of Capivari's brothers, also fazendeiros, became nobles, too: the Visconde da Paraíba, the Barão de Guaribu, and the First Barão de São Luís. Capivari's son, the Visconde de Ubá (Joaquim Ribeiro de Avelar Filho), was also a rich planter. This side of the family was also married to the Wernecks.[12]

Paraíba do Sul had become one of the major coffee producers in the valley by the 1860s. Many families there were second and third sons of the Valença and Vassouras pioneers. The Visconde da Paraíba, born in the city of Rio, began planting in Vassouras, but soon moved to Paraíba, then a booming coffee frontier. The visconde eventually became a local Liberal political chief and sponsored a young Mineiro in politics. This young man, Martinho de Campos, became Paraíba's son-in-law and, in the early 1880s, prime minister of the empire. The Second Barão de Palmeiras (João Quirino da Rocha Werneck), whose main clan interests were in Vassouras, was a prominent planter there. Although Paraíba do Sul never became a center of provincial coffee civilization unlike Valença or Vassouras, at least seventeen titles have been traced to the region.[13]

Of the leading agrarian gentry of Paraíba do Sul, the Alves Barbosa family offers an interesting case of dual residence (also in Valença) and dual economic interests (coffee and trade). Jacinto Alves Barbosa, the founder of this gentry clan, was a muleteer. Having accumulated money through trade between Rio and Minas, he wisely invested in coffee plantations in the 1820s, as the beans were just being sought after in overseas markets. His fortune increased immensely until he was made the Barão de Santa Justa in 1866 and doubly honored only two months later by the title of grandee of the empire. At the time of his death in 1872, he left six highly productive fazendas in Valença and Paraíba do Sul as well as a coffee commission house in Rio, and was among the richest, if not *the* richest, of the coffee planters in the province.[14] His son Francisco took over the family business of coffee cultivating, comissário activities, and money-lending. The Francisco Alves Barbosa Company was one of the best commission houses in the court, and one of its partners was an Avelar.[15] The Alves Barbosas were among about a dozen elite comissários who also invested directly in coffee plantations, exclusively marketing their own products. The family was archetypal of Rio and Paulista planters and merchants, whose idea of the diversification and maximization of economic gains paralleled that of the English gentry.

The second generation Alves Barbosas were honored by the emperor as the Second Barão de Santa Justa in 1876, at the peak of the family's fortune and prestige in the valley. The titular head of the Alves Barbosa clan, however, was Francisco's widow, Bernardina, an energetic *fazendeira* and entrepreneur. This pistol-packing woman was a veritable "amazona bárbara," feared by her neighbors and insolent and overbearing, even toward the imperial family. When her son, José Alves, for example, was awarded a title of the Barão de Santa Justa, the third title obtained by the clan, she chose to carry her personal quarrels with him to an extreme; she opposed the Crown's decision to grant the name Santa Justa. In a letter of protest, the impudent Bernardina wrote the emperor that the granting of this name in José's title without her consent was an invasion of her privacy and chided the Crown for having failed to consult her. The prudent emperor simply ignored the letter. Bernardina wrote again, this time to the princess regent, adding that the confusion resulting from the two Santa Justa titles would hurt her comissário business as well as plantation activities. She pointed out that the princess and her consort, the Conde d'Eu, had been her guests at Fazenda Santa Justa. The Crown continued to ignore her vehement objection; however, a few months later, the Braganzas made the persistent woman the Viscondessa de Santa Justa in a mollifying gesture, some seventeen years after the death of her husband, the Second Santa Justa.[16] As in the cases of Vassouras and Valença, the hypothesis regarding planter politicians based on the northeastern patterns holds here: no titled planter in Paraíba do Sul ever became a prominent mandarin. Political participation at the imperial level was minimal.

Pirai-Mangaratiba-Barra Mansa-Resende

By the middle of the nineteenth century, São João Marcos, Vassouras, Valença, and Resende were the four largest coffee producers in the valley, a supremacy challenged after 1865 by a number of new counties in the valley as well as in the eastern part of the province. A decade later, Valença survived among the province's top five agricultural counties; the others had faded rapidly.[17] In the eighteenth century, this Pirai-Resende region was a supply outpost for the mining region as well as a favorite stopover for mule trains operated by Rio and Mineiro merchants. When the Dom Pedro II Railroad went through this part of the valley, secondary seaports such as Mangaratiba, Estrela, Angra dos Reis, and Parati quickly fell into decay.[18] Porto das Caixas, the outlet for Cantagalo and the eastern part of the province, also declined because the Cantagalo Railroad offered more economical, secure, and direct overland transportation to the court. Railroads played contrasting roles in Rio and São Paulo; in the former, they caused the decline of small urban seaports, and in the latter they pushed the coffee frontier into the western part of the province.

This western part of Rio's Paraíba Valley consisted of a cluster of coffee-growing counties, some of considerable age and productivity during the early years of cultivation history. Pirai, São João Marcos, Mangaratiba, Passa Três, Resende, Barra Mansa, and Rio Claro—the last three being near the Rio-São Paulo border—were the early major coffee cultivators in Rio province. Their inhabitants were typically a mixture of Paulistas, Mineiros, and Fluminenses. Much like their eastern neighbors of the Valença-Vassouras axis, the leading planter clans there frequently intermarried with those of São Paulo and Minas Gerais. Clan association and marriage patterns in the economic and trade practices of this western region can be distinguished from those in the eastern part. The Valença-Vassouras complex used overland routes and mule trains to export coffee beans to the city of Rio, and the western region utilized a sea channel—Mangaratiba, Angra dos Reis, and Parati being its principal intershipping ports to Rio. This rather risky means of transporting cargoes remained in operation until the Rio-São Paulo Railroad was built through the region in the late 1870s.

Through their common pioneering ancestry, Piraí and Barra Mansa shared similar economic development, evolving from way stations for the mule trains that linked Rio with Minas and São Paulo during the eighteenth century to coffee-growing regions in the nineteenth. José Gomes de Sousa Portugal (the future Barão de Turvo) settled there on an eighteenth-century sesmaria that became a productive coffee plantation. Antônio Manuel de Freitas (the future Barão do Rio Claro), born in Cunha, São Paulo, moved to the Piraí region to begin cultivation of coffee in the early nineteenth century; he and his descendants became one of the largest coffee-growing families in that border region. No less than the brother of the future Marquês de Paraná (prime minister, 1853–55) moved from Minas to the Piraí-Barra Mansa region: Nicolau Neto Carneiro Leão (the future Barão de Santa Maria) became as prosperous a planter as his brother in Sapucaia. Other key landowners were José Feliciano de Morais Costa (the future Visconde de Benevente), Luís de Sousa Breves (the future Barão de Guararema), a scion of the empire's largest slave owner, Joaquim José de Sousa Breves, and Francisco de Assis Monteiro Breves (the future Barão de Louriçal), a kinsman of the Sousa Breveses.[19]

The parochial land registry in Piraí and Barra Mansa confirms two major aspects of social history: the supremacy of the titled agrarian clans as the major landowners of the region and the strict regional confinement of their interlocking marriages. (No member of the major agrarian clans of this region, for instance, was married to a member of an equally prestigious family of another economic zone such as Campos, the sugar-growing area of eastern Rio.) In Barra Mansa, the Gomes de Carvalhos, and the Oliveira Roxos were major agrarian holders of nobiliary titles.

The Gomes de Carvalho family, for instance, was founded by a Portuguese merchant, Manuel Gomes de Carvalho (the First Barão do Amparo), whose investment in land led to his rise as an agrarian gentry in the region. Three of his sons, all planters, became nobles: Joaquim (the Second Barão do Amparo), Manuel (the Barão do Rio Negro), and João (the Visconde da Barra Mansa).[20] In addition to these nobiliary elite, the Oliveira Roxo family figured prominently in this region because of its three titles: the Barão de Guanabara, the Second Visconde de Vargem Alegre, and the Barão de Oliveira Roxo. Through marriages, the Oliveira Roxos were related to another key planter family, headed by the Barão de Piraí.[21] As in the case of the Gomes de Carvalhos, the founder of the Oliveira Roxos was a Portuguese merchant, whose four sons were ennobled with Brazilian titles.

In the Freguesia de Santa Ana do Piraí, the Gonçalves de Moraises controlled landholding. The Barão de Piraí and his brother Antônio owned at least five fazendas. But the largest landowner in the freguesia appeared to be the Barão de Vargem Alegre (Matias Gonçalves de Oliveira Roxo), who claimed ownership of four fazendas: Minhocas and Conto Alegre, which he bought; Onça, a gift from the Barão de Piraí, his father-in-law; and Várzea Alegre, which belonged to his father-in-law, but over which Matias exercised usufruct.[22]

The largest landowner in the Freguesia de São João Batista do Arrozal, also a district of Piraí, was José de Sousa Breves; his brother-in-law, the Barão de Piraí, was the next largest holder. A member of the third generation of the Sousa Breveses, José owned six fazendas.[23] The registry offers a glimpse of the landholding pattern among a few of the members of the extended Sousa Breves clan, which included José's two cousins, a half-sister,[24] three in-laws, and the Barão de Piraí.[25] These in-laws owned nine fazendas, not counting those of the Barão de Piraí. One Brites Clara, though married, continued to use her maiden name in all business transactions, such as the parish registry, and was the owner of the clan heirloom, Fazenda Cachoeira.[26] The second largest landowner in Arrozal was the Barão de Piraí. In addition to his five fazendas in the Santa Ana district, he owned three large plantations in Arrozal.

The Sousa Breves clan during the nineteenth century was an archetypal capitalist agrarian gentry of the empire. Although its landholdings were scattered throughout the western part of Rio's Paraíba Valley, the largest concentration was in and around the Piraí-Mangaratiba axis; in addition, the clan owned the island of Marambaia, the reception point and breeding place for African chattels. Afonso de E. Taunay, the foremost authority on the valley's history, did not attempt to trace the clan members, a time-consuming and even futile effort, but did identify the best known, a third-generation Sousa Breves, Comendador Joaquim José. During his heyday as a fazendeiro, he owned at least twenty coffee plantations and more than 6,000 slaves. Containing a minimum of 5 million coffee trees, his fazendas produced more than 200,000 arrobas in 1860 and 250,000 in 1887, but plummeted to only 30,000 after the abolition of slavery.[27] J. J. de Sousa Breves, as he was known, richly deserved his title "King of Coffee."

The career of the founder-patriarch of the Sousa Breves clan paralleled those of the founders of Valença and Vassouras. When the governor-general of Rio ordered in the 1720s that the roads between Rio and São Paulo and between Rio and Minas Gerais be improved for the secure transportation of gold and other cargoes, João Machado Pereira and Antônio de Sousa Breves were chosen to clear the area of Indians. São João Marcos, Piraí, and Resende (formerly Campo Alegre), through which the Caminho Novo passed, had been subject to incessant Indian attacks that hampered settlers in the area as well as communications between Rio and the mining region. The governor-general's aides carried out their duties well; by 1737 João Machado Pereira had obtained a staging ground by establishing a fazenda in São João Marcos, and Antônio de Sousa Breves had set up his plantation in Piraí.[28]

Born in São Jorge, an island in the archipelago of the Azores and Terceira, Antônio de Sousa Breves moved to Brazil soon after his marriage. Taunay was able to identify four of the descendants in Brazil: José (born in São João Marcos in 1748), Domingos (born in 1751), Tomás (born in 1756), and Ana Margarida (birthdate unknown). The titular of the valley's richest family under the empire was Joaquim José, son of José and grandson of Antônio. Joaquim José's brother, José Joaquim, popularly known as José, was the principal landowner in Piraí during the 1850s. The brothers married two daughters of the Barão de Piraí. Because José had no heir, his properties probably passed on to his brother Joaquim José, which would explain why the latter, who owned the most land in Piraí during the last three decades of the empire, did not appear as a landowner in the parish land registry of 1854–56. Described as a "homem do poucas luzes," or "man of dim wit," Joaquim José was a perfect bourgeois gentilhomme.[29] Fond of indulging in an opulent life-style, he maintained a palatial residence in Fazenda São Joaquim da Grama, another sumptuous mansion next to the Imperial Palace of Boa Vista in the court, and a theater in Mangaratiba. Traveling with a large entourage of slaves, he was said to maintain a harem of "white slaves" (*mulatas claras*).

In spite of his outward pretensions, Joaquim José did not seek a Bra-zilian title; according to some, his attitude in this regard was one of utter contempt, for he argued that the only true nobility was that of Eu-rope. His daughter Rita married an Italian noble; a nephew, who was a diplomat in the Brazilian imperial foreign service, married a Russian noble, Vera Haritoff, whose brother Maurice Haritoff in turn married another niece of Joaquim José. The Haritoffs eventually settled in Bra-zil after a brief sojourn in Europe.[30] When slavery was abolished in 1888, the Sousa Breveses, especially the descendants of Joaquim José, ceased to be planters. The family land was either sold off or fragmented among the heirs, the biggest portion being bought by the Rio Light Company, which built a hydroelectric dam and flooded many of the Sousa Breves's magnificent mansions and estates.[31]

The heartland of the "sertões de leste" of eastern Rio was, however, the area of Cantagalo and Nova Friburgo. In the 1880s Cantagalo, in Rio, and Campinas, in São Paulo, emerged as the two biggest coffee producers in the Western Hemisphere. The region was first settled by Swiss immigrants, later by French and German. Nova Friburgo was founded in 1820 by Alpine colonists from the Canton of Friburg who had settled there two years earlier. Sesmarias were given out to both Brazilian and foreign settlers, who prospered as cultivators of such sta-ples as corn and beans and, later, coffee. Despite its steep, hilly terrain and dense pine forest, Cantagalo offered good soil conditions. In the western part of the Paraíba Valley (Barra Mansa, Resende, and Valença, for instance), an average life expectancy of coffee trees ranged between thirty and thirty-five years. In addition, compared to the western part, productivity was superior in Rio's "sertões de leste," but still lower than that in São Paulo. Each thousand trees in Cantagalo produced fifty arrobas; in Campinas, seventy. Prime-aged trees (ten to twenty years old) in Cantagalo yielded only sixty arrobas and trees of twenty to thirty years of age only thirty-five arrobas, compared to the Paulista north and west, where trees of eight to sixteen years produced one hundred arrobas or more and those of twenty to thirty years easily bore fifty arrobas.[32]

The leading gentry plantocracy in Rio province, if not in Brazil, was the clan founded by a Portuguese sesmeiro, Antônio Clemente Pinto (the First Barão de Nova Friburgo). As a youth, he arrived in Brazil and worked as an errand boy in an export-import house in the court, where he met his protector, who started young Antônio in an agricultural enterprise in Cantagalo. According to the parish land registry, Antônio held five properties as of the mid-1850s in the Santíssimo Sacramento district and twenty-one in the Santa Rita do Rio Negro district.[33] In addition to these holdings, he registered fazendas, sesmarias, and tracts of land in the names of four companies or in partnership with members of the local elite. The Nova Friburgo e Jacob Van Erven Company held seven sesmarias and three "posses" of land in the Rio Negro and Sacramento districts. Located in Sacramento, the Nova Friburgo e Belieni Company registered Fazenda Caffés, a sesmaria originally held by three immigrants. In addition to these two companies, the Correia e Clemente Company, in Rio Negro, declared the ownership of three "sítios de lavouras," and in partnership with a French physician, Dr. Troubat, Antônio Pinto also held two more fazendas.[34] Aldéia and Caffés were two of the clan's best plantations by the 1880s. By early in that decade, eight of Antônio's eleven fazendas produced 178,860 arrobas, or 44,715 sacks of sixty kilos. (In comparison, Joaquim José de Sousa Breves produced 250,000 arrobas in 1887 on his twenty plantations.)

Other landowners included one Francisco Clemente Pinto, in Sacramento, who registered four properties: two fazendas and two "situações."[35] Although no Francisco was known to be in the family, this might have been Antônio *fils*, who later became the Conde de São Clemente. Two of his fazendas registered in the parochial registry bore the names of "Sam Clemente" and Mataporcos. The Quartim, Vial, and Ricardo Leão clans each owned fazendas in Sacramento. Antônio Tomás Quartim (the future Barão de Quartim) registered two holdings.[36] The Condessa de São Clemente was a daughter of the Barão de Quartim. Both families branched out into the coffee commission business. Late in the 1880s, another scion of the Fluminense family and the leader of the reactionary slavocrat wing of the Conservative party, Paulino José Soares de Sousa, owned a fazenda in Cantagalo.[37]

In addition to agriculture and commerce, the gentry clan founded by Antônio Clemente Pinto pioneered in railroad building when the First Barão de Nova Friburgo, Antônio, in partnership with the Visconde de Barbacena, organized the Cantagalo Railway Company in 1856. The project was continued by a son, Bernardo, the future Conde de Nova Friburgo. After 1876 traffic between Nova Friburgo and Macaco (Cantagalo) was initiated. In 1883 the Estrada de Ferro Cantagalo was linked to Nova Friburgo and Cachoeira, thus to Rio.[38] Three years before his death in 1868, the First Nova Friburgo spent some 8,000 contos to build the Palace of Catete in the court. The family also owned a palatial residence in Nova Friburgo, in addition to the partially completed seventy-room residence at Fazenda Gavião, the clan redoubt. When the family put Catete up for sale during the early 1890s, the only suitable buyer was the federal government, which turned it into the presidential palace; it is now the Museum of the Republic.[39]

The Clemente Pinto clan accumulated a total of four titles scattered in three generations; besides the founder-patriarch, who held the title of the first Barão de Nova Friburgo, two sons and a grandson became Brazilian nobles. Bernardo, who supervised the family investment in railroads, and Antônio, who went into trade, continued to maintain their joint interests in coffee agriculture. In early 1888 the brothers freed 1,300 slaves shortly before the May 1888 abolition, and Pedro II elevated them to the Conde de Nova Friburgo and the Conde de São Clemente, respectively. Friburgo e Filhos was deemed to be one of the major comissário houses in Rio, principally marketing coffee produced by the family, relatives, and close friends. The family also married its offspring to members of the empire's leading clans in banking (Darrigue de Faro), politics (Sousa Dantas), and commerce (the Barão de Mamoré).[40]

The distribution of nobiliary titles in São Paulo, in contrast to Bahia, Pernambuco, and Rio, tended to be widely dispersed; few families held multiple titles, and it is rare to find in São Paulo cases similar to Rio province in which a single clan held up to ten titles. The province's frontier economy, its importing of many Brazilian and foreign immigrants, and its pioneer mentality from the days of the bandeirantes contributed to the relative absence of entrenched family dynasties, compared to the more sedentary Northeast. The province furthermore was among the empire's fastest-growing regions, a phenomenon guaranteeing a high rate of social mobility and undermining the status quo of the entrenched agrarian interests. Many of the leading landed elite either did not hold a title or did not belong to established clans. Additionally, except in the city of São Paulo—the administrative capital and a commercial center by the 1870s—and a few neighboring towns, the province did not possess sixteenth- and seventeenth-century agricultural establishments. One of the least likely places for Brazilian aristocracy to take root, São Paulo instead proved to be fertile ground for producing the republican gentry and mercantile bourgeoisie of the twentieth century.

The province as a whole accounted for 111 titles under the empire. Only eight families enjoyed the distinction of holding multiple titles. As in Rio, geography greatly influenced agrarian economic organization. For the purpose of identifying the major agrarian nobles, the province can be divided into three regions: the Paraíba Valley; the old traditional staging ground for the pre-eighteenth century *bandeiras*, such as the city of São Paulo, Piracicaba, Itu, and Porto Feliz; and the new coffee frontier of the north and west that came into being in the second decade of the century, Campinas and its hinterland. In contrast to the aristocratic clans of Northeast Brazil, Paulista gentry-nobles did not have fixed residences; rather, their economic investment throughout the province mapped their dual or even triple residential points. As coffee expanded into the hinterland, the gentry-fazendeiros followed the frontier, often establishing a second or third home, or even abandoning the primary residence in the older region and moving to the new area. Within the province, such an "on-the-move" pattern was far more noticeable among the planter clans of Campinas and its hinterland and the old bandeirante staging grounds than among the valley clans, whose mobility was limited by space.

The Paulista Paraíba Valley

This region's economic activities began in two phases. At the littoral, sugarcane planting had been going on since the late sixteenth century. Ubatuba and São Sebastião were two major coastal counties in the valley zone. No families in these sugar counties ever received nobility titles. The valley where the Serra do Mar cuts through from southeast to northeast provided a second region of export agriculture and commerce. A string of isolated farms, governmental check points, and country inns sprouted up to accommodate the expanding mule-train trade between the mines of the "Gerais" and São Paulo. In this region, in the 1810s and 1820s coffee was planted on a commercial scale. By mid-century, the major producers on the Paulista side of the valley were Bananal, Taubaté, Pindamonhangaba, Guaratinguetá, Lorena, and Jacarei.[41]

Of the eight Paulista families holding three or more titles in the province, three came from the valley: the Marcondeses of Pindamonhangaba and Guaratinguetá, with four titles among male family members and three among female (by marriage); and the Chaveses, of Taubaté, and the Limas, of Lorena, who each received three titles. Other coffee planter families never obtained more than two titles. This in part can be explained by the belated appearance of an affluent landed gentry in the province; its "noble families" were still in the first generation during the "golden age" of Paulista coffee, which occurred only toward the end of the monarchy in the 1890s.

The principal coffee producers in the valley during the nineteenth century were Bananal, Jacarei, Guaratinguetá, Lorena, Pindamonhangaba, and Taubaté. These six counties monopolized not only the agricultural history of the valley, but also the titles of nobility. The parish land registries of the 1850s serve as a good source for identifying leading agrarian clans in the region. For Campinas, its north and west, the same source may be less reliable because land occupation and agricultural expansion there took place only after the railroad began to open up the virgin frontiers in the late 1860s and 1870s. The Paulista side of the valley, however, dominated the provincial economy until the end of the Paraguayan War.

In terms of sheer productivity, Bananal, Pindamonhangaba, and Guaratinguetá easily outclassed Campinas until the 1870s. Actually, Bananal ranked second only to São Paulo or Santos in revenues between 1840 and 1870. By the mid-seventies and early eighties, Campinas had replaced Bananal, emerging with Taubaté as among the most important municípios in terms of revenue. Pindamonhangaba, however, continued to hold a respectable second or third place among the counties in the valley.[42] One 1854 provincial census reported that Bananal had 70 fazendas, producing about 150,000 arrobas; the following year, productivity jumped to 554,000 arrobas, inexplicably declining to only 100,000 arrobas in 1857.[43] Taubaté, on the other hand, registered the largest number of fazendas in 1854, 240, producing 354,730 arrobas. Pindamonhangaba's 112 coffee plantations produced 350,000 arrobas; and Lorena's 57 fazendas produced the substantial quantity of 250,000 arrobas.[44] Impressive as these figures were, no one fazendeiro in the valley could match the magnitude of the Sousa Breves brothers or the Clemente Pinto siblings, of Rio province, whose annual production in the 1870s and 1880s reached 100,000 to 300,000 arrobas per planter. The nature of the boom mentality in the coffee business in São Paulo contributed to the eventual fragmentation of land holdings, to the creation of smaller farms of polyculture, and to the emergence of tenancy, which was not common in Rio. The *Almanach de São Paulo de 1888* for the município of Pindamonhangaba lists nine nobles, of whom five were Marcondes clansmen, all practicing a variety of agricultural activities.[45]

By the 1850s the undisputed queen city of the valley was Taubaté. Founded in 1639, the oldest city of the valley was situated in its middle, almost equidistant from the provincial capital and the border coffee counties of Queluz and Areias. As the coffee frontier moved north and west from the valley, the significance of such towns as Areias and Bananal, São Paulo's largest coffee producers in the 1830s, had begun to diminish. Pindamonhangaba, situated between Taubaté and Guaratinguetá, was the third largest bean producer by the 1830s. By mid-century at least a dozen counties in the valley were thriving economically: Lorena and Cruzeiro, both north of Guaratinguetá; Aparecida, Tremembé, and Pindamonhangaba, between the oldest town in the valley and Guaratinguetá; to the south of Taubaté, the counties of Caçapava, Jacareí, Paraibuna, and São Luís de Paraitinga. These were the major producers of coffee beans by the middle of the century.[46] In 1854, by one calculation, the valley counties produced 77 percent of Paulista coffee; the frontier north and west, including Campinas, only 23 percent. Some three decades later, in 1886, the valley was producing only 20 percent; the north and west, 80.[47]

The background of the pioneer settlers on the Paulista side of the Paraíba Valley resembled that of Rio's, but their landholding patterns differed. During the eighteenth century, the entire valley was involved in producing foods and beverages for the mines of Minas Gerais and the city of Rio. The descendants of these small subsistence farmers had become coffee planters by the early nineteenth century. In Bananal, a county bordering Rio province, the three related clans of the Aguiar Valims, the Aguiar Toledos, and the Nogueiras were the major planters. Of the 194 farms and plantations registered, 19 belonged to the Aguiars and 10 to the Nogueiras. The Barão de Bela Vista (José Aguiar Toledo) was by far the largest planter by mid-century, holding 8 plantations. The Barão de Aguiar Valim (Manuel) registered 4 properties. Jorge Nogueira and the Barão de Joatinga (Pedro Ramos Nogueira) were the clan's leaders. Joatinga, uncle of the Barão de Aguiar Valim and the Barão de Almeida Valim (Luciano José), was one of the oldest landowners in the county. His Fazenda Loanda, one of the most productive, was built on a colonial land grant.[48]

Taubaté registered the largest number of plantations and farms in the valley, a total of 886. The Monteiros, the Silva Ramoses, and the Salgados were the principal agrarian clans. The Visconde de Tremembé (José Francisco Monteiro) was a major coffee planter and moneylender.[49] The Barão de Jambeiro (David Lopes da Silva Ramos) held three properties in the county. The Salgados, partners in Sergueira Salgado and Company, were also landowners in Pindamonhangaba. One of the clan's largest planters was the Viscondessa de Paraibuna (Benedita Bicudo Salgado Lessa).

Close rivals of the Salgado clan were the Marcondeses. This clan had two branches: those descended from José Homem de Melo and those from Inácio Marcondes do Amaral. José married Maria Marcondes, and Inácio wedded Maria Justina, daughter of the Viscondessa de Paraibuna. These two branches produced three nobility titles, all landowners in the county. The Barão de Homem de Melo was a Liberal cabinet minister in the 1880s and a railroad builder in the valley. His father, the Visconde de Pindamonhangaba, was a major landowner in the county.[50]

Another distinguished gentry clan with multiple titles in the valley was the Castro Lima family, in Lorena. Joaquim José Moreira Lima was a wealthy Portuguese merchant and landowner, but it was his widow, Carlota Leopoldina de Castro Lima, who continued the family business upon his death and emerged as one of the major landowners in the valley. She received by her own right the title of the Viscondessa de Castro Lima in 1879, probably the first widow to accomplish this feat in the province. Two of her children were ennobled in the 1880s: Joaquim José Moreira Lima (the Conde de Moreira Lima) and Antônio

Moreira de Castro Lima (the Barão de Castro Lima). A rich sugar planter who founded a refinery in 1881 on his land of 2,000 hectares, the conde was also a coffee fazendeiro in Jambeiro, Pindamonhangaba, and Pinheiro. His brother Antônio, a sometime partner in various business ventures, was also a well-off coffee planter in Silveira and Limeira. The viscondessa's daughters—Eulália and Angêlica—married brothers, two leading landowners of the Azevedo family, in Lorena. Eulália became the Baronesa de Santa Eulália; Angêlica's son, the Barão de Bocaina (Francisco de Paula Vicente de Azevedo). Bocaina was an enterprising agribusinessman of his time, whose investments included a sugar refinery, the Banco Comercial de São Paulo, and a directorship of the Rio-São Paulo Railroad. Active in commerce at the court, he later became a major landowner in Minas Gerais.[51]

Two interesting patterns of landholding in the valley can be observed. First, the fazendas held by major planter families, as shown in the 1855–56 land registry, were smaller in size than those on the Rio side, seldom exceeding 750 braças. Second, the valley had a large number of small farms and plantations, thus avoiding the rise of latifúndio by mid-century. It was here in the valley, however, that the coffee economy of São Paulo prospered until the 1870s and served as the harbinger of the province's large-scale capitalist agriculture in the north and west frontier.

The gateway to the expanding virgin land for the moving coffee frontier was the provincial capital. The city of São Paulo sits high "at the crest of the Serra do Mar" at the end of the southwestern part of the Paraíba Valley and controls the entrance to the vast north and west frontier. Although a sixteenth-century town, São Paulo did not expand until the second half of the nineteenth century, Brazil's railroad age. Coffee from the valley had been exported overland to various seaports in western Rio and from there to the city of Rio, the international port of the Center-South. The city of São Paulo remained an administrative and cultural capital, boasting the provincial government and the Faculty of Law. The steep road that connects the port of Santos and São Paulo was, and still is, a main artery to the interior, first by mule train and later by the railroad. The capital city's role in the provincial economy was that of a general store, supplying the needs of the interior coffee plantations—from slaves and foodstuffs to dry goods, manufactured items, and capital. Five highways branched out from the capital, following the colonial paths that the earlier bandeirantes had trekked: to the valley and Rio; to Minas Gerais; to Campinas and its frontier north and west; to Itu and Piracicaba, which connected to Mato Grosso via the Tieté River; and finally to Sorocaba, which served as the livestock emporium and gateway to Paraná and Rio Grande do Sul.[52] In 1867 the eighty-five-mile line of the São Paulo Railway Company was put through the capital, linking Jundiaí and Santos. Another decade was required to tie the provincial capital to the imperial court, the empire's premier port; this line of the Dom Pedro II Railroad was the artery that served the Paraíba Valley of the two provinces. During these decades, the 1860s and 1870s, the city emerged as the true capital of the province, including the seat of government, the law academy, and major banking-commercial activities.

The opening of the north and west came about at an unpropitious time: the international slave trade had been abolished and interprovincial trade in Brazil was being curtailed. Meanwhile, Santos had yet to assert itself as the province's chief export harbor for agricultural commodities, in spite of colonial governors' attempts in the late eighteenth century to force the valley's sugar planters to export their products via Santos. The only result had been the near-collapse of such prosperous communities as Ubatuba and São Sebastião. The Paulista sugar economy was still tied to Rio as an appendage of Fluminense commerce and as a constant reminder to the proud Paulistas of the backwardness of their province. When the slow but steady construction of railroads (financed mostly by private enterprises but subsidized by the imperial and provincial governments) revolutionized much of the pre-1877 economic relationship between the capital and the rest of the province, the valley stubbornly remained Rio's loyal vassal. To a degree, São Paulo province continued to retain a neocolonial relationship with the national capital well into the first decade of the twentieth century.[53]

Campinas and the Hinterland North and West

Although a latecomer to coffee cultivation, this region contained a larger number of older, entrenched gentry-nobles than did the valley. Mobility, both social and physical, did not come about until the 1860s, when the São Paulo-Santos Railroad firmly tied the provincial port to the vast, expanding coffee hinterland of the north and west. Furthermore, the region's several important sugar-producing counties provided agricultural balance, avoiding a skewed monocultural economy. The harbinger of the new economic boom towns in this region was still Campinas, where sugar growing was the principal economic activity until the early 1820s, when planters began to switch to coffee. In the mid-1830s, sugar was still Campinas's single most significant crop and ninety-three mills were in operation; twenty years later, half of them had gone out of business or converted to coffee cultivation, and, by the 1880s, Campinas in São Paulo and Cantagalo in Rio reigned supreme as Brazil's two largest coffee producers. Production in Campinas had risen from only 8,000 arrobas in 1836 to 1,500,000 in 1887,[54] and the town went on to serve as the chief distribution center, proving ground, and model farm for new seedlings and agronomic techniques for the hinterland and the rest of the province in this century.

The largest collection of titleholders was in Campinas itself, where in 1888 the *Almanach de São Paulo* listed no fewer than eleven titles: one visconde and ten barões. Campinas's wealthiest family was the Sousa Aranhas, a clan pioneered by Francisco Egídio de Sousa Aranha, who introduced coffee cultivation in the region. Francisco, who held four fazendas in Campinas at mid-century, was a native of Curitiba, then part of São Paulo province; he was probably a muleteer who settled with his brother in Campinas to grow sugarcane. Married to a Camargo (Maria Luisa), the founder of the clan left an impressive number of titled heirs and landholdings. His widow later became the Viscondessa de Campinas. Of some fifteen noble landowners in Campinas, the three biggest fazendeiros were the Sousa Aranhas: the Marquês de Três Rios (Joaquim Egídio); his brother-in-law the Barão de Itapura (Joaquim Policarpo); and the Barão de Anhumas (Manuel Carlos de Aranha), a nephew of Itapura. This agrarian clan did not confine its economic orbit to Campinas. Três Rios was a prominent planter in Rio Claro and elsewhere. From his father-in-law, he inherited Fazenda Santa Gertrudes, in Rio Claro, founded in 1854 and one of the finest in the province. In addition to agricultural activities in Campinas and Rio Claro, he was active in politics and business, serving as a provincial deputy, vice-president of the province, president of the Paulista Railroad Company, and a founder-director of another railroad, the Jundiaí-Campinas Company. Defying the traditional monocultural landlord mold, Três Rios was a gentry businessman, a frontier entrepreneur who was willing to risk his fortune in a variety of capitalist ventures.[55] The prototype gentry-nobleman, he never forsook the family tradition of mercantile and plantation activities, but rather diversified them to maximize profit.

The Sousa Queiróses were equally, if not more, entrepreneurial in their economic and financial activities, largely because of their extensive linkages to major clans in the province and Rio. The founder of the dynasty was a merchant. He obtained a series of sesmarias in and around the capital at the turn of the century; by 1817, owning some sixteen sugar engenhos in Campinas alone, he was one of the wealthiest men in the empire, certainly in São Paulo. At his death, he left three fazendas in Campinas—Boa Esperança, Tapera, and Monjolinho—as well as some urban properties. His sons—the Barão de Sousa Queirós (Francisco Antônio), the Barão de Limeira (Vicente), and Luís Antônio—were among the largest planters in the province. A senator of the empire from São Paulo (1848–89), Francisco was perhaps the best-known planter-politician in the province. He was the doyen of the imperial senate by virtue of seniority. He was also a son-in-law of Nicolau Pereira de Campos Vergueiro, senator and imperial regent. (A Portuguese comissário and fazendeiro, Nicolau Vergueiro is often remembered for his innovative but unsuccessful attempt to introduce free tenant labor *parceria* in Brazil during the 1840s. His son, also Nicolau Vergueiro, was one of the leading coffee merchants in São Paulo.) In addition to this familial connection in the province, the Sousa Queiróses were in-laws of the Resende family of Valença, Rio, through Francisco's sister, who married the Marquês de Valença (Estêvão Ribeiro de Resende); Valença, the founder of Fazenda Coroa and the owner of several plantations, was a minister of Pedro I and councillor of state in the 1820s. One of his sons, the Barão de Geraldo de Resende, settled in Campinas, where he was known for his innovative farming methods, inheriting the fazenda owned by the mother, which was probably her dowry to the marquês, Fazenda Santa Genebra (Gembra).[56] Much like the Sousa Aranhas, the Sousa Queiróses owned land in several communities, including Limeira, Belém do Descalvado, Constituição, and later Piracicaba.[57]

In Campinas and its frontier north and west, there were several other families whose economic and social prestige was a notch lower than that of the two premier families but were still influential. Many were descendants of merchants and smallholders and made money as coffee began to penetrate the hinterland after 1860. Many dabbled in politics, invested in railroad building, and shared in the growing banking business.[58] Perhaps, the model case of upward mobility from obscurity to fame is the Melo e Oliveira family. It held three titles. The Visconde do Rio Claro (José Estanislau) was a planter, banker, and railroad builder; he was also a major Liberal politician in Rio Claro county; two of his twelve children became nobles and two of the daughters married gentry nobles.[59]

The Capital, Itu, and Its Adjacent Region

The sugar-growing area of Itu, Piracicaba, Monte Mor, and Capivari boasted two sets of multiple titleholders whose family roots antedated the coffee cycle: the Pais de Barroses and the Campos Ferrazes. Holders of colonial sesmarias, these families had become pioneer sugarcane cultivators by the 1780s, the first major competitors to the littoral sugar mills in Ubatuba and São Sebastião. The founder of the Pais de Barros clan was Antônio de Barros Penteado; two of his sons became nobles: the First Barão de Itu (Bento) and the First Barão de Piracicaba (Antônio). Bento was a wealthy sugar planter in Itu. Antônio, an influential landowner in Sorocaba, was one of the province's deputies to the Portuguese Cortes in 1821–22, briefly served as a general deputy, but later confined his political activities to the provincial level. Successful careers in politics and agribusiness simply did not mix.

Bento's son, Antônio de Aguiar Barros, became the Marquês de Itu, an important coffee and sugar planter in Itu county, and married his cousin, Antônia, daughter of the First Barão de Piracicaba. Antônio's son, Rafael Tobias de Barros, became the Second Barão de Piracicaba and married his cousin, Leonarda, daughter of the First Itu; he was active in agriculture and banking. His second wife was a daughter of the Visconde do Rio Claro, and through her inheritance the couple became landowners in Rio Claro county. Partner of Três Rios and Rio Claro, the Second Barão de Piracicaba was a director of the Banco Comércio e Indústria de São Paulo, diversifying his economic stakes in gentry fashion. The clan was also related to the Sousa Queiróses and the Marquês de Monte Alegre, prime minister of the empire and absentee Bahian landowner in Piracicaba.[60] An equally large and wealthy clan with three titles was the Campos Ferrazes.[61] This family followed a similar pattern of gentry diversification, as had others of the province.

Based on the available data on the patterns of economic diversification of the provinces of Rio, São Paulo, and Minas, from sugar to coffee, the inauguration of railroads, the founding of financial institutions, and the history of major pioneer families, several observations can be made on landholding patterns and title distribution in the Center-South. Taunay identified as the major agrarian elite twenty-four families in Campinas and the hinterland north and west and eleven in the valley. Six of the former and two of the latter did not hold titles. In contrast, in the coffee zone of Rio province, the Paulista historian singled out fifteen families as the province's largest landowners. All were titled.[62] The difference between São Paulo and Rio, aside from the obvious pattern of title distribution, suggests that the relative youth of São Paulo's coffee economy and the equally young, obscure origins of the wealthy planters affected the Crown's choices. A "rags to riches" success story did not impress the Crown as the sole qualification for nobiliary incorporation. Furthermore, the golden age of the Paulista coffee economy began in the 1880s, the last decade of the monarchy, allowing little time for the planter class to win titles. In fact, the golden age of the Paulista north and west did not fully bloom until after the fall of the empire; and by 1902 the state (as São Paulo was called under the First Republic) was the king of Brazilian coffee, producing about 65 percent of the total.[63]

Although smaller than those in Rio province, coffee plantations in São Paulo, especially those outside the valley, enjoyed superior soil and outproduced them. (In Rio, planters assigned two seedlings per *pé*; in São Paulo, four per pé was normal. Furthermore, in Rio, thirty to thirty-five years was the average life expectancy of a coffee plant; in São Paulo, more than fifty. In Campinas, for instance, planters obtained seventy arrobas from each 1,000 pés; in Cantagalo, Rio's best farmland, only fifty.)[64] The major coffee-producing clans in Rio possessed one or more titles, often three or more, but in São Paulo several major grower-families either did not have any or held one or two at most. Furthermore, diversified investments in land, trade, banking, and railroads seemed to be more preferred by planters in the north and west than by those in the valley. On the Rio side of the valley, several major families held interests in commerce, banking, commission houses, and manufacturing industries. The more diversified the interests of a clan, the higher the probability of its survival and success, especially after the abolition of slavery in 1888 and the increase in competition at the dawn of this century.

Merchant and Entrepreneur Nobles

Although landowners were the single largest titled group, leading merchants, bankers, and comissários of coffee and sugar also received nobiliary honors. In Rio and Santos, the major bankers, merchants, and comissários expanded their operations after the 1830s, when coffee became a major export item and the imperial family often relied on merchants and bankers in the court for its cash flow. Leading coffee planters in the Paraíba Valley utilized Rio comissários and bankers as their purveyors of credit and slaves, as sources of the latest information on agricultural practices overseas, and as occasional confidants to whom their children were entrusted during their education in the cities. The capital for bankers, merchants, and comissários (often all three rolled into one) came from three different sources: from *tropeiro* activities, as in the case of the Mesquitas, of the court, the Alves Barbosas, of Valença and Paraíba do Sul, and the Sousa Queiróses, of São Paulo; from trade, as with the Pereira Marinhos, of Bahia, the Prados and the Vergueiros, of São Paulo, and the Ferreira Armonds, of Minas Gerais; and from agrarian families who invested in urban commercial and financial activities, such as the Faros, the Clemente Pintos, the Sousa Breveses, and the Teixeira Leites, of Rio province. Regardless of how they accumulated capital, the urban patriciate prospered by serving the needs of Brazilian commercial agriculture. Often fortunes were made and unmade by the constantly oscillating conditions of the export economies.

The entrepreneurial dimension of the northern and western planters is best described as capitalistic. This can be traced to their earlier ties with commerce. If the Sousa Aranhas and the Sousa Queiróses typified new frontier capitalism among the northern and western planters, then it was there that the most daring, risk-taking agribusiness was organized and later expanded. Although Handelman, Taunay, and Cassiano Ricardo have observed that the coffee "civilization" bred a more democratic spirit than the sugar-growing society (more "aristo-cratic"), some scholars dispute this view.[65] The reliance on free labor (Ricardo), the planters' humble origins (Taunay), and the high probability for the success of relatively small fazendas (Handelman) were the principal characteristics that shaped the frontier capitalist mentality in the north and west. However, it should also be noted that the planters lacked any alternative to using free labor—foreign immigrants being preferred to Brazilian freedmen—considering their inability to replenish their plantations with slaves by the 1870s and the subsequent move to turn their slaves into indentured servants by the middle of the 1880s. The progressive subdivision of old sesmarias and latifúndios became more desirable when several railroads made the frontier accessible; that was not the norm in the older sugar region of Northeast Brazil or in the Paraíba Valley. Because of the apparently unlimited, fertile virgin land and the railroad technology available after 1870, however, the Paulista north and west experienced a crushing shortage of labor. The importing of *colonos* as mobile laborers persisted through the decades after its initial failure in the 1840s. Such a step was inevitable for those merchant-fazendeiros who held several properties in the region, namely, the Vergueiros, the Sousa Aranhas, and the Sousa Queiróses, all pioneers in the north and west's social and economic modernization.

It was the entrepreneurial spirit of the merchant-fazendeiro, as opposed to the merchant-turned-fazendeiro, that settled the region and imbued it with a new mentality. In Bahia and the Paraíba Valley, it was a rare planter who held several landholdings in different locations and an even rarer one who continued to exercise the older profession of commerce and trade and to diversify his interests in agriculture, trade, and industry simultaneously. The acquisition of properties in several municípios, especially in noncontiguous counties, strongly suggests that commercial transactions were responsible for the multiple acquisition of plantations, aside from family inheritance and wedding dowries. After 1870 such widespread landholding was immensely facilitated by the expansion of rail transportation. This ability to diversify his economic ventures and yet to remain successful as an entrepreneur marked the quintessential difference between the northern and western Paulista fazendeiro and his counterpart elsewhere.

The Richest Merchant Noble in the North

In the North, the most prominent titled merchant family was the Pereira Marinhos, of Bahia. The Conde de Pereira Marinho, holder of a Portuguese title, was a prominent comissário for the Bahian Recôncavo's major sugar planters, to whom the Pereira Marinho Company supplied foodstuffs, slaves, and capital. Two sons became nobles—one by Portugal and the other by Brazil. The Brazilian noble was the Visconde de Guaí (Joaquim Eliseu Pereira Marinho), who in the 1880s became minister of the navy and a devout protégé of the Barão de Cotegipe. The imperial mandarin was one of several clients of the family firm, whose original profits came from the slave trade.

The *inventários* of a few members of the Pereira Marinhos tell much about the family wealth. When the condessa died, she left assets (*monte mor*) valued at 4.106:744$239; urban properties alone included twenty-nine buildings: six *sobrados* (mansions) and twenty-three houses. Guaí inherited 2.350:610$748 from his father; the other half went to his mother, according to Brazilian law. The older brother, who had lived in Paris, died and therefore did not figure in the financial settlement. When Cotegipe succumbed in 1889, he left 106:748$065, of which 84:364$170 were debts. The Marinho Company held notes on Cotegipe, a total of 79:661$400, which included a takeover (consolidation) of the politician's debts by the Conde de Pereira Marinho in 1881 at the annual interest of 9 percent, practically a favor. On paper, Cotegipe left three engenhos (Cabaxi, Quibaca, and Sapucaia) and a total of sixty-two slaves. Quibaca, including all the tools and slaves, had to be turned over to the Pereira Marinhos as partial settlement of the debt.[66] This family company was also the banker of many Bahian planters, including the best aristocratic and gentry families in the province.

The Southern Merchant Nobles

In the Center-South, the epicenter of the nineteenth-century Brazilian economy, were several outstanding mercantile noble families. The Mesquitas, in Rio, held four titles. The founder of the clan was a Portuguese-born operator of mule trains, Francisco José de Mesquita (the Marquês de Bomfim), who with his partner (Domingos Custódio Guimarães, the future Visconde do Rio Preto) traded between Minas Gerais and Rio. Having accumulated a fortune, the two founded the Mesquita-Guimarães Company at the court, which flourished until the advent of commercial coffee. The firm broke up when Guimarães went into coffee planting, becoming the owner of eleven of the best plantations in and around Valença. Mesquita invested his money in banking. For the next three generations, the family remained major bankers in Rio; the founder's son, Jerônimo José (the Conde de Mesquita), and two grandsons, José Jerônimo (the Barão de Bomfim) and Jerônimo Roberto (the Barão de Mesquita), stayed active in the family business, eventually diversifying their interests in urban properties and capitalist agriculture. Pedro I was thought to have had an interest in the Mesquita group, the favorite banker of the Braganzas. When the Conde de Mesquita died in 1886, he left a mind boggling 9.919:903$159 as the monte mor, almost two and a half times richer than the Pereira Marinhos, in Bahia. His major assets were shares in several banks, railroad and navigation companies, and firms that traded agricultural commodities. His five heirs received 1.322:653$754 each after the expenses of estate settlement and retiring the debts.[67] None of the Mesquitas rose to the rank of imperial mandarin, however.

The Vergueiros, of São Paulo, and the Faros, of Rio, offer good contrasting examples of merchant-planters. Related through marriage, both families were strongly involved in commerce and coffee brokerage, as well as being important planters. Nicolau Pereira de Campos Vergueiro founded the first clan. His son and namesake became the Visconde de Vergueiro, the only title in the family aside from those held by in-laws. Portuguese by birth and a lawyer by training, the founder came to São Paulo in the late eighteenth century, where he obtained sesmarias and also engaged in trade. By the 1820s he had become a major leader in the provincial politics of São Paulo. A diehard liberal in the classic European tradition of his time, he distinguished himself as a senator (from Minas Gerais), regent of the empire, and cabinet minister. More importantly, he was the champion of capitalist agriculture. His plantations, Ibicaba, in Limeira, and Angélica, in Rio Claro, became early models for free labor at the height of the slave-powered economy.[68] Between 1847 and 1874 some fifty planters in the São Paulo north and west experimented with a free labor system (colonos). Vergueiro, his son-in-law (the Barão de Sousa Queirós), and the baron's brother (Comendador Luís Antônio de Sousa Queirós) imported a total

of 2,425 colonos, spreading them among the trio-owned coffee plantations in Campinas, Limeira, Piracicaba, and Rio Claro.[69] This significant experiment with tenancy (parceria) failed, but the undaunted
Vergueiro continued to promote innovative coffee-cultivating methods. His Fazenda Ibicaba was judged to be among the best plantations
in the empire. Three square leagues in size, it employed 300 slaves in
the 1840s (before free labor was introduced), producing 12,000 arrobas
of coffee and 8,000 arrobas of sugar per annum.[70] Vergueiro's firm, Vergueiro & Cia., diversified its holdings, adding banking to its original
brokerage activities. His son, the visconde, was reputed to be Brazil's
largest comissário.

Like their in-laws the Vergueiros, the Faros, of Rio, were also of Portuguese origin, migrating to Brazil in the late eighteenth century. Principally based in Valença, the founder of the clan, Joaquim José Pereira
Faro, was the son-in-law of Regent Vergueiro; the Marquês de Valença,
another son-in-law of Vergueiro and a planter in the same town, was
therefore Faro's brother-in-law (concunhado). Faro, himself ennobled
as the Barão do Rio Bonito, owned Santa Ana and Monte Alegre, two
productive fazendas in the same class as the showpiece plantations of
the Nogueira da Gamas, the Wernecks, and the Teixeira Leites of the
valley. He and his sons organized two comissário and import-export
companies that specialized in the importation of farm machinery in
addition to coffee export: Carvalho, Faro e Cia. and Sociedade Comercial de Faro e Irmãos. Such forward linkage-based business activity
was common among progressive gentry planters and merchants in
nineteenth-century Brazil, a sure sign that a capitalist mentality was
firmly embedded in the dominant agrarian class. When the Barão de
Pati do Alferes, in Vassouras, wanted to modernize his coffee fazendas
with more efficient mills (moinhos), he contracted with the Faros for
the job. A demonstration by an American-made moinho that was able
to prepare twenty kilos of coffee beans per hour, in operation at Faro's
farms, impressed his clientele: Pati do Alferes ordered the gadget for
his operation, and other planters whom the Faro companies served followed suit.[71]

By the middle of the century, the Faros had achieved elite status. The
First Baronesa do Rio Bonito, daughter of Nicolau Vergueiro, died in
1854, leaving to her husband and children four of her own fazendas, two
sítios, and two sesmarias (all in Valença), one sesmaria in Piraí, and the

hefty sum of 1.130:202$233, according to her inventory of the estate. The couple had three children, one of whom, João Darrigue Faro, became the Visconde do Rio Bonito, a prominent local and provincial politician. João Faro was vice-president of the province of Rio de Janeiro between 1849 and 1854, during which time he served as acting president on five separate occasions; it was a critical era for the Fluminense coffee economy, simultaneously facing the end of the African slave trade and the onset of the railroad revolution. When his political career was cut short by his untimely death in 1859, João Faro left an enormous fortune: two very productive plantations (Santa Ana and Monte Alegre); a sesmaria; no fewer than eleven urban properties; more lands; and a substantial number of stocks in private and public companies, including his own, Sociedade Comercial de Faro e Irmãos. His worth was assessed at 2.131:007$019, about double his father's. Two sons, José (the Third Barão do Rio Bonito) and João (no nobiliary title), each received a fortune of a little more than 900 contos from their father's legacy.[72]

The Third Rio Bonito was active in business, in exporting coffee, and in family coffee plantation activities as his brother's partner. Unlike the custom in the Northeast, an increasing number of coffee planters in Rio made innovative use of the family wealth structure, often organizing a closed company system instead of fragmenting the landed properties. The baron was also a director of the Clube de Lavoura e Comércio in Rio, a major organization of coffee brokers in the empire, and was an enthusiastic promoter of agrarian modernization in the 1870s and 1880s. His company was engaged in importing modern farm machinery and selling coffee to overseas markets. Like his uncle, the Visconde de Vergueiro, Rio Bonito was extensively involved in lending capital to planters. Furthermore, like his great grandfather, Regent Vergueiro, he was a tireless advocate of free labor. In the mid-1880s he expanded his investment activities to Campos, the heart of the Rio sugar zone, in partnership with the equally prestigious comissário firm of Furquim, Joppert, and Company. This Faro planter-merchant clan succeeded in diversifying its agrarian interests, and by the third generation fully half the clan wealth was in commerce—a classic example of a planter transformed into an urban bourgeois merchant, gentry in spirit and novo rico in behavior.

The Prados, of São Paulo, and the Ferreira Armonds, of Minas Gerais, exemplify the reverse transformation of merchant into planter elite. When the extraordinary coffee boom in São Paulo's north and west and the Zona da Mata of Minas Gerais created a high degree of social mobility, even plebeian merchants succeeded in consolidating their wealth into landed interests. The Prados, of São Paulo, one of the richest dynastic families in the First Republic, had made their fortune from commerce (mule trains and cattle trade), coffee and sugar plantations, comissário activities, banking, and railroads. The founder of the clan, Antônio da Silva Prado (the First Barão de Iguape), amassed his fortune in Bahia, Mato Grosso, and later São Paulo and Rio.[73] He served as the director of the Bank of Brazil, in São Paulo, and vice-president of the province. Martinho Prado, a son, continued the family tradition of commerce, but branched out to agriculture, first in sugar and later in coffee. When he died in 1891, he left a fortune worth 2.5 million pounds sterling. The family's fazendas, Guatapara and São Martinho, contained more than 5 million pés of coffee trees, constituting two of the largest plantations in the country. A grandson of the paterfamilias, the fourth Antônio, became the minister of agriculture in the 1880s and the mayor of São Paulo in the years before World War I. His brother Martinico (Martinho Júnior) was a coffee comissário, banker, and railroad magnate.[74] Because the clan did not reach the height of its success until the 1890s, it lacked the opportunity to win titles of nobility. Much like the Faros, the Prados were gentry to the core, a modern novo rico family.

The Ferreira Armonds, descendants of Azorian fidalgos, settled in Minas during the first half of the eighteenth century. Barbacena was the clan redoubt. By the 1840s the family had established successful coffee plantations in southern Minas Gerais and in Rio province (Paraíba do Sul). The first Armond to receive a Brazilian title, Marcelino José Ferreira Armond (the First Barão de Pitangui), born at Barbacena in 1786, was one of the pioneer coffee planters in southern Minas. He and his wife, the daughter of another pioneer coffee planter, had four children; three became nobles: Camilo Maria (the Conde de Prados), a prominent politician in the province; Honório Augusto (the Second Barão de Pitangui), a local politician of repute and a wealthy landowner in Juiz de Fora; and Camília Francisca, by her second marriage, the Baronesa de Juiz de Fora. Through this marriage, the Ferreira Armonds became in-laws of the Ribeiro Leite clan (whose titular was the Marquês de Valença), of Minas Gerais, Rio, and São Paulo. Another important planter-entrepreneur of the Armond dynasty was Mariano Procópio Ferreira Lage, nephew of the First Barão de Pitangui. Mariano Procópio was the founder of the União e Indústria, a firm that built the macadamized road between Juiz and Petrópolis.[75]

Little is known about the economic activity of the Armonds, however. The Second Barão de Pitangui was a fazendeiro who owned properties both in Juiz de Fora and the Rio side of the Paraíba Valley, not far from Valença, where he and his partners once established agricultural colonies. The younger brother of the Conde de Prados, the Second Pitangui, died in 1874. Prados was a Paris-trained physician who practiced his profession upon his return to Brazil. Inheriting coffee plantations from his father, he lived at Barbacena until he became a leader of the Liberal Revolution of 1842. Arrested but granted amnesty, he began his political career while marshaling his interests in plantation activities. The founder of the Hospital da Misericórdia de Barbacena, the family was among the elite of the Zona da Mata. In 1878 Prados was appointed as provincial president of Rio and took the occasion to establish his second residence in the court. The following year, he was appointed to the Council of State, in which he served until his death in 1882.[76]

Prados's cousin, Mariano Procópio, who preferred to use his mother's name following the prevalent custom of Minas Gerais, was equally well known and reputedly a good friend of Dom Pedro II. A merchant by profession, Mariano Procópio was also an affluent planter, the owner of Fazenda Fortaleza de Santana, in Juiz de Fora. (This plantation was later passed on to his niece and nephew-in-law, the Visconde de Cavalcanti, Diogo Velho Cavalcanti de Albuquerque, a senator from Rio Grande do Norte and a member of the Council of State.) One foreign visitor to Fortaleza de Santana in the early 1860s marveled at its innovative management practices. Mariano Procópio was a model farmer, building his own roads to transport coffee beans more easily and thereby cheaply, using fertilizers and rotating techniques to improve the soil, and growing much of the family's food. Another foreign visitor in the early 1880s, after the ownership of the plantation had passed to the Visconde de Cavalcanti, would comment on the decline of Fortaleza de Santana. For building the União e Indústria road, a pioneering contribution to the economic development of Minas Gerais, the grateful emperor offered Mariano Procópio the title of barão, which the entrepreneur-planter politely turned down. Instead, he asked the Crown to honor his mother with the title. Dona Maria José de Santa Ana (Ferreira Lage) was made the First Baronesa de Santana in 1861, months after the completion of the macadamized road.⁷⁷

During the heyday of the 1860s, Mariano Procópio represented the third district of Minas Gerais in the imperial chamber of deputies, serving in the eleventh and the fourteenth legislatures (1861–64 and 1868–72). His cousin, Camilo (the Conde de Prados), also represented the same district in the chamber between 1861 and 1881, interrupted only by the Conservative years. Serving in the twelfth, thirteenth, and seventeenth legislatures (1864–66; 1866–68; 1878–81), Camilo presided over the last two years of the twelfth and the entire seventeenth legislature as the speaker of the chamber of deputies. Procópio's political career was cut short by his death in 1872. His contributions as an enterprising agribusinessman were well recognized. The Ferreira Armonds, much like the Faros and their in-laws the Ribeiro Leites, diversified their economic stakes in Minas and Rio and held key elective and appointive political offices. The interlocking clan ties among the major planter and mercantile groups in the three provinces of the Paraíba Valley came about because of the nineteenth century's expanding coffee economy. Such interprovincial dynasties were rare in the sugar-growing Northeast, as seen above. By the 1880s and 1890s, these gentry clans often utilized family and business ties for political purposes, consolidating their power during the first decade of the First Republic.

Several factors seemed to have affected the formation of the two separate sets of Brazilian nobilities, economic and political. Generally speaking, the economic nobility was created by a combination of circumstances: the nature of Brazil's capitalist agriculture and the consequences of economic geography. The location of the imperial court in the Center-South also influenced the patterns of the political system, especially after the investiture of Dom Pedro II in 1841. Specifically, the patterns of political elite recruitment, the training of mandarins, called for an investment in time away from the home province to complete internships for offices that ranged from district judge to provincial president to cabinet officer. The process required on the average fifteen to twenty years, after a five-year absence from home at one of the empire's two law schools, in São Paulo and Olinda (moved to Recife after 1854). Consequently, a successful mandarin left his home (and, indirectly, his economic interests) at about the age of eighteen and spent his adult life elsewhere, often marrying into a family of another region.

Given the family strategy of Brazilian society, especially that treasured by the elite—endogamy being a popular option—the life of a professional politician was not attractive. Agrarian dynasts therefore were compelled to choose between a political career, at the risk of economic loss, and that of a planter, in the family tradition. Educated at home and/or abroad, some children of planters could not accept the rustic life-style, as in the cases of the Marquês de Barbacena, of Minas, and the Marquês de Abrantes, of Bahia. Others had no family wealth on which to build their future and left to seek more profitable urban careers. Still others attempted in vain to combine the two careers, as in the cases of Sinimbu and Cotegipe, running their fazendas through proxy managers or long-distance directive. Cotegipe pushed his fazendas into near-bankruptcy. Abrantes, Paraná, Albuquerque, and a few others simply moved, reestablishing their economic holdings near the court. The Visconde de Albuquerque, of Rio Grande do Norte, settled in Niterói, where he was a major landowner. Abrantes, once the lord of Engenho dos Calmons, in Santo Amaro, transferred his wealth to the court; by the 1860s the clan wealth was subdivided among its numerous scions. In the county of Santo Amaro alone, no fewer than seven Calmons held land, but none of them emerged as important imperial politicians because they stayed in Bahia. Paraná, a native of Minas Gerais and an astute investor, made his coffee plantation in Sapucaia, Rio province, an immense success (see chapter 6).

The nature of capitalist agriculture called for creating the division of labor into the economic and the political nobilities. The export agriculture of coffee and sugar demanded the constant presence and supervision of landlords; the only luxury leave of absence was an occasional visit to provincial capitals and the court, almost always combining business with pleasure. Not until the 1880s did affluent coffee planters in Rio and São Paulo begin to maintain urban residences; few sugar planters in the Northeast adopted this life-style. One foreign visitor in the 1860s remarked that travel by planters and their families involved much preparation and was costly. One marquesa required "thirty-one pack mules" for a trip of a few weeks' stay in town; her caravan carried "all conceivable baggages, besides provisions of every sort, fowls, hams, etc., and a train of twenty-five servants" to look after her. Coffee barons and gentry landowners in the Paraíba Valley frequented the court during the reign of Pedro I, but the cost was so exorbitant that many were forced to stop such pilgrimages to Rio, especially during the second half of the century, when the coffee economy in Rio province commenced its irreversible decline.[78]

If a short visit was a major operation, the complete liquidation of wealth in one province and its transfer to the court (to have a political career) would have been a price too high for the majority of planters to pay. For this reason, no scion of a major agrarian or mercantile dynasty in the northern half of the empire could combine a successful political career at the court with the time-consuming chores of running plantations in the provinces. By comparison, the agrarian and mercantile elite in the provinces of São Paulo, Rio, and Minas were more successful in a dual career and were therefore more willing to enter politics and at the same time retain control over the family business. The geography, as much as the economic boom in the Center-South, simply enhanced the chances for such a combined career for the coffee planters in Rio, São Paulo, and Minas Gerais.

A political career therefore appealed more to those from humble and moderately wealthy origins from the Northeast and the economic elite of the Center-South. On the whole, families rich enough to finance advanced education for their children in law, medicine, and engineering produced the majority of imperial mandarins. Sons of the principal agrarian clans did not need to make a career of imperial politics, which would have removed them from their home provinces and their economic interests. The agrarian dynasties—both aristocratic and gentry—such as the Moniz de Aragãos, the Carvalho e Albuquerques, and the Costa Pintos, to name only the well known in Bahia—confined their political careers to local and provincial levels; no imperial minister or senator came from the ranks of these premier agrarian clans. The province of Pernambuco seems to have been an exception: the Sousa Leãos, the Cavalcanti de Albuquerques, and the Pais Barretos produced ministers, senators, and councillors of state, but the political members of these clans never participated fully in the economic decision making at home. Furthermore, in comparison to their counterparts at home, the political clansmen were never wealthy in their own right.

Therefore, the pattern of amassing a clientele of economic nobility by the political elite (including nobles) for mutual dependence became the norm, not in the form of patron-client but rather lawyer-client relationship. The practice was not uniquely Brazilian. Such an interlocking relationship between the landed gentry and the political elite reinforced English politics as late as the nineteenth century, for example. What was unique about the Brazilian pattern was the fact that such a clientage between families of economic wealth and those of political power never went beyond the forging of clannish interests, and never served as a vehicle to consolidate a regional or national corporation of agrarian-political nobility, aristocracy, and gentry into a national bourgeoisie, a new power elite. Among the factors that discouraged the regional clans of one province from merging with those of another were: the absence of entail; the lack of a national network of economic ties; the regional diversity in commercial agriculture (on the one hand, the atrophying sugar sector and the expanding coffee sector, and, on the other, the slave-run plantations of the Northeast and the Paraíba Valley together with the mixed labor of servile and colono workers in the Paulista north and west by the 1880s); and, therefore, the different life-styles. Marriage patterns among the dominant elites remained remarkably endogamous and intraprovincial until the end of the nineteenth century. Without enlarging a network of marital alliances or expanding interregional business ties, Brazilian society languished in the patriarchal mold, the nobiliary corporation being divided into political and economic branches, and imperial politics became the monopoly of sinecurist mandarins who were removed from the economic and social realities of the empire.

6

Life, Marriage, and Wealth of Noble Families

If office and favor was [sic] lacking, there was always marriage . . .
piling estate upon estate by the judicious choice of brides.
Many of the older peers owed their position very largely to their prudence
in choosing and their skill in capturing rich brides. LAWRENCE STONE

Upper-class Brazilian families in the empire practiced carefully planned family strategies, especially class endogamy and intraclan exchange or the consolidation of properties through marriages. The family life of typical rural gentry and aristocracy evolved around a network of extended kin (*parentela*), instead of a nuclear family. Male heads of families were preoccupied with the succession of lineage and preservation of family wealth. Although the concept of kinship carried less significance among urban bourgeoisie or the submerged classes, it summoned an individual and collective commitment to the honor, respect, patronage, and prestige of the "family." Thus, the head of a family was deemed in fact the leader of a community. As Tristão de Alencar Araripe observed, "The chief of family was domestic magistrate of a small republic."[1] His authority was respected by society at large and revered as absolute by his kinsmen. However, between the mid-eighteenth and early nineteenth centuries, the patriarchal power of the paterfamilias of agrarian clans began to erode as the social and economic fabric of late colonial and independent Brazil was subjected to the strains of modernization, regional diversification of capitalist economies, and other forms of social change. During this time, the mining economy fell into decay and a new plantation economy of coffee cultivation began to emerge. By the early 1830s the Brazilian patriarchal family was once again to serve as the viable social system another century or more, and only by the mid-twentieth century would this system cease to function.[2]

In the nineteenth century, the abolition of colonial primogeniture and entail practices actually helped to expand the power of a family head. Once family property was entailed and could pass only to the first born male heir, the head of the family lacked the capability to dispose of the estate at his will; his economic decision-making power was so restricted that he simply lived off the rents and services from the family holdings. This was a decidedly aristocratic life-style, so well reflected in England before 1850.[3] In this kind of precapitalist economy, the state and law could be of no use in expanding or protecting the collective wealth. In addition, the expansive forces of Atlantic industrial capitalism of the nineteenth century disrupted the stability of traditional social and economic foundations by spurring the rapid growth of Brazilian agriculture in the Northeast and Center-South. Therefore, the new economic opportunities to amass wealth posited absolute power in the hands of family heads. Business decisions often involved such family considerations as marriage, education, and career choices for offspring. As new influences, such as European ideas, capital, technology, and, later, immigrants, were injected into the national economy, the Brazilian agrarian elites experienced oscillations of the export economy, thereby ever greater vicissitudes of financial well-being. The power of a family head expanded as the economy was gradually integrated into the Atlantic world-economy. Even the unrestricted power of family heads was a necessity to deal with the changing realities of social and economic life; successful management of family wealth depended on their ability to anticipate needs as well as to mobilize the kindred and their financial resources at the right time.

In brief, no other intermediate authority existed between the state and the family. In deference to the power that a family head enjoyed, one historian was prompted to comment that "the state is born out of the transgression of the domestic and familial order."[4] The interaction between the state and family during the nineteenth century constituted the core dimension of a Brazilian modernization that by the end of the century would pit society against state. No social history of the agrarian gentry would be complete without a careful analysis of the family structure and its workings, particularly the management of life-style, marriage, and patronage.

The study of the Luso-Brazilian family requires the definition of such terms as "clan," "extended family," and "kin." The origin of "clan" is Gaelic (*clann*, meaning offspring or descendants). Unlike its Roman counterpart, the Gaelic clann included all cognatic descendants, and thus was not restricted to the agnatic, or male line heirs.[5] Over time, anthropologists have come to define "clan" somewhat loosely as a group of offspring who share a common male or female ancestor having a properly identified surname, property, and even collective activity. This unilineality assures group solidarity as well as the means by which wealth and power can be transmitted from generation to generation without upsetting the collective harmony. In some societies, common residency of clansmen is also a requisite for the survival of the group.[6] In New Guinea, for instance, a clan was a "territorially based political unit" that functioned as a corporate landholding group.[7] In earlier chapters of this book, such clan-dynasties as the Albuquerques, of Pernambuco, the Carvalhos e Albuquerques and the Monizes, of Bahia, and the Nogueira da Gamas, of Minas Gerais and Rio de Janeiro, have been identified. In the absence of formalized entail after independence, the economic integrity of a clan-estate was seriously endangered because both legitimate and illegitimate heirs were entitled to shares of the property. After 1842 the necessity to distinguish heirs born of marriage and offspring of casual affection (*filhos naturais*) became legally obsolete in estate division, though it still remained socially desirable behavior. Thus, the commonweal of an upper-class family was left to such devices as class endogamy and intraclan cousin marriages. Clan membership, once it became unable to restrict itself by law, grew rapidly. To retain social and economic power, a clan often adopted internal policing rules and other control measures to manage its corporate interests.

As a result, by the mid-nineteenth century the parentela, or extended family, emerged as a kinsmen's corporation that included members of "both maternal and paternal lines" as well as "individuals who were related by the ceremonial ties of *compadrio*."[8] Godparents, or *padrinho* and *madrinha*, at baptisms and witnesses at weddings often reinforced clan ties, especially those weakened by feeble lineages and slight wealth bases. If the clan shared the same roof, the extended family was often a geographically dispersed congregation of several related clans. In some ways, the clan is an extended family, but not all extended families are clans. The parentela functioned as a social, economic, and political organization, especially during the nineteenth century, when voluntary associations with horizontal interests were a rarity. Wagley reported that in Amazônia, where subsistence agriculture became the mainstay of the regional economy when the natural rubber market collapsed after 1914, no large parentela could survive without the economic foundation that held it together. Instead, the network of ritual kinship "functioned to almost exaggerated proportions" as the basis for social relationships and economic survival.[9] The forces of the capitalist world-system in the nineteenth century helped the clan-plantation system to incorporate its formal and informal dependent population, including poor kinsmen, ritual relatives, and even slaves. At the head of this community stood the paternalistic lord, patriarch in the Brazilian sense, the senhor de engenho in the sugar-growing Northeast and the fazendeiro de café in the coffee-producing Center-South.

Gilberto Freyre and his disciples have studied the historical roots of Luso-Brazilian patriarchalism. The sugar plantation of the sixteenth century became the prototype clan for the elite upper-class family. Hierarchically structured, the plantation sustained a retinue of technical personnel (overseers, masters of sugar, and artisans), an army of slaves and their children, and an indirect dependent population, such as cane growers and tenants who utilized the lord's lands and milling facilities and paid him with shares of their harvest. These people constituted the bedrock of the planter's subject population. A paternalistic, or patron-client, relationship emerged from these economic and social environments, and soon the monopoly of land resources and the work force in and around the clan-plantation allowed the patriarch to exercise his political suzerainty over his domain. The institutionalization of such private social and economic power (ordem privada) continued to expand throughout colonial times.

By the early nineteenth century, a new segment of society was seeking to emulate the traditional elite: parish gentry and even petty landlords learned to manipulate this private order and sought to translate it into public power, laying the basis for Brazilian coronelismo, the golden age of which lasted from 1870 to 1930.[10] In Weberian terms, patriarchalism—rule by the elder of the household or, more specifically, in the Brazilian case, by the landlord—was a functional equivalent of the state. The distinction between patriarchalism and patrimonialism is one of degree; the former lacked a household administrative bureaucracy, and the latter was administered by the privately appointed staff of civil and military servants, often sinecurists.[11] Weber would have gone a step further in defining the Brazilian basis of patriarchalism to be "rule by inheritance."[12] It was the ownership of a capitalist agricultural complex, such as sugar mills and coffee plantations, including slaves, that invested in the planter class the right to rule. Therefore, it was critical for the rural gentry and aristocracy to devise acceptable means to perpetuate their status quo as well as to pass it on to the next generation. Hence, carefully planned marriages, education, and career choices were regarded as such essential building blocks to family strategies that only they could ensure the collective well-being—the lifestyle, wealth, and patronage power of the clan.

The first important social linkage available to a person was the parental selection of ritual godparents at a baptismal ceremony. A closer look at such affluent parishes as Sé and Santa Efigênia in the city of São Paulo during the nineteenth century offers a clear picture of how such a social linkage system worked. Before 1890 the provincial capital was still a sleepy town; the locus of the coffee economy was in the Paraíba Valley until 1870, when the newer frontier of the Paulista north and west began to challenge the valley's economic supremacy. The city of São Paulo, also the provincial capital, therefore provided a stage for the rich provincial gentry and aristocracy to show off their affluence; the centrally located Sé parish became a popular middle- and upper-class residential district, in which agrarian elite and urban bourgeois merchants, public officials, and other liberal professionals maintained residence and mixed socially. The manner in which baptismal parents were selected and the style in which the adoption of such ritual linkages was performed were a key clue to the family life-style that was prevalent in the Sé district. It can be argued that this district reflected a fair representative sample of the provincial rural and urban well-to-do who were eager to reinforce vital social and economic ties for their offspring.

The ceremony of baptism varied from class to class. Although it often took place at the residence of the child's parents, it could also take place at the home of the grandparents, the godparents, or someone else. In 1829 Pedro I and the bastard but later legitimized daughter the Duquesa de Goiás became the godparents of one Pedro, son of Mariano José de Oliveira and Eulália Bonifácia de Toledo. The circumstances that led to this ritual linkage remain obscure. One clue is that the baptized was related to the Marquesa de Santos, whose mother's surname was Toledo. Also a middle name was Bonifácia. Thus, the mothers of both the baptized and the marquesa had the names of Bonifácia de Toledo. The entry in the baptismal log of the parish describes the ceremonies:

> On the eighth day of August of 1829, with the permission of His Excellency the Bishop, at the house of Brigadier Francisco de Lima e Silva, the Most Reverend Cantor Lourenço Justiniano Ferriera baptized and anointed with Holy Oil Pedro, legitimate son of Mariano José de Oliveira and of Dona Eulália Bonifácia de Toledo; godfather was His Imperial Majesty, for whom His Excellency the Bishop stood in, and for godmother, Her Highness Senhora Duquesa de Goiás, for whom the Illustrious Brigadier General Francisco de Lima came. All are from this Parish.
> (signed) Parish Priest Manoel da Costa Almeida[13]

Not everyone had a distinguished cantor of the diocese to baptize one's child. Furthermore, the brigadier, soon to become a regent of the empire in 1831, was the father of the future Duque de Caxias. Social and court protocol would not have allowed the emperor and his mistress (Santos) to appear together for this occasion and become godparents to Pedro de Oliveira; the emperor had just taken an European princess for his second wife. Hence, the Duquesa de Goiás, a love child of the emperor and his mistress, was substituted for the marquesa. Most likely, the marquesa alone was present at the ceremony, however. The use of Brigadier Lima e Silva's house also suggests that no Paulista and Paulistano (of the city of São Paulo) elite were involved in the affair. In fact, the Marquesa de Santos was often despised by provincial politicians and city fathers for her alleged political influence over the emperor as a Brazilian Pompadour. The Andradas of Santos, the port city of São Paulo after which the marquesa's title was named, and their political cronies had snubbed her since the early 1820s; hence, no one from the provincial elite seemed too eager to risk their social standing for a baptismal ritual. Lima e Silva was the commandant of the imperial army in the province and, therefore, along with the provincial president, a top patrimonial servant of the emperor in loco. Either one of the two officials would have been a logical candidate to host such an event, and Brigadier General Lima e Silva accepted the chore.

Instances of the emperor and his family members serving as godparents were rare, but not unheard of. More often, in-laws and relatives of fame and wealth were cultivated by poor members of the clan to build future economic and political connections for their offspring. The godparents saw their role as dispensers of patronage. Thus, the baptismal practices in the parish of Sé fall in the categories of *interclass* as well as *intraclan* ritual alliances. The sample in Sé also reflected the consequences of the expanding provincial economy. Many of the major agrarian, mercantile, and political clans were bonded together by marriage and their relationship was further reinforced by the adoption of baptismal godparenthood. The building of such horizontal linkages was widely practiced by the provincial elite families, especially mobility-conscious gentry and merchants. The families of Sousa Quierós (land and commerce), Sousa Barros (land), Sousa e Melo (politics), Silva Prado (commerce, railroad, and land), Sousa Aranha (land and railroad), Vergueiro (commerce, railroad, and land), Pacheco Jordão (land), Monteiro de Barros (land and commerce), and Sousa Teles (land) were all interrelated by marriage; furthermore, their ties were reinforced by such ritual alliances as baptismal godparenthood and matrimonial witnesses.

Thus, Judge Rodrigo Antônio Monteiro de Barros and his wife, Maria Marcolina Monteiro e Prado, had their first child, Lucas, baptized in 1829. The father was a son of the Visconde de Congonhas do Campo, the grand old man of Minas Gerais politics and a counselor of Pedro I; the mother was a daughter of Capitão Francisco da Silva Prado, a merchant-landowner and brother of the First Barão de Iguape (Antônio da Silva Prado), a well-to-do mule trader and landowner in the province. Lucas's godparents came from both sides of the family: the Visconde de Congonhas do Campo and Ana Vieira da Silva Prado.[14] Some seven years later, when Lucas's sister Maria Luisa was baptized, she had Iguape for godfather and for godmother Ana Vicência Rodrigues de Almeida.[15] Because of the overarching network of in-laws scattered throughout the three provinces of São Paulo, Minas Gerais, and Rio de

Janeiro, the Monteiro de Barros offspring were able to draw on a variety of kinsmen; at the same time, the diverse geographic locales assured the baptized of a choice of region and profession in his adoptive parents.

The Sousa Queirós clan was expert at using in-law and relative connections to ensure social mobility for its offspring. Between 1834 and 1855 Francisco Antônio de Sousa Queirós (the Barão de Sousa Queirós and an imperial senator from São Paulo) and his wife, Antônia Eufrosina Vergueiro de Queirós, baptized eight children. Frederico, born in 1834, was baptized at the house of José da Costa Carvalho (imperial senator for Sergipe and prime minister in 1848), the future Marquês de Monte Alegre. Born in Bahia, Monte Alegre moved to Piracicaba, São Paulo, where he was one of the large landowners. Frederico's maternal grandfather, the former Regent Nicolau Pereira de Campos Vergueiro, and paternal grandmother, Genebra de Barros Leite, served as his godparents.[16] Another son, Luís, was baptized at his parents' home in 1836. No padrinho was selected for the occasion. Instead, his two grandmothers served as godmothers: Maria Angélica de Vasconcelos Vergueiro, wife of the imperial regent and maternal grandmother, and Genebra de Barros Leite, paternal grandmother.[17] Another son, Alfredo, had five godparents: his own brother Francisco Antônio Júnior, Genebra, Maria Angélica, grandfather Vergueiro, and uncle Brigadier Luís Antônio.[18] As the family connections with other clans proliferated, new in-laws were inducted into the ritual parentela. José, another son of the couple, was baptized in 1853. Brother Luís (born in 1836 and studying in Germany) and Agueda de Faro Vergueiro, a cousin living in the court, served as godparents.[19] The Faros were one of the premier agrarian gentry clans in Rio province and later branched out to commerce and railroad building as well. José was the first offspring of Senator Sousa Queirós and his wife to have a godparent outside São Paulo, but the alliance forged was still within the confluence of blood relatives.

The senator himself also served as godparent of his nephews and nieces, a double lacing of blood and ritual kinship that proved to be a sound basis for family strategy. An infant daughter of Brigadier Luís Antônio de Sousa Barros and Ilídia Henriqueta de Sousa Resende was baptized in 1835. The baby girl, also christened Ilídia, had her uncle Francisco Antônio, the vice-president of São Paulo, and her paternal grandmother, Genebra, as godparents.[20] On another occasion, the senator sponsored baptismal festivities at his house for Francisca, daughter of brother Vicente and his wife, Ana Francisca de Paula Sousa. The senator and his wife, Antônia, served as godparents.[21] Vicente's wife was the daughter of Francisco de Paula Sousa e Melo, future prime minister of the empire. The senator's own wife, of course, was the daughter of the imperial regent and Senator Vergueiro. Francisco Antônio de Sousa Queirós was the longest-serving imperial senator from his province. His political career, though confined to the senate for some four decades, certainly was not hurt by such marital and ceremonial ties; on the contrary, they should have helped his career. It can be argued that the Sousa Queirós-Vergueiro-Sousa e Melo group, in São Paulo, was far more extended socially and economically throughout the province than were the Andradas, of Santos and, therefore, that the former should be considered the ruling elite of the province, not the patrician family from Santos City.

The use of family members and in-laws as godparents was not an invention of the Sousa Queiróses. Another moneyed bourgeois clan, the Silva Prados, practiced the building of such ritual alliances and went a step further by extending their patronage to provincial immigrant merchants. An eighteenth-century—some say sixteenth-century—family, the Silva Prados, had become an economic elite at the outset of the nineteenth century. By then, such Silva Prados as Antônio (the Barão de Iguape) and his brothers were the rising bourgeois merchants in the province. Antônio, in particular, had the kind of wide-ranging business ties, stretching from Bahia to Mato Grosso and throughout São Paulo and Rio, that made the Silva Prados attractive godparents for ambitious bourgeois classes.

In the parish of Sé, the records show that at least five Silva Prado offspring were baptized between 1832 and 1854. Sé was the primary residence of Francisco (Iguape's brother) and his wife, Maria Benedita; Martinho and his wife, Verediana (Iguape's brother and daughter, respectively); and Veríssimo Antônio and his wife, Ana Leopoldina (Iguape's son and niece). Three of the children by Martinho and Verediana were given ritual parents; two—Verediana, born in 1842 and named after her mother, and Martinho, or Martinico, born in 1843— had their grandfather and granduncle as padrinhos. Verediana's madrinha was Maria Marcolina Monteiro e Prado, her aunt and the wife of Rodrigo Antônio Monteiro de Barros, a judge, general deputy, and prominent politician in the city.[22] Martinico's godparents were his paternal grandfather Eleutério da Silva Prado and one Maria Cândida Moura Prado.[23] The third baptized was the future imperial mandarin, who would serve as president of Ceará in 1888, Antônio Caio da Silva Prado. Caio was Iguape's grandson on his mother's side and Eleutério's on his father's. His padrinhos were the Visconde de Monte Alegre (the future marquês) and Maria Inocência de Sousa Queirós.[24] The other two Silva Prado offspring—Maria, born in 1842 (daughter of Francisco and Maria Benedita) and Ana, born in 1854 (daughter of Veríssimo Antônio and Ana Leopoldina)—each had relatives as padrinhos. Maria received her maternal uncle Fernando Pacheco Jordão, but had no madrinha. For Ana, Iguape and Maria Hipólita dos Santos Silva Jordão were selected as godparents.[25]

Several Silva Prados descended from the female line were also baptized in the Sé district. Two of the three Monteiro de Barros children were also Silva Prados on their mother's side: Lucas and Maria Luisa, children of Rodrigo Antônio and Maria Marcolina. Both grandfathers—the Visconde de Congonhas do Campo and Eleutério da Silva Prado—served as their padrinhos. One Ana da Silva Prado (not to be confused with the daughter of the same name by Martinho and Verediana) married one Fidelis Nepomuceno Prates Júnior, of Rio Grande do Sul. Their daughter, Eugênia, had her paternal uncle and aunt for her godparents.[26]

Judging from the practices of the Sousa Queirós, Monteiro de Barros, and Silva Prado clans, clearly no hard and fast rule about godparents prevailed. First, ritual parents need not be of the same generation; neither were they required to come from either the same clan or a similar social class. They would be mixed in generation, clans, and/or classes. Furthermore, a child could have a single godparent, either padrinho or madrinha, but this phenomenon was not always common. Second, the bonding of ritual kinship was a more useful social-reinforcing mechanism for the parents of low social and economic status than for the child. The rich and powerful by nature considered the invitation to godparenthood to be a public recognition of their good stead in the clan and social world, and hence a viable form of patronage.

Thus, for families aspiring to move up socially, the adoption of the right godparents for their children meant an opportunity for association with a more established family. To the rising parvenu merchants and gentry planters, therefore, this kind of ritual bonding, as well as marriage, possessed particular significance. In the Sé district registry, two instances of such ritual kinship between socially powerful titled families and immigrant families were recorded. Undoubtedly more occurred. José Antônio Tomás Romeiro was a native of Oporto, Portugal, and his wife, Carlota, came from Rio. Their infant son, Bernardo, enjoyed the honor of having as godparents the Barão and Baronesa de Iguape.[27] Romeiro was probably a business associate of the barão. Similarly, Antônio, son of Manuel José de Azevedo, also a Portuguese merchant in São Paulo, and his Brazilian wife, Gabriela, was adopted by the noble couple as their godchild.[28] The popularity of Iguape as godparent indicated that he was a successful merchant at least in the province, if not in the southern part of the empire, and his willingness to become an adoptive parent demonstrated that he was eager to use such means to reinforce his business ties. Both sets of parents benefited from the relationship.

The socially and politically prominent were also often sought out by acquaintances to be godparents. The parish registry shows two different modes of forming this type of ritual bonding. The first was the cultivating of the powerful by such middle-class professionals as physicians, lawyers, and civil-military officials of relatively obscure pedigree. The second was the establishment of ritual kinship through association in the same occupation; often the father's superior became a padrinho. Brigadier Rafael Tobias de Aguiar, for example, was the provincial president of São Paulo during the early years of the Regency. A staunch antiloyalist, he was the leader of the Liberal Revolt of 1842 that involved São Paulo and Minas Gerais. He and his second wife, the Marquesa de Santos, sponsored a total of nine children, as recorded in the Sé district between 1831 and 1856. Probably others were registered in the city as well as in Sorocaba, their redoubt in the late 1830s and 1840s. The brigadier alone was padrinho on three separate occasions, once each in 1831, 1832, and 1856, the first two while he was provincial president of São Paulo. On all three occasions, the godchildren were not his blood kin.[29] The parents of the baptized were probably of the lower and middle classes, none of whom were readily identifiable as an economic or political elite of the province or the city. The Marquesa de Santos sponsored alone twice: once for the son of Sargento Mor João Feliciano da Costa Ferreira and his wife and another time for her niece.[30] Together, Aguiar and Santos became godparents for another child of the Costa Ferreiras in 1834 while the former was still provincial president. Another couple was honored when the brigadier and the marquesa adopted their daughter in a ritual bonding; the first daughter of the couple was the godchild of Aguiar in 1832.[31] If the ritual alliance meant the first step up in the social ladder for the less fortunate, the popularity of the brigadier and the marquesa reached an ebb during the 1840s. In the Sé district, only one (1849) baptismal ceremony occurred in which the couple took part during the entire decade.[32] The Liberal Revolt of 1842 made Rafael Tobias de Aguiar a social persona non grata among those eager to associate with the winning side, the government. They obviously avoided Aguiar and Santos.

Among the well-known military and political mandarins who became godparents for the children of their subordinates were Brigadier Francisco de Lima e Silva, Marshal Daniel Pedro Muller, Conselheiro Joaquim Inácio da Silveira Mota, Conselheiro Carlos Carneiro de Campos, Brigadier João Francisco Bellegarde, Major Henrique de Beaurepaire Rohan (the future marshal and the visconde), and the Marquês de Monte Alegre. Army Captain Vicente Ferreira da Silva Lisboa and his wife were honored by Brigadier Lima e Silva, who held the baptismal party at his house and arranged with the bishop of the diocese to officiate over the ritual for their child.[33] In a similar fashion, Marshal Muller adopted the son of an army captain.[34] Muller's daughter, Mrs. Beaurepaire Rohan, and her husband sponsored Bento, the son of a free black couple, to be their godchild. Bento's parents could have been among the Beaurepaire Rohan's retinue.[35] In another case, Carlos Carneiro de Campos (the Second Visconde de Caravelas) was president of the province of Minas Gerais when he was asked to be padrinho by a couple in Sé. Unable to attend, he arranged for his counterpart in São Paulo, José Joaquim Fernandes Torres, to stand in for him.[36] As a final example, Brigadier Bellegarde and his wife adopted one Manuel, "son of Antônia Joaquina and unknown father," as godson.[37] Both the child and the mother might have been black as well as household servants.

Ritual alliances in Rio and Minas Gerais provinces revealed patterns similar to those in the city of São Paulo. Such generosity as that shown by the Beaurepaire Rohans and the Bellegardes was rare. By and large, lower social and economic classes and, in particular, slaves confined the selection of ritual kin to their own class and color. Among the exceptions was the Conde de Baependi, an important aristocratic coffee planter in Valença, who in 1853 adopted the daughter of an immigrant couple—Guilherme and Guilhermina Amélia Murdock—as his goddaughter. Murdock was listed in the Valença birth registry as an interpreter at the conde's Fazenda Santa Rosa, where immigrant workers were employed.[38]

In the baptism registry of the diocese of Luz (Abaeté), Minas Gerais, records show that free couples often adopted slave children in the formation of ritual kinship. One of the richest landowners in Abaeté was Antônio Zacarias Alvares da Silva. Bibiana, one of his slaves, gave birth to a boy in 1862 who was given free godparents in April of the following year, certainly by arrangement of his mother's owner.[39] Another example is the case of one Manuel, also the son of a slave couple who belonged to a well-to-do widow, who was adopted by a free couple as a godson.[40] More common for slave children, however, were slave padrinhos. Historians know little about the internalization of the patriarchal customs such as baptism and marriage among Brazil's servile population, but clues in the Abaeté and other parishes suggest that slaves adopted the practices of the free population, especially of their masters.

As in the case of the free population, slaves often sought the powerful and rich as padrinhos for their children, hoping through social and economic ties to obtain freedom for themselves and their children. A few fortunate slaves succeeded in cementing such ritual bonds. The ritual parentela in the world of slaves is yet to be studied, but evidence suggests that the status of a child's mother—her standing within the plantation or ranch as well as the existence of a carnal relationship with the owner—determined the availability of free godparents for her offspring. In theory, free padrinhos could give their adopted children freedom, often paying the price to the mother's owner.

In Abaeté, slaves also practiced the mixed bonding of free and slave godparents, as well as the adoption of slave padrinhos, often from two different owners. This mixed form of ritual parentela suggests that strategic choices were considered by mothers in such a way that the adoption provided the best opportunities for their children. In Brazil, as in other slave societies, the status of slave was inherited from the mother's side. In 1864 the Silva slave Bibiana had another child, who was adopted by two slaves owned by her master, the landholder Antônio Zacarias.[41] The slave Rosa, a ward of Pedro Ordone, another agrarian power in Abaeté, gave birth to a daughter, Eva; Bibiana and Raimundo, slaves of Antônio Zacarias, stood in as the padrinhos for Eva.[42] The data on Abaeté, if they are representative of other rural regions of the empire, suggest that baptismal rituals failed to lead to manumission. In fact, none was recorded in the diocese. In contrast, cases of manumission were common in the Sé district of São Paulo city, often paid for by padrinhos at baptisms.

Freeing slave children at baptisms came in two forms: a grateful owner granted freedom to a child for the faithful services rendered by the slave mother or a free padrinho bought liberty for the adoptive child—strikingly similar to those conditions used by the Crown to grant titles of nobility to sons of first-generation titled elite in the early 1820s. Describing the manumission at baptism of one Francisca, a daughter of a slave Maria, the parish log reads as follows:

> Maria, slave of Ana Maria da Conceição, of unknown paternity; I declare on this occasion for the said Ana Maria da Conceição in writing in which the owner states that in her free will and in appreciation for the services by the same Maria Mulatta that she confers the innocent Francisca freedom. . . .
>
> (signed) Parish Priest[43]

On another occasion, Francisco Xavier de Castro, padrinho of Vicência, daughter of the slave Antônia, bought freedom for his godchild.[44] Still another padrinho, Francisco Fernandes Pereira, paid in 1849 a sum of 32$000 for the liberty of his godson. In this case, the benefactor could very well have been the real father of the manumitted.[45] When slave children were freed without monetary compensation from godparents, the parish record shows that the owner considered the birth to have taken place free—the most popularly used expression in the registry being "as if born of free womb" (como se de ventre livre nascesse). Almost all the cases recorded were of "unknown paternity" (pay [sic] incognito).[46] A final example of ritual bonding between slaves and free men in the Sé district occurred in 1835. Carlos Carneiro de Campos and his wife adopted one Maria, a slave girl, as their goddaughter. Manumitted earlier, the mother of the girl might have been a slave of the Camposes.[47] This type of social patronage by upper-class Brazilians has yet to be studied systematically.

Freeing slaves was cyclical, often tied to economically good and bad times. Manumissions were registered frequently in the 1830s, rarely in the 1840s, and reappeared in the 1850s, according to the Sé registry. If any economic implication can be drawn from these data, it is that, like Rio (the court) in earlier decades when urban slaves were exported to coffee fazendas in the Paraíba Valley, the city of São Paulo must have exported chattels to the expanding coffee fields in the provincial north and west in the 1840s. By mid-century, the province was importing slaves from other sources, such as Rio, Minas Gerais, and provinces in the Northeast, lessening the drain on urban slaves. A secure supply of servile labor to the rural region probably re-created favorable conditions for resuming such manumission at baptisms. Residents in the parish, such as the relatives and in-laws of the Vergueiros, the Sousa Queiróses, and the Sousa Aranhas, once again played the role of paternalistic benefactors to their servile population.

Marriage, not baptism, however, was often the principal foundation of Brazilian family strategy, in some cases figuring more prominently in career planning and in determining social station for life. The upper class on the whole practiced loveless arranged marriages, often involving the exchange, transfer, and/or consolidation of properties. The clan or, more commonly, "the family" was built around common properties that made marriage a communal affair, a concern that far exceeded the affection of the individuals betrothed and the nuclear families of the couple. Marriage carried profound economic, social, and even political implications beyond the contracting parties. The bride and groom were exchanged between two families as a mutually acceptable means of improving their social and economic standing within society at large. If no advantage could be gained from a union, marriage would not take place. In sixteenth-century England, the marriageable age for an upper-class girl was about twenty years old; by the eighteenth century, the most common age of eligibility was twenty-two or twenty-three.[48] The first-born heir was obligated to marry early and to produce successors for the house. The failure to produce heirs often resulted in the dissipation of clan wealth and the disappearance of the line.

In Bahia, the Costa Pinto heirs typically married in their early twenties, though the Conde de Sergimirim (Antônio da Costa Pinto), a first-generation Brazilian Costa Pinto, married at the age of thirty; and his son, the Visconde de Oliveira (Antônio da Costa Pinto Júnior), at eighteen. Oliveira's son (João Francisco) acquired a wife at twenty-one.

Oliveira's sister Mariana (Iaiá) married the Barão de Jeremoabo at twenty-five. The norm was that the groom was slightly older than the bride. Jeremoabo was two years older than Iaiá. Oliveira was five years senior to his wife, Maria Rita Lopes, who was thirteen years old when she married him. João Francisco, who married a cousin, Jerônima Simões de Meireles, was four years older than she. She was seventeen at the time of betrothal.[49]

Part of the larger design for ensuring the continuity of the male line was the preservation of the family wealth and the acquisition of new properties. In some ways, marriage functioned as a vehicle to recruit new financial and human capital for the clan wealth. Thus, when marriage was contemplated for intraclan members, two weighty factors had to be considered: disposable wealth that the bride's family could set aside as a dowry and ecclesiastical dispensation for closely related cousins. Another factor, when complete strangers were involved, was purity of blood line.

The wealthy rural aristocracy, gentry, and urban bourgeoisie practiced at least one of the four distinct patterns of marriages during the nineteenth century: (1) intraclan cousin marriages; (2) unions between political elite and rich bourgeois or gentry families; (3) marriages between the offspring of people in the same profession, especially in the military; and (4) second or third marriages for widows and widowers that involved a merger of the inherited properties, fame, and status of the two contracting parties. Economic considerations probably weighed less in cousin marriages than in nonconsanguineous unions. Although cousin marriages yielded less immediately transferable cash or land, before the deaths of the parents of the married, the ultimate purpose of such unions was to encapsulate the clan wealth, so that the timing of the transfer was deemed to be less vital. The actual division of properties and slaves in the case of rural clans did not occur before one or more of the parents died. Among urban families, partnership in the family business often substituted for the division of clan wealth. Thus, during the life of the bride's parents, the actual transfer of properties, and even dowered properties, was often deferred, though the holder of the dowry enjoyed the usufruct to the properties. However, the transfer of slaves and even fazendas during the lifetime of the parents of the newly married was not unheard of. The Conde de Baependi and his wife began to distribute their wealth to their children well before their wills were prepared; and, similarly, the Marquesa de Santos advanced huge sums of cash to her children, especially to those in dire financial difficulty, such as the Condessa de Iguaçu.

Hence, even among cousins and brothers, the conditions for marriage needed to be precisely worked out beforehand, often in written contracts. Cousin marriage was also employed to thwart an unwelcomed intrusion by an outsider. After 1835, when the mortmain became illegal, upper-class Brazilians viewed marriages among cousins as the most viable means of maintaining the economic and social status quo, which some noble families had previously protected by the voluntary use of primogeniture rules. The announcement of betrothal, then, was a momentous occasion for a clan, celebrated by all the relatives of the two families with colorful festivities. The wedding, most often in church, was a family holiday for the houses involved and their dependent populations. Neighbors were invited to the event, and slaves were freed both conditionally and unconditionally by the parents of the bride and groom. Generous gifts were bequeathed by charity-minded families to such religious institutions as a Santa Casa de Misericórdia and monastic orders. After the wedding, rich newlyweds traveled to foreign countries, most often in Europe, or an out-of-province place. For the not-so-rich, the retreat to a fazenda of relatives or a city residence served as the honeymoon. Upon its conclusion, the bride moved into her husband's house, shared the conjugal bed, and raised a family. Thus, the first leg of matriarchal responsibilities began.

The parish records on marriages in Sé between 1812 and 1900 provide rich data for broad generalizations on family structure and strategies, as well as for comparisons between urban and rural marriages. Of thirty-seven cases of marriage that involved titled families of mercantile, agrarian, military, and political elites of the parish, fifteen, or 40.5 percent, can be classified as endogamous to class, mergers between offspring of parents in similar or the same professions. Thirteen, or 35.1 percent, fall in the category of union between political elite and moneyed classes of agrarian or mercantile origins. Five cases, or 13.5 percent, can be classified as the social unions of rich and famous widowers and widows, often their second or third marriage., And finally, four, or 10.8 percent, are in the category of intraclan cousin marriages.

Generalizations from the Sé samples should be taken with caution, however. Especially after the end of the Paraguayan War, in 1870, that urban district was replaced by such new upper-class residential sections as Santa Ifigênia, Campos Eliseus, and by the end of the empire, Higenópolis, soon to be outclassed by the Avenida Paulista district of old and new money. Nevertheless, the samples demonstrate that marriage was a vehicle for intraclass as well as interclass mobility, a fact that probably held true in various districts, old and new, of São Paulo city. The low instances of cousin marriages in Sé did not mean that such unions were not popular in Brazil; rather, they were preferred by landed aristocracy and gentry with aristocratic pretensions more than by the forward-looking urban bourgeois and profit-minded gentry planters, who viewed marriage as both a system of maintaining their status and a means to expand their wealth and properties.

The intraclan marriages in the district of Sé involved the families of Sousa Queirós, Monteiro de Barros, Silva Prado, and Azambuja. All the married were cousins of second and third degrees removed, meaning that they were descendants of the same grandmother or great-grandmother. When José Bonifácio Nascentes de Azambuja married a third cousin, Maria Adelaide d'Araújo Macedo, in 1837, the bishop's dispensation was required and obtained for the union. Coronel Antônio da Silva Prado (Iguape) and José Manuel França served as the witnesses for the wedding.[50] Veríssimo da Silva Prado, Iguape's son, married his second and third double cousin Ana, daughter of Francisco, Iguape's brother, in another wedding approved by the bishop, as "dispensed from the impediment of the second and third degrees of consanguinity." The fathers of both the bride and groom served as witnesses.[51] Judge Rodrigo Antônio Monteiro de Barros also married his second cousin, Ana Francisca da Silva Prado; and José Egídio de Queirós Aranha wedded his second cousin, Josefina de Queirós Aranha.

These two marriages wove familial ties among the four clans: the Monteiro de Barroses and the Sousa Aranhas, key landowners, and the Silva Prados and the Sousa Queirós, mercantile families whose wealth had been diversified by mid-century to include coffee plantations. The double cousinhood meant that the parents and grandparents of the newly married had also engaged in intraclan marriages. The groom José Egídio was from Campinas, where the family owned several large coffee estates. His mother was a Silva Prado. Josefina, the bride, was from the district of Sé. Her father-in-law was also her uncle, brother of her own father.[52] These families also included major planters, merchants, judges, and politicians of national status. They frequently joined efforts to expand their economic activities, such as importing free European laborers and building railroads. The financial linkages among these families were thus intricately forged, and each family also retained its own ties to other business associates, with whom no marital bonds were formed. Collectively, the upper class of the province constituted a tightly knit community.

Class endogamy (marriages of economically equal partners) as opposed to clan endogamy (marriages of not always economically equal relations) offers a fascinating glimpse of social mobility at the time when São Paulo was emerging as the new economic core of the empire. Of the fifteen class endogamous marriages observed, five took place among political families; four among mercantile clans; three among agrarian gentry; two among agrarian and mercantile families; and one between two military families. In one salient case of clan endogamy, Eliza Carneiro de Campos, daughter of the Visconde de Caravelas, married Francisco Ferreira França, a cousin from Bahia through his father's side, with a proper episcopal dispensation. The Ferreira Franças were a well-known political family in Bahia, and the father of the bride had twice served as provincial president of Minas Gerais, imperial senator (1857–78), Cabinet minister twice, and councillor of state (1870–78). Caravelas's political career, however, matured after he had relocated to São Paulo, married a Paulista, and made a home in the province.[53]

In a similar fashion, the union between a son of the Barão de Sousa Queirós, the senator from São Paulo, and a daughter of Conselheiro José Bonifácio de Andrada e Silva, the patriarch's son, was a classical political marriage of two powerful clans.[54] It should be noted that the Sousa Queirós-Vergueiro-Sousa e Melo alliance formed through marriages and baptismal ties was not expanded to include the Andradas, of Santos, before 1879. The Sousa Queiróses were the chain link to these powerful agrarian, commercial, and political clans. Such an alliance probably was not possible or even desirable during the lifetime of the patriarch, whose difficult relations with the House of Braganza in the 1820s made many ambitious gentry and bourgeois Paulistas maintain their distance from the Andradas. By 1879 the first family of Santos was no longer a political power in the empire, but certainly remained an excellent name that gentry such as the Sousa Queiróses could cultivate.

Other class endogamous marriages involved children of military as well as mercantile families. Major Henrique de Beaurepaire Rohan married Guilhermina Muller das Chagas, daughter of Marshal Daniel Pedro Muller and widow of an army officer. Rohan was one of the most ancient aristocratic names in France. The Brazilian branch was a military family, and Henrique eventually rose to the rank of general and became the Visconde de Beaurepaire Rohan.[55] Nicolau Pereira de Campos Vergueiro, a grandson of the namesake, married one Messias Freire, daughter of a merchant. The groom was from Faxina and the bride from Sorocaba.[56] Both the Vergueiro and Freire families were coffee traders.

Among the most interesting cases of marriage as a vehicle for upward social mobility are the mergers between moderately impoverished political elite families and those of the moneyed class—in particular, novos ricos of agrarian gentry and merchants. Such unions were prudently based on mutual benefit: political prestige for the economically well off and money for the politically powerful. The thirteen cases studied in the district of Sé can be categorized as follows: three marriages between political and agrarian families; six between political and mercantile; three between military and mercantile; and one between political and military. Two Monteiro de Barros offspring thus married into an agrarian and mercantile family, respectively. Manuel José de Castro Monteiro de Barros wedded the daughter of a gentry. The groom was from Minas Gerais and the bride from the city of São Paulo. Marco Antônio, the second Monteiro de Barros, married Leonor Augusta Hambary Luz; the groom's father was Judge Rodrigo Antônio, who resided in the court, and the bride's father was probably a well-to-do merchant from the city of São Paulo.[57]

Other examples of scions of political elite families marrying into landed or mercantile classes include the marriage of Júlio, the son of Cristiano Benedito Ottoni, an imperial politician from Minas Gerais, and Barbara Balbina (a daughter of the Barão do Engenho Novo, a landowner in Valença, Rio) to Paulina de Sousa Queirós, a daughter of the Barão and Baronesa de Limeira. The groom was from the court, and the bride from the Sé parish, but her father, brother of the imperial senator the Barão de Sousa Queirós, was a landowner in the interior.[58] Antônio Carlos Ribeiro de Andrada Machado e Silva, son of the namesake, married a daughter of a rich planter in Itu.[59] The groom was the third Antônio Carlos and a great-nephew of José Bonifácio, the patriarch of Brazilian independence. The Andradas by mid-century had opened up a political clan in Minas Gerais.

The unions of children of ambitious political nobles of humble origin as well as meager wealth and children of rich merchants conjure up shades of Molière's bourgeois gentilhomme. On one level, a Monteiro de Barros (Rodrigo Antônio) married a Silva Prado (Maria Marcolina), a union of money and political fame. Similarly, a son of the Visconde de Caravelas married a daughter of a merchant.[60] And, on another level, one Andrada (Maria Horta) married Henrique João Dodsworth, a mercantile family in the court.[61] By the time of the First Republic (1889–1930), the Dodsworths had become a prominent urban political family in Rio. A final example concerns a thirty-nine-year-old president of São Paulo province who married a sixteen-year-old girl; one inference that can be drawn was that the impoverished politician was attracted to the wealth of the young girl's family because affection mattered little in first marriages. Another inference can be made: physical attraction between them. Brazilian customs would not have permitted professional education for the sixteen-year-old girl, and hence the marriage could not have been forged on mutual admiration for intellectual or professional excellence. The groom was from Campos, Rio, where the family did not figure among major agrarian gentry or aristocracy. The bride was from São Paulo.[62]

The five cases of second marriages by well-known elites registered in Sé parish involved two politicians, one general, and two landowners. Conselheiro José Bonifácio de Andrada e Silva married Rafaela de Sousa Amaral, both widowed and for the second time each.[63] Teófilo Benedito Ottoni, a widower and a senator, wedded Eliza Maria Rosa, of São Bernardino do Campo.[64] Marshal Daniel Pedro Muller's second marriage was to the widow of an army colonel.[65] And, finally, the Barão de Três Rios (the future marquês) married the Baronesa de São José do Rio Claro in 1876, and the Barão de Tatuí wedded the widow of the Barão de Itapetininga in 1881.[66] The last two cases involved mergers of considerable amounts of land as well as urban properties. Três Rios, for instance, was already an important landowner in Campinas and its adjacent area, but his marriage to the baronesa brought him properties in Rio Claro and Sorocaba. He was also the founder of a railroad company, a banker, and a well-established provincial politician, serving as both vice-president and president of São Paulo. Campinas's second marriage undoubtedly extended his political and economic power within the capitalist agriculture of the province.

If the marriages examined from the parish records of Sé give any clues to family strategies for preserving and expanding wealth, they suggest that, in urban areas, interclass marriages were most often preferred as a medium for social mobility. This pattern can also be identified among the English gentry whom Lawrence Stone studied. Similarly, marriages in Bahia served as a way to move upward socially. The Paulistana examples from Sé confirm that in the city of Salvador: more marriages began to function as interclass mergers by mid-century, though the frequency of such instances was considerably lower than in Rio and São Paulo. Enough marriages between money and political power did take place in such provincial cities as Salvador and Recife to warrant the conclusion that the gentry and bourgeois classes' most cherished social values had begun to permeate the provinces in the Northeast by the early 1870s.

The marriage of João Maurício Wanderley (the Barão de Cotegipe) was an exemplary merging of political power with money. He was the chief of the Conservative party in Bahia and prime minister of the empire between 1885 and 1888. Born in the interior town of Barra, in the Middle São Francisco Valley of Bahia (formerly of Pernambuco), of modest origins—his father was known as "the poorest" Wanderley—he began his political career as prosecutor and judge in Bahia. After graduating from the Olinda Law Faculty in 1837, he did not marry, but instead concentrated on his political career for the next twenty years. At the age of forty-two in 1857, he married Antônia Teresa, daughter of the Conde de Passé, one of the richest planters in the province. Although Cotegipe served as Bahia's provincial president in the first half of the 1850s and by 1854 was a cabinet minister, he lacked wealth. In fact, his grandson-biographer went so far as to admit that the baronesa's asset was not her beauty but her dowry, which consisted of at least two fine sugar plantations, scores of slaves, and cash. When she died, she left Cotegipe with four sugar mills, hundreds of slaves, and many rural properties.[67] The marriage was a merger in the fashion of other Bahian politicians, such as the Marquês de Monte Alegre and the Visconde de Caravelas, both of whom settled in São Paulo.

The Conde de Passé did not stop with one politician son-in-law in his family strategy. A daughter married the Barão de Pirajá (José Joaquim Pires de Carvalho e Albuquerque); a son married a daughter of the Visconde de São Lourenço, a planter and mandarin of national reputation from São Francisco do Conde, Bahia.[68] São Lourenço (Francisco Gonçalves Martins) was a Conservative politician who rose rapidly within provincial politics and by the late 1840s was president of Bahia. São Lourenço and Cotegipe were chiefs of the provincial Conservative party for nearly four decades (1840s–1880s); their political ties were further reinforced by their marital linkage to the Passé family.

Compared to interclan marriages, intraclan marriages on the whole seemed to involve the transfer of less wealth, at least at the outset of the unions. For one thing, they yielded smaller dowries. When João Vicente Viana, scion of a Recôncavo planter family that acquired four nobility titles and owned several sugar mills, married his cousin in 1841, for example, her dowry consisted of seven slaves, worth 2:950$.[69] People believed that intraclan marriage was also designed to maintain purity of lineage, as much as to amass new wealth. Another example illustrates the case of a good bloodline over money as an asset for marriage. Antônio da Costa Pinto (Sergimirim) resolved that his thirteen-year-old orphan niece should marry his son, Totônio (the future Visconde de Oliveira and Sergimirim's namesake). The Costa Pintos were a leading agrarian clan in Santo Amaro of eighteenth-century origin. The bride was adequately dowered, but had no major financial or landed assets to bring to the clan. Her virtue and pedigree were sufficient.

Gilberto Freyre contends that, when a member of the parvenu rich in Pernambuco wanted to gain entrance to the established landed class, what mattered most was financial standing, not lineage. As in Bahia, when Portuguese merchants and their offspring married provincial gentry and even aristocracy, money was the essence of the union, which included the transfer of both urban and rural properties as well as a considerable amount of cash.[70]

If marriage did not involve money and political fame, the purity of blood was extolled. The Conde de Carapebus, a prominent courtier noble and planter from Campos, Rio, was a skillful power broker at the court of Dom Pedro II. He was married to a Nogueira da Gama, of Valença. When he contracted marriage for his daughter Chiquita in the early 1880s, he was able to boast to a friend that the groom came "from a clean, stable, and white family."[71] No mention of money was made in the letter. The prestige of acquiring a son-in-law of French lineage alone was sufficient to compensate for the lack of wealth. It was noted earlier in this volume that a few elite families in Bahia married into German families. The Ferreira Bandeiras, of Santo Amaro, and the Moniz branch, of Cachoeira, had offspring marry Teutonic brides and grooms. Carapebus clearly recognized that no amount of money could improve an obscure pedigree. No Brazilian wealth and pedigree could match a good European lineage.

According to the Sé samples, the frequency of marriages between politicians and moneyed groups was about the same as between similar professional families, thirteen and fifteen cases, respectively. Two tentative conclusions can be formed from these cases. First, there was less deep-seated desire to marry *à la intraclan* among the emerging gentry and merchant families in São Paulo, where the moving frontiers of coffee, opportunities for success in trade and crafts, and entry into urban professions made marriage an open avenue to mobility; the aristocratic closed approach to family building was on its way out as no longer warranted. Brazilian historians have argued that marriages such as those of Júlio Benedito Ottoni with a Sousa Queirós and Teófilo Benedito Ottoni (Júlio's uncle) with a wealthy widow, Rosa, fostered a sentiment of class alliance between political elite and landed interests, so that imperial politicians with such linkages were more likely to speak out for the defense of the status quo. In the case of the Ottonis, however, this was hardly the result. In the case of Cotegipe, it can be argued that he, like a Jesuit convert, emerged as one of the staunchest defenders of slavocratic interest. Manuel Pinto de Sousa Dantas was an ardent abolitionist by the 1880s, when one of his sons married a Clemente Pinto, of Cantagalo, Rio. Although the Pintos were among the major slaveholding families of the empire and megaclass coffee planters, the marital bond between the Pintos and Sousa Dantases did not co-opt the prime minister into diluting his abolitionist rhetoric. The intricate workings of a politician's mind during the empire could not be comprehended by a single variable such as a marital alliance.

A second tentative conclusion, based on the cases described, is that in an economically stagnant region such as the Northeast, and even in some parts of Rio province where economic decay had already set in by the early 1870s, marriages often helped delay the disintegration of clan wealth. Evidence of this tendency is apparent among the aristocratic landowning clans in Campos and Macaé, of Rio; Santo Amaro, São Francisco do Conde, and Cachoeira, of Bahia; and the Zona da Mata, of Pernambuco.

The marriage records of Valença's São Pedro e São Paulo parish and Nossa Senhora da Glória parish between 1845 and 1888 also strongly support the above generalizations. Among the major nobiliary families in Valença, only three registered marriages occurred, though the records fail to reflect the many weddings arranged in the court. The Wernecks were a large clan that claimed five nobility titles: the Barão de Pati do Alferes, the Barão de Ipiabas, the Barão de Bemposta, the Barão de Palmeiras, and the Barão de Werneck. Bemposta and Pati do Alferes lived in Vassouras; Ipiabas was born in the court but became a resident of Valença, like his father the Visconde de Ipiabas; Palmeiras was also a planter in Valença; and Werneck was a planter in Paraíba do Sul. The last two were brothers, grandsons of the First Barão de Palmeiras (Francisco Quirino da Rocha). As in the fashion of the older families in the Northeast and Minas Gerais, the Wernecks first practiced intraclan marriages and after 1840 began to branch out by incorporating outsiders. But the frequency of marrying relatives continued to exceed that with outsiders.

Cândida Peregrina das Chagas Werneck married her double cousin Benjamin de Sales Pinheiro. Benjamin was a son of the Visconde de Ipiabas, and the bride was the visconde's niece. The viscondessa was also a Werneck (Chagas). This marriage required an episcopal dispensation, which was granted pro forma for the twenty-one-year-old Benjamin and twenty-seven-year-old Cândida.[72] Sisters Maria and Rita Peregrina Werneck married brothers Manuel and João Vieira Machado da Cunha, also cousins. Manuel, a coffee comissário in Rio and a ranch landowner in Valença, a capitalist gentry planter par excellence, was to become the Barão de Aliança. The two weddings took place in tandem in 1869 and 1870 at the family fazenda, Oriente, the property of Ipiabas. Joaquim de Almeida Ramos, son-in-law of Ipiabas, served as a witness for both.[73] He was the future Barão de Almeida Ramos and a prominent coffee commission agent in the court, responsible for the sale of coffee from the "family" plantations.

Another Werneck married a cousin. Francisco Pinheiro de Sousa Werneck wedded Francisca Guilhermina d'Assunção Werneck, twenty-eight and sixteen years old, respectively, at Fazenda do Oriente. The witnesses of this wedding were the future Second Barão de Palmeiras and João Batista de Almeida Werneck.[74] Only one marriage by the Wernecks during the same period was with an outsider; the thirty-two-year-old Werneck bride married a forty-five-year-old Brazilian from Uruguay.[75] Because the Valença parish registry, unlike that of the Sé, failed to give biographical details about the betrothed and their in-laws, the groom is identified only as a professional, either a lawyer or a physician.

It can be hypothesized that the older families, such as the descendants of the Marquês de Baependi and the Marquês de Valença, registered only the marriages of their dependent population because their children moved away from Valença to cities and provinces, as in the cases of the children of the Marquês de Valença, or entered different urban occupations, as in the cases of the descendants of Baependi. Hence, the offspring of these nobiliary clans lived in many different residences, and marriages took place elsewhere. Thus, in 1867 Coronel Manuel Jacinto Carneiro Nogueira da Gama (Juparanã) witnessed the wedding of one Manuel Jacinto da Silva and Josefina Maria da Conceição.[76] Considering the coronel's proclivity for sex with slaves, he could have been the father of the namesake, if not the padrinho. Inasmuch as the registry did not list the color of the married individuals, as in some of the books in São Paulo and Minas Gerais, it is pure conjecture that the future Barão de Juparanã was related to the groom. Manuel Jacinto was also a witness to another wedding at Fazenda de Santa Mônica, the clan redoubt. The groom was Portuguese and the bride, Presciliana, was presumably Josefina's sister.[77] Stanley Stein pointed out that planters in Vassouras and elsewhere in the Paraíba Valley often hired Portuguese immigrants as foremen of their plantations and of the mule trains that transported coffee to Rio. This Portuguese could very well have been such a foreman or mule-train captain for the Nogueira da Gamas. Still another marriage took place at Santa Mônica, this time involving a groom from Minas Gerais and a local bride; neither was a blood relative of the clan.[78] The marriage was probably one of those involving the dependent population in the fazenda.

Genovese, Gutman, and other North American historians have argued that slave marriage in the Old South was often used to stabilize the restive servile population. In the Caribbean, marriages among slaves were liberally allowed, especially in the English West Indies, as an effective measure of social control—an effort to contain the potential explosion of the black majority in a society ruled by a small white minority.[79] In Brazil, too, slave marriages served such a purpose. In the parish of Sé, São Paulo city, individual slave marriages were as common as free working-class marriages.

In Valença, though individual marriages among slaves were not rare, formalized unions registered in the parish records were less frequent. Rather, the registry showed several multiple marriages of plantation slaves. In 1868, when the Barão de Ipiabas consented to marital union for his slaves, sixteen couples wed on a single day. The baron's son and a foreman bore witness to the mass wedding.[80] In similar fashion, another planter, the Barão de Vista Alegre, permitted twenty couples of his slaves to marry in 1888, a few short months before the abolition of slavery. (Rio province, especially in and around Campos, was plagued by waves of slave violence and flights, forcing abolition in the city of Campos by early 1888. This event set off a sudden upsurge of better treatment of slaves throughout the province, including such co-optive ploys as marriage.)

Five of the forty slaves married were aged above fifty years; ten, between forty and forty-nine; another ten, between thirty and thirty-nine; thirteen, between twenty and twenty-nine; one was in her teens; and one declared his age unknown.[81] Thus, twenty-five of the forty slaves married were older than thirty years, well past their prime when the average age for field hands was between eighteen and twenty-eight years. The age distribution of the married slaves suggests that, first, the labor force of the Barão de Vista Alegre was older than the average and, second, the planter was concerned about the specter of slave violence and found ways to keep his slaves of all ages happy and therefore willing to remain with him. Because the parish record failed to give the age breakdown of Ipiabas's thirty-two slaves, one can only guess that a similar desire on his part was the prime motive for consenting to their mass marriage.

The exercise of patronage power often involved intra- and inter-class social actions. Men of wealth, in particular those holding nobility titles, sought out ways to influence their society. Baptism and marriage often provided a way to grant favors and wishes to less fortunate relatives as well as to strangers. The linkages that grew out of these relationships—such as padrinho, madrinha, and witnesses at weddings—were far more important to the parents when such alliances were made between classes. The intraclass formation of social parentela was often designed to protect clan lineage, purity of blood, and wealth—the primary objective of cousin marriages. The crucial differences between the Center-South and Northeast lay in the nature of the regional economic elite families. Coffee fazendeiros in the Center-South, as creatures of nineteenth-century industrial capitalism, exhibited more profit-minded approaches to their economic and social activities; to borrow the well-chosen expression of Raymundo Faoro, "the lucrative class" came from the ranks of gentry farmers. The titles of nobility that coffee planters amassed with such relish indicate that the novos ricos were determined to erase their obscure pedigrees by an ostentatious show of wealth, titles, and patronage.[82] This gentry, or "lucrative class," mixed intra- and inter-class marriages as an alternative to the continued expansion of their power, wealth, and prestige in society at large.

The nobles, especially the planters, of the Northeast remained tightly knit groups, as demonstrated in Bahia and Pernambuco. In Bahia, the agrarian class did not open its door to outsiders; hence, such clans as the Costa Pintos, the Calmons, the Albuquerques, and the Monizes were by and large intraclan and intraclass bred. In Pernambuco, a recent study shows that the landowning class as a whole was much more diversified than that in Bahia by involving themselves in commerce and other urban economic activities. The most aristocratic clan in the province, the Cavalcantis (de Albuquerque), who at one time owned a third of all the sugar plantations in the Zona da Mata, were not exclusively an agrarian noble house. Bahia and Pernambuco offer a contrast. Planters of gentry and aristocratic origins there did not practice interclass marriage as widely as their counterparts in São Paulo and Rio, but some Pernambucan planters branched out to urban economic ventures, which was not the case with the Bahian planter group.[83]

These regional differences underscore the distinction between the landed classes in the Northeast and Center-South on the one hand, and, on the other, between those in Bahia and Pernambuco. Wealth and patronage were used by the coffee fazendeiros to expand their social and political power in the provinces and then in the nation, and sugar barons viewed them as the inherent perquisites and privileges of their clansmen.

PART III

POWER AND PATRONAGE IN IMPERIAL BRAZIL

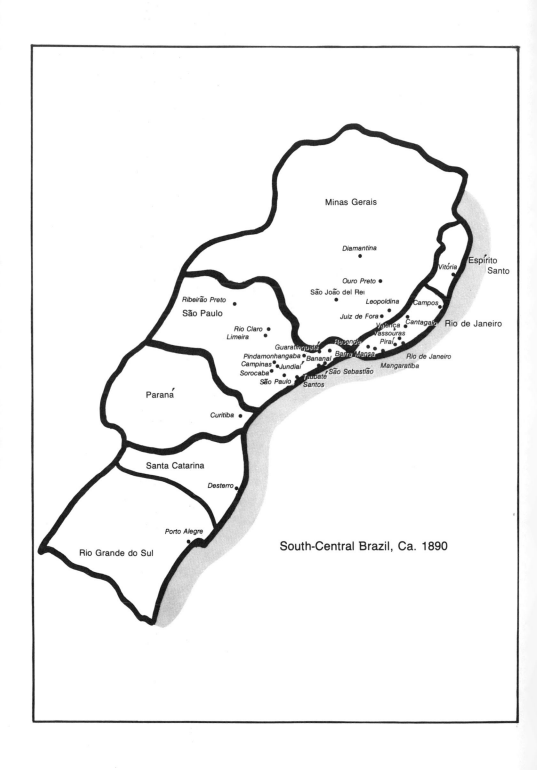

South-Central Brazil, Ca. 1890

7

The Sale of Imperial Honors and Titles

The commonest method of obtaining a peerage . . .
was payment to the Duke of Buckingham, his relatives,
or his followers. LAWRENCE STONE

I have never seen such a diarrhea of so many barons! A BAHIAN MERCHANT

Detractors of the nobility system, both foreign and Brazilian, often accused the Crown of selling titles and other honors. Walsh pointed to the "prostitution" of the titles. One Brazilian historian classified the nobility into two types. that of merit and that of money. José de Alencar likened this class to "a kind of paper money, fiduciary note, the value of which is in inversion to that of the metallic coin." Luís da Gama, a mulatto abolitionist and journalist, condemned the nobility in toto as a slavocracy. And an Argentine diplomat in Brazil observed that the group was a "caricature of aristocracy." According to a popular adage, "He who steals little is a thief *(ladrão),* but he who steals a lot is a baron *(barão).*"[1] How many of the 1,278 titles were actually sold by the Crown is beyond anyone's ken. However, the existing documents reveal that money not only was involved, but was also often a substantial factor in the politics of title awards. Prospective candidates often contributed *before and after* large sums of money to the state, the church, and charities of the imperial couple. Historians, however, have yet to find any evidence that the emperors were avaricious and profited personally by such a practice.

The minister of the empire was the official intermediary in regulating the flow of title concessions, but several personal friends of the emperors, most notably those who had ceremonial or staff roles in the Braganza court, often served as procurers of titles and other honors for their relatives and clients. Customarily, many of the aspiring noblemen hired a go-between to represent them in the court. Money was often turned over to the intermediary, who chose at his discretion whether to contribute to a charitable activity or a religious institution, or to make a direct payment to the state. Pedro I created 146 titles, or 11.4 percent, of the total, during his eight-year reign; and Pedro II ennobled 1,132, or 88.6 percent, during his forty-nine-year rule. In 1825 and 1826, the first two years of the Cisplatine War, the first emperor granted 104 titles. During the Paraguayan War, the second emperor awarded 169 titles between 1865 and 1871. None were issued during the years of the Regency (1831–40).[2] How many of the titles were the result of a monetary contribution cannot be calculated, though some cases can be documented.

Periodically, the minister of the empire instructed the provincial presidents to draw up a list of eligible candidates. One such list, organized in 1857 by the provincial president of Bahia, João Luís Cansanção de Sinimbu, a future nobleman and prime minister, allows a glimpse into the Crown's and the mandarins' decision making. A total of thirty-three names—no women appeared on the list—were selected by Sinimbu for imperial largesse. Only six were recommended for titles of nobility: five barões and one marquês. Antônio da Costa Pinto, described as a "rich planter and a member of a large and respected family in the county," was cited for his contribution to the quelling of the Sabinada Revolt, in November 1837, for which he had been rewarded with the honorary rank of lieutenant colonel in the army. Now, two decades later, he was listed as a candidate for the title of the Barão do Bom Jardim, the name both of his residence in Santo Amaro county and of one of his numerous plantations. Likewise, Francisco Vieira Tosta, "the commanding officer of the National Guard in Cachoeira, a well-to-do landowner, worthy father, and intelligent planter," was recommended for the title of the Barão de São Felix.[3] Not mentioned in the letter to the minister of the empire was that Tosta was a brother of a Bahian noble, the Marquês de Muritiba (Manuel Vieira Tosta), a senator of the empire. No close in-law or relative of Costa Pinto was a noble as of 1857. Joaquim Inácio de Araújo Aragão Bulcão, "brother of the Second Barão de São Francisco, a rich planter and former employee of the imperial legation in Paris," was on the list as the candidate for the baronate of Pitinga.

Two other agrarian elites were named for titles. Sancho de Bitencourt Berenguer César, "a retired colonel of the army, who had served in the War of Independence," was nominated for the Barão do Rio Fundo. The Berenguer Césars, among Santo Amaro's most elite inbred planter families, were as numerous as the Costa Pintos and the Calmons. The other planter, Luís Francisco Gonçalves Junqueira, "an owner of three big sugar plantations, a member of a large family, and a highly respected man," was recommended for the baronate of Paramirim.

In addition to these five wealthy planters, the archbishop of Bahia was nominated for the Marquês de Porto Seguro or Santa Cruz. Religious leaders were usually given the title of conde, but Sinimbu made an exception in the case of the Bahian bishop, who by papal investiture was also the Primate of the Brazilian Church.[4] The title of conde was particularly appropriate for Brazilian bishops, who were automatically made grandees of the empire by virtue of their offices. A grandee held the same status as a conde in court rituals and etiquette.

None of these six were successful in obtaining a title in 1857. In fact, no one from Bahia received an imperial title that year. The following year, the Primate of the Brazilian Church was made the Conde de Santa Cruz. The Barão de Itapicuru de Cima (Manuel de Oliveira Mendes) was elevated to the visconde in February 1858, and, in October, a Bahian-born admiral was honored with the title of the Visconde de Cabo Frio.[5] No planter, no merchant, and no politician from the province was ennobled.

Not until March 1860, some months after the imperial visit to Bahia by Pedro II and the empress in November 1859, were a host of Bahian planters and politicians, along with the archbishop, ennobled or elevated to higher honors. No merchant was so recognized. On the empress's birthday, March 14, twenty titles were either freshly created or passed out as promotions. Four nobles were named *veadores*; two baronesas were made *damas*. Santa Cruz was elevated to marquês, the highest title ever held by a religious elite; the Visconde de Passé, former diplomat and planter, was promoted to conde; two politician-nobles (Cotegipe and São Lourenço) of the Conservative party were given honors of grandees. Furthermore, eight new nobiliary titles were created.[6] None received the original names of the titles recommended in

1857. Costa Pinto became the Barão de Sergimirim; Francisco Vieira Tosta, the Barão de Nagé; Junqueira, the Barão de Jacuípe; and Bulcão, the Barão de Matuim. Costa Pinto would have preferred the Barão da Conceição de Bento Simões or Bom Jardim, the first being the family foro and the second the clan's redoubt.[7] Tosta would have welcomed imperial acquiescence in the name of São Felix, the clan stronghold. The scion of the Bulcão clan wanted to legitimize his lordship of Engenho Pitinga, thus completing the social conquest of São Francisco do Conde county, where the family was the elite of elites. Both his father and brother held nobiliary titles as the First and Second Barão do São Francisco. Similarly, Paramirim was the name of both a river and a plantation that the Junqueira family valued. No Berenguer César was ever ennobled.

The 1860 Bahian case was rather typical. In 1861 the provincial president of Rio recommended for imperial honors a number of citizens who had performed worthy service to the state. Antônio Xavier da Rocha, a rich coffee planter in São João do Príncipe, had paid for the repair of the main church in town as well as for other "beautification" projects, for which he claimed to have spent 50:000$. The provincial president amended the claim: according to the engineer in charge of the work, the cost was considerably lower, 30:000$. The planter was given no honors. On the other hand, five major planters in Valença spent more than 24:000$ to build a road that joined Valença and Vassouras: the Barão do Rio Preto (Domingos Custódio Guimarães) was eventually promoted to visconde; Manuel Jacinto Carneiro Nogueira da Gama years later became the Barão de Juparanã; Peregrino José de América Pinheiro was honored with the title of the Visconde de Ipiabas; and two planters did not receive a title.[8] Similarly, during the years of the Paraguayan War (1864–70), provincial president throughout the empire routinely reported on citizens who had contributed to the war effort, recommending them for titles or other honors. Often, the combination of substantial contributions in money and good political connections at court resulted in ennoblement. Money alone did not open the doors.

Historians have often accused José Clemente Pereira, a Portuguese-born imperial mandarin in the 1840s, of initiating the practice of "selling" imperial honors and titles to finance various social and public work projects, such as schools, hospitals, and asylums for which the state lacked sufficient funds.[9] If titles and honors were auctioned off and if this debased the value of titles, there was little sign that such a trade-off bothered the majority of Brazilians. In fact, titles and honorific commendations after 1850 were often de facto exchanges for money, well disguised in the name of charities, public contributions, and religious activities. During the second half of the nineteenth century, the three most frequently cited reasons for requesting nobiliary titles were monetary contribution to worthy causes, public service to the state, and charitable donations to the church and its pious works.

The sale of titles and lesser honors was not an outgrowth of corruption at the court. The deputies of the constituent assembly of 1823 debated the possibility of establishing a table of fixed prices for imperial titles and honors as a means of financing a national university. The chief proponent of this proposal was Antônio Gonçalves Gomide, deputy from Minas Gerais and later senator of the empire. As he saw the issue, the legislature could create titles and honors in conjunction with the executive branch. In short, the deputies did not perceive the exercise of granting titles and honorific commendations to be the prerogative of the emperor. Under the original scheme, a title of barão would have cost an astronomical 80:000$; Grão Cruz, 40:000$; Dignitário, 10:000$; Oficial, 8:000$; and Cavaleiro, 2:000$.[10] Besides these, an additional schedule fixed prices for titles transferred to sons and grandsons of nobles and fidalgos. While the debate was in progress, Pedro I ennobled a Scottish admiral (Lord Cochrane) as the Marquês do Maranhão, thus breaking his promise that he would not create any titles until the assembly dealt with the issue. The proposal to fix prices officially never became a reality, for in mid-November 1823 the emperor abruptly dissolved the assembly. Over time, titles and other honors carried different "prices," though not sanctioned by the legislature.

As early as the 1820s, even before independence, money played a key role in winning honors. Leading merchants at court, landowners with political connections, and loyalist mandarins were frequently showered with honors. But those on the periphery were also rewarded. One fazendeiro in Mato Grosso was given the honor of the Hábito da Ordem de Cristo in 1822; another landowner in Goiás in 1829 was recommended for a minor honor on account of his monetary contribution to the province.[11] By mid-century, the substantial sum of 10 contos (10:000$) was judged to be a bare minimum for the title of barão, a scant one-eighth of the price suggested by the 1823 assembly. Any sum

below 10 contos would usually net one of the minor honors, such as
Rosa, Cristo, or Cruzeiro. Elevation to visconde, a title of grandee, or
comenda da Rosa would cost 15 contos or more.[12] By the 1860s the two
most favored avenues for acquiring titles were direct donations to Dom
Pedro II Hospice for the Mentally Ill, in Rio, and contributions of
money and slaves to the Paraguayan War.

Hospício de Dom Pedro II, founded in 1846, was practically organized and operated by selling nobiliary titles and lesser honors, supple-
mented by periodic lotteries. Such a financing method, however
precarious it might seem, was common in Luso-Brazilian history,
where the Anglo-American type of private family-run philanthropy
failed to emerge. The hospice's *prevedor* (executive director) was the
Marquês de Abrantes (Miguel Calmon du Pin e Almeida), who during
the last years of his political career was minister of foreign affairs,
minister of finance, and even interim prime minister in the Olinda
Cabinet of May 1862–January 1864. As chief fund-raiser for Hospício de
Dom Pedro II, he had recommended scores of people for titles and honors. Without question, he was the most efficient power broker for nobiliary titles and honors during the life of the empire.

Abrantes always made personal evaluations of the character and family fitness of the candidate under consideration. He passed on both the
receipt of a monetary contribution or a promissory note along with his
letter to proper authorities. In one letter dated 18 December 1860, he
informed the minister of the empire that the hospice had received
three contributions and made appropriate recommendations according
to their size: Antônio Pereira dos Passos, a planter and capitalist in São
João do Príncipe and Mangaratiba, offered 15:000$ to the hospice, for
which he sought the title of barão; João Rodrigues Barbosa and Luís
Antônio da Costa e Sousa, a planter in Piauí and a cattle rancher in Rio
Grande do Sul, respectively, each donated 4:000$ and each was recom-
mended for a Comenda de Cristo, not nobility titles. For Passos,
Abrantes added his personal observation that the candidate was of
"good character" and that the other two candidates from the periphery
were not enthusiastically endorsed, but were acceptable according to
the prevailing standards for imperial honors.[13] Passos became the
Barão de Mangaratiba on 28 December 1860, ten days after Abrantes
wrote to the minister of the empire; and on December 27, the central

administration of Hospício de Dom Pedro II received the "voluntary donation."

The case of the Barão de Mangaratiba was not unique. Dona Francisca de Assis Viana Moniz Bandeira was the widow of a wealthy fazendeiro in Santo Amaro, Bahia. The clan, a nineteenth-century creation of the agrarian family of Viana and the mercantile family of Bandeira, equaled the Calmons and the Costa Pintos in prestige. The lady of the house donated 10 contos to the mental hospital in Rio in 1872. Six months later, she was ennobled as the Baronesa de Alenquer in an imperial decree specifically mentioning the charitable donation.[14] The Barão de Turvo (José Gomes de Sousa Portugal) was an important coffee planter in São João do Príncipe and Barra Mansa, two mid-century coffee producers in Rio province, where he had served as alderman, provincial deputy, and National Guard officer. He chose the legalist side in the Liberal Revolt of 1842 and became the commandant of National Guard units in several key counties in the Paraíba Valley. Abrantes, who wrote an endorsing letter to the minister of the empire, specifically mentioned that, in addition to these political and military services during the last two decades, the nominee gave 10:000$ to the hospice. The letter was dated in July; the title was issued 1 August 1860.[15] Mangaratiba, Alenquer, and Turvo were hardly of aristocratic origin, coming rather from well-to-do novo rico gentry; money was undoubtedly the operative factor in these and similar cases.

On 29 April 1862, a bare month before he was to become minister of foreign affairs, Abrantes presented the lengthiest list to date of contributors to the hospital for the minister of the empire to consider for titles. This letter, more than any other document, confirms beyond doubt that titles and imperial honors often carried fixed price tags, if not sanctioned by the Crown, then in the minds of Abrantes, officials of the Ministry of the Empire, the Crown lawyer (procurador da coroa), and, certainly, prospective candidates: 10:000$ for barão, 6:000$ for Ordem da Rosa, 4:000$ for Ordem de Cristo, and 1:000$ for Hábito da Rosa. (In 1862 a healthy slave in Rio cost close to 1:000$.) When Manuel Nunes da Cunha, of Poconé, and Joaquim José Gomes da Silva, of Albuquerque, both in Mato Grosso, promised cash donations to the hospital, they were told that such gifts would enhance their chances. Cunha paid the customary 10 contos and was made the Barão de Poconé. Silva's case was different. Abrantes observed that this candidate had built a road linking his fazenda and Corumbá; such service alone would not have earned him a title because many planters throughout the country often built their own roads to facilitate exports. When Silva promised to contribute 15:000$, a title was offered: the Barão de Vila Maria. The fazendeiro paid this amount on June 18, and the title was granted three days later.[16]

In contrast, the Barão de Curvelo (Joaquim José de Meireles Freire) serves as a misapplied case. A local bigwig in Sabará, Minas Gerais, he served as alderman and president of the municipal council. In 1849 he gave 4:000$ to the hospício but failed to obtain a title; two years later, he donated 11:000$ and was ennobled as the Barão de Curvelo. For a later series of small donations in Sabará, he asked for the honors of grandee in June 1864. He was turned down. Persistent, he made a 20:000$ donation to the imperial government to be used for the Anglo-Brazilian diplomatic conflict, adding another 2:000$ as a sign of patriotism when the Paraguayan War broke out. For five years, he pursued his goal without success; on a second request, in October 1870, the Crown granted his wish. Curvelo was lucky. A Brazilian with a Portuguese title who donated a total of 12:000$ to the mental hospital was usually neither able to "Brazilianize" his title nor given the honors of grandee, but the two lesser honors of Rosa and Cristo.[17]

Donations to the hospice were not the only avenue to nobility. Direct donations (still 10 contos or more) to the provincial government and the imperial government in the name of public education, war efforts, and other favorite charities of the Crown often resulted in ennoblement of the donors. The Barão de Aracaju (José Inácio Acióli do Prado), of Sergipe, the Barão de Butuí (José Antônio Moreira), of Portugal, the Barão de Gurjaú (José de Sousa Leão), of Pernambuco, and many others donated 10:000$ for school-building funds in their respective provinces.[18] Still others used a more direct approach. Sugar planter Antônio Alves da Silva, of Pernambuco, deposited 12:000$ in the Recife branch of the London and Brazilian Bank for state expenses, so informing the minister of the empire; Joaquim Marinho de Queirós, of Rio province, gave 10:000$ to the imperial treasury "to be used for State urgent matters."[19] Both received titles of nobility: the former the Barão de Amaragi and the latter the Barão de Monte Belo.

Contributing money to the Paraguayan War or to religious charities, freeing slaves, and supporting public works projects were other avenues to the winning of nobiliary titles. The municipal council of Diamantina, Minas Gerais, submitted the name of Antônio Moreira da Costa as a nominee for a title of barão. Fazendeiro and merchant in Diamantina, he was said to have founded a hospital and maintained it at his own expense; additionally, his regular assistance to the poor was a well-known samaritan gesture. The council's recommendation impressed the imperial authorities so much that he was ennobled as the Barão do Paraúna.[20] In Piraí, a key coffee-growing município in Rio province, coffee planter Joaquim José Ferraz de Oliveira spent more than 30:000$ to build a road and clear a canal; furthermore, he contributed generously during a cholera epidemic. He was made the Barão do Guapi.[21] During his tenure as president of the Recife municipal council, Francisco Antônio de Oliveira established a cemetery; built a town water-supply system *(água portável)* as well as the Recife Public Theater; and constructed other public works. Because the city's yellow-fever victims were buried in the cemetery, Recife and probably the whole province avoided the unpleasant consequences of poor public health conditions. Barely two months before he was made the president of the council of ministers, the Visconde de Paraná wrote a highly supportive letter to the minister of the empire pointing out that the candidate was a worthy citizen, "friend of the order, always dedicated to the Government and to the institutions of the land."[22] Comendador Oliveira was made the Barão de Beberibe in December 1853, some months after Paraná became the prime minister. Significantly, no cash contribution to the state was involved in either of these cases. Similar recognition was given the Barão de Capanema (Guilherme Schüch de Capanema), who was honored with the Ordem da Rosa in 1860 for supervising the construction of telegraphic lines and with a baronate in 1882 for his work as director of the imperial telegraphic service—some two decades after he had requested a title.[23]

How many people contributed money, slaves, and special services to the empire's war effort between 1865 and 1870 is not known, though records of individual donations are plentiful. Pedro Ramos Nogueira, a coffee planter in Bananal, São Paulo, gave 10:000$ for the war; seven years later, the grateful empire made him the Barão de Joatinga.[24] Father and son of the Costa Pinto clan, of Bahia, donated 10:000$ each to the war chest; the son, Antônio, was made the Barão da Oliveira in 1866; the father, the Barão de Sergimirim, was not promoted to visconde until 1871, after the war.[25] Numerous other citizens donated their valuables for titles and lesser imperial honors: Vicente de Sousa Queirós, for example, was made the Barão de Limeira, and the Second Barão de Lorena (Estêvão Ribeiro de Resende) was granted the honors of grandee. Both planters had freed six slaves each.[26] The tradition of ennoblement for manumitting slaves continued. In 1884 at least four titles were created for this humanitarian act: the Barão de Três Serros (Anibal Antunes Maciel) freed fifty-eight slaves; the Barão de Arroio Grande (Francisco Antunes Gomes da Costa), sixty-four; the Barão de Correntes (Felisberto Inácio da Cunha), fifty-six or fifty-eight; and the Barão de São Luís (Leopoldo Antunes Maciel) freed seventy-two slaves and gave 12:000$ to the state.[27] Francisco Bonifácio de Abreu, a physician, was made the Barão da Vila da Barra for his services during the war; similarly, another physician, Antônio Cândido Antunes de Oliveira, was made the Barão de Macejana for his work in 1867 and was promoted to visconde after having contributed to a school-construction fund in 1885.[28] A financier-banker, Manuel Antônio da Rocha Faria, was given the title of the Barão de Nioac for having lent the government "significant amounts of money, without interest," for the war effort in Montevideo.[29]

A careful examination of random samples of numerous petitions indicates that the "sale" of titles and honors was most pervasive at the barão level; a few elevations to visconde were also decided on the basis of monetary contributions. Almost certainly higher titles, such as conde, marquês, and duque, called for other requisites, thus becoming status symbols that remained beyond the reach of country bumpkins and gentry. It would be too simplistic to argue that Brazilian titles were freely sold and bought; rather, the Crown condoned such practices during economic crises, war times, and periods of droughts as a means of financing worthy public projects, social welfare charities, and religious as well as educational works. The existing evidence overwhelmingly suggests that, though money was not the sole consideration, it was the major factor.

The cases of near or complete rejection of requests for titles offer a fascinating account of the social history of the nobility. Such a history reflects both the basic tenet of one-life limitation of nobiliary privileges, firmly grounded in the Thomistic philosophy of individual virtues, as well as the persistence with which some candidates pursued membership in the nobiliary corporation. Ennoblement meant access to the world of the imperial elite system. A case in point was that of Felisberto de Oliveira Freire. Although he was one of the richest men in the province of Sergipe, his past was controversial. As the lord of Laranjeira county, he hired two intermediaries (a general deputy and a Rio merchant who had connections at the court) to obtain a title of barão. Having initially spent 22:000$ for religious institutions in the province and advanced an additional 25:000$ as a loan to the provincial government at 8 percent interest per annum, he felt he surely deserved a title. After years of waiting, the irate applicant undiplomatically pointed out that he knew at least two men who were ennobled even before they had donated money to imperial charities. More importantly, he stressed in his letter to the imperial government, they had given less than he had. The deputy-intermediary wrote to Joao Alfredo (minister of the empire) that Freire was ready to give more to any religious institution "that you designate with the amount of contribution that you specify." The imperial government advised that Freire should donate to an educational building fund. The eager candidate extravagantly gave 16:000$. Upon the state's receipt of the donation, he received his title, the Barão de Laranjeiras.

But Freire's travail did not end there. Imperial authorities had been aware, some time before the ennoblement, that he had committed at least one murder in his backwoods fief; a forgiving jury had found him not guilty. A full year after the title was bestowed, anonymous enemies sought to abrogate his imperial honor in a note accusing the "nobleman" of the crime. The Ministry of the Empire ordered the provincial president to forward all pertinent police and judicial papers to Rio. They showed that, some sixteen years before, Freire was alleged to have ordered the murder of his mistress, "publicly being dragged by his goons, being tied to a tree, and ordered to be shot on the same day." For five years, Freire had eluded prosecution, finally submitting to a jury trial in Laranjeiras, where he had become the political boss and economic czar. The jury had acquitted him. The accusing letter had further stated that the intermediary who negotiated a title for Freire had pocketed six to eight of the sixteen contos that the candidate had donated to the imperial government. This unsigned note was obviously dismissed by prudent imperial authorities as a prank. In the end, Freire was allowed to keep the title.[30]

Not everyone fared as well as the Barão de Laranjeiras. In some cases, money was spent in vain. Antônio Homens de Loureiro Siqueira, of Pará, freed twenty-six slaves and donated 10:000$ worth of building materials, but was turned down for a title; Domingos Teixeira de Carvalho, of Minas Gerais, contributed 26:000$ in cash for school- and church-building funds, but no title was given. Goian merchant Antônio Pereira de Abreu not only donated cash (13:936$) and food to the veterans of the Paraguayan War and their families, but the Goian authorities claimed he had also loaned the state 34:000$ without interest to finance the campaign in southern Mato Grosso against the Paraguayan forces. In spite of these "services," the Crown stoutly ignored the recommendation of the provincial authorities: no title was ever granted.[31] More candidates from peripheral provinces were turned down than those from the "core" provinces, possibly because they lacked good connections at the court or were unable to document their lineage, preferably going back to the previous century as well as to Portugal. Thus, a rich cattle rancher in Formosa, Goiás, whose pedigree was obscure, was rejected for a title though he contributed to the Paraguayan War and gave 10:000$ worth of properties to a local school.[32] Possibly, the imperial government also judged the contribution and donation to be overvalued because Formosa was the heartland of the backwoods. Another Goiano, who spent his life improving the navigability of the Tocantins River, which opened north to Pará, was turned down for a title, despite his invaluable service and even a moderate cash contribution to the local government.[33] The record shows that he failed to document his claim to good lineage.

Equally rejectable and often rejected were claims by middle-echelon officials in the outer rim of the empire. Too poor to make substantial cash donations to charities and too nondescript in their pedigrees, many minor officials claimed that their achievements amounted to charitable activity. The former secretary of the provincial government of Ceará contended that, during the Great Drought of 1877–79, he was instrumental in raising some 34:000$ to feed the victims; another official informed the imperial government that he had raised 111:245$800 in relief funds; and a retired army colonel argued that he was responsible for building roads that radiated from the capital of Minas Gerais to the interior in the 1820s and 1830s, a critical period in the consolidation of the empire. Requests for titles from these three men were turned down by unimpressed imperial authorities, presumably on the ground that their services were integral to their official duties, for which they had been paid in salaries and perquisites.[34] Nevertheless, major middle-echelon functionaries in ministries and parliament, both institutions at the "core" of the empire, were frequently ennobled, strongly suggesting that the right political connections at the court and in the power arena were a crucial factor.

The example of a naturalized Portuguese lawyer in Belém, Pará, offers an enlightening contrast among reasons for rejection by the Crown. Alvaro Pinto de Pontes e Sousa was a practicing attorney in the capital of Pará province, a major port of entry to the Amazon region and trading entrepôt with Europe and the United States. Married to a Brazilian, he resided in Brazil for more than sixty years. In 1835 he was wounded in the Cabanos Revolt as an officer of the loyalist army, lost his fazenda in the Marajós Island in a retaliation by the rebels, and continued to support imperialism. Petitioning for a title in 1851, he was rejected. Years later, according to his own testimony, he was considered for a title of barão or "conselheiro" by João Alfredo, but the lawyer politely declined the honor. In spite of the official judgment of the Procurador da Coroa that "he practice[d] the profession of lawyer, is married to a Brazilian . . . , is a man of clean birth *(homem de nascimento limpo)* and friend of the public order," the supplicant was denied a title. In 1889, in his seventy-ninth year, the indefatigable Pontes e Sousa wrote to the Conde d'Eu, husband of the imperial regent, Princess Isabel, renewing his claim that he be given a title of the Visconde de Belém. Aware of the imperial reluctance in granting the viscondado in the first instance, he argued that his days were short and that he would like to die in Brazil a noble. He reminded the French-born consort of the Brazilian heiress to the Bragantine throne that his son had fought with the conde in the Paraguayan War. Still, no title was given, in spite of some four decades of persistent effort.

The case of the Belém lawyer suggests that the Crown often looked into the question of lineage. In particular, the presence of impure elements, often meaning African blood, was frowned upon. But at least two politicians of national reputation, both from Bahia, were mulattoes: Cotegipe and Jequitinhonha. Crown officials, although circumspect about these things, nevertheless insisted on evidence of physical and moral purity. The cases of Cotegipe and Jequitinhonha, as well as probably scores of other imperial mandarins with African blood, though considered exceptions, clearly indicate that the empire did not always view race as a factor in honoring the deserved and moneyed.

Neither were imperial officials always consistent in assessing questions of morality. Customarily, the Crown granted honors to clergy; for instance, one priest in Pernambuco requested and obtained the title of "Canon of the Imperial Chapel" on the basis of his longtime service to the church.[35] In accordance with such customs, another priest, this one in Juqueri, São Paulo, petitioned for the honors of cavaleiro da Ordem de Cristo on the ground that he had served God and the state for more than thirty years. The provincial president, without giving his reasons, recommended the lower grade of hábito. The priest's request was rejected. Three years later, he renewed his petition, this time for hábito, "imploring Your Imperial Majesty to reward me for so many services performed by the supplicant." Under normal circumstances, such a modest request would have been routinely honored. But this was not a normal case. The Bishop of São Paulo, Dom Antônio Joaquim de Melo, filed a separate confidential report with the minister of the empire accusing the priest of "having lived with a mistress" (era concubinado) and only a short time before having dismissed her, presumably to strengthen his claim for the imperial honor. The bishop did not oppose the imperial favor if forthcoming, but also did not recommend it.[36] Likely, the priest's moral turpitude was the basis for his rejection.

Similarly, a Bahian planter's request for a title was not immediately honored for reasons of morality. Having lived with a harem of slaves and never formally marrying any of them, he pursued the peculiar custom of manumitting his slave mistresses only when presented with a son. For whatever the reason and after a series of rejections, he finally succeeded in acquiring a title in his nineties, the oldest man in the empire to be ennobled. Living a year and six days as a noble, he died in June 1867.[37] Such cases represent only a few among numerous similar petitions, evidence that both the physical and moral character of men and women played a significant "other" role in imperial decisions.

Well-known politicians, favorite courtiers of the imperial house, and venerable aristocratic clans fared very well in obtaining titles and other honors not only for themselves, but also for their heirs, in-laws, relatives, and close friends. The facile acquisition of all sorts of honors by the established political, economic, and social elite reflected the intention of the empire to reinforce its power base among the territorial titled clans, loyalist politicians, and regalist courtiers. Francisco de Paula Sousa Leão, colonel in the National Guard in Olinda, Pernambuco, was one of several Sousa Leãos who received imperial patronage. He fought on the legalist side in the Praieira Revolt in 1848 and was awarded the Ordem da Rosa. The sons and nephews of the Barão de Moreno (Antônio de Sousa Leão) were made fidalgos da Casa Imperial in deference to the clan.[38] In contrast to the Cavalcantis, who were among the chief opponents in the Revolution of 1817 against Bragantine imperialism, the Sousa Leãos staunchly supported the empire. The decree that created the title of Moreno explicitly made mention of "the constant proofs of fidelity to the cause of the Empire and to My Person."[39]

Yet, not every supplicant from the distinguished Sousa Leão clan was successful. Antônio de Paula de Sousa Leão, the lord of Engenho Matas, in Cabo, and fidalgo cavaleiro of the imperial house, requested a title of barão in 1857 on the ground that he had contributed to the imperial cause in the 1848 revolt. Yet, the sugar planter had no tangible political service to his credit, according to the reviewing Crown officials. His request in the end was politely turned down. Both Francisco de Paula and Antônio de Paula lacked the regional political prestige and leadership that should have accompanied their social and economic wealth. Here was a case when good names alone could not win imperial nobiliary titles. Furthermore, the general political and social trend was to obliterate the partisan lines that had inflamed regional revolts during the 1830s and 1840s. In the days of the "politics of conciliation," the Crown was more prudent about showing its partisan colors in granting titles and patronage.

In Bahia, a similar claim to a title by an Albuquerque on the basis of his good family pedigree and political partisanism was also rejected. The primogenitor of the Barão de Jaguaripe sought imperial authorization to inherit the title of his deceased father. Seconding the claim, the provincial president of Bahia added that the sole bases for the petition were the father's services to the state and the family name. It was the very family that produced the first Brazilian nobiliary title after independence, Garcia d'Ávila, a name that figured prominently among the empire's most aristocratic clans. The files of the petitioner did not contain a satisfactory explanation for the rejection.[40] However, it is plausible that the ministries of the "politics of conciliation" discouraged any overt show of partisanism by the Crown that could provoke another wave of regional opposition: the concession of a title in such a case could be construed as incendiary to partisan passion. Sinimbu, the provincial president of Bahia, pointedly excluded the name of this Albuquerque in the 1857 list for imperial titles and honors.[41] In a subtle way, politics had become a key guidepost in the creation of titles and imperial honors, a powerful and compensatory means of patronage.

Especially during the second half of the century, the imperial award of honors and titles reflected a gradual politicization or ponderous consideration of partisan views. A strong recommendation from politicians of national reputation considerably strengthened petitioners' chances. Both the Barão do Rio Bonito and the Conde de Baependi, powerful Fluminense politicians at mid-century and members of the premier planter families in the empire, recommended a minor honor for a second son of the Barão de Piraí, one of the richest coffee fazendeiros in the Paraíba Valley. It was granted. Two sons of the Visconde de Maranguape (Caetano Maria Lopes Gama), one of the Conservative party bosses in Pernambuco and a member of the Second Council of State, were made moços fidalgos of the imperial house with the endorsement of the Barão de Vila Bela (Domingos de Sousa Leão) and the future Visconde de Bom Retiro (Luís Pedreira do Couto Ferraz). Ten-year-old Francisco Nicolau de Lima Nogueira da Gama, a grandson of the Duque de Caxias (on his mother's side) and the Marquês de Baependi (on his father's side), was made a moço fidalgo. On a lesser scale, two sons of the Visconde de Jequitinhonha were made fidalgos cavaleiros upon the recommendation of Bom Retiro.[42]

These are only a few of the salient examples which reinforce the hypothesis that political influence in the second half of the nineteenth century came to play a role as indispensable as that of money in the imperial award of titles and patronage. Perhaps the supreme irony was that widows of major politicians were offered titles. Women could neither vote nor hold office, yet, in honor of their political husbands, they were drawn into the partisan exercise of creating titles. Many rejected the offer, as in the case of the daughter of José Bonifácio and the widow of his brother. The widow of the man whom historians have accused of initiating the sale of titles, José Clemente Pereira, was ennobled as the Condessa da Piedade (literally, "Piety"), a fittingly hypocritical misnomer.

Good names, wealth, and political cronyism were no match for courtier brokering when it came to extracting imperial patronage. The imperial couples and their families were surrounded by a coterie of titled and untitled staff, from chamberlains and ladies-in-waiting to cooks and coachmen. The Marquesa de Santos, mistress of Pedro I and lady-in-waiting to the first empress Leopoldina, and Chalaça (Francisco Gomes da Silva), a Brazilian Falstaff and all-purpose confidant to the first emperor, practically regulated the flow of imperial favors. During the Second Reign, José Clemente, Abrantes, Carapebus, Bom Retiro, Baependi (the son), and João Alfredo, to cite the best-known court mandarins, played key intermediary roles in the imperial concession of titles and favors.

But, among the courtier staff, no one rivaled Antônio Dias Coelho Neto dos Reis, the future Conde de Carapebus, when it came to the question of access to the imperial chamber. As early as the mid-1850s, he worked as an effective go-between. A rich sugar planter from Campos, he was educated in Coimbra, lived in France, and dabbled in court social life for more than four decades; however, he never held a political office beyond the provincial level. Urbane, cultured, and polyglot, he was a favorite member of the imperial entourage in soirees and trips. From 1866 to 1889 he was the favorite chamberlain of Pedro II. As such, Carapebus exercised enormous influence and power over the imperial couple, virtually regulating the traffic in titles, honors, office appointments, and other patronage distribution during the last decades of the empire.[43] He knew the "ins" and "outs" of court life, key mandarins, and most importantly, Pedro II and Empress Teresa, whose trust in him was nearly absolute.

Married to a daughter of the Conde de Baependi (Brás Carneiro Nogueira da Costa e Gama), of Valença, Carapebus was a great-grandson-in-law of the dowager courtier the Baronesa de São Salvador de Campos. Related to Caxias through the Nogueira da Gamas, he was also a cousin of the Carneiro da Silva clan, of Macaé-Quissamã, the pioneer in sugar-refinery construction in the empire (see chapter 3). Using such family and political connections, Carapebus could have succeeded in any of several careers that upper-class gentlemen might choose: diplomat or politician, enterprising planter, or international trader and banker. Yet, he preferred the easygoing life-style of the imperial court.

A recognized broker in matters of court connections and influence,

Carapebus was easily accessible to planters, merchants, and other fa-
vor-seekers of both foreign and Brazilian origin. For the right price, he
was available. A Bahian sugar planter, Francisco Moreira de Carvalho
(the future Conde de Subaé), had been a fellow student of Carapebus in
Coimbra, where they had become intimate friends. In 1856 Carvalho
asked his friend to acquire for him a minor honor, probably Ordem da
Rosa, a first step toward eventual ennoblement. The intermediary reported that his father-in-law (Baependi) talked to "Conselheiro Pedreira [Bom Retiro] about the request," and was told that "the price for
these things has gone up: 3:000$ for Oficial da Rosa, 5:000$ for Comenda de Cristo, 6:000$ for Comenda da Rosa, only for those who had
a claim for some services, and 7:000$ for all other citizens."[44] In view
of the inflation in price of honors and titles, Carapebus advised his Bahian friend that he should send to Rio another 1:000$ (thus a total of
6:000$), plus 500$ to take out the certificate. A month later, Carapebus acknowledged the receipt of 1:500$ from the planter. Some eight
years later, Subaé again asked Carapebus to intercede with the Crown,
this time for a title of barão. The courtier replied: "Your aspirations
can be fulfilled if you were disposed to give 15:000$ for the title of
barão (without the honors of grandee)."[45] The planter willingly paid and
was made the Barão de Subaé. It is fair to speculate that there were
hundreds of Subaés throughout the empire, especially affluent coffee
planters in the Paraíba Valley of Rio and São Paulo provinces.

The Carapebus clan was highly conscious of their rightful place in
court society. The children added Carapebus to their names first, using
the title later as the official family surname. José Inácio Neto dos Reis
de Carapebus, a mining engineer who had studied in France, was a son
of Carapebus. In 1885 the young man inherited six slaves from his maternal grandfather and freed them without onus. His proud grandfather, the Conde de Baependi (president of the imperial senate), wrote
to the minister of the empire of the virtuous act, almost casually pointing out that the manumission of slaves was always deemed "relevant
services to the State" by the imperial government, and called for making the young Carapebus an Oficial da Ordem da Rosa; he had been
decorated already by Portugal as Oficial da Ordem de São Tiago and
Hábito de Cristo.[46] When it came to court and political connections,
this young man surpassed them all.

While the Visconde de Carapebus (elevated to conde in 1888) worked "inside" the palace on matters of patronage, the future Visconde de Ourém (José Carlos de Almeida Areias), a lawyer and frequent lobbyist for foreign interests in Brazil, was an "outside" man. In March 1889 Ourém gave three names to Carapebus for possible imperial honors, asking him to see the empress on this matter;[47] a few days later, the conde reported to Ourém that the letter had been hand-delivered to the emperor, but added that "the emperor is becoming difficult and wanting to shut down the treasure chest of titles *(cofre das graças)*."[48] On another occasion, Carapebus boldly suggested to Ourém that "you could render here relevant services as a Councillor of State," as if such an appointment could be arranged with ease.[49] The letters exchanged between Carapebus and Ourém did not mention money, as in the case of Subaé, but it is difficult to discount altogether the possibility that a cash donation was involved. Europeans whom Ourém recommended for Brazilian honors were associated with either economic interests in Brazil or the social elite in their respective countries. The influence of the chamberlain was well attested to by the final elevation of Ourém to a visconde in July 1889. Carapebus reported proudly to his client that he had succeeded where João Alfredo (the Conservative prime minister in 1888–89) had failed.[50]

In brief, Carapebus during the last days of the empire reached the apex of power and influence in court politics, superseding even such mandarins as prime ministers, councillors of state, and senators. The existing documents in the Ourém papers make it clear that the concession not only of imperial titles and honors but also of governmental favors on such public works as dock construction in the port of Salvador, Bahia, and the financial problems of the Santos-Jundiaí Railway often involved the imperial chamberlain and palace staff if the desired results were to be achieved.[51] In addition to Carapebus and Ourém, such courtier staff as the Visconde de Fonseca Costa, also a chamberlain, his wife, the viscondessa, a lady-in-waiting, and the Conde de Mota Maia, the palace physician, exercised enormous influence over the imperial couple.[52] In the anteroom of São Cristóvão or in the hallway of the imperial palace in Petrópolis, the emperor and the empress were often talked into granting honors and patronage. Even affairs of state were resolved in such private meetings between chief ministers and the emperor, not in the more formal setting of imperial cabinet meetings.

In summary, several major characteristics of the Brazilian nobility distinguished it as a social system. Both Pedro I and Pedro II made a conscious effort to build a nobiliary class into a corporate entity that would serve as a buffer and a conduit between the House of Braganza and the powerful regional groups of agrarian and mercantile interests on the periphery. In fact, the first emperor incorporated in the penultimate draft of the Constitution of 1824 a hereditary nobility class, then dropped the idea. Integration, harmony, and uniformity served as the tripod of the imperial political system and its faithful mandarins. The creation of a rival class, such as an independent nobility, could threaten the viability of the Braganza monarchy. The ennoblement of the first-born of the major agrarian nobles, such as the Vianas and Albuquerques, of Bahia, the Pais Barretos and the Cavalcantis, of Pernambuco, the Nogueira da Gamas, in Rio and Minas Gerais, and the Maciel da Costas, of Minas and Bahia, seemed to suggest that the Bragantine crown was committed to strengthening the agrarian basis for the nobility. Yet, during the decades of the 1850s and 1860s, the Crown showed little willingness to grant titles and names preferred by the candidates, as if the imperial concern to thwart moves for the dynastic entrenchment by the powerful regional clans on the periphery overrode the need to establish a regalist corporate class. The political turmoil during the Regency years and a decade later clearly hardened the suspicious attitude of the Crown and its mandarins toward the territorial potentates.

Therefore, the emergence of two sets of nobility—political and economic—seemed inevitable under a monarchy that was a partially bureaucratized and differentiated system. The politico-administrative structure called for a cadre of well-trained legal and clerical personnel over whom the Crown could exercise complete control. This system of bureaucracy led to the creation of mandarins whose ranks were filled by persons of merit, good birth, or both; and the social hierarchy consisted of the territorial economic elite, such as latifundiary planters and ranchers and export-economy-related merchants and financiers. The system thus reinforced the emergence and formation of both an economic nobility and a political nobility growing in separate spheres of the imperial society and polity. Although tangentially related, these two groups often functioned autonomously, possessing two distinctly different world views and yet serving as twin linchpins of the imperial system at large.

Both the political and the economic nobilities reflected the diverse geopolitical and socioeconomic composition of the empire, though the mandarins had been removed from their home provinces to serve at the court or peripheral outposts and the economic nobility remained in its own region, where its hegemony was firmly established. Once uprooted and cut adrift from clan and economic ties, the mandarin nobles became dependent patrimonial servants of the Braganza Crown. As the holders of such sinecures as senators, councillors of state, and high court judges, it was neither possible nor practical for them to foster and retain dependent linkages with regional clans. To complement this system, the nobility functioned on a different level as a cushion between the regional agrarian clans (and interests, if they were articulated) and the imperial government to facilitate both political and social communication, to win patronage and concessions, and to uphold the hegemony of the empire system. To this end, the two nobility systems intermeshed and worked together, so long as political and social tensions between the House of Braganza and the agrarian interests as well as among rival economic regions could be contained.

Unlike the mandarins, many of whom were ennobled during the maturity of their careers, the Brazilian economic nobility exhibited a serious structural flaw. Although recruited from peripheral elites, the noble landowners and merchants lacked a national cohesion; their unified actions would have contributed to the integration of the monarchy on another level. Instead, they remained fragmented. The lack of interregional unions (both marital and business) could be satisfied by the rise of several regionalized export-economy systems, which in turn stymied the integration of the class. Few of the regional agrarian nobles married outside their clan, much less outside their peripheral zone. The absence of extraregional bonds therefore strengthened the barriers between the fossilized export economies, which in turn could account for the late rise of national entrepreneurial activities. Some children of political nobles—mandarins—married heirs of economic nobles outside their region, but these were few. Olinda's daughter married a well-off Rio planter.[53] Monte Alegre, a Bahian mandarin, wedded a rich Paulista; the Visconde de Cavalcanti, of Rio Grande do Norte, married a niece of a rich Mineiro merchant and industrialist; a Sousa Dantas, of

Bahia, wedded an heiress of the Clemente Pinto fortune, of Cantagalo, and so forth. Such marriages between the political elite of one region and the economic overlords of another usually took place in the imperial court, to which the mandarins were removed from their home provinces and where, in many cases, they settled permanently.[54]

The consequence of such economic parochialization among the agrarian and mercantile nobility and of the formation of a political nobility was the duality of the Brazilian elite system. The economic nobility confined its power to provincial turfs: ranches, plantations, commerce, banking, regional railroads, municipal councils, and provincial legislatures. The political nobility, on the other hand, relatively successful in forging national alliances—parties, coalitions, and so forth—were economically powerless and totally dependent on imperial patronage and favors. It can be hypothesized that the dual structure impeded one sector from dominating the other. The economic nobles failed to establish a firm grip on the locus of imperial power. Conversely, the political elite (the Crown and the mandarins) exercised little domination over the regional lords of capitalist agriculture. Because of the technological requirements of the country's modernization during the second half of the nineteenth century, the demands and counterdemands of various regional agricultural groups for governmental favors, subsidies, and subventions increased. In view of the prevailing duality of the nobilities, the mandarins and the Crown were unable to synchronize policymaking and resource allocations to meet the exigencies of the regional economic elites. When this happened, the legitimacy of the mandarinate ceased to exist and so did the monarchy system.

Despite the peculiar nature of the nobility as a corporation, the trepidations of a throne occupied by a prematurely aging as well as diabetic emperor, and the escalating political crises aggravated by the problems of slavery and financial woes, imperial honors and titles remained popular in certain quarters. "Services to the State and Humanity" continued to be the manifest criterion, but it was considerably broadened in scope for political persons. Money contributions to public education, religious organizations, and other favorite charities sanctioned by the Crown still remained effective. In fact, Carapebus gave his good Bahian friend Subaé a surprise gift: a title of comendador.[55] Had the custom of buying honors and titles not remained pervasive, such an unsolicited gift would have had no value and less political meaning for such a palace influence-peddler as Carapebus! By the mid-1880s, when the agrarian foundations of the empire had begun to undergo rapid changes and the popularity of the imperial family plummeted, the panicky ministries of João Alfredo and Ouro Preto sought to prop up their personal prestige and political clout with a mass distribution of titles, especially to former slavocrats. One Bahian comissário bitterly complained:

> I have never seen such a diarrhea of so many barons! The Conservatives used to say that the Lafayette ministry gave the lieutenant colonelcy of the National Guard to anyone who could pay for the commission paper, and now João Alfredo has created barons, about whom the same thing can be said, and such nominations already provide only laughs, while it prompted the *Jornal de Noticias* to question the purpose of the nobility titles.[56]

Egas Moniz Barreto de Aragão, a Bahian planter and entrepreneur of immigration, first asked Cotegipe to intercede with the government for a title: the Barão de Paraguaçu with the honors of grandee.[57] The title the Crown granted was the Barão de Moniz de Aragão. In 1887 the new baron complained loudly that he had lost 186:000$ in an ill-fated colonization scheme, plus another 30:000$ for the church project in Mataripe. Wasn't this sacrifice enough to earn the original title of Paraguaçu, which his uncle held? He further mentioned that one key palace official had told him that, because he had paid only half the going price, the original title was not given.[58] Moniz de Aragão did not ask Cotegipe the whereabouts of the other half of the cash contribution, however. The monetary and social value of titles toward the end of the monarchy was slowly being debased.

This lack of value was further accentuated by the failure of impoverished nobles to legitimize titles by paying proper fees and taking out certificates of nobility *(carta de nobreza)* from the Imperial Chancellery. By the 1880s failure to pay required fees had become pervasive, raising the specter of a collapsing imperial nobility system. Traditionally, the ennobled had been required to pay fees to legitimize their titles. The first step was to take out a certificate of nobility because a decree that created a title often contained more than one name. One imperial decree of 14 March 1860 listed nineteen names of barões, including all the Bahian titles created that year.[59] The practice of mass-listing was not confined to economic nobles. An imperial decree of 2 December 1854 created four of the politically most important marquêses of the realm: Olinda, Monte Alegre, Abrantes, and Paraná, in descending order.[60] Three became prime ministers; Abrantes served as interim prime minister. Caxias's first title appeared in the imperial decree of 18 July 1841 as one of nine created that day.[61]

Thus, it became necessary for the imperial house to maintain an Office of the Scribe of the Nobility and Fidalguia of the Empire. The function of this office was to issue certificates or patents of title, to register the titles, and to design coats of arms. To register, one had to pay 128$ for the scribe's fee, 485$ for the right of title, and 80$ for the stamp, a grand total of 693$, the price of a good male slave in the mid-1860s. Carapebus paid this amount for his first title, barão, in 1868.[62] The Conde de São Salvador, a bishop, paid 569$ for the right, 80$ for the stamp, and 64$ for the scribe's fee, for a hefty total of 713$.[63] One visconde, tardy in registering, was fined 128$, plus 435$ for the scribe's fee, 375$ for the right, and 60$ for the stamp, a total of 998$, or roughly a tenth of the cash donation for a title.[64] By mid-nineteenth century standards, these fees were not a minor expense. The nobility titles granted to military and naval officers were exempt from all fees in various stages of legitimization, beginning in 1850. Thus, the Duque de Caxias, whose title was created on 23 March 1869, was registered on April 10 free of charge. Similar favors were granted all military officers; the largest number of their titles were created during and immediately after the Paraguayan War.[65]

In addition to the title registry, nobles were required to adopt a coat of arms, which in the 1880s cost 170$. A symbolic emblem for them and their house, it had extensive social uses: on calling cards, doors of the family coach, business office walls, and even the rooftops of principal residences. Coats of arms were the all-important sign of titles separating nobles from commoners. The design followed certain basic rules related to the use of the crown, color coordination, and flora and fauna images. The First Barão de Santa Justa, a muleteer-turned-coffee planter, included in his coat of arms both mules and coffee trees! On the whole, nobles wanted to convey their lineage, often basing their coats of arms on Portuguese models. It has been alleged that many Brazilian nobles, in fact, had no blood ties with the established Portuguese houses, though their well-established surnames were often usurped. One such family is the Sousa Leão clan, of Pernambuco, which has no direct blood relationship with either the Sousas or the Leãos in Portugal.

When a noble was elevated, the tedious process of registering needed to be repeated. Many territorial nobles simply utilized their business connections, most often comissários and bankers in Rio, to take care of the paperwork. However, by the 1880s, obedience to this requirement was not widespread, which caused a drop in revenue for the Office of the Scribe of the Nobility and Fidalguia of the Empire. Furthermore, for a fee of 10$ and upon proper show of proof, such as birth certificates, parents' marriage contracts, and baptismal documents, nobles and their offspring could acquire additional copies of papers either to be framed at home or for family archives.[66]

But the most fascinating aspect of the negligence of registry was recorded in 1887, two years before the fall of the monarchy. According to the list compiled by the imperial scribe, many distinguished titles were not formally registered *at that time*. At least eight marquêses appeared on the list; among them were Paranaguá, Muritiba, and Monte Pascoal. The first was prime minister and senator; the second, minister and senator; and the last, the archbishop of Bahia and the Primate of Brazil. Twelve condes, thirty-two viscondes, and many more barões also appeared on the list of nonregistrants. Among the well-known elite of the empire who had not legitimized their titles by taking out cartas and registering were prime ministers (Paranaguá, Cotegipe, Ouro Preto, and Sinimbu), cabinet ministers (Muritiba, Barbacena, Cavalcanti), senators (Sousa Queirós, Taunay, Lima Duarte, Vieira da Silva, Nogueira da Gama), palace staff (Mota Maia, Carapebus, and the Condessa de Pedra Branca), military and naval officers (Tamandaré, Beaurepaire Rohan, Lamare, Tocantins, Gávia), and planters (Subaé, Moreira Lima, Araruama, Aramaré, Ubá), to cite the famous.[67]

Whether the nobles who did not take out new letters of titles when elevated or given the honors of grandees or who failed to register in the first instance held legitimate titles at all constitutes an interesting legal and historical question. Obviously, some of the nobles whose names appeared on the list registered *after* the imperial scribe completed it. In view of the incomplete collection of chancellery records, it may safely be assumed that many of those ennobled complied with the rule of the imperial household by registering their titles. However, there were some salient examples of failure to register.

The most interesting case of declining an honor or of failing to register it concerned Caxias's father, Marshal Francisco de Lima e Silva. Elected to the Triune Regency in 1831, he was one of the most distinguished soldiers of the empire. In fact, he and his son, Luís Alves, were both ennobled on 18 July 1841, the first father and son team to be made barons on the same occasion. Although Caxias graciously accepted the title, the senior Lima e Silva simply failed to formalize his title of the Barão da Barra Grande; he did not register it with the imperial scribe. His two brothers and two sons, all generals, held titles throughout their careers. Historians have speculated that Lima e Silva, the *père*, either refused the honor outright or simply declined to use it.[68] One historian believed that he wanted a title of visconde at minimum and that the name Barra Grande was acceptable to him, for it was the beach where he and his troops landed in 1824 to quell the Pernambucan Revolution.[69] Another historian offers an equipose for the controversy: Lima e Silva never claimed the title by paying the necessary fees.[70] The Barão da Barra Grande simply did not complete the notarial aspect of the title legitimation. The title was invalid. Another case was that of the Visconde de Barbacena, Felisberto Caldeira Brant Pontes, a son of his namesake, the Marquês de Barbacena. The visconde never paid the required fees. Although his title was also invalid, he continued to use it until his death. These two are the best-known cases. Foreign titles from the Vatican State, Italy, Portugal, and other European courts offered an additional source of honors and prestige to Brazilian citizens; those who failed to acquire Brazilian or foreign honors simply invented their own or created nonexistent titles.[71]

The Brazilian nobility system between 1808, the days of Dom João VI, and 1889, the last days of the Braganza monarchy in the New World, went through a remarkably short cycle: birth to maturity to decadence in eighty-one years. Both King João and Pedro I deemed a nobility consisting of aristocratic landowners, wealthy gentry, and urban bourgeois merchants to be a reliable system of the ruling class. Meritorious servants of the empire, both civil and military, pious religious hierarchs, and selected literary and scientific savants were ennobled. Unlike the titles in the Old World, those of the Brazilian nobility carried neither stipend nor office nor hereditary right to pass on to the next generation.

Yet, the demand for titles and honors remained unabated, continuing to rise until the 1880s. Titles and honorific commendations were considered integral to a civilized elite, and the novos ricos and imperial mandarins actively sought and obtained honors. By the late fifties, a new twist had been built into the practice of granting them: the quid pro quo exchange of cash donations for titles and other lesser honors. Public education, religious charities, and other social welfare services were thus receiving "voluntary" contributions, initiating an interesting phase of vanity financing of public services for which the empire lacked material resources. Brokers for the titles were from the ranks of prominent politicians: Bom Retiro, Abrantes, João Alfredo; from palace personnel: Carapebus, Baependi; and from the business world: Ourém. By the 1860s, when the empire found itself embroiled in an expensive foreign war, money had replaced merit as the basis for title concessions. The habit of cash contributions became the object of social opprobrium and scorn; there was open talk about the "price table for titles."

By the early 1870s the social debasement of the nobility was in the offing. Political discontent, the slavery question, and the increasingly conflicting definitions of the role of the state in economic modernization, especially in the capitalist agriculture of various regions, led the Crown and its mandarins to gradually isolate themselves; they became less sensitively tuned to the needs of the territorial clans and rising urban middle sectors. To prop up the declining popularity of both the ruling dynasty and the revolving ministries of Liberals and Conservatives, imperial titles and honors were politically used and abused. Those who freed slaves before formal abolition in May 1888 were ennobled and decorated, for such manumission was viewed as a noble act, "service to the State and Humanity." After abolition, the crumbling monarchy sought to bolster its power base by ennobling former slavocrats now clamoring for postabolition indemnity. Such political use or abuse of titles and honors further depreciated the value and cohesion of the nobiliary corporation. The compulsory registration of titles came to be tacitly ignored by political and social elite alike, a subtle but unmistakable indication that the glamour and corporate spirit of the nobility no longer pervaded. The strength of the nobility, especially the one-life title, depended on the individual virtuosity of the titled and the viability of the monarchy. By the 1880s the Braganza

New World empire was hopelessly ailing. In the end, the pillars of stability—the political elite, capitalist agriculture, the imperial nobility, the rising urban bourgeoisie, and other ancillary groups tied to the principal economic activities of the empire—failed to support the agrarian monarchy. The fall of the Braganzas in November 1889 had been well heralded by the gradual decline of the nobility, the onetime bedrock of the imperial system.

8

Noblemen in the Patrimonial Monarchy

The Emperor will do everything for the people,
but not by the people. PEDRO I

The Emperor reigns, but does not rule. THIERS

The Second Reign would not have been possible without the barons,
colonels, comendadores, and conselheiros. RAYMUNDO FAORO

The question *Who ruled the empire?* was not only of philosophical concern to the various Conservative and Liberal factions of the monarchy,
but has also become a legitimate historiographical inquiry among Brazilian and foreign historians.[1] The structure and function of the imperial political elite, the mandarinate, were shaped on the one hand by
the peculiar combination of the temperament of Emperors Pedro I and
Pedro II; on the other, by the changes in the social and economic systems throughout the nineteenth century. Brazil was a partially *differentiated* and *bureaucratized* patrimonial monarchy that lacked at the
outset either a formal or an informal compact between the Crown and
the people. The political history of the empire can in fact be seen as a
story of how to establish and enforce such compacts.

Although the desire for independence was motivated by the liberal
philosophies of the Enlightenment, the Braganza prince, a symbol of
Portuguese colonialism, led the movement. The highest law of the
land, the Constitution of 1824, was not the product of the Brazilian
will, but a gift from Pedro I. His efforts to reconcile the various demands of political groups, social classes, and economic interests of the
far-flung empire—from the Río de la Plata, in the south, to the Oy-

paoque River, in Amazônia—remained futile at best and always frustrating.

Following Pedro I's sudden abdication on 7 April 1831, the tumultuous Regency decade (1831–40) ushered in a democratic era of reform and the Brazilianization of the empire. The Conservative and Liberal parties were established during these years, and, after 1837, imperial politics was a tug of war between them. Although their political differences grew sharper, their social and economic interests often converged, which made it difficult to distinguish them. The office of prime minister, or the president of the council of ministers, was created in 1847 in a minimal democratization of the political system, followed in 1850 by the enactment of the Commercial Code as well as the abolition of the slave trade; and in 1855 by electoral reform, the high point of mid-century state-building efforts. Partisan conflicts in the 1860s caused a realignment on the fundamental issue of imperial politics and persisted until 1889, when the monarchy fell.

Who ruled the empire? is a question still unanswered, and defining the power relationships between the emperor and the people continues to offer a philosophical challenge. Although some advances were made in political and social reform, the ruling group of the empire remained tightly knit, consisting of the emperors, their faithful mandarins, and the two sets of life-tenure officeholders in the imperial senate and the Councils of State. The dynamics of monarchical politics evolved from two sets of power contenders, the Crown and the agrarian clans of the empire. The Braganzas and their sinecurist mandarins controlled the executive branch of government; elected representatives of major territorial clans, the legislative branch. Conflicts often arose from their respective claims for the supremacy of the institution that each controlled. The sum of imperial politics, therefore, was the uneven battle of these two entities, the Crown and executive branch usually exercising greater authority and power than the agrarian clans and their legislature.

The governmental system that João VI introduced in Brazil and relied on for the thirteen years of his reign was simply structured. It consisted of three ministries: Kingdom, Navy and Overseas, War and Foreign Affairs. The Royal Treasury (Real Erário), a fourth ministry, was initially an office within the Ministry of the Kingdom. Only three men, all Portuguese, served as João's chief ministers (always holding the Kingdom portfolio as their principal responsibility): the Marquês de Aguiar, the Conde de Barca, and Tomás Antônio de Vilanova Portugal.[2] No colony-wide legislature was set up and no major reform was imposed on the existing colonial administrative structure. No Brazilian was ever invited to hold a ministerial portfolio until January 1822, when the prince regent appointed José Bonifácio de Andrada e Silva as the chief mandarin, the Minister of the Empire and Foreign Affairs.[3]

By 1822 the Regency had established five ministries: Empire and Foreign Affairs, Justice, War, Navy, and Finance. By November 1823 the most senior administrative branch, the Ministry of the Empire and Foreign Affairs had been broken up into two separate ministries; Foreign Affairs had become the sixth. The seventh and last ministry under the empire, created in March 1861, was Agriculture, Commerce, and Public Works, until then a bureau in the Ministry of the Empire.[4] Between 1822 and 1889 fifty-nine Cabinets were installed, in which a total of 219 ministers served. Some 189 were Brazilians, 20 Portuguese, and the rest born overseas of Brazilian and/or Portuguese parents.[5] The longest-serving Cabinets were those of Paraná (1853–57) and of Rio Branco (1871–75).[6] Fifty-four ministers served during the years of the First Reign (1822–31) and the Regency (1831–40), and 165 held office under the Second Reign (1840–89). After the formal organization of the two-party system in 1837, Cabinet control alternated between the parties, though the one out of office often participated. The Conservatives controlled fifteen Cabinets, remaining in power for twenty-nine years and nine months; the Liberals organized twenty-one Cabinets and ruled for nineteen years and five months.[7]

The conflict between the agrarian clans of the export economies and the Braganza rulers began with João's establishment of political sinecures. After 1808 a coterie of nobles and fidalgos who had followed their prince to Brazil had to be housed and given jobs. By doling out public employment in the civil and military services to his loyal followers, João created a cadre of sinecurists. Those who had been in the second echelon of the colonial service sought to upgrade themselves by frequenting the court and exploiting their connections. Brazil's rural gentry in Rio, São Paulo, and Minas was attracted to court life and dazzled by the glitter and brilliance of the Braganza presence and its accompanying diplomatic corps in Rio. The court became the seat of political activity during the Joanine years, a kind of "tropical Versailles." The obliging monarch handed out not only nobiliary titles but also lesser royal honors, including 5,610 certificates for the various grades (cavaleiros, comendadores, grão cruzes, etc.) of the Christ, Avis, and Santiago orders.[8] The early recipients of royal largesse, by and large, came from the ranks of the Portuguese and Brazilian urban mercantile bourgeoisie, high- and middle-level functionaries, and religious officials, including a smattering of rural gentry.

In 1821 the Portuguese Cortes was convoked in Lisbon, to which Brazilian provinces were instructed to dispatch their elected representatives. The de facto underrepresentation of Brazilian agrarian interests in the Cortes was glaring; the seventeen-member delegation from Minas Gerais and the three-man group from Rio Grande do Norte never attended the Lisbon congress. Antônio Pais de Barros of Itu, a substitute deputy, and Nicolau Pereira de Campos Vergueiro, a deputy, Portuguese expatriate, merchant, and future senator as well as regent of the empire, were major figures in São Paulo's export economies. From Rio, seven deputies were sent, but none could claim a significant tie to the local agricultural economy. (It can be argued that coffee had yet to bloom as an export economy by the early 1820s, and that, had the principal elite of this sector existed, the budding planter class could have not yet mustered political clout.) By one count, less than 30 percent of some eighty Brazilian delegates (forty-six deputies and the rest substitutes) to the Portuguese Cortes came from the ranks of the agrarian interests. More than half of the delegation represented the professions of magistrates, clergy, and civil-military officialdom, the bureaucracy of the American kingdom of the Luso-Brazilian empire.[9] Thus, the first group of elected political leaders in Brazil had few firm ties to the dominant agrarian interests.

An examination of the delegations from Bahia and Pernambuco, where the sugar economy had begun in the sixteenth century and had been resuscitated in the 1790s after a period of stagnation, reinforces the evidence that no substantial political power was garnered by the dominant economy. From Pernambuco, one Cavalcanti (substitute) and Pedro de Araújo Lima could be looked on as legitimate spokesmen, by slightly stretching the imagination, for planter interests; from Bahia, Domingos Borges de Barros and Alexander Gomes Ferrão represented landed interests. Thus, of the total twenty-three representatives from these two regions (eleven for Bahia and twelve for

Pernambuco), only four can be identified as agrarian-based deputies. Both Bahia and Pernambuco, however, included leaders of the regional revolts as legitimate voices of the urban classes: Cipriano José Barata de Almeida, from Bahia (a leader of the 1789 revolt), and Francisco Muniz Tavares, from Pernambuco (a revolutionary priest in the 1817 revolution).[10] The remaining deputies were members of the middle- and high-echelon military and civil bureaucracy.

The future political elite of the First Reign, however, did come from the 1821 Cortes group. Pedro de Araújo Lima (the future Marquês de Olinda) became a high court mandarin of the empire. A cadre of other imperial sinecurist politicians also came from the ranks of the 1821 Brazilian deputation: Diogo Antônio Feijó, Antônio Carlos Ribeiro de Andrada Machado e Silva, José Feliciano Fernandes Pinheiro, Nicolau Vergueiro, Francisco Vilela Barbosa (the First Marquês de Paranaguá), José Lino Coutinho, and José Martiniano de Alencar. Because their political prestige was well established before the Cortes was convened, these men would emerge as the first generation of Brazilian political leaders in the Constituent Assembly of 1823.[11]

Mutual suspicion and mistrust undermined the congress of the Portuguese kingdoms and colonies. The rivalry between the two "co-kingdoms" of the empire took a nasty tone from the outset; the Portuguese deputies were bent on recolonizing Brazil. The news from Lisbon was angrily received in Brazil, and on 13 May 1822, King João VI's birthday, the municipal council of Rio de Janeiro invested in Pedro (prince regent) the title of the Perpetual Defender of Brazil.[12] By then, the majority of the Brazilian deputies were eager to quit Portugal, but suspicious authorities in Lisbon impounded their passports, which forced them to stay; some succeeded in leaving Portugal, literally smuggled out of the country by sympathetic British consular agents and sailors.[13] Events were unfolding rapidly: on May 23, the Rio municipal council urged Pedro to convoke a General Assembly of the Provinces to draw up a constitution. Accordingly, the prince regent decreed on 3 June 1822 that a constituent assembly be called into session.[14] It was only a matter of time before the court nobles and politicians advised Pedro to take a step further: to declare full and complete independence from Portugal. The declaration came on 7 September 1822 on the banks of the Ipiranga River, São Paulo.

From the outset, the Constituent Assembly showed every sign of forcing a confrontation with the Braganza prince. Meeting on 3 May 1823, it immediately identified issues of conflicting interests: determining the perimeter of the emperor's (executive) power and the constitutional rights of deputies (legislature) on the one hand, and on the other conciliating the diverse regional interests of agrarian clans and those of the sinecurist political servants of the House of Braganza. The constituent assembly was organized on the demographic strength of each province, including slaves. One hundred deputies were to have made up the assembly, but only seventy attended during the six months of its existence.[15] On account of the civil wars, the provinces of Bahia, Maranhão, and Amazonas (Rio Negro), then part of Pará, could not send their representatives to the first meetings in May, though some were able to attend much later. Minas Gerais had the largest delegation: twenty, of whom nineteen were Mineiros. Rio was allotted eight deputies, of whom none was a native. The single largest professional group consisted of lawyers and judges (twenty-six and twenty-two, respectively); other professions represented were nineteen priests, seven military officers, two physicians, and two mathematicians; the rest were public servants and landowners.[16]

Considered to be a liberal body, the assembly reflected a wide range of philosophical views. The Andradas brothers—Antônio Carlos, José Bonifácio, and Martim Francisco—stood in the forefront of legislative liberalism, and two Mineiros—Manuel Jacinto Nogueira da Gama (the future Marquês de Baependi) and João Severiano Maciel da Costa (the future Marquês de Queluz)—championed royalist conservatism.[17] Of several issues that received attention from the deputies, two particularly stood out as contests of will between the Crown and the people: the structure of provincial government and the feasibility of a federalist monarchy.

Antônio Carlos, the orator of the political family and the leader of the radical liberals in the assembly, proposed a bill that would establish a provincial council throughout the empire; larger provinces would have six elected members, smaller ones four. Two ex officio members—the highest ranking officer of the militia (ordenança) and the most senior judge—would sit in the council with two or four members, who were to be elected in the same manner as deputies to the assembly. The emperor would appoint the provincial president, who, together with the council, would govern the province. The duties of the chief executive of the province were well defined in Antônio Carlos's proposal and were by and large administrative.[18]

Deputies from the empire's peripheral provinces were more preoccupied with the "despotism of the center Rio," especially the manner in which the provincial president would be selected. They wanted a local legislature to elect him. One deputy thundered that the people lacked confidence in Rio. Going one step further than the deputy from São Paulo, he demanded that provincial presidents be elected locally and confirmed by the emperor. Another deputy countered with the proposal that the emperor choose a president *only* from the native-born of the province. Still another defended the imperial right of appointment, but sought to reconcile it with the defense of regional interests of capitalist agriculture by suggesting that the Crown select a president from the provincial council. On the question of the organization of provincial government, deputies on the whole leaned toward a liberal solution, placing some sort of "checks and balances" on the appointment process as well as running the government. On the question of the national government, Deputy Francisco Muniz Tavares, of Pernambuco, spoke for the periphery: the cabinet should be subordinate to the parliament.[19]

More divergent views prevailed among the deputies on the issue of centralism versus federalism. One Bahian deputy argued that the constitution should explicitly state that "the empire is comprised *federally* of provinces." Another deputy opposed this proposal on the ground that it would lead to the "dissipation of solidarity and force of this Constitutional Monarchy." Provinces were not independent, he argued; rather, they were integral parts of the monarchy. Nicolau Vergueiro, of São Paulo, cautioned that North American federalism with its distinct republican slant could not be transplanted to Brazil's monarchy. A Bahian deputy stoutly opposed the federalist idea: a "Liberal Constitution" should not be confused with provincial independence. An economic liberal, this disciple of Adam Smith argued that federalism would destory the viability of the constituent assembly and eventually of the monarchy. Other deputies contended that such a discussion should be postponed until the representatives from Pará, Maranhão, and Amazonas were able to participate.[20] This debate on the federalist monarchy as well as that on the structure of provincial government reflected the conflicting stances of Pedro and the elected deputies. Despite the underrepresentation of agricultural interests, the constituent assembly was dominated by Brazilians; it confronted the prince with substantive issues that eventually set the two sides on a collision course.

Other issues touched on the concerns of religion as well as of land. One deputy introduced a bill that would regulate the size of religious orders by controlling recruitment. His principal preoccupation was the loss of manpower to the church; without marriages, there could be no population, and without people, agriculture would suffer.[21] A Bahian deputy proposed that the provincial council be given full powers to make land grants, a position opposed by a Paulista solon, who called for the suppression of future land grants. The sugar-based Bahian economy would benefit from the monopolistic control of land by the council, which according to the assembly's proposals would be firmly controlled by the regional senhores de engenhos. On the other hand, São Paulo in the early nineteenth century had yet to develop capitalist agriculture and was plagued by too many barren sesmarias ("terras maninhas"), forcing poor farmers into the frontier and creating a labor shortage as well as the underutilization of land. Vergueiro, an adopted Paulista, advocated that an agriculture committee be established in the assembly to deal with the problems of public lands and that, until a land law was adopted, sesmarias should not be given out. A politically wise Araújo Lima, of Pernambuco, called for the suspension of all discussion on the potentially nation-splitting issue.[22] A Bahian deputy proposed an end to the Crown monopoly of the brazilwood trade, and still another from the Northeast asked for tax exemption for Bahian agricultural products to resuscitate the sagging provincial economy devastated by the war of independence.[23]

If the agrarian questions clearly reflected the regional hues and divergent views under discussion, no clear-cut regional loyalties emerged over the proposal to establish a national university. Paulista José Feliciano Fernandes Pinheiro proposed to set up at least one university in São Paulo, later modifying the plan to add one in Olinda; Mineiro Nogueira da Gama pushed the idea of Rio as the seat of the national university. Araújo Lima, of Pernambuco, supported the idea of two universities (Olinda and São Paulo) and a law school in Rio. Bahian deputies were split on the issue: the future Visconde de Jequitinhonha thought that, as the demographic centers of Brazil, Bahia and Minas

Gerais should have universities; Cairu considered the imperial capital to be the proper location for this institution. Miguel Calmon supported the São Paulo and Olinda option. And still another deputy called for one university in Maranhão and another in São Paulo. One deputy wondered if the two-university plan would cost too much.[24] It must be remembered that, soon after the transfer of the Braganza court to the New World, two medical schools were organized, one in Bahia and another in Rio. The choice of São Paulo and Olinda seemed to gain wide political support as a means of balancing regional distribution of the education system.

By October 1823 the conflict between Pedro I and the constituent assembly had taken a sudden turn for the worse. While discussion of the new constitution was still in progress, the emperor broke his promise to the assembly that he would not create nobiliary titles. In fact, deputies were startled to learn that Pedro had made Lord Cochrane the Marquês do Maranhão on 12 October 1823. No one questioned the merit of the Scottish admiral and his service to Brazil; after all, he had defeated the remnants of the Portuguese royal forces in the northern province, hence the title of Maranhão. What bothered the deputies was not the ennobling itself but the imperial abuse of power in nonchalantly breaking the promise. (Antônio Gonçalves Gomide had not long before proposed a legal basis for vanity financing of various worthwhile projects, including raising funds for the national university. For instance, a title of barão would be priced at 80:000$.[25] Had this proposal been incorporated into the constitution, the structure of the Brazilian imperial nobility would have acquired both legislative and executive sanction. Titles could have carried more clout and even attained official status as a formal corporate group. But this was never realized.

The gap between imperial absolutism and the assembly's political liberalism was too wide to bridge; the deputies saw themselves as Brazilians, and Pedro regarded them as radical anti-Portuguese. At least a few intransigent deputies, such as the Andrada brothers, José Joaquim da Rocha, and others, were later deported from the empire; Nicolau Vergueiro was arrested, but freed.[26] Palace hangers-on condemned the deputies as "anarchists" who threatened the security of the nation as well as that of the imperial person. On 2 November 1823, Pedro I himself led troops to close down the recalcitrant constituent assembly.[27] The dismissal of the body constituted a victory for Braganza centripetalism *(imperialismo)* over the attempt by regional agrarian clans to impose constitutional constraints on the Crown. On one level, the dominant economic interests of the empire were completely ignored and remained unheard; on still another level, the patrimonial emperor succeeded in consolidating his control over the process of the sinecurization of political offices. However, from this group of dismissed deputies would come future mandarins, including thirty-three senators, twenty-eight Cabinet ministers, seven councillors of state, and four regents.[28]

The Constitution of 1824 was neither written by the "people" nor approved by them. A committee of ten men (the Council of State), all trusted lieutenants of the emperor, was commissioned to write the magna carta of the land.[29] Pro forma ratification was accomplished by the municipal councils of the provincial capitals. Essentially a Crown-centered executive form of government, incorporating few checks and balances, the document's unique feature was the insertion of a moderating power *(poder moderador)*, to be vested in the hands of the emperor, the chief executive of the government. The other three powers were in accordance with a Montesquieu constitution: bicameral legislature, supreme tribunal, and executive branch. Both the moderating and executive powers were exercised by the emperor. He was his own prime minister until 1847, when the office of the president of the council of ministers was set up. Under the moderating power, the emperor could dismiss parliament, appoint and remove ministers, and intervene in state affairs when national security was threatened. The philosophical and political debate over this fourth power raged from time to time throughout the monarchical period, dividing Liberals and Conservatives and often pitting politicians of all persuasions against the Crown and its supporters. Voting was carried out indirectly by electoral colleges; in 1881 a direct election system was adopted by Liberals. Income, not literacy, was a constitutional requirement for voting and holding office, higher incomes being required for officeholders; women, conscripts in the armed forces, members of regular orders of the church, slaves, and various marginal elements of society were excluded from the electoral franchise.

The Brazilian parliament (Parlamento Brasileiro) was organized on a two-chamber system. The chamber of deputies, the lower house, was made up of general deputies *(deputados gerais)* elected in proportion to the population of each province; thus, Minas Gerais, the empire's most populous province, held the largest number of seats. In the last legislature (the twentieth, 1886–89), 125 deputies represented twenty provinces; Minas sent 20, Bahia 14, Pernambuco 13, Rio (the court and the province) 12, and São Paulo 9.[30] In the lower house, 1,331 men served between the first legislature of 1826 and the twentieth in 1889.

The upper chamber, or senate, whose members were called senators of the empire *(senadores do império)*, had exactly one half the total number of the general deputies, or a minimum of 1 senator per province. Minas Gerais had the largest number of senators, with 10, followed by Bahia with 7, Pernambuco and Rio with 6 apiece, and São Paulo with 4. Eight provinces had a single senator. Between 1826 and 1889 some 234 life-term senators served in the upper house. A senador do império held office for life, first elected by the people and then appointed by the emperor from a list of the three candidates who received the largest number of votes. The emperor often chose the second or even third on the list to suit his personal needs as well as to demonstrate his "independence" by supporting or opposing a party or a faction. General deputies served for four years, unless the chamber was dissolved by the emperor. To all the empire's provinces, the single electoral law was applied; after 1861 no province had fewer than 2 deputies and 1 senator. The Brazilian parliament met annually in May and closed its session by October. At the inaugural session of each legislature, the emperor or a regent customarily delivered an opening speech, the Speech from the Throne, usually prepared by the prime minister in consultation with the Council of State.[31]

Its formal organization notwithstanding, parliament's effectiveness was heavily influenced on the one hand by the rapid bureaucratization of the patrimonial state, and, on the other by the recruitment of elite whom the Crown allowed to hold office, especially those "reelected" for a number of terms. Major agrarian clans, or their interests, rarely enjoyed direct representation in parliament. Furthermore, the liberal impulses of the chamber of deputies, especially after 1840, were often checked by the more conservative senate, a cadre of patrimonial sinecurists whom the Braganzas had groomed and whose political careers the emperors had personally molded. As the empire matured, the differences between the two houses became more glaring in terms of their stands on various social, economic, and political issues.

If power in the imperial chamber of deputies was measured by the ability to be reelected, the offspring of the empire's major agrarian clans were sadly lacking. According to Taunay, 1,421 men served in the constituent assembly of 1823 and the twenty legislatures of the chamber of deputies between 1826 and 1889. Some 925 of the deputies, or 65 percent, served only one term.[32] As has been shown, only 2 deputies were elected ten times, and 21 (1.47 percent) more than seven times. Of these 21 men, partisan affiliation was about evenly divided: 11 Liberals and 10 Conservatives, including 1 prime minister (Martinho Álvares da Silva Campos), 7 senators, 10 cabinet officers, and 5 elected in two or more provinces. The overwhelming majority, 16 (76 percent), were trained in law or served in a judicial office. The remaining 5 were a priest, an army officer, a civil servant, a journalist-lawyer, and a physician-landowner. Only 2 (Martinho Campos and the Conde de Baependi) were legitimate voices of capitalist agriculture, representing Valença, Paraíba do Sul, and Zona de Mata. Sebastião do Rego Barros, the only one from the Northeast (Pernambuco), reelected eight times, came from a latifundiary rural clan. If this small cadre of deputies had a common interest at all, it was their undying loyalty to Braganza imperialism; they were the Crown's favorite political mandarins.

Only men of substance could afford to hold elective offices because the pay was low, and they could donate four months a year out of noblesse oblige or for the sheer pleasure of working politics. Deputies and senators did not earn salaries, but they were paid expenses; in 1824 a deputy received 2:400$ and in 1889 the amount was 6:000$ for a four-month session. A senator was paid 3:600$ in 1826 and 9:000$ by the end of the monarchy.[33] As a rule, a political career, especially an elective office, did not offer an avenue for amassing fortune; rather, it often served as a first step toward higher offices. However, few scions of the major agrarian clans dominated the imperial legislature. By some stretch of the imagination, it can be argued that the political prestige of only one agrarian clan rivaled that of the Braganzas: the Cavalcanti de Albuquerques, of Pernambuco. For the entire period of the monarchy, at least one was seated in each house. Inbred and widely dispersed throughout the Northeast, however, the clan never mobilized its agrarian interests to create any clout on the national level. Even if one hypothesizes that the agrarian clans in Rio, Minas Gerais, and São Paulo, physically closer to the court and therefore able to dispatch their offspring to the imperial parliament at a lesser cost than those in the Northeast, were more likely to participate in imperial politics, none of the major clans in the Center-South succeeded in dominating electoral offices. The planter families of capitalist agriculture had no better chance than professional politicians to be elected and reelected to national offices. A closer look at the agrarian representation in parliament is in order.

The contrast between the patterns of agrarian representation in the Bahian and Pernambucan deputations is a logical point of departure because it offers some clue to intraregional economic and social differences. Between 1821 and 1889 Pernambuco sent 153 deputies to the Lisbon Cortes and the Brazilian chamber of deputies, and Bahia sent 156. Apart from the deputies to Lisbon, Pernambuco had 145 and Bahia 148 between 1823 and 1889. Of these, 31, or 21.4 percent, of the Bahian deputation were reelected more than four times; 33, or 22.8 percent, of the Pernambucan deputies fall in this four-time category. In spite of these superficial similarities, Pernambuco had marshaled better representatives for its agrarian interests than had Bahia; 10 Albuquerques, 6 Cavalcantis, and 4 Rego Barroses served as solons. No major agrarian clan in Bahia enjoyed multiple representation. (The Ferreira Franças had four deputies, but they were not a major agricultural clan.[34] Furthermore, only Eduardo represented Bahia four times, in the period 1848–60.[35] Although his brother Ernesto was also a four-time deputy, he served one term for Minas Gerais, another for Pernambuco, and only twice for Bahia.)

Of the eight six-term deputies from Pernambuco, only two—Pedro Francisco de Paula Cavalcanti de Albuquerque (the future Visconde de Camaragibe) and Francisco do Rego Barros (the future Conde de Boa Vista)—were the bona fide representatives of provincial commercial agriculture. Only one of Pernambuco's seven five-term deputies, Francisco Xavier de Pais Barreto, and four of the seventeen four-term deputies—the Visconde de Albuquerque, the Barão de Vila Bela, Inácio J. de Sousa Leão, and Francisco de Almeida e Albuquerque—were members of the province's agrarian clans.[36]

In Bahia, only one of the eight six-term deputies was a legitimate agrarian spokesman: Francisco Gonçalves Martins (the future Visconde de São Lourenço). Also a six-termer, Manuel Pinto de Sousa Dantas, the future prime minister of the 1880s, was not from a major planter family, certainly not of a sugar clan of the Recôncavo. Three of the eight five-term deputies—the Barão de Cotegipe, José Antônio Saraiva, and João Ferreira Moura—could claim ties to the sugar interests. All three were engaged in the modernization of sugar refineries in Bahia. Of the fourteen four-termers, only three—Inocêncio Marques de Araújo Góis, the Barão de Jeremoabo, and Pedro Moniz Barreto de Aragão—were sugar planters in the bay area of Bahia. The eight-term deputy from Pernambuco—Sebastião do Rego Barros—was a landowner, but Bahia's nine-termer José Augusto Chaves was not.

Of the thirty-one Bahians who served in the chamber more than four times, four became prime ministers: Barão de Uruguaiana, Saraiva, Cotegipe, and Sousa Dantas, in that order. Of Pernambuco's thirty-three deputies who were reelected four times or more, only two—Olinda and João Alfredo—became prime ministers. Of the nine Bahian-born prime ministers, only two—Cotegipe and Saraiva—held direct interests in the province's sugar plantations. The only two Pernambucanos who became prime ministers were not legitimate offspring of the province's major agrarian clans.

The comparison between the Bahian and Pernambucan cases offers significant evidence of the relative absence of the agrarian influence in electoral politics. The Albuquerques, the Paes Barretos, the Cavalcantis, and the Rego Barroses had established both horizontal (interfamilial) and vertical (interclass) ties in economy and society at large, however. Unable to elect themselves, they were able to influence the election of kinsmen. Sugar was cultivated throughout the littoral of the province and then spread into the interior. The penetration and saturation of cane cultivation therefore offered the key to the hegemonic crisis of the monocultural clans of capitalist agriculture in social and economic life. Marriages within and without the clans further strengthened vertical and horizontal linkages, thus consolidating the political supremacy of the agrarian families. Recife, with its law academy, and Olinda, with a seminary, in the second half of the century served as the regional urban system that combined international and interprovincial trade and elite training. The web of influence radiating from Recife toward other northeastern cities and towns was far greater than Salvador's. The provincial capital was a natural magnet not only for the Pernambucan agrarian elite, but also those of the neighboring provinces: Alagoas, Paraíba, Rio Grande do Norte, and even Ceará, over which Pernambuco held suzerainty. Urbanizing the agricultural wealth in Recife was an inevitable consequence for the elites of the provinces in the Northeast, especially those of capitalist agriculture, whose exports passed through Recife. During the second half of the century, this process of integration was accelerated and became more intense, as railroads and refineries began to change the traditional economic and social relationship of the region. This process of modernization enhanced the consolidation of the political position of Pernambuco's major agrarian clans as the legitimate spokesmen for the regional capitalist agriculture.

In Bahia, the opposite pattern existed. Sugar was, and still is, cultivated on a large scale in and around the Recôncavo, which radiates about 150 kilometers from Salvador. From colonial times until the end of the nineteenth century, the diagonal axis of Salvador-Santo Amaro was the major artery of the sugar economy, where the major agrarian clans settled and spread. South of the capital, the old Comarca de São Jorge dos Ilhéus, today's cacao country, was an area of subsistence agriculture, typically owned by family-unit labor groups cultivating manioc, beans, and other cash crops to feed the capital and Recôncavo plantations. Farther into the up-country, Feira de Santana, the province's cattle-trade emporium, served as the secondary economic pole for the pastoral economy of the sertão. However, Bahian plantations often imported jerked beef, *charque*, from as far away as Rio Grande do Sul and Río de la Plata countries. Plantations outside the port city of Salvador often relied on Feira de Santana; thus, the urban market of Salvador did not function as the regional hub for all Bahia, as in the case of Recife, but as one serving the capital and its adjacent region.[37]

Reflecting such economic-geographical considerations, the clans of capitalist agriculture of the Recôncavo were compactly concentrated in a narrow strip of the bay plantation corridor (Salvador-Santo Amaro), which stretched some 100 kilometers in length and about 20 in width. Many families engaged in endogamous and intraclan marriages, thus strengthening their horizontal ties but further limiting their group's vertical links in terms of their ability to reach out within the provincial population, especially to those segments not directly involved in the sugar economy. The medical school in Salvador served an integrating function as a regional center of learning for the Northeast, but its political and cultural importance never surpassed that of the law fac-

ulty in Recife. By nature, more persons with legal training and backgrounds went into imperial politics than physicians. Sixteen (76
percent) of the empire's twenty-one deputies who were reelected more
than seven times came from the lawyer and judge class.

In contrast, the clan electoral representation in the coffee-growing
areas in Minas Gerais, Rio de Janeiro, and São Paulo throughout the
nineteenth century differed substantially from the patterns thus far
observed in the Northeast. No major coffee-planting family, except the
Nogueira da Gamas of Valença among the Rio Paraíba Valley landowners, succeeded in forging a successful political (electoral and appointive) career. Of Rio province's 136 deputies (not counting 7 to the
Lisbon Cortes), 18 (13 percent) were reelected more than four times. No
major planter family from such key coffee- and sugar-producing counties as Vassouras, Resende, Barra Mansa, Valença, Campos, and Macaé
managed to match the uninterrupted political representation in the
imperial parliament of the Albuquerques, of Pernambuco. The Conde
de Baependi, a Nogueira da Gama and a seven-term deputy, was the sole
political representative of provincial agriculture. João Manuel Pereira
da Silva, a ten-termer and historian-lawyer, was a professional politician and a power broker of the Conservative party in Rio province.

Similar observations can be made on the lack of electoral representation by the major regional agrarian clans in São Paulo and Minas
Gerais. In São Paulo, Monteiro de Barros, elected four times as deputy,
was a scion of a major planter family. In Minas Gerais, the Zona de
Mata was represented by the Conde de Prados (Camilo Maria Ferreira
Armond), whose family owned a major mercantile-agrarian fortune, a
typical post-1850 gentry of the coffee zone. There, too, no major clan
could succeed in monopolizing imperial elective offices.[38]

The dearth of electoral offices held by local and regional leaders in
the Center-South, the dynamic "core" area of the empire after 1840,
raises some nagging questions about the nature of imperial politics
and the patrimonial state system. If the economic class that produced
the wealth and revenues for the monarchy did not monopolize political
offices, as in a liberal bourgeois state, then who did? Either the imperial government was fraught with organizational defects or it possessed a special cadre of patrimonial bureaucrats and sinecurist
politicians who remained at least partly outside normative politics beyond the reach of influence by the dominant agrarian interests. Except

for Pernambuco, where the major landed families also functioned as
major political clans, sets of Crown-sponsored politicians were imposed upon key provinces. These men did not depend on ties to the local or regional economic clans for their political prestige; their
retention was based on their acceptance into the *corpus politicum imperium* by the Braganza Crown; they were actually manorial mandarins of the House of Braganza. The Sousa Dantases, the Cotegipes, and
the Calmons, all of Bahia, the Soares de Sousas, the Ferreira Vianas,
the Rodrigues Torreses, and the Nogueira da Gamas, all of Rio, the Andradas, of São Paulo, and the Ottonis and the Assis Figueiredos, of
Minas Gerais, made up the empire's leading political clans, whose
prestige rested on their being among the chosen few of the Crown.[39] Of
these, the Nogueira da Gamas were the only *major* practicing capitalist agriculturalists, who acquired the status of a courtier noble family
at the same time. Although many of these clans at one time had roots
in agrarian backgrounds, wealth in land did not sustain them in power.
It was their entry into the imperial mandarinate that guaranteed power
elite status in the empire.

The capstone to a career in the mandarinate was an appointment to
the imperial ministry. The emperor's power to appoint and dismiss
ministers, to call and dissolve the chamber of deputies (the senate
could not be dismissed because it was a life-tenure body), and to for-
mulate politics had its origin in his moderating and executive powers.
Under these two constitutional duties, the emperor exercised enormous control over the organization of the upper house, the council of
state and, after 1847, the ministry. These three institutions—the senate, the council of state, and the cabinet—often functioned as a counterweight to the popularly elected chamber of deputies. Furthermore,
these three bodies were at the service of the Crown, responsible neither to parliament nor, by extension, to the people. The emperor
groomed, rewarded, and controlled the members of these power
groups, who often doubled as court advisers and formed the highly select body of patrimonial mandarins.

Essential to the success of the imperial mandarinate was the gradual
transfer of dependency/loyalty of the elected and appointed officials
from regional agrarian clans to the Braganza Crown.[40] Because the ruling house completely lacked familial or matrimonial links with the
major Brazilian agrarian or mercantile clans, an awkward problem

arose over the legitimacy of the patrimonial state system when Dom Pedro II did not have a male successor. To maintain the hegemony of the Braganza emperors at the head of the patrimonial monarchy, the Crown had to establish a cadre of loyal officials whose devotion was directed to the state, not to regional overlords of the dominant export agriculture. Thus, the mandarin concept was born: a scion of an important family, typically trained in law at one of the two academies, in São Paulo or Recife, who was willing to serve the imperial cause—the centripetalist patrimonial monarchy. Once inducted into the service, he was carefully groomed, molded, and promoted through the hierarchy of elective and appointive offices. During his years of initial service in low-ranking offices, he was gradually but definitively separated from both his family and his regional roots; his career advancement depended totally on the patrimonial whims of the imperial house. In service to the cause of imperial unity and hegemony, he was a foremost Crown agent and was expected to act like one. Partisan affiliation mattered little, as a myriad of social, economic, and political issues constantly tested his loyalty. The viability of the empire system depended on his faithful execution of the imperial will, his skill in conciliating between Braganza principles and the demands of regional oligarchies, and his ability to resolve conflicts in the name of imperial harmony.

Key to the intricate workings of the imperial body politic is an understanding of the patrimonial elite system, the mandarinate, in terms of its recruitment, career patterns, and co-option process. The principal training ground of Brazilian mandarins was Coimbra University, in Portugal, which produced the pre-1850 political elite of the empire; thereafter, the two Brazilian law academies, in São Paulo and Recife, took over such training. The five-year study in a law school became the first stage of elite recruitment. From various parts of the empire, students possessing different social and economic values were corralled into Coimbra, São Paulo, or Recife, where their provincial attitudes and loyalties were synthesized and restructured into a set of common values, ideals, and perceptions to promote the nation-state concept, the broad national political culture of *Brazilianness*. This process of national acculturation prepared the graduates to be ideal agents of the empire, once they were scattered and posted to various provinces. Equally important, the informal aspect of their integration and the psychological experience shared by graduates of the same class *(turma)* created a lifelong bond that reinforced their formal training. The combination contributed to the emergence of an ideologically homogeneous elite devoted to administering a far-flung empire and to consolidating the monarchy's supraregional needs.

Often launched by his family's political and economic connections, a mandarin's typical career began with his first appointment to office after graduation. After a brief tenure as district judge *(juiz de direito)*, public prosecutor *(promotor público)*, district police chief (delegado de polícia), or another provincial or imperial appointive office in the capital, he could run for an elective office, typically in the provincial assembly, but possibly in the imperial parliament. Another avenue for advancement would be transfer to a different province; thus, a Bahian *bacharel* on the move might be transferred to a post in Sergipe, a Paulista to Mato Grosso, Goiás, or Paraná, and so forth. At this stage, if not earlier, political parties began to recruit worthy candidates to run for higher elective offices. By the time a prospective mandarin reached this second stage, he was looked upon as a good risk for Crown favors. His patrimonial career, either as an administrative bureaucrat or a political mandarin, was well underway.

Election to the chamber of deputies, appointment to a provincial presidency, or nomination by the emperor to the senate marked the final phase of mandarin grooming. Travel to the capital permitted a deputy to appear in the court, where the emperor, senior counselors, and leading politicians could evaluate his performance and that of other novitiates. Once selected, he would be groomed for higher political office in the appellate court's judicial bureaucracy or the post of provincial police chief or president. If he was among the luckier ones who had powerful connections at the court, he would receive a minor cabinet post. In either capacity, the chosen one became a patrimonial agent of the Crown. Successful completion of his assignments in these offices sped his advance within the service and his induction into the ranks of the mandarins. Throughout the empire, as a rule, the majority of senators had served in the chamber of deputies more than two terms, either under Crown sponsorship or through their own prestige as regional elites. Cabinet ministers came from the ranks of senators, occasionally from those of deputies, and almost all prime ministers had been senators; the council of state drew its members from the senate and from former ministers.

In short, the most coveted status for an imperial mandarin was the office of senator, a life-term post that was first popularly elected and then selected by the emperor. A senator was a politician whose prestige people recognized and whose value to the Crown the emperor treasured. Senators performed any duty called for by the exigencies of the centralist authority. Although provincial presidencies had been at one time a major stepping-stone for mandarin careers, after the late 1870s senators were dispatched to key provinces where the prime minister's party required bolstering. The Marquês de Paranaguá, senator and minister, served as president of Bahia in 1881–82 and from that post became the prime minister in 1882–83. A Mineiro and Rio coffee planter in Paraíba do Sul, Martinho Campos was made the provincial chief executive of Rio in 1881–82; from this post, the nine-term deputy became prime minister and senator in 1882. Florêncio Carlos de Abreu e Silva, senator from Rio Grande do Sul, was made the provincial president of São Paulo in 1881.[41]

It would nevertheless be a gross misjudgment to classify all the senators of the empire as a bunch of subservient mandarins of the House of Braganza. Although many were blindly loyal to the cause of imperialism, some proved to be ardent defenders of regional economic interests, asserting the independence protected by their life-tenure offices. Such a pattern of change in the composition of the upper chamber, however, did not take place until the end of the 1860s. At the beginning, senators were selected from the ranks of the emperor's trusted friends, devout churchmen and loyal military-naval officers. Whether or not a senator represented the economic interests of the province in which he was elected was and still is debatable. Some scholars argue that the senator in fact represented both the province and the empire.[42] Pedro I often imposed his own choices on peripheral provinces to assert his centripetalist proclivity. Dom Pedro II, however, cautiously compromised the autocratic tendencies of his father and the needs of the realpolitik in selecting senators. On the whole, the traditional Crown imposition of its own candidate, a sign of the supremacy of the imperial poder moderador, was on the wane by the 1870s.

An examination of the first senatorial election in 1826 offers a helpful point of reference in comprehending the political dynamics of the patrimonial state system. Many of Dom João's Brazilian and Portuguese advisers remained in the service of Pedro I after their monarch's return to Lisbon in 1821. Young Brazilian counselors joined the older group of Portuguese to form the core of the imperial political elite of the First Reign. With a few exceptions, such as the Andrada brothers, the majority of these court advisers became senators. Some candidates ran for senator from more than one province. Queluz, for instance, competed for the office in six different provinces at once, including his home, Minas Gerais; the emperor picked him to represent Paraíba. Caravelas ran from three provinces—Bahia, Minas, and Rio—and was nominated to represent his home province, Bahia. Baependi, a Valença planter, competed in Minas and Rio, and was selected to serve Minas, the province of his birth, not of his residence. Peripheral provinces, such as Pará, Maranhão, and Mato Grosso, were represented not by native sons but by Pedro's intimate advisers, civil and military, who were "elected" from them. Bahia was the only province completely represented by its own sons, and they were all highly loyal court advisers. In fact, for the first senate in 1826, Baianos represented four provinces: Pará, Piauí, Pernambuco, and Rio de Janeiro.[43] This strategy of placing an outsider (but an emperor's confidant) in senatorial posts became an integral tradition of patrimonial service. In one Mato Grosso senatorial election, Pedro II passed over his boyhood friend, the Visconde de Bom Retiro, to select the Visconde do Rio Branco, the then rising star in imperial politics and diplomatic service. In 1826 Pedro I failed to name Nicolau Vergueiro, the favorite in São Paulo's triple list, preferring to name him as senator for Minas Gerais in 1828.[44]

Both political and personal friendship as well as enmity played substantial roles in the emperor's nomination of senators. Vergueiro, an outspoken liberal and an opponent of centripetalism in the constituent assembly, was obviously excluded by the displeased emperor; some of the major imperial counselors, such as Aracati, Queluz, and Santo Amaro, were not permitted to represent their home provinces, though they were elected there. Pedro I placed these men as senators in provinces where they did not have social and economic roots, a strategic dispersal of key advisers that reinforced patrimonial ties and the dependency of the life-tenure servants on the Crown. At the same time, it stifled the rise of powerful rivals, potential threats to imperial hegemony.

A point worth reemphasizing is that no recognized scion of a major agrarian clan represented his home or province where a candidate had economic interests in the senate of 1826. None of the six senators of Pernambuco came from the Albuquerques, the Rego Barroses, or the Sousa Leãos.[45] In Bahia, six native sons were named to represent the *terra boa*, but none were related to the province's major clans of capitalist agriculture. Of the ten senators from Minas Gerais, two were legitimate planters: the Marquês de Valença and the Marquês de Baependi. Both were born in Minas Gerais, but were major coffee planters in Rio province long before independence. In Rio and São Paulo, each represented by four senators, the majority of the senators selected by the emperor were recognized politicians, not planters or merchants. An exception was Lucas Antônio Monteiro de Barros, named as senator for São Paulo, who was a prominent landowner in Minas. Hence, the assertion that the regional agrarian elite dominated the imperial parliament simply does not hold up.

The pattern of the dispersed appointment of trusted counselors as senators for outlying provinces neatly complements the Weberian concept of a patrimonial (mandarin) ideology. The principal function of the Braganza mandarins was to uphold the monarchical hegemony of the ruling house by supporting national unity and directing unquestioned loyalty to the Crown. The senate, "the other half" of parliament, in practice served as the Praetorian guard for imperial values, often checking the abuses and liberalism of the chamber of deputies.

Not until the first decade of Pedro II's reign would a second pattern emerge, as regional clans succeeded in seating their offspring in the senate, though not always for their own provinces. Only under the Pernambucan regent Pedro de Araújo Lima did two brothers of the Albuquerques, of Pernambuco—the Visconde de Albuquerque and the Visconde de Suassuna—enter the senate, in 1838 and 1839, respectively; and the Conde de Boa Vista, also of Pernambuco and from an important agrarian clan, took a senatorial seat in 1850. In Bahia, no major agrarian clan succeeded in electing one of its members to the august upper chamber. Instead, in-laws and gentry landowners entered the senate, not as landowners but as accomplished mandarins. Thus, the Visconde de São Lourenço, a sugar planter in the Recôncavo, was elected to the body and won imperial appointment in 1851; and, in his turn, Cotegipe became senator in 1856. In Minas Gerais, a well-known landowner and mandarin, the Visconde de Jaguari, entered the senate in 1853. In São Paulo, it was also at mid-century, in 1848, that a landowner-mandarin took a seat in the senate: the Barão de Sousa Queirós, a prominent landowner in Campinas and an in-law of Nicolau Vergueiro and the Marquês de Valença.

During the late 1870s and the 1880s, a third pattern emerged when the importance of the coffee economy smoothed the way for a small number of capitalist agriculturists to enter the senate: the Barão de Santa Helena and the Barão de Leopoldina, both local politicians and planters in Minas Gerais; and Antônio da Silva Prado, a planter, banker, and railroad magnate in São Paulo's burgeoning northwest.[46]

The composition of the senate in 1826 can be seen as a patrimonial state's attempt to apportion equitably life-term offices among the various corporatist groups constituting the empire system. Emphasis was on balancing the exigencies of consolidating the imperial system, as the Braganza emperor and his courtier advisers saw them, and the patronage granted by the patrimonial prince to his regional (and corporatist) interests. The personality of Dom Pedro I, contemporary political situations and, more importantly, the mandarins' overall perception of what constituted a Brazilian empire system played crucial roles in senate organization.[47]

Of the first fifty senators seated in 1826, the single largest group (sixteen) came from the ranks of magistrates. Some of the better known were the Marquês de Queluz, the Marquês de São João da Palma, and the Marquês de Caravelas. The second largest group (twelve) consisted of governmental officials. Nine of them were members of the First Council of State, Pedro's most trusted advisers. Some were military officers whose careers had matured under Portuguese tutelage and continued after independence, among them the Marquês de Aracati, the Marquês de Barbacena, the Marquês de Baependi, and the Marquês de Paranaguá. Aracati and Barbacena served in foreign wars, the first as governor-general of Portuguese (French) Guiana and the second as the commander of the Brazilian forces in the Cisplatine War. Barbacena and Baependi served in numerous administrative and diplomatic assignments and were rich planters; both were Mineiros. The former moved to Bahia, married a daughter of a wealthy merchant, and invested in sugar plantations. The latter settled in Valença, founding a major coffee-planting clan.[48] The clergy constituted the third largest group (eight) in the senate of 1826. The bishop of Rio, Dom José Caetano da Silva Coutinho, became senator from São Paulo;[49] significantly, the bishop (who also served as Chaplain Major of the imperial house) was not allowed to hold the senatorship from the court and its province, over which his ecclesiastical authority reigned. The Crown often strove to transfer a patrimonial elite of one region to another during the mandarin-training process. Only Ceará, in the Northeast, was represented by priests in the senate; eight south-central provinces, including the Cisplatine province, had a senator-priest each. Minas Gerais was the only major province represented by a native son-priest of a major clan (the Monteiro de Barroses).[50]

Other professional men were also included in the 1826 senate. At least four senators were high-ranked public servants: the Marquês de Caravelas, the Marquês de Santo Amaro, the Marquês de Maricá, and José Carlos Mayrink da Silva Ferrão. One diplomat-poet (the Visconde de Pedra Branca), three landowners, two physicians, and a lawyer represented other corporate groups. The overwhelming representation of the civil, military, and religious bureaucracy in Pedro's senate is convincing evidence that a patrimonial empire system was built on the personal loyalty directed to the Crown and, more importantly, to the emperor himself. Hence, the empire system was not an intellectual offspring of the Enlightenment, despite its constitutional facade. On the contrary, its patrimonial emphasis on the participation of various corporatist groups further legitimized its imperial structure and strengthened the personal authority of its emperor.

Modifications in the pattern of dispersing seasoned mandarins as provincial senators did take place. The economic and social importance of certain groups coincided with the paramount concern of the empire. The occupational breakdown of those senators of 1826 can be readily identified. The magistrate group retained their dominance over the senate. During the second half of the nineteenth century, professors of law and practicing attorneys increased their share of seats. Proportionately, the clergy lost offices, and landowners and "capitalists" increased their hold on senatorial seats, especially after 1870. By Taunay's count, 34 of the 234 senators were landowners, or 14.4 percent. Of these, the five major provinces of capitalist agriculture claimed 20 whose fulltime economic interest was export agriculture: Pernambuco (4), Bahia (1), Minas (6), Rio (5), and São Paulo (4). These 20 constituted 59 percent of the total planter and rancher category in the senate.[51] This trend simply attests to the changing realities of the Brazilian economy and society after 1850, when Rio, Minas, and São Paulo emerged as an important appendage of the Atlantic world-economy, the principal locus of the empire's capitalist agriculture and the producer of provincial and imperial revenues.

Along with the entrenchment of corporatist representation in the patrimonial state was the dynastic domination of senatorial seats by several sets of fathers and sons, brothers, and in-laws. Taunay's contention that the Albuquerques were·the only Brazilian clan that had a continued presence throughout the imperial period in the senate (1826–89)[52] is a slight exaggeration. In 1826 Albuquerque Maranhão, the first of that distinguished name, was selected to serve as senator from Rio Grande do Norte (his home province), not from Pernambuco. This Potiguar family was probably a relative of the mainline clan, the Albuquerques of Pernambuco, a family that produced three senators (all brothers), the only Brazilian agrarian clan enjoying such a distinction. There were nineteen other sets of dynastically related senators (see table 3). The Monteiro de Barroses, of Minas Gerais, could claim five senators, including their kinsmen the Barão de Santa Helena and the Barão de Leopoldina, both planters in Minas. The Duque de Caxias could claim his in-laws (the Nogueira da Gamas) and father, together producing four senators. The Visconde do Uruguai (born in France) was a concunhado of another Conservative cacique in Rio province, the Visconde de Itaboraí, and could claim three senators for the visconde's family. Nicolau Vergueiro and the Marquês de Valença were in-laws of the Barão de Sousa Queirós, thus constituting a threesome. In addition, distant relationships gave other clans sets of three senators: the Nabucos and the Carneiro de Campos, both of Bahia, and the Rego Barroses, of Pernambuco. This surname analysis gives the Albuquerques ten senators.[53] A point to underscore is that only in Pernambuco did agrarian interests attain political power at the national level.

Although the Constitution of 1824 invested the power to nominate senators in the emperor from a list of three who had won the most votes, the exercise of this moderating power remained a potent source of conflict between the Crown and its detractors. The power was often abused to favor a partisan faction loyal to the emperor or to advance the career of a particular imperial ward. Especially after 1860, the Liberals clamored for reform in the senate as well as in the moderating power itself. In 1868 the third Zacarias Cabinet resigned in protest when

Table 3 Senators of Close Kinships in Brazil, 1826–1889
(in alphabetical order)

Name	Relationship	Province	Party	Years in office
Visconde de Albuquerque	Brother	Pernambuco	Liberal	1838–63
Visconde de Suassuna	Brother	Pernambuco	Liberal	1839–80
Visconde de Camaragibe	Brother	Pernambuco	Conservative	1869–75
José Tomás Nabuco de Araújo	Father	Espírito Santo	Liberal	1837–50
José Tomás Nabuco de Araújo	Son	Bahia	Liberal	1858–78
Marquês de Baependi	Father	Minas Gerais	Conservative	1826–47
Conde de Baependi	Son	Rio de Janeiro	Conservative	1872–87
Marquês de Caravelas	Brother	Bahia	n.a.	1826–37
Francisco Carneiro de Campo	Brother	Bahia	Conservative	1826–42
Marquês de Caravelas	Father	Bahia	n.a.	1826–37
Visconde de Caravelas	Son	Bahia	Conservative	1837–55
Visconde de Congonhas do Campo	Brother	São Paulo	Liberal	1826–51
Marcos Antônio Monteiro de Barros	Brother	Minas Gerais	Liberal	1826–52
Visconde de Congonhas do Campo	Father	São Paulo	Liberal	1826–51
Antônio A. Monteiro de Barros	Son	Minas Gerais	Liberal	1838–41
Teófilo Benedito Ottoni	Brother	Minas Gerais	Liberal	1864–69
Cristiano Benedito Ottoni	Brother	Espírito Santo	Liberal	1879–89
Marquês de Paraná	Father-in-law	Minas Gerais	Conservative	1842–56
Visconde do Cruzeiro	Son-in-law	Rio de Janeiro	Conservative	1873–89
Francisco de Paula Pessoa	Father	Ceará	Liberal	1848–79
Vicente Alves de Paula Pessoa	Son	Ceará	Liberal	1881–88
Joaquim Franco de Sá	Father	Maranhão	Liberal	1849–51
Felipe Franco de Sá	Son	Maranhão	Liberal	1882–89
Marquês de São João da Palma	Father	São Paulo	Liberal	1826–43
Manuel de Assis Mascarenhas	Son	Rio Grande do Norte	Conservative	1850–67

Table 3 Senators of Close Kinships in Brazil, 1826–1889
(in alphabetical order)—continued

Name	Relationship	Province	Party	Years in Office
Visconde de Sepetiba	Brother	Alagoas	Liberal	1842–55
Saturino de Sousa e Oliveira	Brother	Rio de Janeiro	Liberal	1847–48
Francisco de Lima e Silva	Father	Rio de Janeiro	Conservative	1837–53
Duque de Caxias	Son	Rio Grande do Sul	Conservative	1845–80
Joaquim Vieira da Silva e Sousa	Father	Maranhão	Conservative	1859–64
Visconde de Vieira da Silva	Son	Maranhão	Conservative	1871–89
Visconde do Uruguai	Concunhado[a]	Rio de Janeiro	Conservative	1849–65
Visconde de Itaborai	Concunhado	Rio de Janeiro	Conservative	1844–72
Visconde do Uruguai	Father	Rio de Janeiro	Conservative	1849–65
Paulino José Soares de Sousa	Son	Rio de Janeiro	Conservative	1884–89
Marquês de Valença	Brother-in-law	Minas Gerais	Conservative	1826–56
Barão de Sousa Queirós	Brother-in-law	São Paulo	Liberal	1848–89
Bernardo Pereira de Vasconcelos	Brother	Minas Gerais	Conservative	1838–50
Francisco Diogo P. de Vasconcelos	Brother	Minas Gerais	Conservative	1857–63
Nicolau Pereira de Campos Vergueiro	Father-in-law	Minas Gerais	Liberal	1828–59
Barão de Sousa Queirós	Son-in-law	São Paulo	Liberal	1848–89

	Brothers	Father/Son	Brother-in-Law	Father/Son-in-Law	Concunhado
Number of Kin Sets: 6		10	1	2	1

Sources: Affonso de E. Taunay, *O senado do império*, 2nd ed. (Brasília, 1978), pp. 147–160; Arquivo Nacional, *Organizações e programas ministeriais: regime parlamentar no império*, 2nd ed. (Rio, 1962), pp. 407–416.

[a] Sister-in-law's husband.

Pedro II failed to pick the (Liberal) candidate who had gained the most votes and nominated instead a Conservative for the senate.[54] The manifest goal of the Liberals during the late sixties and early seventies was to cast this aspect of reform as the prelude to a constitutional monarchy in which, to paraphrase Thiers, the "king reigned but ruled not."[55] To the end of the empire, Liberal desire to reform the life tenure *(vitalicidade)* in the senate and the council of state and of the poder moderador mounted steadily and by the mid-1880s still remained the reformists' unfulfilled dream.

The defenders of imperialism or of the centripetalist prerogatives of the emperorship argued that the life-tenure system not only was necessary for a polity made up of various orders such as Brazil, but also provided an imperial corpus of men who had "wisdom, ability, virtues, and services to the fatherland"; decisions of state made by such men could not be easily influenced by partisan passions and petty local strifes.[56] According to such Conservative politician-intellectuals as the Marquês de São Vicente (José Antônio Pimenta Bueno) and the Visconde do Uruguai (Paulino José Soares de Sousa), a state was a political society designed to impose order and to promote "fixed, general interests" on the one hand and on the other to foster "local aspirations and well-being."[57] To São Vicente, the elected chamber of deputies represented local and regional interests, and the senate was the custodian of higher national values and purposes. If life tenure was removed, the difference between the upper and lower chambers would disappear. Furthermore, he pointed out, the Brazilian senate was not an aristocratic body representing the "bastion of the territorial wealth, entails (morgados), or the privileges of a hereditary nobility. Neither was it a simple creature of the crown."[58] To Uruguai, Brazilian society was made up of many "different bodies" *(corpos diferentes)* with distinctly identifiable interests, constantly in competition and often in conflict among themselves. To maintain checks and balances and to conciliate the various corporatist forces, the state then must possess institutions empowered to promote and defend its long-term interests as well as to satisfy its short-term needs. The requisite order and stability made life tenure for senators and councillors of state an absolute essential.[59] Both São Vicente and Uruguai, among many other Conservative and Liberal politicians, subscribed to this view of the state, the perfect epitome of the Weberian patrimonial and Thomistic corporatist model.

To help stabilize the monarchy system, the writers of the Constitution of 1824 considered imposing income requirements on the electoral franchise that would have excluded virtually all working-class people from the process who had no corporatist identities: 150 *alqueires* of manioc flour for voting, 250 for elector, 500 for deputy, and 1,000 for senator.[60] The final draft of the document chose to substitute monetary for the commodity requirements: 200$ for voting, 400$ for deputy, and 800$ for senator. This income requirement for the exercise of voters' rights continued until the end of the monarchy.

A voter roster of Valença in 1879 offers a glimpse into the income distribution of informal social corporations. Landowners registered the highest annual income range: 40:000$ to 1:000$. Physicians and surgeons were the next richest group, with a range of 6:000$ to 1:200$. Pharmacists and merchants had similar income ranges: from 5:000$ and 4:000$, respectively, to 400$ and 200$. Of the eight lower-class occupational categories, goldsmiths and coffin-makers earned the highest incomes: 400$ and 200$ each.[61] Based on the sample of Valença, the incomes correlate positively with the social categorization of corporate groups. Yet, income requirements alone could not ensure the stability of the monarchy system. As Brazilian economic realities changed, so did the size and composition of the electorate. In the 1880s one calculation is that less than 3 percent of the empire's male population actually exercised the electoral franchise.[62] Because the intent of state managers was to strike a balance between encouraging democratic participation and guaranteeing imperial prerogatives, the adoption of life-tenure offices (senate and council of state) became a prudent way out.

The second institution involving life tenure, the council of state, was a pillar of imperial authority that has not been fully explored by historians. Contrary to popular belief, however, the council was neither a "kitchen cabinet" for Pedro I and Pedro II nor the Brazilian version of a privy council. Its harbinger was the Conselho de Procuradores Gerais das Províncias, created by the decree of 16 February 1822, a body of local citizens elected to advise on governmental reform and organization taking place in the hiatus between the departure of King João VI and the independence of the empire. In July 1822 this body became the First Council of State, only to be abolished by the constituent assembly in October 1823. The council was reinstated by the decree of 13 November 1823 and the Constitution of 1824, which fixed the total number of councillors at ten.[63] Six of the first councillors came from the ranks of the imperial cabinet, and four new members were added by Pedro I. These same men, charged with the writing of the constitution months earlier, were all noblemen.

In political importance, the First Council of State (1824–34) reflected the imperial notion of a political institution. It lacked partisanism and strong personalities. All ten members were loyal creatures of Pedro I, and their political career patterns reflected the sinecurism of the monarchy. None came from the ranks of politicians who enjoyed independent regional power bases, such as the Andradas, of São Paulo, and the Albuquerques, of Pernambuco. Nine of the ten were titled functionaries, all marquêses and one a visconde. All the council's characteristics contributed to a rising Lusophobia among Pedro I's subjects; to thwart it, he appointed Brazilians to the presidencies of provinces and even permitted one radical liberal, "almost republican," to hold the executive position of Ceará.[64] Such outspoken opponents of Braganza imperialism as José Bonifácio, Nicolau Vergueiro, and others were exiled or silenced. The patronizing emperor, however, granted pensions to the persecuted: 1:200$ for married men and 600$ for those who were single.[65] In spite of such gestures, the balance of political power remained in the hands of Pedro's Portuguese advisers, and the First Council of State never gained the popular confidence that it sorely needed among Brazilians. An easy target for nationalists, it was abolished by the Ato Adicional of 1834.[66]

Historians have often contended that the Regency period (1831–40) represented a true transition in Brazilian politics, an era frequently cited for its "experiments with republicanism" and "provincial revolts."[67] Republicanism and secessionist ideas erupted during the turbulent decade, when both the empire and the new emperor, Pedro II, suffered growing pains. Such a staunch regional dynast-politician as Holanda Cavalcanti de Albuquerque proposed in 1832 a sweeping administrative reform transferring economic decision-making power to the provinces, an idea immediately attacked by life-tenure senators. Liberals in São Paulo and Minas Gerais proceeded to draft a "reformed constitution," which they printed in Porto Alegre and then circulated clandestinely in the court. This constitutional amendment served as the basis for the Ato Adicional of 1834.[68]

At the heart of the Additional Act was an attempt by the elected chamber of the parliament to disperse imperial power, then concentrated in the hands of the Crown, to the provinces. The act established a provincial legislature to replace the old Conselho Geral, an advisory body to the president of a province. Popularly elected, every provincial legislature would have a chamber of deputies. Such major provinces as Rio, Minas, São Paulo, Bahia, and Pernambuco were also to have a senate, and minor provinces possessed the option to create an upper house.[69] Provincial control of judicial and police powers was beefed up by shifting it from the município level to the provincial president, an appointee of the Crown. The legislature was to act as a counterweight to the president. To the considerable credit of the Regency ministers, many political, social, and administrative reforms were created, including establishment of a citizen army, the National Guard; abolishing the First Council of State (but not the moderating power of the emperor); and suspending the award of nobiliary titles and lesser honors.

From Rio's standpoint, the reforms implemented administrative decentralization, making provincial governments stronger and more democratic. From the perspective of the lowest administrative unit of the monarchy, the município, however, the Regency period represented a loss of power to the provincial capital, especially of judicial and police power. It should be pointed out, however, that the current tendency in Brazilian historiography has been to stress the "decentralization" aspect, at the loss of a balanced interpretation of the power adjustment among the three levels of the monarchical government system. Thus Rio's decentralization was deceptive. Its agents, the provincial presidents, held greater power than had their predecessors before 1834.

The Regency decade was torn on the one hand by political strife between Liberals and Conservatives, and on the other by a series of internal wars: in Pará, in the North; Bahia, in the Northeast; and Rio Grande do Sul, in the South.[70] Between April 1831 and July 1840, the ten-year rule was managed by four regencies—two triune and two single regencies—and some thirteen cabinets were formed and disbanded. The Ato Adicional of 1834, a milestone in the history of the empire, established some of the most basic reforms, among them the introduction of a strong single executive system of government.

Two leading contenders for regent were Pedro Diogo Antônio Feijó, bishop of Mariana and senator from São Paulo, and Antônio Francisco de Paula e Holanda Cavalcanti de Albuquerque, deputy from Pernambuco.[71] In a heated contest, the Paulista priest defeated the Pernambucan dynast. Between October 1835 and September 1837, Feijó had three cabinets; his administration was plagued with nascent partisan struggles. The death of Pedro I in Portugal turned the "partido de regresso" into the Brazilian Conservative party, of which Bernardo Pereira de Vasconcelos, of Minas Gerais, became the leader. The regent was the leader of the anti-Pedrista Liberals. By 1837 Feijó was being attacked by the Conservatives, and he was replaced by Pedro de Araújo Lima, a rising Conservative party star whom Feijó had just nominated as senator from Pernambuco over Holanda Cavalcanti and his brother Paula Cavalcanti, both leaders of the Pernambucan delegation. Both these men had received more popular votes than Araújo Lima, but Feijó picked the least objectionable of the three Conservatives and made him minister of the empire in May 1837.[72] By September, Pedro de Araújo Lima had been elected as regent to replace his patron, Feijó. The Pernambucan regency was administered by four cabinets, the last one in 1840. The continuing political instability, compounded by debilitating regional revolts as well as power struggles between the senate and the chamber of deputies, prompted politicians to initiate a movement to return power to the teenage emperor.

The idea of making Pedro II a "major" eligible for the full power of emperor, as required by the constitution, had been discussed from time to time in parliament: in 1835 by Luís Cavalcanti, in 1837 by Vieira Souto, and in 1839 by Montezuma. Inasmuch as the chamber of deputies was controlled by Regent Araújo Lima in 1840, Liberals feared the rising political power of the northerners (nortistas), led by the Pernambucan politicans, and began to revive the idea of "restoration." One plan was to offer the throne to Princess Januária, who could rule as imperial regent, a ploy especially attractive to the Liberals, who thought that such a move would stymie the Conservative attempt to declare the majority of Pedro, who was still a minor. In the end, thinking politicians of both parties accepted the "majority" plan for Pedro, and, by early April 1840, José Alencar had organized the Clube Maiorista. Holanda Cavalcanti, the Andrada brothers (only Martim Francisco and Antônio Carlos), and others joined the club. The senate introduced a bill to declare Pedro a major, and, after considerable debate on the floor, the bill was finally approved by both chambers.[73]

Adherents of the Maiorista movement won only half the battle, however. Originally, José Alencar presented two bills in tandem: one to make Pedro "maior desde já" and another to create a council of state with a representative from each of the empire's provinces, nominated by the emperor to help him run the country until he reached twenty-one. A different bill proposed by opponents incorporated the two goals in one, slightly modifying the council's organization as the Privy Council of the Crown, a ten-member, permanent institution. Strong differences of opinion among the maioristas over the issue resulted in the presentation of two more separate bills. Finally, the majority bill was passed, and the privy council bill was rejected. Among those casting "nay" votes were such major mandarins as Nabuco, Pedra Branca, Lopes Gama, Lages, and Alves Branco. The president of the senate, the Marquês de Paranaguá, was not counted among the authors of the privy council bill but supported it. In the final tally, sixteen in favor and eighteen against, the idea of the privy council died in the senate.[74]

The movement to return Brazil to a centripetal regime was in part a reaction against the failures of Liberal experiments during the Regency years. Politics had been severely marred by the arbitrary, autocratic tendencies of two holders of the office: Feijó and Araújo Lima. When the death of Pedro I in 1837 terminated the dream of restoring Braganza hegemony, Liberals campaigned for further democratization of the empire, a prospect that struck Conservatives as bordering on anarchism. The latter perceived placing a teenage emperor on the throne as just a first step in the arduous struggle toward restoring a strong government system. This was done in 1840. On 3 May 1841, the fifteen-year-old Pedro in his first Speech from the Throne to the Brazilian parliament implored the tribunes to reestablish the Council of State to help him administer the empire.[75]

The fate of the council was intricately tied to the poder moderador granted in the constitution to the Crown and which was deemed to be "inviolable and unanswerable" by the elected legislature. This power was to serve, especially after 1840, as the cornerstone of the Brazilian imperial state, whose Thomistic perception of patrimonial-capitalist statehood it clearly expressed.[76] The Crown was the head of the *corpus politicum* of the monarchy. As in the Catholic church model, the emperor was expected to behave like a pontiff, a supreme fount of authority, the arbiter of various social and economic "orders" that were stitched into the hierarchy of the empire, and as the governing authority. To reconcile the conflicting demands of various corporations of the social and economic interests in the monarchy's diverse regions, the emperor exercised the moderating power, the quintessence of patrimonial lordship. The parliamentary system of government that the monarchy adopted was basically the offspring of a different kind of philosophy, though Brazil was commonly compared to England in the nineteenth century.

Parliament's response to the imperial appeal in the Speech from the Throne was the passage of Lei No. 234 of 29 November 1841, creating the Second Council of State, a bill initiated in the senate, not in the temporary chamber. To some historians, the council epitomized the supremacy of imperial authority, thus ending the Liberal Age in Brazil. The creation of the council effectively suppressed the "checks and balances" system inherent in all democratic, constitutional regimes. Other measures fostered centralization. The Código do Processo (Criminal Trial Code) of 3 December 1841 nullified provincial control over the judicial and police power, restoring it to the central government. The adoption of this code finalized the collapse of the Liberal experiment that had spanned more than a decade—a period of turbulence, internal wars, and near-anarchy.[77] The re-creation of the council in 1841 was meant to assign the power to rule to the Crown; it also foreshadowed the strengthening of the moderating power as the principal fount of all governmental authority. The council was to play a major role for the next half century.

The Second Council of State (1842–89) was composed of twenty-four members, twelve regular (ordinários) and twelve alternate (extraordinários).[78] The working members of the council, whether regular or alternate, drew an annual stipend of 4:000$. Frequently, councillors were appointed to cabinet posts and in such cases were disqualified from the council's decision making. Meeting in plenary sessions, the council issued advice (consulta), recommended specific actions (ata), and rendered decisions (resolução imperial) on specifically referred issues. The council heard and decided myriad cases, ranging from the constitutional rights of slaves, pardon and clemency, and judicial review to the extent of provincial legislative power, the eligibility of double officeholding, the proper manner of law enforcement, and the conduct of foreign relations.[79]

The council's volume of work steadily increased over the years, as the complexity of administering the far-flung empire required constant attention from the imperial authorities in the court. Additionally, the inadequately trained patrimonial officials and bureaucrats often contributed to the council's workload because, for example, any improperly worded decrees or laws, sloppy administration of good decrees and laws, egregious judicial errors, and out-of-bounds actions by provincial legislatures required corrective measures by the council. The vicissitudes and vagaries of imperial administration, from Amazonas to Bahia to São Paulo to Rio Grande do Sul and then to Minas Gerais to Mato Grosso, tended to strengthen the Crown's power by providing continual opportunities to intervene and reinforcing the legitimacy of the moderating power through remedial decisions and advice that the council often handed down in the name of the emperor.

In accordance with the Liberal-Conservative compromise, the "reactionary cabinet" of 1841–43 appointed only half the total regular and alternate members of the council: seven ordinários and five extraordinários, all Conservatives. Three appointments each went to Bahia, Minas, and Portugal; Pernambuco received two and Rio one. By the end of monarchical rule in 1889, six provinces had received one appointment each, but seven had never been represented at all. It is interesting to observe that São Paulo, the bastion of liberalism, did not have a councillor until 1845, when the first nomination went to Paula Sousa, the persistent doubter and opponent of the council idea in 1841.[80] A total of seventy-two persons served in the Second Council of State between 1842 and 1889. Several interesting clues support their geographical distribution. The only provinces gaining ten or more appointments were Bahia (seventeen), Rio (fourteen), and Minas (thirteen). Neither Bahia nor Minas received any appointment during the second decade of the council; Bahia won five seats during the decade of 1861–70, and Minas accounted for the same number during the decade 1881–89. The economic power of Minas province was on the rise after 1870, and that of Bahia was in decline. São Paulo went for two decades (1861–80) without a single appointment, gaining one seat during the following decade. It is also noteworthy to observe that Pernambuco, Bahia's arch-rival in the Northeast, netted only five appointments, both sets of appointments occurring during the first and last decades of the council, leaving a hiatus of three decades (1851–80).

Although too much cannot be read into this pattern of geographical distribution of council seats, it does convey where the trustworthy patrimonial councillors came from and, secondarily, suggests that a strong relationship existed between the distribution of ministerial portfolios and that of councillorships. As might be expected, fifty-three of the seventy-two councillors, or 73.6 percent, were trained in law, followed by a distant second, the military, with eleven councillors, of 15.3 percent. Lawyers and soldiers were the foundation of the patrimonial empire system, their services being indispensable for administering justice as well as maintaining order and stability.

Of the twenty-three men who held the coveted post of president of the council of ministers, only four did not become councillors of state: two ardent proslave mandarins and two radical Liberals, three of them from Bahia and one from Piauí. José Antônio Saraiva and the Barão de Cotegipe were slavocrat-planters, Liberal and Conservative, respectively. Both were known for their zeal in modernizing sugar plantations; Saraiva was a full partner in a refinery project in Bahia in the early 1880s.[81] Zacarias de Góis e Vasconcelos, three-time prime minister, also from Bahia, was denied appointment to the council. His relations with the Conservative party and the Crown were turbulent, to say the least; his conflict with Caxias and his objection over Pedro's choice for a senator caused his fall from imperial grace and his dismissal from the highest office in the land. The fourth, Francisco José Furtado, was a native of Piauí and, like Zacarias, a Liberal. A scant three weeks after Furtado was chosen for senator, the emperor appointed him to the presidency of the council of ministers as a compromise candidate between radical Liberals and himself. His short tenure in office (less than a year, from August 1864 to May 1865) was attributable to political differences between the two dominant parties as well as his unpopular propeace policy at the outset of the Paraguayan War (1864–70). Much like Zacarias, his colleague in the senate, Furtado believed in a weakened Crown, constitutional checks on the poder moderador, and more autonomy for parliament. He was also one of the founders of the radical Centro Liberal in 1868, which called for a series of reforms or, in the absence thereof, a revolution. The following year, he died without knowing the outcome of the radical Liberal programs.[82] The exclusion of these four prime ministers from the council, therefore, was political, as in the cases of Cotegipe and Saraiva, when viewed against an 1880s backdrop of the rising antislavery tide. It simply was not prudent for the patrimonial emperor to side with any particular interests, especially those of the slavocratic planters. Conceptually, slavocracy was only one among several corporatist entities in the empire.

Sixty, or 83 percent, of the councillors who served in the Second Council of State were senators, thus holding two life-tenure offices. Fifty-three of these, an overwhelming 96 percent, held a portfolio of minister of state once or more during their sinecurist political careers. Nineteen of the fifty-three quadruple officeholders became presidents of the council of ministers. The Crown made a deliberate attempt to create a pool of mandarins in two life-tenure offices: the senate and the council of state. That the council of ministers was dominated by the holders of one of these two offices is a significant clue to the actual practice of imperial patrimonialism as conceived by the Braganzas. The stability of their ideas and institutions was assured by the loyalty and devotion of seasoned mandarins, as was the legitimacy of the Crown itself. Not all cabinet ministers were drawn from this pool between 1847 and 1889, however. The induction into cabinets of carefully selected nonlifers, such as deputies, career military men, and even planters and merchants, regularly replenished the dwindling "pool." This pattern significantly affected the formation of the political elites of the monarchy in two ways.

First, an appointment to a ministerial portfolio was a process of mandarin-making when it involved a relatively low-ranking deputy or a career military man. The system of reward and co-optation of mandarin elites was continually at work, and the search for prospective patrimonial officials was a perennial process. Those who failed to measure up to the expectations of the Crown, even at the ministerial and senatorial levels, could still be eliminated from the highest sinecurist office of councillor of state. Saraiva, Cotegipe, Zacarias, and Furtado were just four of those rejected from the rank of prime minister. Of 219 ministers of the empire, only 57, or 27 percent, reached the apex of the mandarinate. Countless other candidates were eliminated well before they reached ministerial rank.

Second, by the inclusion, however occasional, of promising upstarts, the Crown assured some balance between the "general interests" and the "specific interests," the former being the concern of the empire and the latter that of its myriad regions. The corporatist notion of distributing power, or permitting various groups to participate in decision making, was firmly embedded in such appointments.

The emperor thus exercised both the moderating and executive powers after 1842 through two different sets of patrimonial agents, ministers of state and councillors of state; as the empire system reached maturity, the fusion of these two sets of mandarins became a fact. By 1889, when the monarchy fell, Brazil still had thirty-seven double life-term officeholders who had been ministers of state and deputies. Almost half a century was required to complete the process, but the Braganza monarchy toward its end successfully forged a loyal cadre of patrimonial mandarins of the highest order, sufficiently large to form five separate cabinets in succession. It should be pointed out that the interdependency of the emperor and his sixty senator-councillors (fifty-three of whom were ministers of state) in the exercise of the moderating and executive powers was a two-way street: the holders of double life-tenure offices drew a senator's stipend of 9:000$ and that of a councillor, 4:000$, or enough to buy twelve or fifteen healthy slaves in the 1880s. The Crown in turn took advantage of their financial dependence on the patrimonial state by turning them into docile bureaucrats of the House of Braganza. Political careers in nineteenth-century Brazil were never designed to be well compensated, rather to have their expenses be paid. But the mandarins of the highest order were financially well looked after by the Crown as worthy wards of the patrimonial state. Zacarias, who advocated the thesis that the moderating power must be subject to the constitutional control of the people, contended that the council of state was the center of gravity of imperial political power.[83] To Nabuco de Araújo, it was a "crucible of our statesmen and the arch of the traditions of government."[84]

If the council of state under the direction of the emperor functioned as the head of the Brazilian body politic, the council of ministers provided the limbs to carry out the decisions of the council of state and the imperial will. It was created by Decree No. 523 of 20 July 1847.[85] The first president of the council was a Bahian Conservative, the Visconde de Caravelas; the last, in 1889, was a Mineiro Liberal, the Visconde de Ouro Preto. Because historians and political scientists have accepted the concept of mandarins and their role both in the empire and republic, it is not necessary to repeat the story. However, the emergence of conflicts between the centripetal state and regions, and in particular the resolutions thereof, should be examined as one aspect of how the mandarin system functioned.

After the crowning of Dom Pedro II in 1841, the Conservatives masterminded the passage of the Reinterpretive Law of 1842, under which much of the existing political, judicial, and police power reverted from the provinces to the imperial government. The political power of the provinces, the bastion of capitalist agriculture and its wealth, was systematically stripped away by imperial fiats, decrees, appointments as well as removals of officials, and judicial reforms. By mid-century, the imperial authorities in Rio had succeeded in tilting the keel of the government toward centripetalism, or what Joaquim Nabuco called *imperialismo*. The persistent loss of local autonomy and power, once guaranteed under the Ato Adicional and even under the Constitution of 1824, during the decades following 1860 corresponds to the weakening of the territorial aristocracy. The shift of power occurred precisely during the decades when the northern sugar economy found itself at its lowest ebb and the south-central coffee industry was busily expanding and forming a politically awakened gentry class.

Therefore, the major conflict between the imperial government and the provinces evolved around how to shape and discipline the provincial legislatures and municipal councils, the seats of local power.[86] Savoring the autonomy granted by the 1834 Additional Act, provincial legislators passed at will laws that would be beneficial to the local hegemonic classes and at the same time were detrimental to the general interests of the monarchy. This conflict between "the particular interests" and "the general interests" needed to be resolved without dissolving the empire. The council of state played a key role in dealing with such conflicts.

Provinces often adopted generous retirement pensions for public employees that could not only drain the public exchequer but also breed rampant nepotism. The imperial government struck down every law that provincial legislatures enacted without regard for the empire's finances. Such peripheral provinces as Pará, Sergipe, Santa Catarina, and Rio Grande do Sul were more assertive with their legislative power, thus committing greater perfidy. The distance from the court gave them false psychological security in their autonomy, though at times their assertiveness worked. On the whole, the imperial government urged its provincial presidents to exercise better supervision over the legislatures that tended to be protean, eager to deviate from the general will of the monarchy.[87] The consistent imperial vetoing of provincial legislative actions over the decades practically destroyed most local autonomy. By the 1880s several provinces had failed to convoke legislatures for lack of interest. In 1885 no legislatures met in Sergipe and Santa Catarina; some provinces were forced to delay the opening of the assemblies for lack of a quorum; and in Bahia, after no fewer than seven extensions, the legislature still failed to produce a quorum or to pass a single law. The disgusted president of the province refused to set a date for a new session.[88]

The indifference so pervasive among provincial deputies reflected an aging patrimonial state that was increasingly less sensitive and responsive to the divergent needs of its provinces and that was saddled with a ruling political elite becoming gerontocratic in its thinking and performance. Out of touch with reality, some of this group openly rebelled against imperial conformity; and others, like Sousa Dantas and Prado, pushed for reforms. One historian, recognizing this process of ideological disintegration among the mandarins, concluded that Brazil after 1870 lacked a cohesive ideology to survive.[89] Additionally, the mandarin ideology had become superfluous. Its philosophy was designed to hold the empire together, to emphasize the general welfare over the particular interests of the provinces or of a certain class. It insisted on administrative and judicial uniformity in governing a territory more vast than the continental United States.[90] What was suitable for Amazônia in 1870 could hardly be appropriate to Rio Grande do Sul. Yet, the empire lived under one law, one government, and one mandarinate that exercised total power. Such a patrimonial state was a creature of the Braganza court and its agents before 1830, not that of the regions of diverse and often conflicting economic as well as social interests that made up the Brazil of the post-1870s. The dysfunctioning of the patrimonial state system was by then a fact. One frustrated minister of the empire broached the idea of setting up a remedial school for provincial presidents to improve the efficiency of imperial administration. The same minister also suggested that the tenure of the president's office be extended.[91] The authorities in Rio were aware of this disintegrative process. That the imperial parliament and the Crown government could not produce the reforms necessary to revive the aging monarchy was a sure sign that regional and class demands were too diverse and even antithetical to be reconciled.

At the heart of the erupting conflict was a jungle of laws, decrees, and regulations with which the imperial government had inundated the country—each instructing provincial presidents, legislatures, and municipal councils how to enforce imperial laws. A simple index of orders *(ordens)*, circulars *(avisos circulares,* or often just *avisos)*, decrees *(decretos)*, and instructions *(instruções)* as issued by the ministries for the period 1850 to 1884 required five volumes. The *Coleção das Leis do Brasil* and the *Decisões do Governo,* the principal codes of the monarchy, consisted of several hundred volumes. No administrator could possibly remember the intricacies of such myriad procedures. In fact, the infamous avisos often repeated themselves in content as well as wording, whenever a new minister took up his portfolio.[92]

A few examples of the limitations placed on regional action by imperial interests can help show how the gap between the core and periphery widened. The power invested in provincial legislatures was tightly regulated by the imperial government and often revised from time to time to reflect the philosophical bent of each ministry. The provincial assembly could create administrative posts on city councils, but it was barred from interfering with the operation of the councils themselves.[93] The provincial legislatures were expressly prohibited from passing laws that were incompatible with imperial laws.[94] Laws that sought to regulate church properties, the function of judicial officials, and the management of mineral wealth fell outside the purview of regional legislatures.[95] An 1871 aviso of the Ministry of Agriculture prohibited provincial deputies from adopting any law that could delay the enforcement of the metric system. In some northern provinces, this provoked peasant revolts that appeared both archaic in motive and a bit antimonarchical in character. These revolts were called "Quebra Kilos," or "break the metric system," and were surreptitiously organized and supported by local agrarian overlords.[96] By mid-century, the many imperial decrees of "can do" and "cannot do" had so hamstrung the provincial legislatures that they had degenerated into ineffectual regional bodies. Such decay was more pronounced in economically decadent regions.

The role of the provincial chief executive was also carefully monitored, in spite of the wishes of the imperial government to use him as a counterweight to the local elite and as a watchdog on the legislature. He was a frieze on the imperial edifice, not a pillar of the administrative-judicial bureaucracy. No financial authority was ever invested in him. An 1862 minister of finance instruction explicitly stated that the provincial president had no power to authorize any payment from the treasury. A few years later, the original instruction was reissued in more emphatic terms that stripped the provincial president of all authority on matters of "the administration of the treasury."[97] By 1871 the minister required that the provincial chief report all financial transactions, such as the budgets of the province and counties, to the imperial authorities *before* they could be put into effect.[98] The provincial president could not remove any employee of the imperial government from his domain, though he was the highest Crown authority. Neither could he authorize any alteration in the budget for a project previously sanctioned by the imperial government without checking with the appropriate ministers.[99] Even with the provincial legislature's approval, the president could not issue contracts for mineral and water exploration. And he could not fine municipal councils for infractions of their own ordinances.[100] In the words of one Liberal reformer, the provincial administration was in "an anarchy."[101] Often, the misgovernment brought about by frequent breakdowns and administrative bottlenecks was attributed to the legislature belonging to one political party and the president to another, a frequent occurrence after 1870.

The imperial regulations governing municipal councils outnumbered those for provincial assemblies and presidents by three to one. This excess simply on one hand confirms the gerontocratic nature of the imperial authority, and, on the other, the escalating power struggle between the state and society. The sheer number of prohibitive decrees and orders was staggering. By 1870 the local government considered itself the real government of the county and began to eye suspiciously the meddlesome imperial government as a usurper. The rise of Republican movements on the county level in Rio, São Paulo, Minas Gerais, and Rio Grande do Sul was a sure sign of the sentiment that a state which interfered with the governance of local affairs by the dominant elite was an undeserving political institution that society at large must be rid of. Like the agricultural clubs of the 1860s, 1870s, and

1880s, the Republican clubs represented the resistance of society against a state malfunctioning in the political arena. The revolt of society against the state was therefore in the offing by the onset of the 1870s amid the nation's unexampled economic growth and expansion in the Center-South and its equally unprecedented economic decay in the Northeast.

The imperial authorities were particularly preoccupied with the rampant abuse of nepotism on the county level, especially in the areas of public finance, double and triple officeholding by one person, and internal maladministration. In the matter of finances, the municipal government was given no leeway whatsoever. Its ordinances *(posturas)* required the sanction of the provincial legislature before they could be enforced, though many municipios enforced posturas and then reported to the legislature, which declared them, more often than not, unconstitutional. For instance, the municipal council could not tax or dispose of Indian lands nor could it mortgage, rent, or lease municipal properties, especially land grants earmarked by the imperial government for public use.[102] Counties were deprived of sources to generate revenues. Santo Amaro, for example, once a rich sugar county in Bahia, complained that little was left in its coffers after paying taxes to the provincial and general governments. Itu, a prosperous polycultural county in São Paulo, had a meager budget of a little more than eight contos per annum, still about five times that of Santo Amaro, after turning over fifteen contos annually to the provincial and imperial treasuries.[103] The gentry class and aristocracy resented the decades-long diversion of local resources for which they received little in return, a resentment that even united various agricultural clubs and Republican movements.

The imperial government sought to curb abusive nepotism on the local level, where the most common double officeholding involved a combination of alderman with a judicial post, such as a municipal judge, justice of the peace, or any of the substitute judges of the county. Imperial laws were already very succinct on the qualifications for alderman: a male above twenty-one years having an annual income of 400$. New laws barred an alderman from holding one of the following offices concurrently: substitute judge, public teacher, postal agent, police delegate, deputy police delegate, officer of the provincial police brigade, active officer of a National Guard unit, county prosecutor, justice of the peace, municipal judge, and commander of a volunteer unit during the Paraguayan War.[104] Most members of the regular and secular clergy were also prohibited from holding offices in the municipal council: village priest (*pároco* or *vigário geral*), canon (*cônego*), cochaplain (*coadjutor do vigário*), and secretary to the local bishop.[105]

Those holding judicial posts were also faced with innumerable prohibitions against double and triple officeholding. A justice of the peace, for instance, could not hold any of the following offices: active National Guard officer, municipal judge, alderman, president of an electoral board, and a National Guard officer *together*; officer of the provincial police brigade; notary public; and president of the municipal council.[106] In 1860 the minister of the empire, the chief watchdog for provincial and county administrative matters, granted justices of the peace the right to hold the alderman's post, but in 1882 another minister revoked the 1860 rule: the two posts could not be held by the same person.[107] Police delegates and subdelegates were equally barred from holding certain offices concurrently: county public health physician, vice-president of the province, and alderman.[108] A district prosecutor (*promotor público*) was prohibited from holding any of the following: substitute municipal judge, secretary of the municipal council, alderman, and provincial inspector.[109] This legal maze of prohibitions that imperial, provincial, and local officials had to cut through to discharge their duties meant that the local elite could ignore the prohibitions with impunity; more importantly, flaunting their resistance and escaping imperial retaliation strengthened the local elite position.

Confusion was compounded by additional rules and edicts that were routinely issued by zealous mandarins on the top of the existing corpus of laws and decrees. For instance, the municipal government could not remove an alderman who held a second public office, even in direct violation of the law, without the prior consent of the imperial government.[110] An alderman could not accept a substitute municipal judgeship, but could serve as municipal judge in the event that the county had no such magistrate. In this case, while serving as a judge, the alderman could not draw the second salary.[111] A president of a municipal council could not become a substitute municipal judge, but he who refused to serve as a municipal judge could not remain in the presidency.[112]

The rules that sought to curb nepotism seemed equally bizarre and chaotic. A municipal judge could not marry a daughter or a sister of a district prosecutor, but could wed a niece. Two brothers-in-law were barred from serving as a substitute municipal judge and a substitute district judge concurrently. Two brothers could not serve as a deputy police delegate and a substitute municipal judge. Two brothers could not hold offices of a substitute probate judge and secretary of probate court, nor could two brothers serve as a district prosecutor and as a police delegate. Finally, when two brothers were elected to a municipal council, the one who received fewer votes and/or the younger brother must resign.[113] No mention was made of father and son or father-in-law and son-in-law, who presumably could hold any offices in the same county concurrently. At the same time, serving in the imperial senate was a set of brothers (the Cavalcanti de Albuquerques, of Pernambuco), of father and son (Caxias and his father), of father-in-law and son-in-law (Vergueiro and Sousa Queirós), of brothers-in-law (Itaboraí and Uruguai). No prohibition was ever imposed on imperial mandarins.

Imperial laws and regulations also restricted the internal administration of the municipal corporation. An illiterate or an ex-convict could hold the office of alderman, but a convicted criminal who was making an appeal could not.[114] A *freguesia* (parish) had to have a council and it was required to set a fixed number of sessions, but it could not close sessions in contravention to an 1828 law. It was empowered to regulate the activities of a justice of the peace, but it could not validate or refuse his election. In its capacity as an "administrative corporation," it could not hear contentious cases involving municipal affairs. Absent aldermen would be fined an amount set by the president of the council.[115] Although these restrictions on the council, its members, and county and provincial officials certainly had the effect of imposing the centripetal will, not only is it doubtful that they were ever fully enforced but also that they were even enforceable. The local elite flouted imperial authority with the relish of defiance. As the breakdown and disruption of local law enforcement increased after 1870, the cynicism and contempt of the local agrarian elite for the Bragantine patrimonial monarchy grew.

The separation between the imperial mandarin elite and the local elite was not just structural; their diverging definition of the state and its power produced a series of irreconcilable differences between them. This pitted the core against the periphery and hence the empire against antimonarchist interests. As shown earlier in this chapter, 65 percent of the Brazilian deputies between 1823 and 1889 were one-termers. Only 2 of 1,421 deputies were reelected ten times; 21, or 1.47 percent, of the total were reelected more than seven times. The majority (76 percent) of the reelected were trained in law, and though their social and economic origins could very well have been agrarian, their political careers were molded and remolded by the patrimonial Crown and its agents, not by family or class interests. Their promotion and career advancement were determined by their performance as bureaucrats in the service of the House of Braganza. Of the 21 seven-termers, 10 became ministers of state, 7 senators, and 1 prime minister. Only 2 (both were senators and ministers) were legitimately linked to capitalist agriculture: the Conde de Baependi, of Valença, and Martinho Campos, of Paraíba do Sul, both Mineiro expatriates established in the coffee zone of the middle Paraíba Valley. What is being strongly suggested here is that historians should look at the process of elite-making, not at the elites' social origins, as the determining factors in Brazilian state-building.

One historian claimed that no landowner was ever appointed to the Second Council of State,[116] that Pedro II was forced to appoint powerful landowners to the senate ("Senatorial Siberia"),[117] and that the presence of the landowners in the senate made that institution more conservative.[118] This view must be taken with a grain of salt. However, the dependency, in particular the financial dependency of high-ranking mandarins, or the "governmental group" in the imperial government, was a fact. This was precisely the aim of a patrimonial state with strong centripetalist proclivities as in the Brazil of the nineteenth century, when the empire became a peripheral adjunct to the expanding Atlantic industrial capitalism. The process of elite formation, from academic preparations in Brazilian law academies to eventual selection to the senate or the council of state, involved a gradual social and economic weaning from the home province. Those born into wealthy planter families were simply forced to cut their ties or to delegate the management of plantations and ranches to others at times. In either case, the usual outcome was to drive the business into bankruptcy, as exemplified by Sinimbu, of Alagoas; Olinda, of Pernambuco; Abrantes, Saraiva, and Cotegipe, of Bahia; and Paranaguá, of Piauí.

Such a break with economic and social roots was more prevalent among northerners than southerners. Perhaps this willingness to embrace a new patrimonial-political career, or sinecurism, was prompted by the ever-sagging economies of northern sugar, though in the expanding frontier-like coffee provinces of Rio, São Paulo, and Minas such an attitude was rare. As the internal transportation network improved in and around the court, politician-planters became a new but familiar breed among the Brazilian imperial elite, especially after 1877 when Rio and São Paulo were linked by a railroad. This new group of politicians, whose political socialization was firmly grounded in capitalist agriculture, came from the southern provinces that specialized in coffee and cattle. For most of this generation, their careers bloomed only after 1889.

Brazil, like China, required a highly skilled cadre of Crown agents to hold the far-flung empire together, to administer imperial justice, and to satisfy conflicting regional demands. But, unlike China, Brazil enjoyed the advantages of being located on the periphery of the Atlantic world-economy and having a common language and official religion to forge itself into a viable state. Further, China did not have political parties as in Brazil, and its mandarins were "household" servants of a particular emperor—differences that can be explained by China's multiple dialects and languages as well as by its national concept of property ownership. Again unlike China, where the state kept private properties weak to the extent that the central government created a "hydraulic civilization," to borrow the expression of Karl A. Wittfogel, Brazil fostered the ethos of capitalism, incorporating its private-propertied economy as an appendage of Atlantic world-capitalism.[119] That a society with capitalist agriculture, however unevenly developed and distributed, had adopted a mandarin-like corps of patrimonial bureaucrats at the outset of the nineteenth century simply reinforces the thesis of this book: the monarchy was an artificial imposition at best and the absence of dynastic linkages between the Braganza House and the empire's leading agricultural clans through marriages considerably weakened its legitimacy and eventually contributed to its demise. The expansion of the Atlantic "core" economy during the second half of the nineteenth century reshaped Brazil's economy, whose vibrant metamorphosis in turn held the key to the survival of the empire.

Vagaries of Rich Nobles, Poor Nobles

Niggardliness is the worst evil that can befall noble persons.

MARQUIS OF ARGYLE

Not all rich nobles in the empire inherited their wealth. Many were self-made magnates whose backgrounds were obscure. Although such a newly amassed fortune did not always open doors in the traditional, or aristocratic, Northeast, it was the key to public recognition as an established family in the Center-South. One historian flatly states that the "400-year old family" in São Paulo was nothing but a myth. If a family possessing money is not old, it "soon will be."[1] The societal distinctions between aristocratic and gentry planters were based partly on a clan's wealth management. A planter's use of human, financial, and landed capital indicated either a gentry or an aristocratic mentality. Coffee fazendeiros as a whole, for example, were gentry-minded in their thinking, for they were integrated into the Atlantic world-economy during the expansion of industrial capitalism in Europe and the United States. Money-making in the Center-South was looked upon as a respectable activity. Other evidence of wealth management are provided by wills and inventories, which clearly indicate whether or not a noble family chose to diversify its wealth. The purpose of this chapter is to show how regional differences in capitalist (gentry) and precapitalist (aristocratic) mentalities affected the clan fortunes of the Brazilian nobility.

Brazilian law required that an estate be divided among the surviving heirs in the following manner: the partner (widow or widower) received one half *(meição)*, and the other half was divided among a number of eligible heirs, both consanguineous and nonconsanguineous relatives. The total, always valued in monetary terms, was called *monte mor*. The amount deducted from the monte mor in debts, legal fees, and probate court expenses was called *dedução*. The remaining amount, called *líquido*, was portioned out to all the eligible heirs. Each portion inherited was called a *quinhão*, or a share. When people died intestate, the inventory of their wealth took longer. Any heir could, and often did, contest the manner in which the estate was settled, and the resulting dispute prolonged probate. Once the estate was settled, the law did not require that properties be sold. Two or more siblings who inherited one plantation, for instance, could choose to designate one of them as the in loco manager, while the others remained as partners.

Women were legally eligible to become executrices *(inventariantes)* of their husbands' or fathers' estates, to serve as tutoresses to their children, and to work as partners in family businesses. However, because women, even daughters of the rich, were not taught to read and write, were seldom educated in professional schools during the nineteenth century, and were more often cloistered at home,[2] few sought professional careers. No women merchants, bankers, or *comissárias* existed; brothers, uncles, husbands, and other male relatives ran women's inherited businesses. However, women commonly succeeded their husbands as planters. One such case was the Viscondessa de Santa Justa (Bernardina Alves de Barbosa), a fazendeira in Paraíba do Sul, Rio province, and a partner in the family-run coffee brokerage firm in the court. A careful look at inventories, wills, and probate decisions on amicable dissolutions of marriages can shed light on the contrasting styles of Brazilian noble families—both gentry and aristocratic—in their wealth management.

It should be remembered that what made a planter a member of the gentry or the aristocracy in Europe was historically determined by the age of pedigree, purity of blood, and even marital alliances. The lineages and purity of blood among the Luso-Brazilian nobles were difficult to establish, for they were at times obscured by unsubstantiated and often oral claims to fidalguia, or nobility of blood, and further complicated by the intrusion of African and Amerindian blood. Hence, in the empire, a planter holding a title of nobility was determined to be gentry or aristocrat by his wealth management. The transmission of wealth from father to children and grandchildren entailed a carefully orchestrated family strategy during the nineteenth century. Such a strategy was appropriate and even necessary in a society based on capitalist agriculture whose economic frontier was continually on the move, which offered expanding opportunities for new and greater wealth.

A typical planter-aristocrat invested less than 10 percent of his wealth in urban properties, public debentures, stocks and bonds in commercial firms, and manufacturing industries. The Barão de Guanabara (José Gonçalves de Oliveira Roxo), for instance, one of the richest landowners in the Rio-São Paulo border region, died in 1875, leaving 686:256$920 that included Fazenda Ponte Alta, in Vassouras. The baronesa and two sons were his sole heirs. The widow received 403:108$690, including the sale of the coffee harvested, and the two sons each inherited 159:302$855. The brother of the deceased bought the fazenda; one half of the sale price (567:722$) went to the sons, the other to the widow. Another kin agreed to buy a house in Rio, valued at 50:000$, and paid the heirs with public-debt certificates. The late barão's inventory showed no urban wealth. Thus, his legacy had been increased by property sales and a good return from coffee futures.[3]

The Ferreira Bandeira family of Santo Amaro, Bahia, was also a typical landowning clan that did little to diversify its wealth. Pedro Ferreira de Viana Bandeira, who died in 1831, left a legacy of 223:155$576 that consisted of one sugar mill, fifty slaves, and ten shares of Banco do Brasil stocks. The wealth, divided among his widow and three sons, continued to increase through the years. One of the sons, Custódio, when he died, left an impressive legacy of 1.556:408$433, including four sugar mills and two cattle ranches; the six properties employed more than 400 slaves. Custódio's inventory showed no urban wealth. His son, the Visconde de Ferreira Bandeira (Pedro), died in 1916, leaving 419:762$264, nearly double his 1872 inheritance of 259:401$330. His wealth consisted of four sugar plantations, houses in Salvador, shares in Santo Amaro waterworks, and family jewelry. (The visconde's will was contested by one of the heirs, who claimed that he had been promised the clan's sugar mills left by the will in the custody of an unmarried daughter.)[4]

The founder of the Ferreira Bandeiras, Pedro, was a merchant during the first decade of the nineteenth century who married into a landowning family, the Vianas. The first provincial president of Bahia in 1822 after independence was a Viana. Later, the Ferreira Bandeiras established marital ties to other latifundiary families, the Bulcãos and Monizes. Pedro Ferreira de Viana Bandeira's children were educated in Hamburg; at the time of their father's death, Custódio and Francisco, aged fifteen years and ten years, respectively, were in a German boarding school. Pedro's grandson and Custódio's son, the Visconde de Ferreira Bandeira, was also educated in Germany; he married Maria Sophia Schmidt. His mother, a Moniz, was ennobled as the Baronesa de Alenquer for her charitable works. The visconde's uncle Francisco wedded a Bulcão. In spite of European education and marriage with a German family, the Ferreira Bandeiras continued to remain closed. By extended family ties, the Monizes and Bulcãos were also cousins of the Ferreira Bandeiras. All these clans remained agrarian, though one in-law of the Ferreira Bandeiras, the Visconde dos Fiais (Luís Paulo de Araújo Basto), was a merchant and banker. Unlike agrarian families in Pernambuco and Rio, the Ferreira Bandeiras and their cousins, the Monizes and the Bulcãos, did not retain ties to the mercantile occupations of their ancestral founders. The Bahian landed class seemed eager to erase such linkages, instead of using them for economic gain.

More typical precapitalist landlords were the Barão de São João da Barra, of Rio province, and the Barão de Saubara, of Santo Amaro, Bahia. The Barão and Baronesa de São João da Barra, whose wealth was inventoried in 1863, were planters in São João da Barra, where they owned three sugar plantations near Campos and a town house. Their total wealth was assessed at 1.404:852$741, including more than 200 slaves; the house in Campos alone was valued at 40:000$. At Fazenda de Cactá, the largest of the three plantations, 123 slaves lived in forty-two slave shacks *(senzalas)*. Ten heirs divided the wealth, each of the three principal heirs receiving 286:000$ and the remainder being distributed among grandchildren, each of whom received 73:000$. The inventory listed no urban properties except the house in Campos.[5] Rarely did a sugar planter in Rio province leave such a fortune. The heirs, however, chose to diversify their legacies by risking them in entrepreneurial projects, in the 1880s pioneering sugar-refinery construction in Rio province.

The Barão de Saubara (José Joaquim Barreto), a sugar planter in Santo Amaro, had the dubious distinction of becoming the oldest man to be ennobled. When he died in 1867, he left 166:926$635, of which 47:740$, or 28 percent, constituted the value of his ninety slaves. He never married; his two sons by slave women were legitimized before his death, thus earning them the right to share in the will. Two-thirds of Saubara's wealth went to the sons (Torquato José and João José) and the remaining third was distributed to his nephews and grandnephews. The family property of Engenho Gonçalo do Poço was jointly held by the two heirs. Torquato José received 67:593$497 and João José 68:202$303, a difference explained by the shifting value of slaves from the time of their assessment until probate was completed. Although the inventory and will identified the mothers of Saubara's sons and they were living when the estate was inventoried, he made no provision for them. In his will, he placed his purveyor in Salvador in charge of his finances, and made a well-known Santo Amaro politician the executor of his estate. He also stipulated that at least a dozen faithful slaves were to be manumitted when his will was probated. No mention was made of annual pensions for the freedmen, however.[6] The baron had no shares in urban businesses, city mansions, or public bonds.

The successful builders of Brazil's capitalist agriculture were gentry planters, among them the Visconde and Viscondessa de Ipiabas, major landowners in Valença with holdings also in Vassouras and elsewhere in Rio province. When the viscondessa died in 1892, she left eight heirs, among whom were the Barão de Ipiabas, the Baronesa de Almeida Ramos, the Baronesa de Potengi, the Baronesa de Aliança, and the Baronesa de Palmeira. Two other daughters were married to the Cunha family (Aliança). The major family farms, Fazenda do Oriente and Fazenda dos Campos Elísios, in Valença, were valued at 142:463$ and 92:122$. The viscondessa also owned other rural properties. But the fortune she and her husband had amassed was in urban wealth. More than a third of the total estate inventoried consisted of houses in Rio and shares in the Banco Metropolitano, public-debt certificates, and federal bonds. Out of 553:334$548, some 197:595$ was in nonagrarian properties.[7] The Visconde de Ipiabas was active in the improvement of local agriculture and a strong supporter of railroad building in Valença. He consented to the mass marriage of his slaves in 1867, an action that was deemed to be innovative.

The landowner-politician par excellence was the Second Visconde de Jaguari (José Ildefonso de Sousa Ramos), a rich coffee planter in Minas

Gerais and Rio province. He began his political career in his home province; in 1843 he was provincial president of Piauí, of Minas in 1848, and of Pernambuco in 1850. In 1853 the emperor honored him with nomination to the imperial senate. By 1870, when he was named to the Council of State, Jaguari had been a cabinet minister three times; in 1874–81 he was president of the imperial senate. Few politicians of national stature could boast such impeccable credentials. Extraordinarily successful in combining the careers of a capitalist agriculturalist and a mandarin, he died in 1883, leaving an impressive estate of 1.194:912$881. His principal rural property was still Fazenda de Três Barras, in Paraíba do Sul, though he was also a fazendeiro in Valença, where his wife was born and held plantations. The viscondessa (executrix) and their four children were the heirs to the estate. Of the eleven separate types of assets listed in the inventory, Fazenda Três Barras was the only rural holding. The urban properties, valued at 703:500$, or 58.8 percent of the total, included thirty-four houses and buildings, and some twenty lots *(terrenos)*, all in the court.[8] The visconde's political career after 1853 as a senator of the empire, a cabinet officer, and a councillor of state moved him and his family to Rio and gave them the stability of a permanent residence, thus enabling them to diversify the family wealth in urban holdings. Jaguari, a gentry planter to the core, skillfully urbanized his income and learned to multiply it.

The Resende family, in Valença, was another expatriate Mineiro landowning clan that produced a distinguished imperial mandarin. The Marquês de Valença (Estêvão Ribeiro de Resende) was a confidant of Pedro I, who appointed him to various cabinet posts during the 1820s. In one of his numerous dalliances, the marquês sired a son, also called Estêvão, and soon acknowledged his paternity by legitimizing the birth. This son married into a landholding family in Piraí, Rio province, became a coffee planter, and was ennobled in 1854 as the Barão de Lorena. The Baronesa de Lorena died in 1864, leaving the widower and six children an estate of 403:105$172. After the court expenses and payment of minor debts, one half of 397:331$372 went to Lorena and each of the other heirs received 33:110$947. A house in the county seat was listed at 50:000$, and the family fazenda, Santo Antônio, in Piraí, was valued as 29:696$. The couple owned 216 shares of public bonds, worth 216:000$, or 54 percent of the total assets.[9] Lorena therefore met the criteria for becoming a gentry planter. Similarly, the Barão do Rio Preto (Domingos Custódio Guimarães) was a gentry farmer. He died in 1876, leaving his wife 1.659:817$ after taxes and court expenses were deducted. Of this amount, 220:143$, or 13.3 percent, was in stocks and bonds, including those of a local railroad company. The single largest asset listed in the inventory was slaves, worth 35.4 percent of the total, or 588:860$.[10] Lorena, Rio Preto, and others like them built Brazil's modern capitalist economy during the nineteenth century. Their commitment to diversification of wealth diverted surplus capital from agriculture to urban commerce and manufacturing, thus laying the foundation for modern Brazil.

The best example of a gentry planter family that diversified its wealth over more than one generation is the Faros, of Rio province. The family was an important landowner in the first generation, and by the third its wealth had substantially been invested in urban businesses, especially in railroad and export houses. The First Baronesa do Rio Bonito died in 1854, leaving in Valença, Vassouras, and Piraí four coffee plantations, two colonial land grants (sesmarias) and two sítios, underdeveloped ranches or plantations. A total of some 600 slaves worked on the four plantations. The biggest, Santa Ana, covered 2,590 braças and employed 270 slaves "more or less." The monte mor reached 1.130:202$333, the bulk of which consisted of rural holdings and slaves. The inventory mentioned stocks, bonds, town houses, and cash that totaled 106:600$, or about 9.4 percent of the total estate.[11]

The inventariante of the late baronesa was her son the Visconde do Rio Bonito (João Pereira Darrigue Faro), one of three brothers who received 223:277$556 each. When the visconde died in 1859, the monte mor was 2.131:007$019, almost double his parents'. Heading coffee comissários in Rio, the visconde and his brothers owned the Sociedade Comercial de Faro e Irmãos; at the time of his death, the visconde's share in the firm was worth 115:194$690. He also owned two plantations: Santa Ana, an heirloom, and Monte Alegre, a new addition, both magnificent coffee estates. Santa Ana was worth 514:060$, Monte Alegre a whopping 872:070$440. The visconde also owned eleven urban properties valued at 161:000$ and shares of private firms and public-debt certificates; he held 114:186$ in the "stocks of public companies," among which were 100 shares in the newly formed Rio-São Paulo Railroad, of which Rio Bonito was president until his death. Each of his two heirs received 900:318$661 from the estate, after deducting court and lawyers' expenses.[12] The Third Barão do Rio Bonito (José Pereira Darrigue de Faro), his father's executor, continued the visconde's business. By the 1870s and 1880s, the Third Rio Bonito was a completely transformed urban businessman whose economic interest in agriculture remained only as a faint family tradition. The Faros were an outstanding case of generational transformations during the age of capitalist agriculture in the nineteenth century.

One broad generalization can be formulated by comparing 250 inventories of landowners in Santo Amaro, Salvador, Valença, São Paulo, Itu, and the city of Rio: the noticeable tendency among Rio coffee planters to invest in urban properties was rare among Bahian planters. It is almost tempting to argue that this was the rule among the south-central gentry planters; the exception for those in the Northeast. This should have affected the availability of surplus capital for nonagrarian activities, such as manufacturing, trade, and banking. Incipient industrialization was already taking place in São Paulo and Rio by the late 1820s, thanks to this transfer of capital. Once this diversification was in motion, a multiplier effect also took over in both positive and negative senses. The average net return from urban investments in Rio and São Paulo later in the 1880s was considerably greater than that in Recife or Salvador, according to inventories. Just when the stagnant rural economy in the two northeastern provinces should have encouraged some diversification of wealth, the contrary was the case. Landowners in Bahia, for instance, heavily in debt, lacked surplus capital for urban investment. In Rio, where the presence of the court turned the city into both the social and the financial capital of the empire, as well as its political hub, economic opportunities were more diverse. Successful planters maintained city residences for their seasonal visits as well as for housing their children who studied in the court. The expansive coffee economy therefore stimulated urban investments.

Differences in the social and economic origins of the northern and southern planters also influenced their urban investment patterns. Many of the leading families in Rio and São Paulo came from mercantile backgrounds, such as the Barão de Santa Justa, of Paraíba do Sul, the Barão do Rio Bonito, of Valença, the Barão de Iguape, of São Paulo, and the Barão de Sousa Queirós, of São Paulo. The highly clannish Bahian planter families, whose agrarian roots extended back to colonial times, probably looked down on urbanized wealth. Those families that started in trade, such as the Ferreira Bandeiras, once married into a landowning clan, did their best to remove all the vestiges of urban commerce and trade from the family tree. Wealth management in the provinces of south-central Brazil was therefore free of clan and social restrictions, and that in the Northeast was inhibited by tradition and familial philosophies. The coffee planters possessed the group *mentalité* of entrepreneurial capitalism by the early 1850s, a secular trend that did not take place in the Northeast until the mid-1870s. By the second and third generations of nobles, many planters in Rio and São Paulo had reverted to the original professions of the clan founders, such as urban trade and commerce, but retained agrarian interests. This process of "coming home" to their roots led to the diversification of their newly acquired wealth, which ensconced Brazil's capitalist agriculture in the best entrepreneurial tradition.

The inventories of major politicians, courtier nobles, and leading military officers also offer rich data for understanding the dynamics of Brazilian society during the nineteenth century. Of forty-five mandarins holding nobiliary titles that were studied, only three left estates of 500:000$ or more, demonstrating either that career politicians were poor or that opportunities for graft and corruption were not abundant. The Second Visconde de Jaguari left the largest estate, 1.194:912$881. The next largest was that of the Condessa da Piedade, the widow of Senator José Clemente Pereira, her second husband, a total of 697:704$ to two heirs from her first marriage. (José Clemente and the condessa had no children.) Her widowed son-in-law, Eusébio de Queirós Coutinho Matos, received half of the estate, 309:791$. Three grandchildren divided the remainder. Their father, the condessa's son and executor, Manuel Marques de Sá, had also died by the time the inventory was concluded. Condessa da Piedade held one fazenda worth 105:365$500, including slaves; "various houses in the court" were assessed at 222:500$; 50 shares of the Dom Pedro II Railroad Company were worth 5:500$.[13] The condessa's second husband had been a Portuguese merchant-turned-politician, whose early career was rooted in the municipal council of Rio. The widow had probably fostered good relations with the city's merchants and commercial houses, thus enabling her to marshal her wealth prudently.

The third largest estate left by a nineteenth-century political noble belonged to the Marquês de Paraná. Of the monte mor of 580:629$410, which included one big coffee fazenda in Sapucaia, his "houses and chácaras" were valued at 107:000$. The marquês and marquesa lived in grand style.[14] Furniture, carriages, dinner settings, silverware, and glassware were valued at 15:334$. The slave household staff in Rio alone was assessed at 7:100$. Fazenda Lordelo employed 190 working slaves, whose total value came to 192:590$, or 1:000$ each.[15] The marquesa assumed the administration of the fazenda until her death. Much like Jaguari, his compatriot from Minas Gerais, Paraná did well with his urban investment, which amounted to 388:039$, or 67 percent of the estate. The marquesa received the customary meiação of 321:039$476, and four surviving heirs divided the other half into four equal portions.

Not all politicians fared as well as Paraná, Jaguari, and José Clemente. Most well-known imperial mandarins were impoverished; others left only moderate sums to their heirs; and still others died bankrupt. By European standards, Brazilian politicians were virtually free of corruption. No clues to illicitly amassed fortunes have surfaced in the inventories of leading politicians, courtier nobles, and military officers. In fact, many of the major imperial politicians squandered their inherited fortune while serving in political office. The commitment to noblesse oblige in politics led to the pauperization and even bankruptcy of many scions of the empire's rich rural gentry and aristocracy.

The Marquês de Barbacena (Felisberto Caldeira Brant Pontes) was one such case. A Mineiro by birth, he married the daughter of a wealthy Bahian merchant, Salvador's major slave importer. Barbacena became a prominent landowner in southern Bahia and the Recôncavo, where he held sugar mills. One of the few Brazilian politicians of the First Reign (1822–31) whom Pedro I took into his confidence, he was a general, statesman, and sometime diplomat, a several-time cabinet officer, briefly commanding general of the Brazilian forces in the Cisplatine War (1825–28), and negotiator of the second marriage of Pedro I, with Amelia of Leuchtenberg. When he died in 1842, he left a paltry 3:455$640 to be divided among three of his heirs: the Conde de Iguaçu, who married a daughter of Pedro I and Santos; the Visconde de Barbacena; and the Viscondessa de Santo Amaro. Barbacena bequeathed one fazenda, a sugar mill, 115 slaves, and shares in the Imperial Society of Brazilian Mining of Congo Soco, the total value of which came to

88:000$, probably only on paper. However, the marquês also was in debt 41:618$ to nine merchants and bankers. To the Visconde dos Fiais (the then barão), Barbacena owed no fewer than eight separate notes, or 16:237$. By the time all the debt claims had been met and the expenses of probate services for the inventory paid, the principal heirs had little to inherit.[16] In fact, both of Barbacena's sons died poor.

The Visconde do Bom Retiro (Luís Pedreira do Couto Ferraz), a boyhood friend of Dom Pedro II and his adviser for decades, died in 1886 with no direct heirs, leaving 78:018$690. His brother, Dr. João Pedreira do Couto Ferraz, was the estate executor. The single most valued item in the inventory was his house ("sobrado/chácara") in Rua Barão do Bom Retiro, in Rio, valued at 35:000$. Another town house in Rua Ajuda, also in the court, was assessed at 20:000$, and a third house, in Boa Vista, was valued at 6:000$. Furniture was the fourth most important asset, worth 2:676$700. Bom Retiro also owed much. The deduction allowed in the inventory came to 48:617$010, which included probate court expenses.[17] Considering the connections, political prestige, and social influence that Bom Retiro enjoyed as a confidant of the emperor, cabinet minister, senator of the empire, and councillor of state, he would have been an ideal man from whom foreign investors and national merchants would curry imperial favors. A man of impeccable scruples, he never abused his friendship with Dom Pedro II to enrich himself, as his small legacy testified.

Few politicians possessed wealth of any significance. In the same league with Bom Retiro was the Barão de Pindaré (Antônio Pedro da Costa Ferreira), imperial senator from Maranhão. When he died in 1860, he left 100:819$390, of which 61 percent, 61:880$, was the value of his slaves. After expenses, his ten heirs divided 96:974$758, which came mostly from his slaves and rural properties in Maranhão.[18] The Barão de Uruguaiana (Ángelo Muniz da Silva Ferraz), a Bahian who had served as prime minister, died in 1867, leaving 137:404$058 for the four children from his three marriages. He owned seventeen slaves (10:050$) and modest properties valued at 92:404$.[19]

Another Bahian and former prime minister, the Barão de Cotegipe, inherited a meager sum of 2:393$916 from his father in 1841, consisting of one slave and cattle but no land.[20] However, he married into a wealthy landowning family, the Pita e Argolos; the head of that clan, the Conde de Passé, became his father-in-law. When the Baronesa de

Cotegipe died in 1868, she left her husband and three children the hefty sum of 749:666$442, including four sugar mills. The baron's share (meiação) came to 374:272$271. Two older children received one plantation each and the baron held two for himself: Engenho Quibaca, valued at 159:380$282 with 66 slaves; and Engenho Sapucaia, worth 99:892$. When Cotegipe died in 1889, he was heavily in debt, almost all to one commercial house, the Pereira Marinho Company, in Salvador. At the time of his death, Quibaca had been mortgaged to the Pereira Marinho Company for eight years. It was valued at 79:661$400 and Sapucaia at 107:052$900. Years of neglect and inadequate management, coupled with the economic woes of the sugar industry actually devalued Quibaca by half. The company seized Quibaca by legal action. In addition to this mortgage, Cotegipe owed the same firm 48:124$115 for supplies for his sugar mills, including food for his slaves and cash advanced on sugar futures. The company held a third note of 25:120$780, which Cotegipe had borrowed in 1884 at the annual interest of 9 percent and was to be paid off in six months. When he could not pay it, the loan ballooned to 36:078$170, which was to be collected from his estate. Of the baron's legacy of 106:385$555, creditors claimed the staggering total of 64:364$710, or 79 percent of the entire estate. Each of his children, therefore, received 14:221$811. (One of the children was married to a future governor of Bahia, João Ferriera de Araújo Pinho, a rich sugar planter and sometime in loco manager for Cotegipe's estate.)[21]

Although Cotegipe's case cannot be considered typical, it underscores the fact that career politicians seldom amassed fortunes. The Marquês de Monte Alegre, a Bahian who married a wealthy widow in São Paulo, left 317:608$791, consisting only of rural properties in Piracicaba, São Paulo. His heirs were two sisters and ten nephews.[22] Like Cotegipe and Uruguaiana, he had been prime minister. The Visconde de Niterói inherited from his wife in 1880 a sum of 352:277$560. The couple had little debt. The visconde received one half, 176:083$780, and seven children inherited 25:636$968 each.[23] A still less fortunate mandarin was the Marquês de Sapucai (Cândido José de Araújo Viana), who was born in Congonhas de Sabará, Minas Gerais, in 1793. His fifty-two-year uninterrupted legislative career set a record among Brazilian legislators. First elected to the constituent assembly of 1823 from his home province, he was made an imperial senator in 1839. He served in the cabinet three times between 1833 and 1843 and was honored with a seat in the imperial council of state in 1850. A lifelong Conservative, he was the archetypal mandarin. When he died in 1875, he left 8:229$774, including seven slaves (4:500$) and a magnificent library valued at 2:256$200, the second most important asset after the slaves. The family was pauperized. One of the impoverished heirs implored a judge to award him "whatever share that he could be entitled to." The Marquesa de Sapucai died the following year, leaving a total of 4:782$511 to six of her children. Her five slaves were valued at 3:228$800.[24]

Such a democratic distribution of inheritances made it virtually impossible for the traditional elites to survive without risking the loss of wealth and power. Hence, cousin marriages were one way to avoid dissipating the family wealth; another was diversification. The first avenue was practiced by all, but the second was preferred only in the Center-South, where the economic growth of coffee allowed it. The consequences were interesting.

Imperial mandarins without noble titles also fared poorly. João Alfredo Correia de Oliveira, of Pernambuco, was the head of the last Conservative Cabinet in the empire, which abolished slavery in May 1888. Possessing a brilliant legal mind, he received a doctorate in law two years after he graduated from the Recife Law School. In 1857 he married a cousin, Maria Eugênia da Cunha Rego Barros, a daughter of the Barão de Goiana, one of the richest sugar planters in the province. João Alfredo and Maria had eleven children. His political career blossomed in the 1860s and required an additional financial outlay that he could ill afford. The maintenance of a residence in the court and trips to Europe bled him financially. Heavily in debt well before the monarchy was overthrown in 1889, he owed numerous merchants and bankers in Recife and Rio. Among his chief creditors was the Conde de Mesquita, perhaps the richest man in the empire, to whom João Alfredo owed close to ten contos by June 1889, when he left office. (When Mesquita died, his heirs sold João Alfredo's note to another banker, the Barão de Itacuruçá.) João Alfredo's annual income until 1889 had been only thirteen contos as an imperial senator and councillor of state. After the Republic was established in November 1889, he lost his sole source of income. He speculated on the rising demand for land in the western part of São Paulo, where he bought a fazenda and then sold it for profit. But he never became a planter or land speculator. He lived in penury, so destitute that his former political foe, Manuel Pinto de Sousa Dantas, president of the Banco do Brasil during the early years of the Republic, offered him a loan. The proud Pernambucano turned it down. The penultimate prime minister of Brazil died in abject poverty.[25]

In contrast to landowners and, in particular, to politicians, most of the merchant nobility were affluent. Money played a major role in obtaining merchants' titles in the first place. Probably the richest merchant-banker-planter family in the empire was the Mesquitas. The founder of this banking clan, which later diversified into commerce and agriculture, was the Marquês de Bomfim (José Francisco de Mesquita). Born in Minas Gerais in 1790, he made his fortune in trade between Rio and the interior provinces, wisely investing his money in banking and urban commerce (retail and wholesale) at the time that coffee was just emerging as the empire's single most valuable export item. At one time a director of the Caixa de Amortização in Rio, José Francisco was ennobled in 1841 as the First Barão de Bomfim, a title one of his grandsons would inherit in 1888. At the age of eighty-two in 1872, he was honored with the title of marquês and the following year died.[26]

His son, the future Conde de Mesquita (Jerônimo José de Mesquita), inherited the family business. Dabbling in the city politics of Rio, Jerônimo José was a city alderman, president of the Rio Commercial Association, and director of the Banco do Brasil. These positions widened his acquaintance with key imperial politicians and he eventually became the banker of many mandarins, including prime ministers, cabinet officers, and senators. The conde had two sons who also became nobles: the Barão de Mesquita (Jerônimo Roberto) and the Second Barão de Bomfim (José Jerônimo). The former continued in the family trade as a banker, and the latter became a planter, a new family economic activity. The conde held several coffee plantations and cattle ranches in the Paraíba Valley, especially in Itaguaí.

When the Conde de Mesquita died in 1886, he left the fabulous sum of 9.919:903$159. His major assets included 2,270 shares of stocks in seven banks and companies; the single largest block of stocks was in the Banco do Brasil: 614 shares, worth 171:920$. He owned 250 shares of the Leopoldina Railway Company (33:750$), 500 shares of the Banco Comercial in the court (109:000$), 240 shares of imperial and provincial debentures (232:676$), 416 shares in his own Companhia Lavoura e Indústria (83:200$), and 250 shares in the Navegação Paulista (27:500$). His voluminous inventory reads like the social history of a Rio merchant. Six heirs, including his wife, divided the gargantuan estate. One half went to the condessa, and each of the other five heirs received 1.322:653$754.[27]

Less affluent than the Mesquitas were the Figueiredos. The Viscondessa de Figueiredo, widow of a leading merchant, died, bequeathing the huge sum of 2.244:814$983. Her husband (Francisco de Figueiredo) was the future Conde de Figueiredo. The couple had eight heirs, each of whom inherited 160:407$498.[28] The Conde de São Mamede (Rodrigo Pereira Felício), also a merchant, left his heirs 1.860:177$651, and another merchant, the First Barão de Alegrete (João José de Araújo Gomes), passed on the hefty sum of 1.080:597$779 to his children.[29]

Merchants in the provinces were also affluent. The Conde de Pereira Marinho, a Portuguese title, was probably the richest man in northern Brazil. His sole surviving heirs were his wife and a son, the Visconde de Guaí (Joaquim Elísio Pereira Marinho), a protégé of Cotegipe and one-time navy minister in João Alfredo's cabinet. Guaí inherited an immense fortune because, unlike planters, he was unaffected by the abolition of slavery. The conde's legacy was 5.862:000$, plus £10,000 life insurance with an English firm. He had no debts. The condessa received the customary half and Guaí the other half.[30] When the condessa died, she left her sole heir the impressive sum of 4.106:543$400. The inventory process alone lasted for two decades, draining the legacy of unprecedented probate and legal costs, amounting to 967:543$400, a sum considerably larger than the estate of a well-to-do coffee planter in Rio or São Paulo.[31] In a more modest way, another banker, the Visconde dos Fiais (Luís Paulo de Araújo Basto), an expatriate from Rio residing in Salvador, left 680:777$276, which included one sugar mill and sixty slaves. Among the urban slaves were tailors, sailors, and distillery workers.[32]

Inventories of Brazilian nobles as well as those of the untitled rich offer data for social history. Most of the homes of nobles in the Bahian sugar-growing counties were built of "stone and limestone" (pedra e cal); and those in São Paulo, where building stone was scarce, were constructed of mud and wood. This led to a regional contrast in lifestyles. Many plantation houses in São Paulo were poorly built, including those in Campinas, the province's richest county in the nineteenth

century. Some landlords' mansions in Itu, a sugar-growing county, bore
a strong resemblance to good slave quarters in opulent Santo Amaro
and São Francisco do Conde.[33] Both sugar and coffee planters' assets
were slaves and land under cultivation. Gentry planters naturally acquired more assets because of their proclivity to diversify and recycle
their capital in urban properties, commerce, and industrial projects.
Merchants' wealth was subject to less oscillation on account of diversification. Litigations against planters usually involved defaulted loans
and mortgages, much of which were unsalvageable. When a person died
owing money to a merchant, the creditor automatically registered his
claim in probate court for settlement, which meant the inventory took
longer; such an action assured the merchant a legal right to collect; and
the monte mor (total asset) was calculated first and then the debt was
subtracted before the heirs could divide the estate.

A careful study of the inventories reveals details of a wealthy family's house furnishings, eating habits, and personal hobbies. Sapucai, for
example, had an excellent library on law and history. Most furniture,
bed frames, chairs, dressers, dining tables, and desks were made of the
fine jacaranda wood. To accommodate the humid climate of the country, furniture was simple and airy in style. Silverware, glassware, and
linens were specially made for the household, often engraved with a
coat of arms. Many of these items were imported from Europe, though
Brazil did have a few skilled European jewelers and engravers. One noble in Vassouras spent 40:000$ to refurnish his house for a single visit
of the imperial princess and her consort, the Conde d'Eu.[34] The Barão
de Resende (Estêvão Ribeiro de Sousa Resende), of Valença, rang up a
hotel bill of 12:090$ for Vichy water and French wine, which exceeded
his debt to a Rio comissário of 1:422$176.[35] Inventories also show dif-
ferent types of jewels, silk dresses of various designs, custom-made
household goods, and specialty items such as sedan chairs, carriages,
and ladies' cosmetic equipment.

Inventories also reveal that it was common for rich planters and merchants, either titled or untitled, to give a portion of their wealth to
charity or to set up funds for religious ceremonies for their loved ones.
The Barão de Itapororoca (José Joaquim Moniz de Barreto e Aragão), a
rich planter in São Francisco do Conde, Bahia, not only freed scores of
slaves in his will, but also established pension funds for the duration
of their natural lives.[36] In Santo Amaro, the county gentry and nobles

preferred to be buried on their own plantations, but left money for the Santa Casa to celebrate Masses for them, for their parents, favorite slaves, and friends as well. The will of the Conde de Sergimirim was filed in June 1879; and in September the following year, when it was opened, it stipulated prayers for himself, his parents, his relatives, and his slaves.[37] No money was provided for Santa Casa charities, only expenses for the prayers. The Barão de Pirajá ordered a thousand prayers for himself, his dead uncle, his mother-in-law, and her children.[38] A small charitable donation was set up. The Baronesa de Alenquer died in 1867, stipulating in her will the award of 1:200$ to the Santa Casa for charity and an additional 600$ for "the poor of Santo Amaro," but requested no prayers for her soul.[39]

Details of the wealth and life-styles of Braganza's favorite courtier nobles can be deduced from their inventories. The Condessa de Itapagipe (Ana Romana de Aragão Calmon) was the *dama* at the imperial house during the years of Pedro I, the Regency, and the first two decades after Pedro II's investiture. A Bahian of the Moniz and the Calmon clans, she married a wealthy man, who died in 1820. Her son Francisco later became a lieutenant general in the army, and her daughter Maria Francisca married Nicolau Antônio Nogueira Vale da Gama (the future Visconde de Nogueira da Gama), a nephew of the Marquês de Baependi. Like Itapagipe, the visconde was a courtier noble, a majordomo in the imperial house. The condessa was a power broker by nature of her position and was often asked by men of wealth and politicians to intercede with the emperors. Two of her sons were schooled in Munich and were "taken care of" by those who needed her patronage.[40] When she died in 1862, her entire estate was valued at a meager 6:498$816; she owned no house, no rural or urban properties. The most valued item in the inventory was sixteen shares of Banco do Brasil stock (3:040$). After probate expenses, five of her heirs divided 4:517$096.[41]

Another court favorite, the Conde de Carapebus, was a born aristocrat. The scion of a rich sugar planter and banker, he was educated in Coimbra and chose to live both in Europe and Brazil. He dabbled in business as a broker for European investors in Brazil and later served on the staff of the imperial house. Son-in-law of the Conde de Baependi, Carapebus was a grandson-in-law of the Marquês de Baependi, the founder of the Nogueira da Gama clan, in Valença. Hence, Carapebus was also related to both Itapagipe and the Duque de Caxias. The duquesa was a niece of Baependi (the marquês), and a daughter of Caxias married her cousin, the Barão de Santa Mônica, who in turn was a son of the marquês. Carapebus was a nephew-in-law of Caxias's daughter and her husband, Santa Mônica. Carapebus fared better than others financially, leaving the moderate sum of 204:774$ when he died in 1896. This amount contrasted sharply with his substantial inheritance from his father and other relatives in Campos. His wife died in Paris three years later and also bequeathed a moderate sum, 200:393$057. Although after the 1870s Carapebus had frequented Europe and maintained a house in Paris, nothing was mentioned of the couple's European estate in the Brazilian inventories.[42]

The inventories of two of Pedro I's courtier mistresses tell us much about their lives, too. The Marquesa de Santos and the Baronesa de Sorocaba were sisters. Sorocaba bore a son for the emperor, but Santos was his principal concubine, giving him four children: three girls and a boy. Sorocaba died in 1851, leaving seven sons, whose conflicting claim to the estate of 62:042$670 tied up probate for six years.[43] One of the seven children was Pedro's. (Sorocaba had married once; at one time, her husband, Boaventura Delfim Pereira, was an administrator of one of the imperial family's farms.) Little is known about the son, Rodrigo, whose paternity has widely been attributed to the first emperor. The family was obviously poor.

Sorocaba's sister Santos died in 1867, leaving an estate as complicated as her marriage and turbulent dalliance with the first emperor. The heirs of the two marriages and of Pedro I contested the will, and the probate court took eight years to settle the matter. Her estate was inventoried in five volumes, close to 3,000 pages of documents. From her first marriage, to an army officer, she had three children. She divorced him by an ecclesiastical court ruling, but had become Pedro's mistress before the marriage was dissolved. Santos and Pedro had four children: son Pedro and daughter the Duquesa do Ceará died in infancy; the two surviving daughters were the Condessa de Iguaçu and the Duquesa de Goiás. Iguaçu married a son of the Marquês de Barbacena; Goiás, a European noble. From Santos's second marriage, to Brigadier Rafael Tobias de Aguiar, six children were born. Santos had a total of thirteen children, fathered by three men, not counting miscarriages in between. Only seven of the thirteen children survived.

Officially, the executor of Santos's inventory was her first-born, Felício Pinto Coelho de Mendonça e Castro. The inventory was contested by all three sets of offspring, forcing the court to divide the estate into three portions. Because the shares were not equal, the heirs fought among themselves for an equitable distribution of the legacy. The Condessa de Iguaçu, already impoverished, had been receiving subsidies from her mother. On one occasion, the marquesa gave her daughter a sum of 40:000$ from the wedding endowment of Santos's second husband. The Conde de Iguaçu, Santos's son-in-law, was less than successful in his career as a politician and businessman. His brother, the Visconde de Barbacena, was equally unsuccessful as a diplomat and businessman and so indigent that, at the age of 101, he petitioned the Republic's national congress to grant him a pension of 500$ per year; he died at the age of 104. Iguaçu also died poor. Not one of the children of Santos and Pedro I became a social success. Throughout the inventory, the name of Pedro I was not once mentioned, not even as the father of Santos's children. The children from Santos's second marriage also lived off their mother's generosity. The youngest son, Basílio, was heavily in debt; Santos had cosigned one note for 11:274$160. In all, the marquesa cosigned notes for her children and other kin for a total of 108:321$820. Because the borrowers at the time of the marquesa's death were unable to meet their obligations, creditors besieged Santos's estate.

The Santos estate totaled 1.308:848$600. After deducting court expenses, lawyers' fees, and debts for which the marquesa was accountable, the líquido was still a hefty 838:480$452. Each group of siblings from the three unions ended up with 279:493$484. One complication that delayed the probate process was that Santos had been supporting her children financially. No complete records existed of the money she had given them over the years; furthermore, part of the cash Brigadier Aguiar had given Santos as a condition for their wedding had been spent to support the Condessa de Iguaçu, who was obviously unable to pay it back yet refused to count the amount toward her share of the legacy; and, finally, the inventory revealed that the estate of the first marriage had never been settled. The marriage was practically annulled by the imperial wish of Pedro I, and the first husband was unwilling to settle the estate amicably during his lifetime.

Santos had lived in a grand style that few of her aristocratic detractors could match. The bulk of her assets was in cash and urban properties. In addition to her various houses in São Paulo, she was also a big landowner in Sorocaba, an interior coffee county. She engaged as heavily in money lending as some small banks: no less than 544:117$475 was loaned out, and the inventory listed 57:584$181 in uncollectable loans.[44] Her generosity was much abused by relatives and kin because scores of godchildren and other ritual offspring swelled the ranks of her clientage. The marquesa was a rich woman, unlike the majority of courtier nobles and even of important political nobles. She was actually richer than most of the prime ministers of the empire.

Inventories also reveal other human foibles that afflicted the nobility. The Visconde de Santa Teresa (Polidoro da Fonseca Quintanilha Jordão) was a lieutenant general in the imperial army when he died in 1879. He listed his marital status in the will as single, yet the executor of the inventory was his "natural son," identified in the inventory as an illegitimate son. The visconde left him the modest sum of 88 contos. Again, not all nobles died rich. The Marquês de Santo Amaro (José Egídio Alvares de Almeida), of Bahia, was a cabinet minister in 1825, and the following year was nominated for the imperial senate. His widow, the marquesa, died in 1846, leaving two heirs: the Visconde de Santo Amaro, son, and the Condessa do Rio Pardo, daughter. The marquesa's estate was inventoried twice. In the first tally carried out in 1847, her total assets were valued at 14:489$944, and her debts came to 25:018$145. In 1852 a new probate calculated the monte to be 4:657$600, the debts 25:029$346, the amount the marquesa owed to her son and son-in-law. Because the marquês died in 1832, probably poor, possibly the widow inherited many of his debts. Had this been the case, her son and son-in-law could have very well retired them by assuming the notes. A final example, the Viscondessa de Uberaba, who died heirless in 1880, listed no landed properties, but eleven slaves. She owed 600$ to her sister, who was also her executrix.[45] Although poor, the viscondessa made the aristocratic gesture of freeing her slaves, but died unable to pay off her debt to her sister. Such were the vagaries in lifestyles of some nobles. Santo Amaro and Uberaba were not the only cases; one can postulate that the aristocratic way of life forced many Brazilian titleholders to behave like nobles, often beyond their means.

In their daily business, nobles behaved no differently than commoners. As creditors, they were quick to ask local courts to render favorable decisions, a natural resort in view of the social and political influence they exercised over local government. In Valença, the Barão do Val Formoso and the Barão de São Luís took their commoner debtors to the local courts and won favorable decisions, thus permitting them to seize properties of the debtors by court action.[46] The Judicial Documentation Section, of the National Archives, in Rio, is full of court papers recording such financial disputes in which nobility was involved and often won. The examples of Valença, Rio, and Santo Amaro, Bahia, suggest that such key offices as juiz de direito and juiz de orfãos were often held by kinsmen of the dominant local elite, often titled noble clans or recipients of their patronage. In Valença, for example, a Bahian Moniz was a juiz de direito in the 1880s; it should be noted that the Visconde de Nogueira da Gama was married to a Bahian Moniz. In Santo Amaro, the county probate judge was a Ferreira Bandeira, a scion of a prominent local landowning family. To a certain extent, the control of local government was far more important for maintaining the status quo for the nobility than for any measure of dominance over the imperial government. Throughout the monarchical period, the administration of estate distribution, such as inventories, opening of wills, and amicable partitioning in divorce, remained in the hands of the local judiciary. In brief, the monarchy never directly controlled the management of wealth held by the local elite. This allowed a measure of political independence for the provincial and local elites.

Other facets of personal life-style also show up in the inventories. During the late eighteenth and early nineteenth centuries, many well-to-do unmarried couples lived together. Scores of inventories of both agrarian gentry and merchants in Bahia listed many offspring as "emancipated children."[47] This suggests that both the urban and rural rich lived with their slaves and decided to free children born of such informal unions, a tradition that persisted throughout the nineteenth century and was later widely practiced among the urban and rural poor. However, exceptions did exist, such as the case of the Barão de Saubara, of Santo Amaro, already presented. Some fathers preferred to sell their slave offspring. Luís da Gama, an abolitionist journalist in the 1880s, was the victim of an unusual circumstance: his free father gave him as payment for a gambling debt to a ship captain, who raised the boy. Such a Byzantine way of life was inevitable in a society where there was a small elite class and a huge dependent and servile population.

For upper-class men, interracial and interclass sex was a fact of life in Brazil. Slave owners routinely claimed their right to monopolize the sex lives of male and female members of the servile and free but dependent people. One Bahian planter nobleman lived with two slave women at once; another was known for his interest in young slave boys; and still another persuaded a local priest to give his surname to his slave child, Teodoro de Sampaio. Even such aristocratic nobles as the Nogueira da Gamas and the Cavalcantis interbred with servile females freely. It was not until 1835 that mortmain was dissolved by law; by 1842 all children, legitimate, legitimized, and natural, were entitled to share their parents' wealth.

Contrary to popular belief, the landowners of Brazil were not without debts. In fact, the average planter, rancher, and farmer in the nineteenth century was heavily in debt. In Pernambuco, a quarter of all planters were in arrears, often having to borrow beyond their means. In the Northeast, some 60 percent of all the agricultural capital, slaves, and equipment employed in the plantation economy came from borrowed money. In the south-central provinces of Minas, São Paulo, and Espírito Santo, the heartland of Brazilian coffee, plantations numbered 773, of which 726 were mortgaged in the amount of 42,000 contos, or approximately U.S. $21 million.[48]

An examination of the family strategy of one agrarian clan should provide insight into how landowners typically managed their wealth. The Nogueira da Gamas were considered to be one of the most aristocratic families and were certainly among the most affluent planters in the empire.[49] One local historian of Valença traces the first Nogueira da Gama to settle in that Paraíba Valley town to 1797. But it was another Nogueira da Gama (Manuel Jacinto, the future Marquês de Baependi) who obtained a giant land grant from Dom João VI and prospered there. Manuel Jacinto, a courtier politician, was reputedly encouraged by his king to cultivate coffee at that place.[50] The 10,800 alqueires (540 Km²) of the royal land grant became the basis for several family plantations in the nineteenth century. By 1826 Manuel Jacinto, already the Marquês de Baependi and an imperial senator, had carved out three of the best coffee fazendas in the empire: Santa Mônica, Santa Rosa, and Santa Ana.

Baependi married well, too. A thoroughgoing patrimonial mandarin (he was a general as well as a Crown official), he chose the daughter of a super-rich Portuguese merchant to be his wife: Francisca Mônica, whose parents were Brás Carneiro de Leão and his wife, later the Baronesa de São Salvador de Campos. Baependi and Francisca Mônica had three sons: Brás Carneiro (the Conde de Baependi), Manuel Jacinto (the Barão de Juparanã), and Francisco Nicolau (the Barão de Santa Mônica). By the 1850s the Nogueira da Gama clan in Valença held a veritable agrarian fortune. But, unlike gentry clans such as the Sousa Queiróses and the Prados of São Paulo, the Nogueira da Gamas practiced clan endogamy when it came to the marriage of their offspring. None of the children of the marquês and marquesa married an outsider. Brás Carneiro wedded Rosa Maria, a daughter of his uncle Coronel José Inácio Nogueira da Gama (Baependi's brother) and his aunt, the future Baronesa de São Mateus. Manuel Jacinto never married. Francisco Nicolau also wedded a cousin, Luisa do Loreto, a daughter of Caxias.[51] Francisco Nicolau and Luisa had one son. Manuel Jacinto sired a score of children, all born of slave women and freed lower-class women. Therefore, it was the offspring of the Conde and Condessa de Baependi, eight in all, who continued the succession of the clan.

The second Nogueira da Gama to settle in Valenća was a son of José Inácio and the Baronesa de São Mateus: Nicolau Antônio Nogueira Vale da Gama. The future Visconde de Nogueira da Gama was also a landowner in Valença. He married his cousin Maria Francisca, a daughter of the Condessa de Itapagipe. Within two generations, the expatriate Mineiro clan had succeeded in ensconcing itself as the ruling Valencian elite throughout the nineteenth century.

The Marquês de Baependi was a Coimbra graduate, the holder of a doctorate in mathematics. Entering military service upon graduation, he had risen to the rank of general by the time of Dom João VI. A court favorite, he served as royal finance inspector and in other upper echelon posts. By the time of Brazilian independence, he was already a key counselor to his king and crown prince Dom Pedro. In 1823 he was elected to the constituent assembly to represent his adopted province of Rio and he became the third man to hold the portfolio of the minister of finance after independence. A signer of the Constitution of 1824, he firmly established his niche as a reliable loyal mandarin at the court of Pedro I. Serving three times as minister of finance between 1823 and 1831, he was also one of the original appointees to the First Council of State (1823–34). By 1826 he was an imperial senator from Minas Gerais.

He had begun his career during Dom João's time and served his country for more than four decades.

The marquês died in 1847 a wealthy man. Although his inventory, filed in the county probate court, was incomplete,[52] the inventory of the marquesa, who died in 1868, gives an indication of how rich the couple was. According to the inventory, they owned properties in Portugal and in the province of Espírito Santo, in addition to fazendas in Valença and houses in the court, and were virtually free of debt. Her estate was calculated at 841:054$899. After deducting the customary court expenses and clearing outstanding accounts with Rio commission houses, the inheritable legacy (líquido) came to 776:531$578, or 258:843$859 each for the three principal heirs. The first-born was already a conde and was president of the province of Pernambuco at the time of inventory. The other two had yet to be ennobled.[53] On the basis of the marquesa's inventory, which was made some two decades after the death of the marquês, his estate should have been in the neighborhood of 1.000:000$, a veritable fortune in pre-1850 Brazil.

The Barão de Juparanã was the first of the marquês's heirs to die. Never married, Juparanã was the capitalist fazendeiro of the clan. Owner-administrator of Santa Mônica and Santa Ana for himself and his brother, the Barão de Santa Mônica, Juparanã was an enterprising planter. Local court documents show that he was active in moneylending as well. When he died in 1876, he left 467:764$164, which included two fazendas and 404 slaves. Torres & Cia. of Rio was his commission agent for coffee, to which the planter owed little. A total of 37:423$422 was taken out of his estate to pay lawyers, accountants, and probate expenses. Based on the evidence of the barão's bequests, sibling rivalry was apparently severe, especially between the first-born and Juparanã; the deceased left the meiação to his favorite brother Santa Mônica, and to his older brother the Conde de Baependi he bequeathed only the dividend income from ten shares of imperial bonds, the value of which was a scanty 10:000$, or 1:000$ per share. The other half of the estate went to Juparanã's natural heirs: a total of sixteen children, all born between 1857 and 1872 of various slave women. At least two of the children were born in the same year, 1872, only a month apart. The inventory mentioned nothing of the legitimization of the children, and, though paternity was acknowledged in the will, they (filhos naturais) were barred from using the name of Nogueira da Gama. There was no evidence that Juparanã urbanized his wealth. For that matter, his parents (the marquês and marquesa) had failed to urbanize their wealth, except houses in the court. The Barão de Santa Mônica received a sum of 111:595$, consisting of slaves, lands, coffee trees, houses, and jewelry.[54] In some ways, Juparanã was a more thoroughgoing agrarian aristocrat than his father in terms of the total absence of wealth diversification.

The Barão de Santa Mônica, in contrast to Juparanã, died poor. In 1853 the young man petitioned the Crown for authorization to marry Luisa do Loreto, as Luso-Brazilian nobiliary practices called for. Both the bride and groom were children of the Brazilian nobility, which the Braganza Crown created, and hence it was customary for the children of nobility, especially fidalgo moço and fidalgo cavaleiro, to request imperial sanction for marriage, but close cousins would require an episcopal dispensation.[55] Of this union, only one heir, Francisco Nicolau de Lima Nogueira da Gama, survived. In spite of the inheritance from his parents and brother, which should have come to a minimum of 500 contos, Santa Mônica failed to expand the estate. His ability as an estate administrator was publicly questioned, at least once, when some citizens sued him for inefficient administration of a church property.[56] One local historian reaffirms that he was a poor businessman. It was Juparanã who managed the inheritance of Santa Mônica from the parents; after the death of his brother-manager in 1876, Santa Mônica was unable to hang on to the family fortune. In 1884 the baron mortgaged Fazenda Santa Mônica, the family heirloom and the centerpiece of the Nogueira da Gama fortune, for 436:315$600, a debt he was unable to pay off before his death in 1887. The baronesa and his only son petitioned the court for permission to liquidate Santa Mônica's estate. The inventory shows that not only had the Barão de Santa Mônica died in abject poverty, but also that the amount of the estate the widow and son wished to dispose of was one share of public bond, valued at 1:000$.[57] Not only did he drive the family business into the ground, but he forced it into bankruptcy.[58] The Brazilian adage of grandfather peddler, son planter, and grandson shoemaker allows three generations to complete the cycle from rags to riches to rags. In the case of the Nogueira da Gamas, two generations were required to establish aristocratic domination in Valença and to end Nogueira da Gama's hegemony.

Little information is available on the wealth management of the last surviving brother, the Conde de Baependi, who also died in 1887. His will specified that his wife, children, and grandchildren would be his heirs, but failed to stipulate how the estate would be divided. The document also failed to state how rich he was.[59] Historians have maintained that he was wealthy, often giving generously to charities in Valença. However, he also had a harsh side. In 1876 two of his slaves were to be freed by the emancipation fund created by the imperial government. After he received compensation from the state, the conde insisted that the two slaves work for him until 1881. Such conditional manumission was frequently associated with a voluntary emancipation, but not with one compensated by the state. The slaves ran away instead of accepting the terms of manumission.[60]

In addition to such incidents, Baependi, like brother Juparanã, also sired several children by slaves in addition to his eight legitimate offspring. None was recognized. One Isabel Congo gave birth to a son, Pedro Henrique da Silva; another slave woman gave birth to Amélia Mateus da Costa. Although these two were publicly accepted as the conde's children, the will provides no evidence that he had set aside portions of his wealth for the offspring of his casual affection. Local historians say that the Nogueira da Gamas kept a harem of mulatta slaves *(rapaziada afidalgada)*. The fathers as well as patrons of these girls and women were presumed to be well-known local gentry and aristocrats, hence the term "nobiliary damsels."[61] Obviously, the fathers were unwilling to claim their paternity, but paid for the upkeep of the children.

The last of the Nogueira da Gama nobles to die was the Visconde de Nogueira da Gama, nephew of the marquês and son-in-law of the Condessa de Itapagipe. A rich landowner and a general deputy from Minas Gerais, Nogueira da Gama's political career failed to blossom. Instead, he entered the courtier staff service, like his mother-in-law. By the 1880s he was the emperor's chief aide, in charge of all external correspondence and managing the court's daily business.[62] His finances must have been shaky because, in 1880, he sold off parts of his property in Valença. The Barão de Santa Justa bought Fazenda Independência from him. In the next few years, Santa Justa, a rich planter-merchant in Paraíba do Sul, was engaged in a dispute with Nogueira da Gama about its exact size. The conflict ended up in court.[63] When the visconde died in 1897, the inventory stated that "they [the visconde and viscondessa, who died in 1885] had no estate." In fact, well before the deaths of the couple, they had begun to dispose among their heirs the family wealth, which came to 260:000$. By 1862 a third of the family estate had already been parceled out to the children. The remainder was disposed of before 1897. On one occasion, 110:000$ was given to a daughter; on another, a son received 40:000$ in land.[64] Furthermore, like other patriarchs, the visconde also knew how to exercise patronage for kin. In 1876 Salvador Antônio Moniz Barreto de Aragão was appointed as a county prosecutor in Valença. This Bahian was the visconde's grandson.[65] The appointment was likely arranged by the courtier noble, and Moniz was accepted in Valença as a Nogueira da Gama.

The case of the Nogueira da Gama clan illustrates a contrasting paradigm, probably typical of the aristocracy, in family strategies of marriage, wealth management, and the exercise of patronage. Both branches of the clan (the children of the marquês and Coronel José Inácio) were denied free career and marriage choices that offspring of gentry planters and merchants normally enjoyed. As an emerging aristocracy, the Nogueira da Gamas opted to practice clan endogamy and sought to encapsulate the clan's wealth by avoiding marriages and business ties with outsiders. Children of the Marquês de Baependi remained in the family business as coffee planters, and only one son entered politics. The marquês's nephew failed to make his name in imperial politics and followed his mother-in-law's career on the courtier staff. From the standpoint of wealth diversification, none of the Nogueira da Gamas succeeded. By 1887, the time of the deaths of Santa Mônica and Baependi, the family wealth had already been dissipated. The income of courtier nobles was too small to allow the Visconde de Nogueira da Gama to amass a fortune.

In fact, the entire imperial house, from the emperor to the household staff, was earning small salaries. Itapagipe earned 110$ per month at the peak of her career, 1:320$ per annum, which helps explain her meager estate. Her son-in-law, the visconde, could not have received much more. A career at the court bore a strong resemblance to that of a mandarin in terms of economic rewards. One was expected to spend his or her own funds to sustain the social and political status required of courtier nobility. Even the court lacked sufficient funds to maintain its

own household staff in style. In 1859 the imperial household had to borrow to pay for the impending trip of the royal couple to the northern
provinces. In 1860 Pedro II received 800:000$, the empress 96:000$, and
imperial princes 6:000$ each as their annuities. That year, the house-
hold staff collectively received 6:400$.[66] In 1827 the first emperor was
receiving 1.000:000$ per year, considerably more than Pedro II's salary
(dotação). Between 1844 and 1882 the Brazilian population increased
by 125 percent, agricultural production by 85 percent, and governmental expenditures by 514.99 percent, yet the court budget under Dom
Pedro II decreased and was smaller than that under Pedro I.[67]

The richest segment of the Brazilian nobility was clearly composed
of merchants. Landowners were rich as a group, but they were by and
large debt-ridden. The case of debt contracts in Santo Amaro and São
Francisco do Conde reinforces this view: of the nineteen nobles who
contracted loans, totaling 2,618 contos, only one family (Costa Pinto)
borrowed money for an entrepreneurial purpose. The 750 contos borrowed constituted 29 percent of the total debt incurred by Bahian nobles in Santo Amaro county. The remaining eighteen families were
forced into debt to maintain certain socially expected living standards.
Such aristocratic families as the Albuquerques (Pirajá), the Monizes
(Mataripe), and the Vianas (Rio das Contas) found themselves in gen-
teel poverty by the third generation. Careers in imperial politics permitted few to fare well in wealth management. Generals and admirals
also fared poorly. Widows of military and naval officers routinely requested state pensions to survive.[68] Because agriculture throughout
the nineteenth century functioned in a capitalist milieu, more successful wealth managers came from gentry planters and merchants
than from the status-conscious aristocracy. It was these groups of
bourgeois capitalists who by the 1870s had become increasingly vocal
in their opposition to the *status quo imperium* and who began to
search for a political solution to end the patrimonial monarchy. A liberal republic could better accommodate their needs and allow them to
rise to the status of a national political elite.

Conclusion

Dom João de Braganza, first the prince regent of Portugal and later the ruler of the United Kingdom of Portugal, Brazil, and the Algarve, introduced nobiliary titles and lesser honors to the New World in part to show his gratitude to the worthy Portuguese and Brazilian subjects who facilitated his transatlantic voyage and settlement in Rio, and in part to surround himself with the trappings of a European court. Rio de Janeiro was no tropical Versailles, but it was the only city in the New World where a European monarch resided. The king liked to ridicule his own creation, the New World nobles, who often struggled with ill-fitting vestments and strange court rituals. The spectacle of a Molièrian bourgeois gentilhomme also provided endless amusement to visiting European diplomats, merchants, and scientists. Despite such defects, Dom João relied on the Portuguese letrados to administer the realm and on the Brazilian nobility to broaden his social ties with the growing body of men of wealth. He was parsimonious in granting titles, however. In contrast, his son, Pedro I, was generous; and his grandson, Pedro II, almost indulged his subjects by undertaking a mass distribution of titles and honors. Both Pedro I and Pedro II discovered the social and political importance of ennoblement and exploited this imperial prerogative to shore up their popularity among their subjects. The second emperor distended the eligible pool of candidates by appointing future nobles from all walks of life. All three Braganza monarchs in the New World found the creating of titles and the bestowing of honors to be a useful and integral part of their lives, for it at once legitimized their rule and reinforced their ties with the elite.

The nobility exhibited several internecine characteristics during its natural life, which spanned almost seven decades. It functioned as an informal corporate group of Crown-selected elite which represented the major social, political, and economic interests that constituted the empire. Rich landowners and merchants, high-ranking generals and admirals, pious prelates, meritorious veteran civil servants, faithful courtier staff, and even leading intellectuals of the empire were inducted into this corporation. Although the attempt to formalize it by law failed in the wake of the dissolution of the constituent assembly in 1823, the imperial creation of titles granted de facto corporate status and privileges to the nobility by virtue of its place in society. Once recruited into this closed group, a nobleman ceased to be only of his profession and instead transcended it as a key intermediary between the Crown and the family or profession of which he was part.

The twin factors of ennoblement—"service to the State and Humanity"—were never rigorously enforced and became difficult to maintain, especially after 1850, when Brazil became a flourishing peripheral capitalist economy in the Atlantic world-system. Money, ambition, and avarice replaced merit guidelines as influential courtiers and imperial politicians flouted the original intent with impunity. Powerful political and court brokers expanded their ever-widening circles of networks of patronage by usurping imperial prerogatives. The sale of imperial honors and titles became inevitable, all in the name of charitable activities and noble causes. Hospício Dom Pedro II in Rio was practically funded by "voluntary donations" from ambitious citizens, who expected the Crown to reciprocate their largesse with titles and honors. By mid-century, the sale was formalized, the prices of various titles and honors became a matter of public record, and the abuse grew rampant. The title of barão cost about ten contos, if the candidate had a "good connection" at the court. Rich up-country bumpkins who lacked such an advantage wasted a "river of money" in hiring intermediaries. Stories of misapplied funds and disheartening results abound. Money, along with political power, still played a major role in the creation of titles.

Noblemen as a collective entity lacked a corporate esprit de corps because they reflected diverse social, economic, political, and geographical backgrounds. As such, they often represented a microcosm, or mosaic, of a larger society. Their values, habits, and thoughts reflected multiclass, provincial, and heterogeneous origins. They emulated their older cousins in Europe in life-styles. When a lineage needed bolstering or "whitening," they used their privileged status to contract for brides and grooms from the Continent, but not always of noble origin, however. Europeans of the humblest background, as one Brazilian count extolled, were still superior to the "chocolate barons" of the empire, a self-inflicted derisive remark on the racial miscegenation of Brazilians. One of the richest court merchants in Joanine times was married to a daughter of an Irish washwoman. Also, a noble in Pedro II's court rejoiced at his daughter's betrothal to a Frenchman, whose purity of blood far exceeded money and the clan prestige that a Brazilian title could add. And, in yet another example, a Bahian sugar plantation mistress inquired about the purity of the bloodline of a young girl, with whom she was contemplating a contract as a bride for her son.

By contrast, in the gentry-dominated provinces of Rio and São Paulo, not all nobles sought to indulge in clan or class endogamy, a residue of aristocratic behavior. A growing number of the titled gentry planters and bourgeois merchants learned to maximize their social status by recruiting brides and grooms from new-money families. Marriage served the purpose of preventing an unwarranted intrusion of outsiders and at the same time functioned as a network of power, money, and influence. The south-central gentry used marriage for this dual purpose, and the older aristocratic northerners continued to review it as a social-control mechanism. An incorporation of fresh human and financial capital often resulted in the creation of a new power group regionally and nationally, and titled gentry in Rio and São Paulo prudently practiced profitable family strategies.

The titled elite of the empire also suffered their share of the vagaries of life. Many struggled to maintain a life-style that was beyond their means, thus forcing themselves into debt. One coffee planter in Vassouras squandered 40:000$ for a single visit by the imperial princess and her husband. Such an extravagant outlay of a small fortune seemed fitting to maintain image. Bon vivant nobles drank French wine, dressed in Italian silk, adorned their women with jewels, and ate their dinner from Limoges china. But the majority of nobles lived ignoble lives. A Bahian planter bedded his slave women and manumitted them occasionally when he was presented with a son. One Nogueira da Gama, never married, sired a score of illegitimate children, all born of slaves and lower-class black women. A priest in São Paulo who broke the vow of celibacy and lived in sin for decades conveniently abandoned his concubine to qualify himself for an imperial honor, and presumably expiated himself in the eyes of God as well. Such examples of checkered life-styles of nobles and prospective nobles are endless.

The esprit de corps so vital and necessary to build up any cohesive institution and ideology never materialized. The monarchy lasted only sixty-seven years and drew its nobles from too diverse regions and classes. The forging of a corporate mentality and value system became impossible, especially in such a short period of time. Few individuals even bothered to obey the extant rules and rituals of the nobility: custom called for the children of nobles and gentlemen of the imperial house to seek imperial sanction for betrothal and marriages; holders of imperial honors were obliged to pay necessary fees and to take out titles by registering them at the Imperial Chancery of Nobility and Fidalguia; and the chosen few were required to create a family coat of arms to symbolize their elite status. Few complied with these rules, however. Those who resided in and near the court did their best to observe these rules and rituals, but those who lived in the provinces hardly cared. The Crown lacked the means to enforce these rules and never attempted to punish those who violated them. Such a lax attitude bred secular behavior and eventually debasement of the institution. For instance, the Barão da Barra Grande, an imperial regent and the father of Caxias, and the Visconde de Barbacena, a prominent businessman and sometime diplomat, either forgot to register their titles or chose to ignore the nobiliary rules. Prime Minister Barão de Cotegipe (1885–88) never established a coat of arms for his title. Such perfidy was unthinkable among European nobilities and would not have been tolerated by a Romanov or a Bourbon king.

If merchants and landowners constituted the richest segment of the Brazilian nobility, they were not the most powerful. In a patrimonial state system, offices were selectively distributed to those obsequious servants of the Crown, especially the life-tenure posts in the council of state and the senate. Political power was tightly held and exercised by the emperor and his sinecurist mandarins. This group of the Braganza household servants made up the most influential elite of the

monarchy. The Crown frequently ennobled cabinet ministers, senators, and councillors of state to forestall any potential disloyalty. As
such, they exchanged their political and personal loyalty for sinecures
and livelihood. No fewer than sixteen of the twenty-three men who
served as prime ministers between 1847 and 1889 were political nobles.
As a whole, loyal mandarins lacked independent economic resources to
support themselves. If they had money at the outset of their careers, it
tended to dissipate toward the end. Cotegipe, who inherited four sugar
mills and hundreds of slaves from his wife, squandered the wealth and
was heavily in debt; Sinimbu, another sugar planter, also led a modest
life at the end of his career. João Alfredo, a son of Pernambuco and the
prime minister who presided over the abolition of slavery in May 1888,
died in abject poverty. The sole source of income for sinecurist senators
and councillors of state was the gratuity from the Crown, and after
1889 the Republic failed to establish pensions for these elite politicians
of the ancien régime.

The most fascinating aspect of the nobility as a social group, however, is its emergence as a dichotomous political and economic institution. The titled politicians usually came from the older established
families and hence were infatuated with a sense of noblesse oblige,
often using up their inheritance to remain in politics. The younger of
the nobility were gentry planters and their ancillary merchants and
bankers, many parvenu to begin with, whose foremost preoccupation
was to guard and expand their newly gained wealth. To this end, they
often indulged in interclass marriages (when and where such unions
were profitable), viewed politics as a necessary means to their economic ends, and often risked their capital on unknown enterprises.
Typically, these two nobilities—the economic and the political—seldom merged as a single corporate elite; rather, they remained as two
separate groups of the corporation, often espousing conflicting claims
and interests within the empire.

The decay of the nobility system in the matter of a little more than
six decades cannot be attributed solely to the banal sale of titles and
honors. The induction of the lesser qualified as well as the parvenu rich
simply destroyed the prestige of the institution, and this unwarranted
vulgarization dissipated the corporation's clout. An increasing number of politicians, such as the Andradas, the Nabucos, the Sousa Dantases, and the Saraivas, refused to accept titles and honors as a show of

defiance to the Crown and its mandarins. But what ultimately destroyed the nobility of imperial Brazil was the change in general society and economy after 1870: the emergence of a new society dominated by gentry values and bourgeois culture that undermined the aristocratic, corporatist pillars of the patrimonial monarchy. The gentlemen of the Southern Cross outlived their usefulness in the days of steam engines, telephones, and electricity. The nobility died with its patron, the Braganza, when the monarchy was overthrown in 1889. The passing of Dom Pedro II in 1891 not only marked the end of a political experiment with patrimonial monarchy, but also closed an era of the social engineering of a status group as the foundation of the imperial system.

Notes

Abbreviations Used in Notes

PUBLIC AND PRIVATE ARCHIVES

AAA	Arquivo de Alencar Araripe. Rio de Janeiro.
ABC	Arquivo do Barão de Cotegipe. Rio de Janeiro.
ACS	Arquivo do Conde de Subaé. Rio de Janeiro.
AEAB	Arquivo de Ernesto Aleixo Boulanger. Rio de Janeiro.
AHGO	Arquivo Histórico de Goiás. Goiânia.
AIGHBa	Arquivo do Instituto Geográfico e Histórico da Bahia. Salvador.
AIHGB	Arquivo do Instituto Histórico e Geográfico Brasileiro. Rio de Janeiro.
AJFAP	Arquivo de João Ferreira de Araújo Pinho. Rio de Janeiro.
AJWAP	Arquivo de José Wanderley de Araújo Pinho. Rio de Janeiro.
AMI	Arquivo do Museu Imperial. Petrópolis.
ANG	Arquivo de Nogueira da Gama. Rio de Janeiro.
APCI/SP	Arquivo Público da Câmara de Itu. São Paulo.
ASCMSA	Arquivo da Santa Casa de Misericórdia de Santo Amaro, Bahia.
AVO	Arquivo do Visconde de Ourém. Rio de Janeiro.
DG/GSU	Department of Genealogy, Genealogical Society of Utah, Salt Lake City.
PP/SH/AEB	Presidência da Província, Seção Histórica, Arquivo do Estado da Bahia. Salvador.
PRO/FO	Public Record Office. Foreign Office. London.
SAP/ANRJ	Seção de Arquivos Particulares, Arquivo Nacional, Rio de Janeiro.
SDE/DAE/SP	Seção de Documentação Escrita, Departmento do Arquivo do Estado. São Paulo.
SDH/AMP/USP	Seção de Documentação Histórica, Arquivo do Museu Paulista, Universidade de São Paulo.

SH/AEB Seção Histórica, Arquivo do Estado da Bahia. Salvador.
SJ/AEB Seção Judiciária, Arquivo do Estado da Bahia. Salvador.
SM/BNRJ Seção de Manuscritos, Biblioteca Nacional, Rio de Janeiro.
SPE/ANRJ Seção do Poder Executivo, Arquivo Nacional, Rio de Janeiro.
SPH/AERJ Seção de Pesquisa Histórica, Arquivo do Estado do Rio de Janeiro, Niterói.
SPJ/ANRJ Seção do Poder Judiciário, Arquivo Nacional, Rio de Janeiro.

JOURNALS AND SERIALS

ACIHA *Anais do Congresso Internacional de Historia da America.* Rio de Janeiro.
AGB *Annuário Genealogico Brasileiro.* São Paulo.
AMHN *Anais do Museu Histórico Nacional.* Rio de Janeiro.
AMP *Anais do Museu Paulista.* São Paulo.
CSSH *Comparative Studies in Society and History.* Cambridge, England.
HAHR *Hispanic American Historical Review.* Durham, N.C.
HGCB *História Geral da Civilização Brasileira,* 12 vols. São Paulo.
JEH *Journal of Economic History.* Wilmington, Del.
JIH *Journal of Interdisciplinary History.* Cambridge, England.
MAN *Mensário do Arquivo Nacional.* Rio de Janeiro.
MJC *Mensario do Jornal do Commercio.* Rio de Janeiro.
RA *Revista de Administração.* São Paulo.
RFSP *Revue Française de Science Politique.* Paris.
RIEB *Revista do Instituto de Estudos Brasileiros.* São Paulo.
RIHGB *Revista do Instituto Histórico e Geográfico Brasileiro.* Rio de Janeiro.

Introduction

1 The petition file at the National Archives, in Rio, is known as Requerimentos de Graças Honoríficas. No exact figure is available as to how many requerimentos were actually filed with the imperial government. This collection is therefore not complete by any means. Some petitions are also in the Manuscript Collection at the National Library, in Rio, and in collections of personal papers at the Instituto Histórico e Geográfico Brasileiro, also in Rio.

2 Estate inventories support this assertion. See Eileen Keremitsis, "Workers and Industrialization in Rio de Janeiro, 1870–1930," Ph.D. Dissertation, Columbia University (1981), Chap. 3; Joseph Earl Sweigart, "Financing and Marketing Brazilian Export Agriculture: The Coffee Factors of Rio de Janeiro, 1850–1888," Ph.D. Dissertation, University of Texas, Austin (1980), pp. 94–98; and Richard Graham, "Slavery and Economic Development: Brazil and the United States South in the Nineteenth Century," *CSSH* 23:4 (October 1981), pp. 633–34, 643.

3 Many works represent the revisionist view that a slave economy was capitalistic: Immanuel Wallerstein, *The Modern World-System: Capitalist Agriculture and*

the *Origins of the European World-Economy in the Sixteenth Century* (New York, 1974), p. 127; and Ciro Flamarion S. Cardoso has been a strong advocate of this view: *Agricultura, escravidão e capitalismo* (Petrópolis, 1979) and *Economia e sociedade em áreas colonais e periféricas: Guiana Francesa e Pará (1750–1817)* (Rio, 1984). For the cases of Bahia and Rio, see Eul-Soo Pang, "Modernization and Slavocracy in Nineteenth-Century Brazil," *JIH* 9:4 (Spring 1979), pp. 667–88. Maria de Nazareth Baudel Wanderley, *Capital e propriedade fundiária* (Rio, 1978), deals with Pernambuco.

4 In addition to Wallerstein, a similar idea is also suggested by Stefano Fenoaltea, in "Slavery and Supervision in Comparative Perspective: A Model," *JEH* 44:3 (September 1984), pp. 635–68. Perhaps the most interesting point about the nature of Brazil's slavery system was that the nonexport economies also relied on chattel labor. For the case of Minas Gerais, see Roberto Borges Martins, "Growing in Silence: The Slave Economy of Nineteenth-Century Minas Gerais, Brazil," Ph.D. Dissertation, Vanderbilt University (1980); later, parts of this dissertation were published (with Amílcar Martins Filho) as "Slavery in a Nonexport Economy: Nineteenth-Century Minas Gerais Revisited," *HAHR* 63:3 (August 1983), pp. 537–68.

1 The Luso-Brazilian Court in Rio de Janeiro

1 Stuart B. Schwartz, *Sovereignty and Society in Colonial Brazil: The High Court of Bahia and Its Judges, 1609–1751* (Berkeley, 1973), p. 239; C. R. Boxer, *Four Centuries of Portuguese Expansion, 1415–1825: A Succinct Survey* (Berkeley and Johannesburg, 1969), pp. 48–55.

2 Francisco António Corrêa, *História económica de Portugal,* 2 vols. (Lisboa, 1929), 1:299.

3 On the problem of private trading, see Schwartz, *Sovereignty,* p. 328; and C. R. Boxer, *The Portuguese Seaborne Empire, 1415–1825* (New York, 1969), pp. 322–23.

4 Schwartz, *Sovereignty,* pp. 375–79; Appendix II, pp. 382–95; Appendix III.

5 On the rise of the Caribbean as a sugar producer and its impact on Brazil, see Celso Furtado, *The Economic Growth of Brazil: A Survey from Colonial to Modern Times,* trans. Ricardo W. de Aguiar and Eric Charles Drysdale (Berkeley, 1963; 1968 paper-back edition), pp. 71–77.

6 Boxer, *Portuguese Seaborne Empire,* p. 324.

7 The best work in any language on the Pombaline economic policies is Kenneth R. Maxwell, *Conflicts and Conspiracies: Brazil and Portugal, 1750–1808* (Cambridge, Eng., 1973).

8 According to one study on the import of slaves into the New World, more were imported during the eighteenth century, or the "mining cycle," though the "sugar cycle" of 1550–1650 is said to have produced more revenues (taxes) for the Portuguese Crown. Philip D. Curtin, *The Atlantic Slave Trade: A Census* (Madison, 1969), p. 268, table 77, assigns 1.89 million for the period 1701–1810, as opposed

to 610,000 from the discovery to 1700; Roberto C. Simonsen, *História econômica do Brasil (1500/1820)*, 4th ed. (São Paulo, 1962), p. 115 states that sugar produced more than 300 million pounds sterling, and the minerals less than 200 million.

9 On Guaratinguetá, see Lucilla Herrmann, "Evolução da estrutura social de Guaratinguetá num período de trezentos anos," *RA* 2 (March–June 1948), pp. 3–326; for the growth of the Fuminense cities in the Paraíba Valley, see Alberto Ribeiro Lamego, *O homem e a serra*, 2nd ed. (Rio, 1963); for the reversed role of Minas as a food supplier to Rio, see Alcir Lenharo, *As tropas da moderação (o abastecimento da corte na formação política do Brasil, 1808–1842)* (São Paulo, 1979).

10 A complete bibliography on coffee is too long and diverse to be presented here. The most comprehensive, but somewhat disorganized, work is Affonso de E. Taunay, *Historia do café no Brasil*, 15 vols. (Rio, 1939–43). There are two coffee-growing community studies: Stanley J. Stein, *Vassouras: A Brazilian Coffee County, 1850–1900* (Cambridge, 1957); and Warren Dean, *Rio Claro: A Brazilian Plantation System, 1820–1920* (Stanford, 1976). See also Odilon Nogueira de Matos, *Café e ferrovias: A evolução ferroviária de São Paulo e o desenvolvimento da cultura cafeeira* (São Paulo, 1974); and Emília Viotti da Costa, *Da senzala à colônia* (São Paulo, 1966). For export figures from Rio, see "A missão tutelar de Associação Comercial do Rio de Janeiro em defesa do café (notas historicas coligidas pelo secretario geral da Associação Comercial do Rio de Janeiro)," in Brasil, Departamento Nacional do Café, *O café no segundo centenário de sua introdução no Brasil*, 2 vols. (Rio, 1934), 1:281.

11 For the sugar economy during this period, see Omer Mont'Alegre, *Um século na história do açúcar. Brasil-Cuba 1760/1860*, separata de *Brasil Açucareiro* (June 1969) (Rio, 1969).

12 John Lynch, *The Spanish-American Revolutions, 1808–1826* (New York, 1973), Chap. 1; C. H. Haring, *Empire in Brazil: A New World Experiment with Monarchy* (Cambridge, Mass., 1958), pp. 4–5.

13 C. R. Boxer, *The Golden Age of Brazil, 1695–1750: Growing Pains of a Colonial Society* (Berkeley, 1962), pp. 323–24. Such a suggestion was first made in 1738, at the peak of the Brazilian gold boom.

14 Eneas Martins Filho, *O Conselho de Estado Português e a transformação da família real em 1807* (Rio, 1968), p. 46; Maria Odila Silva Dias, "The Establishment of the Royal Court in Brazil," in *From Colony to Nation: Essays on the Independence of Brazil*, ed. A. J. R. Russell-Wood (Baltimore, 1975), pp. 89–108; Alan K. Manchester, "The Transfer of the Portuguese Court to Rio de Janeiro," in *Conflict and Continuity in Brazilian Society*, ed. Henry H. Keith and S. Fred Edwards (Columbia, S.C., 1969), pp. 148–83.

15 Martins Filho, *O Conselho de Estado*, pp. 70–71.

16 Haring, *Empire*, p. 5.

17 Martins Filho, *O Conselho de Estado*, pp. 7–9.

18 Ibid., pp. 30–31 (*assento* of 2 September 1807), 9.

19 Ibid., p. 11.

20 Waldemar Mattos, *Panorama econômica da Bahia, 1808–1960* (Salvador, 1961), pp. 12–13.

21 Pinto de Aguiar, *Bancos no Brasil colonial* (Salvador, 1960), pp. 31–33.

22 Pinto de Aguiar, *A abertura dos portos do Brasil: Cairu e os inglêses* (Salvador, 1960), p. 98.

23 Maximiliano (Principe de Wied-Neuwied), *Viagem ao Brasil*, trans. Edgard Sussekind de Mendonça and Flavio Poppe de Figueiredo, 2nd ed. (São Paulo, 1958), p. 23; Omer Mont'Alegre, *Capital & capitalismo no Brasil* (Rio, 1972), pp. 31–33.

24 Mont'Alegre, *Capital*, pp. 33–34.

25 T. von Leithold and L. von Rango, *O Rio de Janeiro visto por dois prussianos em 1819*, trans. Joaquim de Sousa Leão Filho (São Paulo, 1966), p. 53.

26 Alberto Carlos de Araujo Guimarães, "Acção cultural e politica no governo de D. João VI," *Anais do Terceiro Congresso de Historia Nacional* 3 (October 1938), pp. 274–79.

27 Ibid., pp. 263–64, 279.

28 Agenor de Roure, "Politica economica de D. João VI," *ACIHA* 6 (1922), pp. 639–40; Mont'Alegre, *Capital*, p. 80.

29 Charles Lydon Chandler, "Commercial Relations between the United States and Brazil," *ACIHA* 1 (1922), pp. 401–11.

30 Technically, the Royal Treasury was part of the Ministry of the Kingdom, but it was formed as a separate unit in 1817. Max Fleiuss, *Historia administrativa do Brasil*, 2nd ed. (São Paulo, 1922), p. 72.

31 Miguel Arcanjo Galvão, *Relação dos cidadãos que tomaram parte no govêrno do Brasil no período de março de 1808 a 15 de novembro de 1889*, 2nd ed. (Rio, 1969), pp. 13–14.

2 The American Braganzas and Court Life

1 H. V. Livermore, *A New History of Portugal*, 2nd ed. (Cambridge, Eng., 1976), pp. 260–65.

2 Ibid., pp. 265–66.

3 Sergio Correa da Costa, *Every Inch a King: A Biography of Dom Pedro I, First Emperor of Brazil*, trans. Samuel Putnam (New York, 1950), pp. 105–06.

4 Canning to Stuart, London, 14 March 1825, General Correspondence (Brazil), PRO/FO 13/1.

5 A full text of the treaty is in E. Bradford Burns, ed., *A Documentary History of Brazil* (New York, 1966), pp. 219–22; Canning to Stuart, London, 2 December 1825, PRO/FO 13/2.

6 On João, see Gilberto Freyre, *The Mansions and Shanties (sobrados e mucambos): The Making of Modern Brazil*, trans. Harriet de Onis (New York, 1963), p. 4; on Pedro I, see Charles Ribeynolles, *Brasil pitoresco*, 2 vols. (3 in 2), 2nd ed. (São Paulo, 1976), 1:103; on Pedro II, see Affonso de E. Taunay, "Visita a Dom Pedro II (1886)," *MJC* 27:3 (September 1944), p. 574.

7 Costa, *Every Inch a King*, pp. 9–10.

8   Ibid., p. 53.

9   T. von Leithold and L. von Rango, *O Rio de Janeiro visto por dois prussianos em 1819*, trans. Joaquim de Sousa Leão Filho (São Paulo, 1966), pp. 12, 136.

10 Mary Wilhelmine Williams, *Dom Pedro the Magnanimous: Second Emperor of Brazil*, 2nd ed. (New York, 1966 [1937]), p. 5.

11 Costa, *Every Inch a King*, p. 21; Octavio Tarquínio de Sousa, *História dos fundadores do império*, 10 vols., 3rd ed. (Rio, 1957–58), 2: *A vida de D. Pedro I*, 71.

12 Costa, *Every Inch a King*, p. 26.

13 Ibid., p. 52.

14 Freyre, *The Mansions*, p. 4.

15 Cybelle de Ipanema, org., *D. Pedro I, proclamações, cartas e artigos de imprensa* (Rio, 1972), pp. 14–15.

16 Alberto Rangel, *Dom Pedro I e à Marquesa de Santos a vista de cartas íntimas e de outros documentos públicos e particulares*, 3rd ed. (São Paulo, 1969), pp. 20–24.

17 Ipanema, *D. Pedro I*, p. 11.

18 Sousa, *História dos fundadores*, 2:91–94.

19 "Familias reaes: familia imperial brasileira (reinante no Brasil, de 1822 a 1889)," *AGB* 1 (1939), pp. 5–140.

20 Rangel, *Dom Pedro I*, p. 63.

21 Ibid., p. 64; Costa, *Every Inch a King*, pp. 67–68.

22 Rangel, *Dom Pedro I*, pp. 82–85.

23 Ibid., p. 80.

24 "Familias reaes," pp. 5–7.

25 Alberto Rangel, *Marginados: anotações às cartas de D. Pedro I a D. Domitila* (Rio, 1974).

26 Williams, *Dom Pedro*, p. 14; *Veja* (31 October 1979), p. 67; Rangel, *Dom Pedro I*, p. 147.

27 Rangel, *Marginados*, p. 213; the letter was dated 12 October 1827.

28 Ibid., p. 403; the letter was dated 21 June 1829.

29 Rangel, *Dom Pedro I*, pp. 124–25.

30 Ibid., pp. 288–91; "Familias reaes," pp. 5–7.

31 Decreto—Canto e Melo, Domitila de Castro, Livro de Registro de Decretos do Ministério do Império, Códice 15, SPE/ANRJ.

32 Rangel, *Dom Pedro I*, p. 288; Emília Viotti da Costa, "José Bonifácio: homem e mito," in *1822: dimensões*, org. Carlos G. Mota (São Paulo, 1972), pp. 102–59.

33 Rangel, *Dom Pedro I*, pp. 291–92.

34 Ibid., pp. 276–79.

35 Pedro Calmon, *História de D. Pedro II*, 5 vols. (Rio, 1975), 1: *infância e mocidade 1825–1853*, pp. 195–99.

36 Ibid., pp. 200–01.

37 Ibid., pp. 203–04, 214, the remark is from p. 239; Williams, *Dom Pedro*, p. 86.

38 "Familias reaes," pp. 7–8.

39 Calmon, *História de D. Pedro II*, 1:204–05 (footnote 9).

40   Ibid., pp. 245–55; Taunay, "Visita," p. 572.
41   Calmon, *História de D. Pedro II*, 1:216–19, 226–27 (footnote 40); Williams, *Dom Pedro*, p. 89.
42   Williams, pp. 91–97.
43   Ibid., p. 207.
44   Ibid., pp. 259–60

3   Noblemen of the Southern Cross

1   James Lockhart, *Spanish Peru, 1532–1560: A Colonial Society* (Madison, 1968), p. 47.
2   Doris M. Ladd, *The Mexican Nobility at Independence, 1780–1826* (Austin, 1976), pp. 8–17, esp. 13.
3   Alberto Ribeiro Lamego, *O homem e o brejo* (Rio, 1945), pp. 60–75, and *A terra goyataca*, 4 vols. (Rio, 1941), 4:269–93. For Duarte Coelho, see Francis A. Dutra, "Centralization vs. Donatarial Privilege: Pernambuco, 1602–1630," in *Colonial Roots of Modern Brazil*, ed. Dauril Alden (Berkeley, 1973), pp. 19–60. Duarte de Albuquerque Coelho, a grandson, was born in Lisbon (1591) and died in Brazil as the Marquês de Basto. Another grandson of the donatário-founder, Matias de Albuquerque Coelho, was born in Olinda (1593), became the Conde de Alegrete, and died in Lisbon. For details on the viscondessa, see Viscondessa de Cavalcante, "Pequeno Diccionario Biografico Brasilciro" (ms), n.d., n.p., ff. 59–62, I–12, 2, 29, SM/BNRJ. For Azurara, see Francisco Augusto Pereira da Costa, *Diccionario biographico de pernambucanos celebres* (Recife, 1882), pp. 443–45. For colonial Mexico, see David A. Brading, *Miners and Merchants in Bourbon Mexico, 1763–1810* (Cambridge, Eng., 1971); and Ladd, *The Mexican Nobility*, pp. 50–58.
4   For France, see Robert Forster, *The Nobility of Toulouse in the Eighteenth Century: A Social and Economic Study* (Baltimore, 1960). For Portugal, see Luiz da Silva Pereira Oliveira, *Privilegios da nobreza, e fidalguia de Portugal* (Lisboa, 1806).
5   Stuart B. Schwartz, *Sovereignty and Society in Colonial Brazil: The High Court of Bahia and Its Judges, 1609–1751* (Berkelcy, 1973), pp. 13–21.
6   Pedro Calmon, *Historia da Casa da Torre* (Rio, 1939), pp. 106–07.
7   João Antônio Andreoni (pseud. André João Antonil), *Cultura e opulência do Brasil*, intro. by Alice Piffer Canabrava (São Paulo, 1967), pp. 41, 139.
8   Auguste Saint Hilaire, *A segunda viagem a São Paulo e outro histórico da Província de São Paulo* (São Paulo, 1954), p. 16; Sebastião da Rocha Pita, *História da América Portuguesa*, 3rd ed. (Bahia, 1950); Luís dos Santos Vilhena, *A Bahia no século XVIII*, 3 vols. (Bahia, 1969); José Antônio Caldas, *Noticia geral de toda esta capitania da Bahia desde o seu descobrimento ao prezt* anno de 1750, facsimile ed. (Bahia, 1951).
9   Registro Geral das Mercês e Títulos: Cargos Honoríficos: Índice 1808–1889, Códice 116, SPE/ANRJ.

10 Ibid. The third title was awarded to Antônio Ramires Esquivel, the Barão de Arruda.

11 Conde de Baependy, *Apontamentos biographicos da familia Braz Carneiro Leão do Rio de Janeiro*, separata da *Biographias de brasileiros ilustres por armas, letras, virtudes, etc.* (n.d., n.p.), pp. 365–84; J. F. de Almeida Prado, *D. João VI e o início da classe dirigente do Brasil 1815–1889 (depoimento de um pintor austríaco no Rio de Janeiro)* (São Paulo, 1968), pp. 135–36, 152–53. Two of Fernando's nieces were married, one to Belens and the other to Faria, both merchants. Alberto Ribeiro Lamego, *O homem e a serra*, 2nd ed. (Rio, 1963), p. 336.

12 Baependy, *Apontamentos*, pp. 365–84; Prado, *D. João VI*, pp. 154–61.

13 Prado, *D. João VI*, pp. 118–19, 150–51; Maria Odila Silva Dias, "A interiorização da metrópole (1808–1853)," in *1822: dimensões*, ed. Carlos G. Mota (São Paulo, 1972), pp. 171–72.

14 Lawrence Stone, *The Crisis of the Aristocracy, 1558–1641*, abridged ed. (New York, 1967), pp. 135–38, 161–69; David Spring, ed., *European Landed Elites in the Nineteenth Century* (Baltimore, 1977), Introduction.

15 E. J. Hobsbawm, *Industry and Empire from 1750 to the Present Day* (Harmondsworth, Eng., 1974 [1968]), pp. 28–31, 80–82.

16 Barrington Moore, Jr., *Social Origins of Dictatorship and Democracy: Lord and Peasant in the Making of the Modern World* (Boston, 1966), pp. 15–38; F. M. L. Thompson, "Britain," in *European Landed Elites*, pp. 25–26. J. H. Hexter, *Reappraisal in History: New Views on History and Society in Early Modern Europe* (New York, 1963 [1961]), Chap. 6, "Storm over the Gentry," esp. 140–49, reviews the historiographical debates.

17 See Jerome Blum, "Russia," in *The European Nobility in the Eighteenth Century: Studies of the Nobilities of the Major European States in the Pre-Reform Era*, ed. Albert Goodwin (New York, 1967), pp. 92–93, for the distinction between a society of order and a society of class. This concept was further refined in his most recent book, *The End of the Old Order in Rural Europe* (Princeton, 1978), pp. 3–8.

18 An excellent statistical study on the structure of the nobility is Laura Jarnagin, "The Role and Structure of the Brazilian Imperial Nobility in Society and Politics," *AMP* 29 (1979), pp. 99–157. Carlos G. Rheingantz, *Titulares do império* (Rio, 1960), provides a roster of the nobility. An informative, short piece on the subject is Roderick J. Barman, "Uma nobreza no novo mundo: a função dos títulos do Brasil imperial," trans. Stanley E. Hilton, *MAN* 4 (June 1973), pp. 4–21; this work later appeared in English: "A New-World Nobility: The Role of Titles in Imperial Brazil," in *University of British Columbia Hispanic Studies*, ed. Harold Livermore (London, 1974), pp. 39–50.

19 Nobreza e Condecorações no Brasil: Notas pelo Conselheiro Alencar Araripe, Lata 316/Doc. 18, AAA. For the various imperial orders and commendations extant in the late 1880s, see Arthur Sauer, org., *Almanak administrativo, mercantil e industrial do Imperio do Brazil para 1886* (Rio, 1886), pp. 84–90.

20 Mercês, Nomeações e Promoções: Relação de Oficiais da Casa Imperial, Grandes

do Império, Titulares, Mercês, Nomeações e Promoções 1822–1874, Códice 502, SPE/ANRJ.

21 Requerimentos de Licença para Pessoas Nobres Se Casarem 1823–1887, Códice 577, SPE/ANRJ; Rui Vieira da Cunha, *Estudos da nobreza brasileira*, 2 vols. (Rio, 1966–69), 2:115–22.

22 Rheingantz, *Titulares do império*, p. 99. He gives a total of 1,211 titles shared by 986 persons. The discrepancy is accounted for by the definition that is used in determining the size of the nobiliary corporation and therefore the counting method. However, because the records of the Imperial Chancellery survive only in fragments, no one will ever know *exactly* how many titles were legitimate and legal, let alone the total number of imperial decrees issued.

Part of the confusion lay in bureaucratic carelessness in announcing the award of titles. An imperial decree came in several forms. On slightly larger than legal-sized paper, it usually contained a minimum of information: name of the honored, title created, status as current noble or not, reasons for being ennobled (not always given), date of award, and signature of the emperor counterendorsed by a minister of the empire. But the decrees never followed a uniform format. Some listed only one title, others several. On occasion, decrees of creation were issued separate from a list of the ennobled. Consequently, the counting of decrees according to the number of folios does not give the precise total. Furthermore, the real total should equal those titles formally registered, and this figure is not available. Although no one will ever know the exact number, for the purpose of drawing broad social implications about the nobility as an upper class and as an elite representing both urban and rural groups as well as aristocracy and gentry, the following figure will suffice: about 1,200 titles held by about 1,000 people between 1822 and 1889.

23 *Memoria sobre a nobreza no Brasil, por hum brasileiro* (Rio, 1841), pp. 12–19; José Jansen, "Introdução ao nobiliário maranhense," *AMHN* 21 (1969), pp. 165–69, esp. 166; Paulo Braga de Menezes, *As constituições outorgadas ao Império do Brasil e ao Reino de Portugal* (Rio, 1964), pp. 36–38. For Portugal's nobility, see Albano da Silveira Pinto, *Resenha das familias titulares e grandes de Portugal*, 2 vols. (Lisboa, 1885).

24 Conselheiro Francisco Gomes da Silva (O Chalaça), *Memórias*, 2nd ed. (Rio, 1959); Cunha, *Estudos da nobreza*, 2:96–99.

25 Cunha, 2:99–106.

26 Affonso de E. Taunay, "O nobiliario do primeiro imperio," *MJC* 1:3 (March 1938), pp. 1–5.

27 Ibid., pp. 2–3.

28 Decreto—Albuquerque, Antônio Joaquim de Carvalho e, Códice 15, SPE/ANRJ.

29 Decretos, Códice 15; Rheingantz, *Titulares do império*, p. 41 (Rio Seco), p. 63 (São João Marcos), p. 86 (Itanhaém).

30 Rheingantz, p. 41.

31 Rheingantz, passim.

32 R. de Magalhães Junior, *O império em chinelos* (Rio, 1957), pp. 2–3.

33 See the appropriate decretos of the ennobled in Códice 15, SPE/ANRJ.

34 Cunha, *Estudos da nobreza*, 1:30.

35 Decretos, Códice 15, SPE/ANRJ.

36 Taunay, "O nobiliario do primeiro imperio," p. 1. The registry of the chancellery only shows Goiás. For details on the titles granted to the imperial siblings, see note 42 just below.

37 Decretos, Códice 15, SPE/ANRJ.

38 These figures are compiled from Brasil, Arquivo Nacional, *Organizações e programas ministeriais: regime parlamentar no império*, 2nd ed. (Rio, 1962).

39 Jarnagin, "The Role and Structure of the Brazilian Imperial Nobility," pp. 99–157.

40 Monte Alegre to Feijó, São Paulo, 4, 5 July 1842, D-502/I-2-11, SDH/AMP/USP; Octavio Tarquínio de Sousa, *História dos fundadores do império*, 10 vols., 3rd ed. (Rio, 1957), 7:11–12, 342–49.

41 Magalhães, *O império em chinelos*, pp. 4–5.

42 Jarnagin, "The Role and Structure of the Brazilian Imperial Nobility," pp. 99–157.

43 Joaquim Nabuco, *Um estadista do império*, Volume único (Rio, 1975), p. 968, for Nabuco de Araújo; Carolina Nabuco, *A vida de Joaquim Nabuco*, 3rd ed. (Rio, 1943), p. 230, for Joaquim Nabuco; for Dantas and Saraiva: Egas Moniz to Cotegipe, Bahia, May 19, 1879, Lata 4/Pasta 145, ABC; Aureliano Leal, *Historia constitucional do Brasil* (Rio, 1915), p. 197; Alvaro Paulino Soares de Souza, *Três brasileiros ilustres* (Rio, 1923), p. 109; Barão Homem de Mello, "Conselheiro Paulino José Soares de Souza," *RIHGB* 66 (1905), pp. 71–79; Rui Vieira da Cunha, *Figuras e fatos da nobreza brasileira* (Rio, 1975), pp. 16–18, 151–53.

44 Anyda Marchant, *Visconde Mauá and the Empire of Brazil* (Berkeley, 1965). This work includes a good bibliography on the Brazilian businessman.

45 The Barão do Rio Branco was foreign minister under the administrations of Rodrigues Alves, Afonso Pena, Nilo Peçanha, and Hermes da Fonseca.

46 Taunay, "O nobiliario do primeiro imperio," p. 5.

47 Roberval Francisco Bezerra de Menezes, Médicos—Titulares do Império do Brasil, ms, Códice 1139, SAP/ANRJ. For a biography of Motta Maia, the last physician of Pedro II, see Manoel Augusto Velho da Motta Maia, *O conde de Motta Maia, medico e amigo dedicado de d. Pedro Segundo* (Rio, 1937).

48 Decreto—Bueno, José Antônio Pimenta, Códice 15, SPE/ANRJ. A short biography of the statesman is in *A Republica* (Rio), 21 February 1878.

4   Aristocratic Clans of Brazil

1 A. J. R. Russell-Wood, *Fidalgos and Philanthropists: The Santa Casa da Misericórdia of Bahia, 1550–1755* (Berkeley, 1968), p. 62. For this distinguished clan, see Pedro Calmon, *Historia da Casa da Torre* (Rio, 1939).

2 Affonso Costa, "Genealogia baiana," *RIHGB* 191 (April–June 1963), pp. 3–279; for the Monizes, pp. 31–43; for the Araújos, pp. 49–50.

3 Ibid., for the Calmons, pp. 152–55; for the Góises, pp. 119–23; for the Albuquer-

ques, pp. 13–16; for the Bulcãos, pp. 200–06; Antônio de Araújo de Aragão Bulcão Sobrinho, *Famílias bahianas: Bulcão*, 3 vols. (Salvador, 1961).

4 Stuart B. Schwartz, *Sovereignty and Society in Colonial Brazil: The High Court of Bahia and Its Judges, 1609-1751* (Berkeley, 1973), p. 112; João Antônio Andreoni (pseud. André João Antonil), *Cultura e opulência do Brasil*, intro. by Alice Piffer Canabrava (São Paulo, 1967), p. 228; Luís dos Santos Vilhena, *A Bahia no século XVIII*, 3 vols. (Bahia, 1969), 1:174; J. B. von Spix and C. F. P. von Martius, *Através da Bahia*, excerptos da obra *Reise in Brasilien*, trans. Manuel A. Pirajá da Silva and Paulo Wolf (Bahia, 1916), p. 80; José Antônio Caldas, *Noticia geral de toda esta capitania da Bahia desde o seu descobrimento ao prezt^e anno de 1750*, facsimile ed. (Bahia, 1951), p. 438.

5 Caldas, *Noticia geral*, pp. 429–39.

6 Ibid., pp. 445–48.

7 Ibid., pp. 522–33; Brant's father-in-law, Antônio Cardoso dos Santos, is listed in ibid., p. 526; J. F. de Almeida Prado, *D. João VI e o inicio da classe dirigente do Brasil 1815–1889 (depoimento de um pintor austríaco no Rio de Janeiro)* (São Paulo, 1968), pp. 135–36, 152–53.

8 Matrícula dos engenhos da Capitania da Bahia pelos dízimos reais administrados pela Junta Real Fazenda, 1800–1874, SH/AEB.

9 C. R. Boxer, *The Golden Age of Brazil, 1695–1750: Growing Pains of a Colonial Society* (Berkeley, 1962), p. 154; Pierre Verger, *Flux et reflux de la traite des nègres entre le Golfe de Benin et Bahia de Todos os Santos du dix-septième au dix-neuvième siècle* (Paris, 1968), p. 653, which lists a number of ships that were engaged in the slave trade between Africa and Bahia from 1678 to 1704; Caldas, *Noticia geral*, pp. 522–33. Several names appeared more than once under different categories, such as capitalists, export-import merchants, and so forth.

10 Caldas, *Noticia geral*, p. 525.

11 Ibid., p. 534 (José Carneiro de Campos).

12 These figures are compiled from Carlos G. Rheingantz, *Titulares do império* (Rio, 1960), which provides a calendar of the nobility. It suffers from an inaccurate cross-listing of titles by surnames and provinces of births.

13 Rui Vieira da Cunha, *Figuras e fatos da nobreza brasileira* (Rio, 1975), pp. 70–71; Gilberto Freyre, *The Masters and Slaves (Casa Grande e Senzala): A Study in the Development of Brazilian Civilization*, trans. Samuel Putnam, 2nd ed. (New York, 1966), p. 270, footnote 196, p. 439.

14 Antonio José Victoriano Borges da Fonseca, *Nobiliarquia pernambucana*, 2 vols. (Rio, 1935); Affonso de E. Taunay, "O archivo nobiliarchico brasileiro," *MJC* 1:2 (February 1938), pp. 175–79.

15 Freyre, *The Masters and Slaves*, pp. 267–69.

16 Carlos Xavier Paes Barreto, *Os primitivos colonizadores nordestinos e seus descendentes* (Rio, 1960), p. 136.

17 Freyre, *The Masters and Slaves*, pp. 267–68.

18 Ulysses Lins de Albuquerque, *Um sertanejo e o sertão: memórias* (Rio, 1957), pp.

42–44; Costa, "Genealogia baiana," pp. 152–55; Frederico de Barros Brotero, *A família Monteiro de Barros* (São Paulo, 1951), p. 19.

19 Freyre, *The Masters and Slaves*, pp. 268–69, footnote 191.

20 Strictly speaking, it was the Barão de Goiana (José Correia Pianço), a physician in the imperial service, who was the first Pernambucan to be ennobled in 1821, a year before Brazil's independence. Recife was, of course, the first Pernambucan to become a noble from the agrarian elite. Rheingantz, *Titulares do império*, p. 75.

21 Freyre, *The Masters and Slaves*, p. 270.

22 Peter L. Eisenberg, *The Sugar Industry in Pernambuco, 1840–1910: Modernization without Change* (Berkeley, 1974), pp. 130–33; Manuel Diegues Junior, *O banguê nas Alagoas: traços da influência do sistema econômico do engenho de açúcar na vida e na cultura regional* (Rio, 1949), pp. 164–65.

23 Barreto, *Os primitivos colonizadores*, pp. 238–41; Diegues Junior, *O banguê*, p. 168.

24 Augusto Victorino Alves Sacramento Blake, *Diccionario bibliographico brazileiro*, 7 vols. (Rio, 1883–1902), 1:172–73; 1° Barão Smith de Vasconcellos (Rodolpho Smith de Vasconcellos) and 2° Barao Smith de Vasconcellos (Jayme Luiz Smith de Vasconcellos), *Archivo nobiliarchico brasileiro* (Lausanne, Switzerland, 1918), pp. 31–32; Pasta—Albuquerque, Antônio Francisco de Paula e Holanda Cavalcanti de, Documentos Biográficos, C962,2, SM/BNRJ. The Barão de Albuquerque was a son of the visconde of the same name, was born in Rio, and served as a local political boss in his place of birth, not in Pernambuco.

25 Vasconcellos and Vasconcellos, *Archivo nobiliarchico*, pp. 98–99; Pasta—Albuquerque, Pedro Francisco de Paula Cavalcanti de, Documentos Biográficos, C1039,45 and C810,30, SM/BNRJ.

26 Vasconcellos and Vasconcellos, *Archivo nobiliarchico*, pp. 490–91; Pasta—Albuquerque, Francisco de Paula Cavalcanti de, Documentos Biográficos, C1007,78, SM/BNRJ.

27 Vasconcellos and Vasconcellos, *Archivo nobiliarchico*, pp. 242, 303–04; Pasta—Cavalcanti, Manuel Francisco de Paula, Documentos Biográficos, C1038,76, C987,17, SM/BNRJ.

28 The fifteen titles are: Albuquerque (V), Suassuna (V), Camaragibe (V), Muribeca (B), Atalaia (B), Buique (B), Gindaí (B), Merepi (B), Pirapama (B), Tracunhaém (B), Timbauba (V), Cavalcanti (V), Guararapes (V). The Conde de Boa Vista and the Barão de Ipojuca (João do Rego Barros) were grandsons of Coronel Suassuna. Boa Vista, as noted above, was Muribeca's father-in-law.

29 José Antônio Soares de Souza, "O Barão de Vila Bela e a história de uma família," *RIHGB* 294 (1972), pp. 179–89, esp. 181–82. The plural form for "leão" is "leões," but for the surnames, I decided to deviate from this grammatical rule by preserving the original form and add "s," thus Sousa Leãos, not Sousa Leões.

30 Vasconcellos and Vasconcellos, *Archivo nobiliarchico*, pp. 93–94 (Caiará), p. 103 (Campo Alegre), p. 175 (Gurjaú), pp. 226–27, (Jaboatão), pp. 298–99 (Moreno), p. 487 (Sousa Leão), p. 493 (Tabatinga), pp. 537–38 (Vila Bela); Barreto, *Os primitivos colonizadores*, p. 138.

31   Eisenberg, *The Sugar Industry*, pp. 130–32.

32   Some of the scholars who contend that the agrarian elite monopolized Brazilian politics are: C. H. Haring, *Empire in Brazil: A New World Experiment with Monarchy* (Cambridge, Mass., 1958), Chap. 4 (pp. 63–84, esp. 66–70); Luis da Camara Cascudo, *O Marquez de Olinda e seu tempo (1793–1870)* (São Paulo, 1938), pp. 142, 320–22; Craveiro Costa, *O Visconde de Sinimbu: Sua vida e sua atuação na politica nacional (1840–1889)* (São Paulo, 1937); and E. Bradford Burns, *A History of Brazil*, 2nd ed. (New York, 1980), Chap. 4, esp. 212–27.

33   José Wanderley de Araujo Pinho, *Cotegipe e seu tempo: Primeira phase 1815–1867* (São Paulo, 1937), is the first half of the biography by a grandson; the second volume was never published.

34   Biographies of some of these mandarins are available: José Antônio Soares de Souza, *A vida do Visconde do Uruguay (1807–1866) (Paulino José Soares de Souza)* (São Paulo, 1944), written by a grandson of the namesake; José Wanderley de Araujo Pinho, *Politica e politicos no imperio: Contribuições documentaes* (Rio, 1930), pp. 5–54; Álvaro Valle, org., *José Antônio Saraiva (Conselheiro Saraiva): Discursos parlamentares* (Brasília, 1978), pp. xiii–xxx; Alberto Venâncio Filho, org., *Zacarias de Góis e Vasconcelos: Discursos parlamentares* (Brasília, 1979), pp. 15–36.

35   Cascudo, *O Marquez de Olinda*, pp. 33–34. The family was related to the Cavalcantis on both sides of Olinda's parents. In Serinhaém, the Araújo Limas were a political elite, but not the richest clan. Cascudo (p. 247) makes an explicit point on the social and economic origin of Olinda: "Olinda nunca poude ser chefe supremo pela razão do nascimento. Diziam-no 'chefe politico do norte.' " Antônio da Rocha Almeida, *Vultos da pátria*, 4 vols. (Rio, 1965), 3:199–205; Augusto Tavares de Lyra, "Os ministros de estado da independência à república," *RIHGB* 193 (October–December 1946), pp. 88–89.

36   Dieguos Junior, *O banguê, p.* 166.

37   Affonso de Carvalho, *Caxias* (Rio, 1976), is a solid biography that stresses the military career of the general. See also Alberto Ribeiro Lamego, "O tronco de Caxias," *MJC* 4:1 (October 1938), pp. 133–36; Francisco Klors Werneck, *Historia e genealogia fluminense* (Rio, 1947), chap. on Caxias; Vasconcellos and Vasconcellos, *Archivo nobiliarchico*, pp. 126–27; and Pasta—Silva, Luís Alves de Lima e, Decretos de Titulares, SPE/ANRJ.

38   Gileno Dé Carli, *A evolução do problema canavieiro fluminense* (Rio, 1942), pp. 6–8.

39   Ibid., p. 10.

40   Livro de Registro de Terras, No. 24—Freguesia de Santo Antônio dos Guarulhos, Campos, 1854–1857, SPH/AERJ.

41   Ibid., Entries 808 (Castro/Coutinho), 812 (on three sesmarias), 814 (S. Manuel).

42   Ibid., Entries 812, 823; M. Vianna de Castro, *A aristocracia rural fluminense* (Rio, 1961), p. 13; Affonso de E. Taunay, *Historia do café no Brasil*, 15 vols. (Rio, 1939–

43), 8:252, which states erroneously that the Barão de Carapebus was a son of the Viscondessa de Muriaé.

43   Taunay, *Historia do café*, 8:252.

44   Ibid.

45   Ibid., Entries 821, 1038, 1040.

46   Livro de Registro de Terras, No. 24, Entries 1218, 1219, 1220, 1221; Livro, No. 25—Freguesia de São Sebastião, 1854–1857, Entries 801, 802; Livro, No. 50—Freguesia de São Gonçalo, 1854–1856, Entries 121, 221, 280, 352 (heirs), 278, 283 (heirs), 408 (heirs), 434, 436, 437 (heirs), 438 (heirs), 574 (with another person), 575, 588 (heirs), 592, 623, 633, 634, 656, 673, SPH/AERJ.

47   Alberto Ribeiro Lamego, *O homem e o brejo* (Rio, 1945), pp. 60–75, gives much information on the Visconde de Asseca and his heirs. In two freguesias (São Sebastião and São Gonçalo), the Assecas held twenty-five holdings, of which four (Entries 801, 802, 803, and 804) were listed as "sold." For details, see Livros Nos. 25 and 50, SPH/AERJ.

48   José Carneiro da Silva, *Memoria topographica e historica sobre os Campos dos Goitacazes, com huma noticia breve de suas producções, e commercio offerecida ao muito alto e muito poderoso Rey e Senhor Nosso D. João VI* (Rio, 1819), is a credible little book on economic conditions in the Campos region.

49   Livro de Registro de Terras, No. 32—Freguesia de São João de Macaé, 1854–1856, Entry 7, SPH/AERJ.

50   Maria Isaura Pereira de Queiroz, *O mandonismo local na vida política brasileira e outros ensaios* (São Paulo, 1976), pp. 43–47; Livro, No. 81–Freguesia de N.S. de Desterro de Quissamã, 1857, ff. 2-6v (no entry numbers), SPH/AERJ.

51   Taunay, *Historia do café*, 5:239–40.

52   Manuel Martins do Couto Reyes, "Memoria de Santa Cruz: Seu estabelecimento e economia primitiva, seus sucessos mais notaveis, continuados do tempo da extinção dos denominados Jesuitas, seus fundadores, até o anno de 1804," *RIHGB* 5 (1843), pp. 143–86. According to one document, Fazenda Santa Cruz was 4,923 palms by 4,512.6 palms: Manoel Jacintho Nogueira da Gama to Pedro I, Ofício apresentando parecer sobre a Fazenda de Sta Cruz e Engenho de Taguaí, Maço 50/ Doc. 2317, AMI. For technical and historical reports on Santa Cruz, see José da Saldanha da Gama, "Historia da Imperial Fazenda de Santa Cruz," *RIHGB* 38 (1875), pp. 165–230; and Marfa Barbosa Vianna, "Antiga Fazenda Real de Santa Cruz—um pouco de história e lendas," *AMHN* 15 (1965), pp. 267–75.

53   Vianna, "Antiga," pp. 267–75; Taunay, *Historia do café*, 5:257–59.

54   Alberto Rangel, *Marginados: anotações às cartas de D. Pedro I a D. Domitila* (Rio, 1974), pp. 46–47.

55   Taunay, *Historia do café*, 5:164.

56   Ibid., pp. 257–59.

5   Gentry Planter and Merchant Families

1   Afranio Peixoto, "Vassouras," in *O café no segundo centenário de sua introdução no Brasil*, 2 vols. (Rio, 1934), 1:51.

2   A. C. D'Araujo Guimarães, *A corte no Brasil* (Porto Alegre, 1936), pp. 224–26.

3   Affonso de E. Taunay, "Vergueiro e Ibicaba," *MJC* 3:3 (September 1938), pp. 647–651.

4   Taunay, "Cafesaes cariocas," *MJC* 3:2 (August 1938), pp. 405–09.

5   Alberto Ribeiro Lamego, *O homem e a serra*, 2nd ed. (Rio, 1963), p. 334; Afranio Peixoto, "Vassouras," in *O café no segundo centenário*, 1:51–57, esp. 55.

6   Lamego, *O homem e a serra*, p. 335. For the political career of Valença, see Miguel Arcanjo Galvão, *Relação dos cidadãos que tomaram parte no govêrno do Brasil no período de março de 1808 a 15 de novembro de 1889*, 2nd ed. (Rio, 1969), p. 20. For Geraldo, see Affonso de E. Taunay, "Landlords cafeeiros da terra roxa e do oeste paulista na era imperial," *MJC* 23:1 (July 1943), p. 8; and José Maria Lisboa, org., *Almanak de Campinas para 1873* (Campinas, SP, 1872). For Resende, see Jorge Seckler, org., *Almanach da Provincia de São Paulo administrativo, commercial e industrial para 1888* (São Paulo, 1888), p. 547. For Lorena, see Inventário da Baroncsa de Lorena (Barao de Lorena, widower/inventariante)—1864, Cx 2641/No. 634, SPJ/ANRJ.

7   Lamego, *O homem e a serra*, p. 335; 1º Barão Smith de Vasconcellos (Rodolpho Smith de Vasconcellos) and 2º Barão Smith de Vasconcellos (Jayme Luiz Smith de Vasconcellos), *Archivo nobiliarchico brasileiro* (Lausanne, Switzerland, 1918), p. 244 (Juiz de Fora), p. 382 (Retiro), p. 399 (Rio Novo). For this clan, see also *O Pharol* (Juiz de Fora, Minas), 28 June 1883. For sister Leonarda, see "Titulares usados no Brasil e concedidos no extrangeiro," *AGB* 1 (1939), p. 209.

8   Stanley J. Stein, *Vassouras: A Brazilian Coffee County, 1850–1900* (Cambridge, Mass., 1957), p. 16, and in Portuguese, *Grandeza e decadência do café no vale do Paraíba* (São Paulo, 1961); Peixoto, "Vassouras," p. 54.

9   Lamego, *O homem e a serra*, pp. 340–41; Affonso de E. Taunay, *Historia do café no Brasil*, 15 vols. (Rio, 1939–43), 2:250–51, 4:389; Vasconcellos and Vasconcellos, *Archivo nobiliarchico*, p. 67; Taunay, "Barões do café," *MJC* 1:3 (March 1938), pp. 189–93.

10 Taunay, "Uma irmandade de grandes cafesistas e civilizadores: Os Teixeira Leite. Nascimento, vida e morte de Vassouras," in *O café no segundo centenário*, 2:484–89; *Historia do café*, 4:399–406, 5:201–04. Taunay contradicts himself for the total number of the Teixeira Leite siblings: in *Historia* (4:399) he gives six and in "Uma irmandade" (p. 485) seven. See also Lamego, *O homem e a serra*, pp. 340–42; and Vasconcellos and Vasconcellos, *Archivo nobiliarchico*, p. 532.

11 Lamego, *O homem e a serra*, pp. 345–46; Taunay, *Historia do café*, 5:215, 7:293 (for the adage); "Barões do café," *MJC* 1:3 (March 1938), p. 192; Peixoto, "Vassouras," p. 53; Honorio Silvestre, "A colonização mineira nos grandes latifundios de café do Estado do Rio de Janeiro," in *O café no segundo centenário*, 2:605–17, esp. 615.

12 Lamego, *O homem e a serra*, pp. 346–57; Peixoto, "Vassouras," pp. 51–52; Taunay, "Barões do café," p. 192.

13 Lamego, pp. 359–60.

14 Taunay, *Historia do café*, 5:162.

15 Ibid., 7:41–42. The Conde de Avelar was Francisco's chief partner.

16 Taunay, *Historia do café*, 5:162–64; Vasconcellos and Vasconcellos, *Archivo nobiliarchico*, pp. 419–21, for the four titles; Lamego, *O homem e a serra*, pp. 359–360; Agripino Grieco, "Paraíba do Sul, do fastígio agrícola a estagnação dos burocratas," in *O café no segundo centenário*, 1:123, for the remark on "amazona bárbara"; Pasta—Barbosa, Bernardina Alves, Graças Honoríficas: Requerimentos e Propostas—Documentos Biográficos, SPE/ANRJ.

17 HGCB 4:87–89; Eduardo von Laemmert, ed., *Almanak administrativo, mercantil e industrial da corte e provincia do Rio de Janeiro 1875* (Rio, 1875).

18 Taunay, *Historia do café*, 7:38.

19 Lamego, *O homem e a serra*, pp. 301–07, 332.

20 Ibid., p. 317.

21 Ibid., p. 331.

22 Livro de Registro de Terras, No. 40—Santa Ana, Piraí, 1854–1856, SPH/AERJ.

23 Taunay, *Historia do café*, 8:261–65.

24 Her name did not appear on the official family roster, according to Taunay.

25 Livro de Registro de Terras, No. 66—São João Batista do Arrozal, Piraí, 1854–1856, SPH/AERJ.

26 Ibid., f. 36, 42, 44.

27 Ibid., f. 45, 58, 59, 60.

28 Taunay, *Historia do café*, 8:261–62, 266–78.

29 Lamego, *O homem e a serra*, pp. 313–14.

30 Ibid., p. 314; Guimarães, *A corte*, p. 228; José Wanderley de Araújo Pinho, *Salões e damas do segundo reinado*, 4th ed. (São Paulo, 1970), pp. 234–35.

31 Lamego, *O homem e a serra*, pp. 314–16.

32 Taunay, *Historia do café*, 7:170–71.

33 Ibid., 8:208 (Clemente de Pinto) and 8:259–78 (Souza Breves); Livro de Registro de Terras, No. 14—Freguesia de S. S. Sacramento, Cantagalo, 1856 (Entry 183); Livro de Registro de Terras, No. 17—Freguesia de Santa Rita do Rio Negro, Cantagalo, 1855–1858 (Entry 54), SPH/AERJ/Niterói.

34 Livro de Registro de Terras, No. 89, Sacramento, 1854–1856, SPH/AERJ.

35 Entries 166, 227, 228, 229 in Livro de Registro de Terras, No. 14, SPH/AERJ.

36 Ibid., Entries 19 (Vial Quartim), 100 (Ricardo Leão), 53 and 98 (Antônio Tomás); Taunay, *Historia do café*, 7:360.

37 Taunay, *Historia do café*, 8:84, 196.

38 Rui Vieira da Cunha, *Figuras e fatos da nobreza brasileira* (Rio, 1975), p. 123; Lamego, *O homem e a serra*, pp. 366–67.

39 Lamego, pp. 366–67.

40 Taunay, *Historia do café*, 7:84; Lamego, *O homem e a serra*, pp. 371–73.

41 Augusto Emílio Zaluar, *Peregrinação pela Província de São Paulo (1860–1861)* (São Paulo, 1975), pp. 41–122, deals with the major towns in the valley.

42 Orçamento das camaras municipaes da provincia de São Paulo, Coleção João Batista C. Aguirra, SDH/AMP/USP.

43 *Informações sobre o estado da industria de mineração, da agricola e da fabril nos*

municipios da Provincia de S. Paulo, mencionando os principaes estabelecimentos, e a importancia aproximada de seus productos nos ultimos três annos, comparando-se com os que foram dados no cadastro de 1854; as causas do atrazo ou progresso destes estabelecimentos, e os melhoramentos de que são susceptiveis; e contemplando nas informações acerca dos dous primeiros ramos as que forem concernentes ao estado da criação de gado em suas diversas especies (São Paulo, 1854), p. 1.

44 Ibid., pp. 1–2.

45 Taunay, *Historia do café*, 8:249; Vasconcellos and Vasconcellos, *Archivo nobiliarchico*, p. 354 (Visconde de Pindamonhangaba); *Almanach de São Paulo para 1888*, pp. 541–42; *Almanak da Provincia de São Paulo administrativo, commercial e industrial para 1873* (São Paulo, 1873), pp. 194–200; Zaluar, *Peregrinação*, p. 91; Carlos Eugênio Marcondes de Moura, *O Visconde de Guaratinguetá: Um titular do café no vale do Paraíba* (São Paulo, 1976), pp. 89–90.

46 Aroldo de Azevedo, "O vale do Paraíba (trecho paulista)," in *Anais: IX Congresso Brasileiro de Geographia 1940* (Rio, 1944), 5:573–87, esp. 580–83.

47 Richard M. Morse, *From Community to Metropolis: A Biography of São Paulo, Brazil*, new and enlarged ed. (New York, 1974 [1958]), p. 167.

48 Registro de Terras—Bananal, 1855–1856, No. 52, SDE/DAE/SP.

49 Registro de Terras—Taubaté, 1855–1856, No. 84; Registro de Terras—Jacarehy, 1854–1856, Nos. 38, 39, 40; Registro de Terras—Lorena, 1855–1856, Nos. 90, 91, SDE/DAE/SP.

50 Registro de Terras—Pindamonhangaba, 1855–1857, Nos. 56, 57, 58, SDE/DAE/SP; Pasta Pindamonhangaba: Patentes, Provisões e Sesmarias de Pindamonhangaba, 1721 a 1820, Coleção Aguirra, SDH/AMP/USP.

51 Taunay, *Historia do café*, 8:250; Moura, *O Visconde de Guaratinguetá*, pp. 89–90; *Almanach de São Paulo para 1888*, pp. 484, 541–42, 647; Frederic H. Sawyer, *Estudos sobre a industria assucareira no estado de S. Paulo comparada com a dos demais puizes* (Sao Paulo, 1905), pp. 46–69; for Bocaina, see Vasconcellos and Vasconcellos, *Archivo nobiliarchico*, pp. 82–83; and Taunay, *Historia do café*, 5:365; for the Viscondessa de Cavalcante, see "Pequeno Diccionario Biografico Brasileiro" (ms), n.d., n.p., p. 359, I-12, 2, 29, SM/BNRJ; for Santa Eulália, see Aroldo de Azevedo, *Arnolfo Azevedo: parlamentar da primeira república 1868–1942* (São Paulo, 1968), pp. 5–7. See also Registro de Terras—Guaratinguetá, 1855–1858, Nos. 12, 13, 14, SDE/DAE/SP; and Pasta Lorena: Patentes, Provisões e Sesmarias de Lorena, 1721 a 1820, and Pasta Pindamonhangaba, ibid., SDH/AMP/USP.

52 Morse, *From Community to Metropolis*, pp. 20–22.

53 C. F. van Delden Laerne, *Brazil and Java: Report on Coffee-Culture in America, Asia, and Africa to H.E. the Minister of the Colonies* (London, 1885), divides the Brazilian coffee region into two: the Rio Zone, comprising Espírito Santo, Minas, Rio, and the Paulista side of the Paraíba Valley; and the Santos Zone, made up of the new northwestern region that was served by the Santos-São Paulo Railway Company.

54 Taunay, "Landlords cafeeiros," pp. 7–8; Maria Thereza Schorer Petrone, *A lavoura canavieira em São Paulo: Expansão e declínio (1765–1851)* (São Paulo, 1968), pp. 45–47.

55 Taunay, *Historia do café*, 2:327, 8:247–48, and "Landlords cafeeiros," p. 8; Warren Dean, *Rio Claro: A Brazilian Plantation System, 1820–1920* (Stanford, 1976), pp. 138, 165; *Almanach de São Paulo para 1888*, p. 378.

56 Taunay, *Historia do café*, 5:174, 7:196, 8:12, 53–54, and "Landlords cafeeiros," p. 8; Registro de Terras, No. 114—Campinas, 1854–1857, Entry 164, SDE/DAE/SP; *Almanak de São Paulo para 1873*, pp. 475–79; *Almanach de São Paulo para 1888*, pp. 381, 495.

57 Taunay, "Vergueiro e Ibicaba," pp. 647–51; Pasta Piracicaba, Coleção Aguirra, SDH/AMP/USP. Luís Antônio, the son, held Fazendas Serra Dura and Tauaral in Piracicaba, Entries 43 and 44. For the origin of the Sousa Queirós economic fortunes, see Nanci Leonzo, "Um empresário nas milícias paulistas: o Brigadeiro Luís Antônio de Souza," *AMP* 30 (1980/1981), pp. 241–54.

58 Taunay, *Historia do café*, 8:248; Moura, *O Visconde de Guaratinguetá*, pp. 89–90; Maria Thereza Schorer Petrone, *O Barão de Iguape: Um empresário da época da independência* (São Paulo, 1976), p. xviii; *Almanach de São Paulo para 1888*, pp. 515–18.

59 Dean, *Rio Claro*, pp. 42–47, 117, 122, 143, 178, 207; Vasconcellos and Vasconcellos, *Archivo nobiliarchico*, p. 359; *Almanak de São Paulo para 1873*, p. 508; *Almanach de São Paulo para 1888*, p. 569; Taunay, *Historia do café*, 8:248.

60 Taunay, 8:247–48, and "Landlords cafeeiros," pp. 9–10; Dean, *Rio Claro*, p. 46; Vasconcellos and Vasconcellos, *Archivo nobiliarchico*, p. 223 (Barão de Itu), p. 224 (Marquês de Itu), p. 358 (First Piracicaba), p. 359 (Second Piracicaba), and p. 499 (Barão de Tatuí); *Almanak de São Paulo para 1873*, pp. 462–65; *Diario do Norte* (Pindamonhangaba), 10 November 1878; Leandro Guerrini, *História da Piracicaba em quadrinhos*, 2 vols. (Piracicaba, 1970).

61 Taunay, *Historia do café*, 8:248; Dean, *Rio Claro*, pp. 65, 147, 206–09; Vasconcellos and Vasconcellos, *Archivo nobiliarchico*, pp. 116–17 (the Barão de Cascalho), pp. 294–95 (the Barão de Monte Mor), and p. 371 (the Barão de Porto Feliz); *Almanach de São Paulo para 1888*, p. 524; Reynaldo Kuntz Busch, *História de Limeira* (Limeira, 1967), pp. 25–48.

62 Taunay, *Historia do café*, 5:219–220. Elsewhere ("Barões do cafe," p. 191) the distinguished Paulista historian argues that more than 200 titles were created for the coffee planters of the Center-South.

63 Simon Schwartzman, *São Paulo e o estado nacional* (São Paulo, 1975), p. 94.

64 Taunay, *Historia do café*, 7:170, 184; Laerne, *Brazil and Java*, p. 289

65 Morse contends in *From Community to Metropolis* (pp. 113–14) that the coffee-growing area of Costa Rica is as aristocratic as Brazil's sugar region, thus countering the theses advanced by Handelman and Cassiano Ricardo. It should perhaps be noted here that the predominant social structure of any economy is less influenced by the kinds of crops it cultivates than by the landholding patterns, credit mechanism, export linkages, and transportation network. See Jonathan

Levin, *The Export Economies: Their Pattern of Development in Historical Perspective* (Cambridge, Mass., 1958).

66 Inventário da Condessa de Pereira Marinho (Visconde de Guahy, son-inventariante) 1889–1919, Capital–Maço 130/Doc. 1, 130A/Doc. 2, 130B/Doc. 1, SJ/AEB; Inventário do Barão de Cotegipe (Antônia Thereza Wanderley, daughter/inventariante)-1889, SPJ/ANRJ.

67 Taunay, *Historia do café*, 5:183–85; Inventário do Conde de Mesquita (Jerônima Elvira de Mesquita Martins, daughter/inventariante)-1886, Cx 2760/no. 1754, SPJ/ANRJ. The five heirs were: Jerônima Elvira (married), Eliza Jerônima (married), Francisca Eliza (single), José Jerônimo (single), and Jerônimo Roberto (single).

68 Taunay, *Historia do café*, 8:19–20, 53–54, 247. For the early experiment with the parceria system, see Thomas Davatz, *Memórias de um colono no Brasil (1850)*, intro. by Sérgio Buarque de Holanda (São Paulo, 1972), pp. xxxviii–xxxix, which lists 23 planters who imported a total of 3,918 colonos between 1847 and 1857 using a provincial subsidy.

69 Taunay, "Vergueiro e Ibicaba," pp. 647–51; Davatz, *Memórias*, passim.

70 Taunay, *Historia do café*, 7:203–04, 368, 8:247, and "Barões do café," p. 193; one Lindolfo Carvalho, partner, was José's son-in-law; Joaquim José Pereira de Faro to Intendente Geral da Polícia, Valença, 31 January 1827, II, 34, 19, 21, SM/BNRJ; Peixoto (the future Barão de Paty do Alferes) to João Pereira Darrigue Faro, Monte Alegre (fazenda), Vassouras, 6 September 1852, Vol. 3, Códice 112, AFW, SAP/ANRJ.

71 Inventário da 1ª Baronesa do Rio Bonito (Barão do Rio Bonito, widower/inventariante)-1854, Cx 2641/No. 107 and Inventário do Visconde do Rio Bonito (José Pereira Darrigue Faro, son/inventariante)-1859, Cx 2759/No. 964, SPJ/ANRJ. For the business expansion in Campos, see *Monitor Campista* (Campos), 11 February 1886.

72 Inventário de 1ª Baronesa do Rio Bonito.

73 Historians and others have said that the Prados came to Brazil in the sixteenth century with Martim Afonso. For details, see Pedro Tacques d'Almeida Paes Leme, Nobiliarchica paulista, genealogia das principaes familias da Provincia de Sao Paulo, MS, Lata 22/Docs. 10–11, AIHGB. For a good biography of Iguape, especially his business activities, see Petrone, *O Barão de Iguape*.

74 Pierre Monbeig, *Pionniers et planteurs de São Paulo* (Paris, 1952), pp. 122–23.

75 Cunha, *Figuras e fatos*, pp. 14, 65–66; Vasconcellos and Vasconcellos, *Archivo nobiliarchico*, p. 365 (First Pitangui), p. 366 (Second Pitangui), pp. 373–74 (Prados); Pasta—Barão de Pitangui, C1034, 19, Pasta—Conde de Prados, C999, 43, and Pasta—Second Barão de Pitangui, C1011, 2, Documentos Biográficos, SM/BNRJ. For the business activities of Mariano Procópio, see Albino de Oliveira Estêves, "Mariano Procópio," *RIHGB* 230 (January–March 1956), pp. 3–398. The Cia. União e Indústria was incorporated in 1852 and the principal partner of Mariano Procópio was his wife, Maria Amélia Ferreira Lage. Mariano began his business career

in Rio at his father-in-law's firm, Ferreira Lage, Maia e Cunha, an importer and distributor of fabrics.

76 Estêves, passim; Cunha, *Figuras e fatos*, pp. 65–68; Taunay, *Historia do câfé*, 5:174; Galvão, *Relação dos cidadãos*, p. 213. Prados was the thirtieth president of Rio province.

77 Louis and Elizabeth Agassiz, *A Journey in Brazil* (New York, 1969; Boston, 1868), pp. 63–64, 102–16; Estêves, "Mariano Procópio," passim; Taunay, *A câmara dos deputados sob o império* (São Paulo, 1950), pp. 94, 96, 105–06, 171, 177, 184, 192, 210; Laerne, *Brazil and Java*, pp. 224–25; Cunha, *Figuras e fatos*, p. 14.

78 Agassiz, *A Journey in Brazil*, pp. 55–56; Taunay, "Velhas casas grandes," *MJC* 29:3 (March 1945), pp. 519–22. For a comprehensive list of property holders, merchants, and capitalists in Santo Amaro in 1857, see José Ozorio da Fonseca Penna Leitão to Camara, Santo Amaro, n.d., Pasta—Governo/Camara/Santo Amaro, 1846–1870, No. 1427/Doc. 14, PP/SH/AEB.

6   Life, Marriage, and Wealth of Noble Families

1   Tristão de Alencar Araripe, "Pater-familias no Brasil nos tempos coloniaes: memoria lida em sessão do Instituto Historico e Geografico Brasileiro de 4 de Setembro de 1880," *RIHGB* 52:2 (1893), pp. 15–16.

2   Charles Wagley, "Luso-Brazilian Kinship Patterns: The Persistence of a Cultural Tradition," in *Politics of Change in Latin America*, ed. Joseph Maier and Richard W. Weatherhead (New York, 1964), p. 188.

3   Lawrence Stone, *The Family, Sex, and Marriage in England, 1500–1800*, abridged ed. (New York, 1979), p. 112.

4   Sérgio Buarque de Holanda, *Raízes do Brasil*, 3rd ed. (Rio, 1956), p. 199.

5   Robin Fox, *Kinship and Marriage: An Anthropological Perspective* (Hammonsworth, Eng., 1967), pp. 48–50.

6   F. L. K. Hsu, *Clan, Caste, and Club* (Princeton, 1963), p. 61; Morton H. Fried, *The Evolution of Political Society: An Essay in Political Anthropology* (New York, 1967), pp. 124–25. The collective desire for survival was also found to be strong in Germanic clans, or *sippe*. Reinhard Bendix, *Kings or People: Power and the Mandate to Rule* (Berkeley, 1978), p. 25.

7   Andrew Strathern, "Kinship, Descent, and Locality: Some New Guinea Examples," in *The Character of Kinship*, ed. Jack Goody (Cambridge, Eng., 1973), pp. 25–26.

8   Wagley, "Luso-Brazilian Kinship Patterns," pp. 175, 187.

9   Ibid., pp. 182–83.

10 Eul-Soo Pang, *Bahia in the First Brazilian Republic: Coronelismo and Oligarchies, 1889–1934* (Gainesville, 1979), pp. 3–4.

11 Max Weber, *Economy and Society*, ed. Guenther Roth and Claus Wittich, 2 vols. (Berkeley, 1978), 1:231–35.

12 Ibid., 1:231.

13 Diocese de São Paulo, Registros Paroquiaes de N. S. da Assumpção, Cidade de São

Paulo, 8 August 1829, Livro de Batismos, No. 13, 1829–1849, f. 2v, microfilm, DG/GSU.

14 26 September 1829, Batismos No. 13, ff. 5-5v, DG/GSU.

15 24 December 1836, Batismos No. 13, f. 147, DG/GSU.

16 1 September 1834, Batismos No. 13, f. 106, DG/GSU.

17 20 August 1836, Batismos No. 13, f. 142v, DG/GSU.

18 21 October 1849, Livro de Batismos No. 14, 1849–1859, f. 13, DG/GSU.

19 4 December 1853, Batismos No. 14, f. 100, DG/GSU.

20 20 August 1835, Batismos No. 13, f. 126, DG/GSU.

21 6 April 1843, Batismos No. 13, f. 221v, DG/GSU.

22 18 June 1842, Batismos No. 13, f. 213v, DG/GSU.

23 24 December 1843, Batismos No. 13, f. 227v, DG/GSU.

24 29 August 1853, Batismos No. 14, f. 94, DG/GSU.

25 15 April 1832 (Maria), Batismos No. 13, f. 57v; 19 September 1854 (Anna), Batismos No. 14, f. 118, DG/GSU.

26 29 June 1857 (Eugênio Prates), Batismos No. 14, f. 188, DG/GSU. Both godparents came from the father's side in Rio Grande do Sul.

27 23 August 1856, Batismos No. 14, f. 166v, DG/GSU.

28 6 October 1856, Batismos No. 14, f. 170v, DG/GSU. Because no entry was made for Gabriela's surname, this might mean that she was of low birth, even that her mother was a former slave.

29 4 December 1831 and 9 April 1832, Batismos No. 13, f. 47, 80, and 5 June 1856, Batismos No. 14, f. 187, DG/GSU.

30 6 July 1832 and 28 February 1832, Batismos No. 13, f. 85v, 93v, DG/GSU.

31 10 November 1834, Batismos No. 13, f. 107v, DG/GSU.

32 3 August 1849, Batismos No. 14, f. 12v, DG/GSU.

33 18 November 1829, Batismos No. 13, f. 18, DG/GSU.

34 15 December 1829, Batismos No. 13, f. 19v, DG/GSU.

35 10 November 1850, Batismos No. 14, f. 32v, DG/GSU.

36 13 March 1858, Batismos No. 14, f. 205v, DG/GSU.

37 17 November 1848, Batismos No. 13, f. 295v, DG/GSU.

38 17 July 1853, Registros Paroquiaes: Valença, Rio de Janeiro: N.S. da Gloria, Livro de Batismos No. 13, 1867–1871, f. 9, DG/GSU.

39 8 April 1863, Registros Paroquiaes: Diocese da Luz, Minas Gerais: Abaeté: N.S. das Dores do Indaiá, Livro de Batismos No. 6, 1861–1871, f. 15, DG/GSU.

40 30 April 1865, Batismos (Minas/Indaiá), No. 6, f. 33, DG/GSU.

41 29 August 1864, Batismos (Minas/Indaiá), No. 6, f. 22v, DG/GSU.

42 19 April 1865, Batismos (Minas/Indaiá), No. 6, f. 36, DG/GSU.

43 16 April 1830, Batismos (São Paulo/Assumpção), No. 13, 1829–1849, f. 14, DG/GSU.

44 19 May 1830, Batismos (São Paulo/Assumpção), No. 13, f. 17v, DG/GSU.

45 16 September 1849, Batismos (São Paulo/Assumpção), No. 14, 1849–1859, f. 13, DG/GSU.

46 13 July 1832 (Gabriel), f. 63, 13 September 1837 [?] (Delfina), f. 94v, 10 April 1835

(Maria), f. 128, Batismos (São Paulo/Assumpção), No. 13; 24 May 1850 (Brazilia), f. 23v, 1 June 1850 (Maria), f. 24, 8 November 1850 (Narcisco), f. 32v, and 8 September 1851 (Barbara), f. 50v, Batismos (São Paulo/Assumpção), No. 14, DG/GSU.

47 4 October 1835, Batismos (São Paulo/Assumpção), No. 13, f. 128, DG/GSU.

48 Stone, *The Family, Sex, and Marriage*, pp. 38–44.

49 Eul-Soo Pang, *O Engenho Central do Bom Jardim na economia baiana: alguns aspectos de sua história 1875–1891* (Rio, 1979), pp. 185–222, covers the genealogical information on the principal members of the Costa Pintos.

50 Registros Paroquiaes: Parochia da Sé, São Paulo, Livro de Casamentos, No. 5, 1833–1862, f. 21, DG/GSU.

51 18 March 1845, Casamentos (São Paulo/Sé), No. 5, f. 55, DG/GSU.

52 25 December 1855 (Monteiro de Barros), Casamentos (São Paulo/Sé), No. 5, f. 129v and 1 May 1879 (Queiroz Aranha), Casamentos (São Paulo/Sé), No. 8, 1878–1883, f. 10, DG/GSU.

53 3 November 1876, Casamentos (São Paulo/Sé), No. 7, 1868–1878, ff. 160–160v, DG/GSU. The information on the political career of Caravelas is compiled from Brasil, Arquivo Nacional, *Organizações e programas ministeriais: regime parlamentar no império*, 2nd ed. (Rio, 1962).

54 25 January 1879, Casamentos (São Paulo/Sé), No. 8, f. 5v, DG/GSU.

55 10 August 1848, Casamentos (São Paulo/Sé), No. 5, f. 70, DG/GSU.

56 24 March 1881, Casamentos (São Paulo/Sé), No. 8, f. 50, DG/GSU.

57 13 May 1856 (Manuel José) and 7 November 1856 (Marco Antônio) Casamentos (São Paulo/Sé), No. 5, f. 132, 137, DG/GSU.

58 15 July 1879, Casamentos (São Paulo/Sé), No. 8, f. 15v, DG/GSU.

59 13 May 1856, Casamentos (São Paulo/Sé), No. 5, f. 132, DG/GSU.

60 18 February 1854, Casamentos (São Paulo/Sé), No. 5, f. 111v, DG/GSU.

61 11 November 1868, Casamentos (São Paulo/Sé), No. 7, ff. 7v-8, DG/GSU.

62 17 February 1872, Casamentos (São Paulo/Sé), No. 7, ff. 67-67v, DG/GSU.

63 21 January 1875, Casamentos (São Paulo/Sé), No. 7, f. 123, DG/GSU.

64 6 September 1877, Casamentos (São Paulo/Sé), No. 7, f. 183, DG/GSU.

65 10 September 1829, Casamentos (São Paulo/Sé), No. 4, 1812–1833, f. 222, DG/GSU.

66 19 February 1874 (Três Rios), Casamentos (São Paulo/Sé), No. 7, f. 142v and 16 July 1881 (Tatuí), Casamentos (São Paulo/Sé), No. 8, f. 54v, DG/GSU.

67 José Wanderley de Araujo Pinho, *Cotegipe e seu tempo: primeira phase 1815–1867* (São Paulo, 1937), pp. 622–24.

68 Ibid., p. 616, footnote 1.

69 Certidão passada a pedido do testamenteiro Doutor João Vicente Vianna como o theor do registro do testamento a baixo transcripto-1871, Cx 1, AJWAP.

70 Gilberto Freyre, *The Mansions and Shanties (sobrados e mucambos): The Making of Modern Brazil*, trans. Harriet de Onis (New York, 1963), pp. 9–10.

71 Carapebus to Subaé, Paris, 3 January 1883, Lata 552/Pasta 92, ACS.

72 Registros Paroquiaes: N. S. da Gloria, Valença, Rio de Janeiro, Livro de Casamentos, No. 4, 1845–1872, 26 October 1867, ff. 64v-65, DG/GSU.

73   18 September 1869 (Manuel and Maria) and 15 October 1870 (João and Rita), Ca-
     samentos (Rio/Valença), No. 4, f. 91v and f. 109, DG/GSU.
74   15 October 1870, Casamentos (Rio/Valença), No. 4, f. 109v, DG/GSU.
75   18 September 1869, Casamentos (Rio/Valença), No. 4, f. 91v, DG/GSU.
76   8 February 1867, Casamentos (Rio/Valença), No. 4, f. 54v, DG/GSU.
77   30 November 1867, Casamentos (Rio/Valença), No. 4, f. 65, DG/GSU.
78   21 April 1868, Casamentos (Rio/Valença), No. 4, f. 67v, DG/GSU.
79   Eugene D. Genovese, *Roll, Jordan, Roll: The World the Slaves Made* (New York,
     1972), pp. 458–75, esp. 464, 471–75. Genovese states that slaves were often forced
     to marry those on the same plantation at an early age. On the whole, slaves wed-
     ded younger than the children of the master. Hubert G. Gutman, *The Black Fam-
     ily in Slavery and Freedom, 1750–1925* (New York, 1976), pp. 318–23; Richard S.
     Dunn, *Sugar and Slaves: The Rise of the Planter Class in the English West Indies,
     1624–1713* (New York, 1973), p. 251.
80   24 May 1868, Casamentos (Rio/Valença), No. 4, ff. 71v–72, DG/GSU.
81   29 January 1888, Casamentos (Rio/Valença), No. 3, 1887–1911, ff. 1–4v, DG/
     GSU.
82   Raymundo Faoro, *Machado de Assis: a pirâmide e o trapézio* (São Paulo, 1976),
     pp. 205–06.
83   Nancy Priscilla Naro, "The 1848 Praieira Revolt in Brazil," Ph.D. Dissertation,
     University of Chicago (1981).

7   The Sale of Imperial Honors and Titles

1   Magalhães Junior, *O império em chinelos* (Rio, 1957), pp. 1–2, 6–7, 16.
2   These figures were calculated by Roderick J. Barman, "A New-World Nobility:
    The Role of Titles in Imperial Brazil," in *University of British Columbia His-
    panic Studies,* ed. Harold Livermore (London, 1974), pp. 45–47. Affonso de E. Tau-
    nay, "O nobiliario do primeiro imperio," *MJC* 1:3 (March 1938), pp. 1–5 states
    that a total of 98 titles were created between 1822 and 1830.
3   Sinimbu to Olinda, Bahia, 20 November 1857, Ofícios do Govêrno da Bahia ao
    Ministério do Império, IJJ⁹-340, SPE/ANRJ.
4   Ibid.
5   Carlos G. Rheingantz, *Titulares do império* (Rio, 1960), pp. 68, 71.
6   Dom Pedro II, *Diário da viagem ao norte do Brasil,* annotated by Lourenço Luiz
    Lacombe (Salvador, 1959), pp. 26–27. Bahia received a total of 256 honors: 1 mar-
    quês, 1 conde, 4 barões with the honors of grandee, 7 barões without the honors
    of grandee, 1 conselheiro, 2 grandes dignitários, 48 comendadores, 77 oficiais, and
    115 cavaleiros of Cruzeiro, Avis, Rosa, or Cristo orders.
7   Antonio da Costa Pinto to Cotegipe, 26 February 1856, Lata 56/Pasta 184, ABC.
8   Herculano Ferreira Pena to Minister of the Empire, Bahia, 22 February 1860, Of-
    ícios da Bahia, IJJ⁹-341, SPE/ANRJ. In 1860 Costa Pinto was recommended for the
    Barão da Conceição or the Comenda da Rosa. Luis Alves Leite de Oliveira Bello
    to José Ildefonso de Souza Ramos, Niterói, 21 February 1861, Ofícios do Govêrno

do Rio de Janeiro ao Ministério do Império, IJJ⁹-383, SPE/ANRJ. The president of the province (Bello) was a son-in-law of Joaquim José de Souza Breves, a megaplanter of the valley.

9 Magalhães Junior, *O império em chinelos*, p. 14.

10 Brasil, Assemblea Constituinte, *Diario da Assemblea Geral, Constituinte e Legislativa do Imperio do Brasil* (Rio, 1823), 29 October, 6 November 1823.

11 Francisco de Paula Maggessi de Araujo Costa to Thomas Antonio de Villanova Portugal, Matto Grosso, 3 July 1820, Pasta—Mello, Caetano da Costa Araujo, Requerimentos de Graças Honoríficas—Documentos Biográficos, SPE/ANRJ. This is a collection of some 20,000 individual files of Brazilians who requested imperial honors. One part of the collection is in the SPE/ANRJ and the other in the SM/BNRJ. No códice number is assigned to this collection in the SPE/ANRJ. José Clemente Pereira to Presidente da Província de Goiás, Rio, 16 March 1829, Livro de Registro de Decisões e Despachos que Sua Magestade O Imperador, Houver de Dar Representações e Requerimentos dos Habitantes de Goiás, 1825–1833, AHGO.

12 Barão da Laguna to Cunha Figuereido, Rio, 29 May 1876, stated that the Barão de Arari offered 15:000$ for the elevation to a visconde. Pasta—Silva, Henrique José de, Documentos Biográficos, SPE/ANRJ. The going price for elevation from barão to visconde ranged between 10:000$ and 15:000$, depending on the prestige and clout of the broker.

13 Abrantes to Minister of the Empire, Rio, 18 December 1860, and Recibo for 15:000$ ("donativo voluntario"), Pasta—Passos, Antônio Pereira dos, Documentos Biográficos, SPE/ANRJ.

14 José Francisco de Figueiredo to Senhor, Rio, 19 July 1872, Pasta—Moniz, Francisca de Assis Viana, Documentos Biográficos, SPE/ANRJ. Her son Pedro Francisco later became the Visconde de Ferreira Bandeira.

15 Abrantes (a handwritten note), Rio, 30 July 1860, Pasta—Portugal, José Gomes de Souza, Documentos Biográficos, SPE/ANRJ.

16 Abrantes to Minister of the Empire, Rio, 29 April 1862, and Recibo—Hospicio de Pedro II, Rio, 18 June 1862, Pasta—Silva, Joaquim José Gomes da, Documentos Biográficos, SPE/ANRJ. The "price list" of titles and other honors is also in the pasta.

17 Requerimento by the Visconde de Mira-Goya, Rio, 26 February 1855, Pasta—Pinto, Antônio Gonçalves da Silva, Documentos Biográficos, SPE/ANRJ.

18 Recibo—Thesoura Nacional, Rio, 9 August 1872, and President of the Province of Sergipe to Minister of the Empire, Aracaju, 11 July 1877, Pasta—Prado, José Inácio Acióli do; Recibo—Thesoura Nacional, Rio, 9 July 1873, Pasta—Moreira, José Antônio; Recibo, n.d., n.p., Pasta—Leão, José de Souza, Documentos Biográficos, SPE/ANRJ. Other nobles who had contributed to public education were: the Barão do Dourado (José Antônio da Silva Freire, 10:000$), the Barão de Arariba (João Luís Gonçalves Ferreira, 10:000$), the Barão de Camorogi (Antônio Felix de Carvalho, 10:000$), and the Barão da Engenho Novo (Antônio Pereira de Souza Barros, 10:000$), Documentos Biográficos, SPE/ANRJ.

19 Antônio Alves da Silva to Minister of the Empire, Recife, 24 April 1867, and Recibo—London and Brazilian Bank, Recife, 24 April 1867, Pasta—Silva, Antônio Alves da; President of the Province of Rio to Minister of the Empire, Niterói, 1 March 1867, Pasta—Queirós, Joaquim Marinho de, Documentos Biográficos, SPE/ANRJ.

20 Antonio Gonçalves Ferraz to Minister of the Empire, Ouro Preto, 2 March 1889, and João Raymundo Ourão et al. to Minister of the Empire, Diamantina, 8 March 1889, Pasta—Costa, António Moreira da, Documentos Biográficos, SPE/ANRJ.

21 Requerimento, n.d. (Received at the Ministry of the Empire 31 December 1860), Pasta—Oliviera, Joaquim José Ferraz de, Documentos Biográficos, SPE/ANRJ.

22 Requerimento, n.d. (1853), and Paraná to Minister of the Empire, Rio, 9 July 1853, Pasta—Olivicra, Francisco Antônio, Documentos Biográficos, SPE/ANRJ.

23 Requerimento, Rio, 6 November 1860, Pasta—Capanema, Guilherme Schüch de, Documentos Biográficos, SPE/ANRJ.

24 Internal Memo, Rio, 28 March 1877, Pasta—Nogueira, Pedro Ramos, Documentos Biográficos, SPE/ANRJ. *Internal Memo* is an evaluation note by officials at the Ministry of the Empire and the imperial household *for* or *against* granting the petitioner's request. Often these memos reveal much about the rationale for the positive or negative recommendation.

25 Recibo, Bahia, 23 May 1877, Pasta—Pinto, Antônio da Costa, Documentos Biográficos, SPE/ANRJ; the provincial president reported to the minister of the empire that Costa Pinto was prepared to pay 10:000$ in five installments. Manuel Pinto de Sousa Dantas to Olinda, Bahia, 4 October 1865, Oficios da Bahia, IJJ⁹-550, SPE/ANRJ.

26 Decreto—Queiróz, Vicente de Souza, and Decreto—the Barão de Lorena, Códice 15, SPE/ANRJ.

27 The information on all four is found in Pasta—Maciel, Anibal Antunes, Documentos Biográficos, SPE/ANRJ.

28 Decreto Abreu, Francisco Bonifácio, Códice 15, and Internal Memo, Rio, 25 July 1885, Pasta—Oliveira, Antônio Cândido Antunes de, Documentos Biográficos, SPE/ANRJ.

29 Decreto—Faria, Manuel Antônio da Rocha, Códice 15, SPE/ANRJ.

30 Felisberto de Olivcira Freire to Fiel José de Carvalho, SC (Sua Casa) de Belém, 20 December 1871, Carvalho to João Alfredo, Bahia, 7 February 1872, Freirc to Carvalho, Belém, 10 April 1872, Internal Memo, Rio, 13 March 1873, Antonio Pereira Espinheiro e Cia. to Carvalho, Bahia, 24 March 1873, and an unsigned accusatory note, n.d., n.p., Pasta—Freire, Felisberto de Oliveira, Documentos Biográficos, SPE/ANRJ.

31 Internal Memo, Rio, 28 November 1887, Pasta—Siqueira, Antônio Homens de Loureiro, President of the Province to Minister of the Empire, Ouro Preto, 18 July 1885, Pasta—Carvalho, Domingos Teixeira de; João Bonifacio Gomes de Siquᵃ to Minister of the Empire, Goyaz, 7 October 1867, Pasta—Abreu, Antônio Pereira de, SPE/ANRJ.

32 Requerimento, n.d., and Oliveira to José Florentino Meira de Vasconcellos, For

mosa, 13 January 1885, Pasta—Oliveira, Firmino Soares de, Documentos Biográficos, SPE/ANRJ. The candidate also claimed that he freed all his slaves, the number of whom was not given.

33 Requerimento, Rio, 5 November 1888, Pasta—Morais, João José Correia de, Documentos Biográficos, SPE/ANRJ.

34 Internal Memo, Rio, 24 January 1887, Pasta—Silva, Fausto Domingos da; Memorial, Rio, 13 March 1889, Pasta—MacKee, João; Requerimento, n.d., Pasta—Coutinho, Ambrósio de Sousa, Documentos Biográficos, SPE/ANRJ. MacKee was a British merchant who had long resided in Fortaleza. In addition to the money he raised for the victims of the Great Drought, his firm loaned 185:000$ to the provincial government without interest. In 1881 the deputies from Ceará recommended that he be given a title.

35 Requerimento, Iguassu (Pe), 22 November 1886, Pasta—Coutinho, Floriano de Queirós, Documentos Biográficos, SPE/ANRJ.

36 Requerimento, n.p., 24 November 1856; President of the Province of São Paulo to Minister of the Empire, São Paulo, 14 November 1856; Requerimento, n.d.; Dom Antonio to Minister of the Empire, São Paulo, 4 December 1856, marked "confidencial," Pasta—Silva, Joaquim José de, Documentos Biográficos, SPE/ANRJ.

37 Requerimento, n.d., Pasta—Barreto, José Joaquim, Documentos Biográficos, SPE/ANRJ. Inventário do Barão de Saubara (1867), 2° Ofício do Forum do Município de Santo Amaro, Bahia.

38 Requerimento by Capistrano Bandeira de Mello (procurador), n.d., Pasta—Leão, Francisco de Paula Souza, and Requerimento—Filippe de Souza Leão (procurador), Rio, 18 June 1858, Pasta—Leão, Antônio de Paula Souza, Documentos Biográficos, SPE/ANRJ.

39 Decreto—Leão, Antônio de Souza, dated 24 August 1870, Códice 15, SPE/ANRJ.

40 Requerimento, n.d., and Sinimbu to Olinda, Bahia, 23 July 1857, Pasta—Albuquerque, Francisco Pires de Carvalho e, Documentos Biográficos, SPE/ANRJ.

41 Sinimbu to Olinda, Bahia, 20 November 1857, Ofícios da Bahia, IJJ⁹-340, SPE/ANRJ. As shown earlier, the majority of those recommended were members of economic elites with no known partisan radicalism.

42 Baependy to Abrantes, São Christóvão, 9 October 1860; Rio Bonito to Couto Ferraz, Nictheroy, 22 August 1854, Pasta—Morais, Joaquim José Gonçalves de; Villa Bella to Minister of the Empire, Rio, 21 October 1878, and Couto Ferraz to Minister of the Empire, Rio, 2 March 1857, Pasta—Gama, Caetano Maria de Paiva Lopes; Requerimento—Francisco Nicolau Carneiro Nogueira da Gama (procurador), Rio, 12 September 1873, Pasta—Gama, Francisco Nicolau de Lima Nogueira da; Requerimento—Visconde de Jequitinhonha, Rio, 23 September 1856, Pasta—Montezuma, Harmonio de Toledo Marcondes, Documentos Biográficos, SPE/ANRJ.

43 Antonio Dias Coelho Neto dos Reis to Francisco Moreira de Carvalho, Rio, 11 September 1856, Lata 552/Pasta 79, No. 2, ACS.

44 Ibid.

45 Reis to Carvalho, Rio, 12 October 1865, February 22, 1864, Lata 552/Pasta 79, No. 3 and 81, ACS.

46 Baependy to Mamoré, SC, 8 October 1885, and Internal Memo, Rio, 12 March 1885, Pasta—Carapebus, José Inácio Neto dos Reis de, Documentos Biográficos, SPE/ANRJ.

47 Carapebus to Ourem, Petropolis, 17 March 1889, Lata 147/Pasta 41, AVO.

48 Carapebus to Ourem, Petropolis, 14 March, 24 March 1889, AVO.

49 Carapebus to Ourem, Petropolis, 7 March 1889, AVO.

50 Carapebus to Ourem, Rio, 21 July 1889, AVO.

51 Barão de Pereira Marinho to Ourem, Bahia, 28 May 1871, and Carapebus to Ourem, Petropolis, 26 February 1889, AVO.

52 For Fonseca Costa (viscondessa), see Dom Pedro II, *Diário da viagem*, p. 33; and Manoel Augusto Velho da Motta Maia, *O conde de Motta Maia, medico e amigo dedicado de d. Pedro Segundo* (Rio, 1937).

53 Affonso de E. Taunay, *História do café no Brasil*, 15 vols. (Rio, 1939–43), 5:188–89.

54 Taunay, *Historia do café*, 7:84, and Alberto Ribeiro Lamego, *O homem e a serra*, 2nd ed. (Rio, 1964), pp. 372-73 (on Sousa Dantas); and C. F. van Delden Laerne, *Brazil and Java: Report on Coffee-Culture in America, Asia, and Africa to H.E. the Minister of the Colonies* (London, 1885), pp. 224–25 (on Cavalcanti).

55 Reis to Mathias de Carvalho e Vasconcellos, Paris, 12 October 1880, ACS.

56 Aristides Novis to Araujo Pinho, Bahia, 14 November 1888, AJFAP. This archive also includes the papers of the father of Governor Araújo Pinho.

57 Egas Moniz to Cotegipe, Cassarangongo, n.d., Lata 4/Pasta 9, ABC.

58 Egas Moniz to Cotegipe, Maracangalha, 28 October 1887, Lata 5/Pasta 2, ABC.

59 Decreto—14 March 1860, Códice 15, SPE/ANRJ. Some agrarian nobles listed in this decree were Sergimirim, Matuim, Jacuipe, Traripe, and Bom Jardim, all of Bahia.

60 Decreto—2 December 1841, Códice 15, SPE/ANRJ.

61 Decreto—18 July 1841, Códice 15, SPE/ANRJ. Those who appeared with Caxias were his father (Barra Grande), Boa Vista, Fiais, Suassuna, and Cajaíba, among others—all members of political and military elites.

62 Registro de Cartas de Títulos dos Titulares da Casa Imperial 1867—1889, 3 vols., I: Cartas de Títulos, II: Títulos de Conselho, and III: Imperial Licença para Casamento, Códice 310, SPE/ANRJ. I: Cartas de Títulos, p. 7.

63 Registro de Cartas de Titulos, I: Cartas de Títulos, p. 15v.

64 Registro de Cartas de Títulos, I: Cartas de Títulos, p. 2.

65 These laws and decrees were: Lei No. 586 of 6 September 1850 (art. 16), Lei No. 719 of September 28, 1853 (art. 22), Decreto No. 4356 of 24 April 1869, Decreto No. 4505 of 9 April 1870, and Decreto No. 7540 of 15 November 1879.

66 Livro Segundo do Registro das Cartas de Brazãos de Armas de Nobreza e Fidalguia d'este Imperio, Lata 186/Pasta 25; Avisos do Ministerio dos Negocios do Imperio dos Srs. Titulares (de 1855 a 1861), Lata 186/Pasta 23, and Avisos da Secretaria de

Estado dos Negocios do Imperio dos Srs. Titulares (1880–1883 e 1887), Lata 186/ Pasta 24, AEAB.

67 Lista dos Titulares de Marqueses, Condes, Viscondes, e Barões que não Tem Carta de Nobreza, Rio, 30 May 1887, Lata 186/Pasta 1, AEAB.

68 Rui Vieira da Cunha, *Figuras e fatos da nobreza brasileira* (Rio, 1975), p. 54.

69 Taunay, *Historia do café*, 8:222–23.

70 Cunha, *Figuras e fatos*, pp. 58–59.

71 For foreign titles, see "Títulos usados no Brasil e concedidos no extrangeiro," *AGB* 1 (1939), pp. 209–28, which lists a total of thirty-seven titles. This figure is not accurate. For some false claims for titles and honors, see Rubem Amaral Júnior, "Os falsos títulos de nobreza do império do Brasil na Cisplatina," *MAN* (March 1979), pp. 11–17; and Carlos G. Rheingantz, "O título de Visconde com grandeza de Serro Azul: uma falsificação inqualificável," *MAN* (February 1975), pp. 3–8.

8 Noblemen in the Patrimonial Monarchy

1 Eul-Soo Pang and Ron L. Seckinger, "The Mandarins of Imperial Brazil," *CSSH* 14 (March 1972), pp. 215–244, first presented a patrimonial-bureaucratic model of Brazilian elite formation by which the empire created a cadre of trained Crown officials, detached from their home bases and made dependent on the Crown for their political careers, to serve as the linchpin of the imperial high administration. This chapter presents a revised version of that argument on the basis of a careful rereading of Max Weber and recent research. The Brazil Session of the 1979 American Historical Association meeting in New York City addressed the question of "Who ruled the empire?" by examining the extent of political power exercised by landlords. This question has steadily received the serious attention it deserves. Some of the major "views" on this subject follow. Francisco José de Oliveira Vianna, *Instituições políticas brasileiras*, 2 vols. (Rio, 1949), 1:175–316, argues that the territorial lords of regional clans ruled Brazil. Raymundo Faoro, *Os donos do poder*, 2 vols., 2nd ed. (Porto Alegre/São Paulo, 1975), was one of the first syntheses that perceptively presented the nonexclusivity of the agrarian domination of Brazil, pointing out the existence of a powerful bureaucratic class (*estamento burocrático*) that ruled the country. Oliveira Vianna and Faoro have been two of the well-known post-1945 pioneers of these two historical schools. It should be pointed out that neither of these two has forthrightly stated that the monarchy had organized a patrimonial bureaucratic corps of mandarins to administer the empire.

2 Fernando Uricoechea, *The Patrimonial Foundations of the Brazilian Bureaucratic State* (Berkeley, 1980), pp. 16–20; this book was first published in Portuguese under the title *O minotauro imperial* (São Paulo, 1978).

3 Miguel Arcanjo Galvão, *Relação dos cidadãos que tomaram parte no govêrno do Brasil no período de março de 1808 a 15 de novembro de 1889*, 2nd ed. (Rio, 1969), p. 15; Emília Viotti da Costa, "José Bonifácio: homem e mito," in *1822:*

dimensões, org. Carlos G. Mota (São Paulo, 1972), pp. 122–23. The latter work was also published under the title "José Bonifácio: mito e histórias," in Emília Viotti da Costa, *Da monarquia à república: momentos decisivos* (São Paulo, 1977), pp. 53–108

4 Galvão, *Relação dos cidadãos*, pp. 16, 18, 40.

5 Augusto Tavares de Lyra, "Os ministros de estado da independência à república," *RIHGB* 193 (October–December 1946), pp. 3–104, offers brief but good biographical data on 219 ministers.

6 Faoro, *Os donos do poder*, 1:354. On the administration of Paraná's "Conciliation Cabinet," see Roderick James Barman, "Brazil at Mid-Empire: Political Accommodation and the Pursuit of Progress under the Conciliation Ministry, 1853–1857," Ph.D. Dissertation, University of California, Berkeley (1970).

7 Faoro, *Os donos do poder*, 1:354.

8 Luis Marques Poliano, *Ordens honorificas no Brasil* (Rio, 1943). A slightly lower figure (4,642) is given by Faoro, *Os donos do poder*, 1:258–59.

9 Faoro, 1:365–66.

10 Fernando Tomaz, "Brasileiros nas Cortes Constituintes de 1821–1822," in *1822: Dimensões*, pp. 74–101, esp. 99–101

11 Ibid.

12 Costa, "José Bonifácio," p. 124; José Honório Rodrigues, *A Assembleia Constituinte de 1823* (Petrópolis, 1974), pp. 22–24.

13 H. V. Livermore, *A New History of Portugal*, 2nd ed. (Cambridge, Eng., 1976), pp. 262–64.

14 Costa, "José Bonifácio," p. 126; Rodrigues, *A Assembleia Constituinte*, pp. 31–34.

15 Rodrigues, p. 29.

16 Ibid., pp. 25–29; E. Bradford Burns, *A History of Brazil*, 2nd ed. (New York, 1980), pp. 161–62. Rodrigues and Burns disagree on the total number of the deputies who *attended* (Rodrigues 70 and Burns 90) and the number of priest-deputies (Rodrigues 16 and Burns 19). A third set of figures is provided in Aureliano Leal, *Historia constitucional do Brazil* (Rio, 1915), p. 49, which cites the work by Homem de Mello: of the 100 elected deputies, 45 were trained in law, 22 desembargadores, 7 canons, 3 doctors, 19 priests, and 7 military.

17 Rodrigues, *A Assembleia Constituinte*, pp. 44–45, 263–68, 274.

18 Brasil, Assemblea Constituinte, *Diario da Assemblea Geral, Constituinte e Legislativa do Imperio do Brasil* (Rio, 1823).

19 *Diario da Assemblea*, 17 June 1823. For a detailed analysis of the debate on the organization of the provincial government, see Leal, *Historia constitucional*, pp. 58–61. For the provincial views on Brazil's independence and the organization of government, see Brasil, Ministério da Justiça, Arquivo Nacional, *As juntas governativas e a independência*, 3 vols. (Rio, 1975), which treats all correspondence between 1821 and 1823 on the subject.

20 *Diario da Assemblea*, 18 September 1823.

21 Ibid., 23–24 May 1823.

22 Ibid., 14 July 1823.

23 Ibid., 23 June (on Brazilwood trade), 5 August 1823 (on tax exemption).

24 Rodrigues, *A Assembleia Constituinte*, pp. 84–99.

25 *Diario da Assemblea*, 29 October, 11 November 1823; Leal, *Historia constitucional*, pp. 72–73.

26 Rodrigues, *A Assembleia Constituinte*, p. 245.

27 Conselheiro Francisco Gomes da Silva (O Chalaça), *Memórias*, 2nd ed. (Rio, 1959), pp. 70–73; Costa, "José Bonifácio," pp. 147–49; *HGCB*, 3:242–52.

28 *HGCB* 3:243.

29 Leal, *Historia constitucional*, pp. 97–98. For the municipal councils' attitudes toward independence and the constitution, see Brasil, Arquivo Nacional, *As câmaras municipais e a independência*, 2 vols. (Rio, 1972).

30 Brasil, Ministério da Justiça, Arquivo Nacional, *Organizações e programas ministeriais: regime parlamentar no império*, 2nd ed. (Rio, 1962), p. 398.

31 Brasil, *Falas do trono desde o ano de 1823 ate o ano de 1889*, 2nd ed. (São Paulo, 1977), pp. 7–10.

32 Afonso de E. Taunay, *A câmara dos deputados sob o império* (São Paulo, 1950), p. 54.

33 Ibid., p. 10.

34 Afonso E. Taunay, "Representantes de Pernambuco e Bahia," *MJC* 11:2 (August 1940), pp. 305–09.

35 Eduardo Ferreira França, a physician, was a Conservative politician. Because of his death in 1857, he was unable to finish his fourth term. *Organizações e programas*, p. 323.

36 Manuel Correia de Andrade, *A terra e o homem no nordeste*, 3rd ed. (São Paulo, 1973), pp. 23–26. The three major areas of Pernambuco are the *litoral*, the Zona da Mata, and *agreste*. Cane has been cultivated in the first two zones; the *agreste*, or *sertão*, is dry, not suitable for capitalist agriculture.

37 Kátia M. de Queirós Mattoso, *Bahia: a cidade do Salvador e seu mercado no século XIX* (São Paulo, 1978), pp. 26–39, 115–49, points out that Salvador was a city with little expansive and incorporative features during the nineteenth century.

38 Taunay, *A câmara dos deputados*, pp. 51–52.

39 Taunay, "Representantes do centro," *MJC* 1:2 (August 1940), pp. 399–403.

40 The mandarin is a patrimonial-sinecurist bureaucrat. Lower-level civil servants, or administrative elite, are not considered to be mandarins. Magistrates, such as the juiz de direito or *desembargador of relação* (appellate court judge), provincial presidents, and police chiefs should be viewed as low mandarins; and ministers, senators, and councillors of state as high mandarins.

41 A. C. Tavares Bastos, *A província: estudo sobre a descentralização no Brasil*, 3rd ed. (São Paulo, 1975), p. 93, states that "the president of province is in Brazil an electoral instrument." *Organizações e programas*, p. 443 (Paranaguá), p. 446 (Campos), and p. 448 (Abreu e Silva). Afonso de E. Taunay, *O senado do império*,

2nd. (Brasília, 1978), p. 99 points out that Martinho Campos was named on the same day as prime minister and senator.

42 Taunay, *O senado,* p. 54.

43 Ibid., pp. 85–87; *Organizações e programas,* pp. 407–13.

44 Taunay, *O senado,* pp. 88–91.

45 The first Cavalcanti de Albuquerque of Pernambuco entered the senate in 1838. In fact, the three brothers (Antônio Francisco, Francisco, and Pedro Francisco) were elected to that body in 1838, 1839, and 1869, respectively. *Organizações e programas,* pp. 411–12.

46 Ibid., pp. 407–16.

47 Taunay, *O senado,* p. 73.

48 See chapters 2 and 3.

49 Taunay, *O senado,* p. 73; *Organizações e programas,* p. 413.

50 Frederico de Barros Brotero, *A família Monteiro de Barros* (São Paulo, 1951), p. 25, lists Padre Marcos Antônio as one of the eight brothers.

51 Taunay, *O senado,* pp. 76–77.

52 Afonso de E. Taunay, "Synopse senatorial," *MCJ* 12:1 (October 1940), p. 48.

53 Taunay, *O senado,* pp. 148–59. The Albuquerque group included one Albuquerque Maranhão and one Lacerda Albuquerque.

54 Heitor Lyra, *Historia do Dom Pedro II, 1825–1891,* 3 vols. (São Paulo, 1938), 1:493–95.

55 *Manifesto do Centro Liberal* (Rio, 1869).

56 José Antonio Pimenta Bueno, *Direito publico brasileiro e analyse da constituição do imperio* (Rio, 1857), p. 57.

57 Ibid., p. 56.

58 Ibid., p. 57.

59 Paulino José Soares de Souza (Visconde do Uruguai), *Ensaio sobre o direito administrativo* (Rio, 1960), pp. 165–66.

60 Caio Prado Júnior, *Evolução política do Brasil e outros estudos,* 4th ed. (São Paulo, 1963), p. 53.

61 Brazil, Rio de Janeiro Province, Câmara Municipal de Valença, *Lista dos cidadãos qualificados da Freguezia de N.S. da Gloria do municipio de Valença no anno de 1879* (Rio, 1879); *Lista . . . Freguezia de Santo Antonio do Rio Bonito . . . .* (Rio, 1879), *Lista . . . Freguezia de Santa Isabel do Rio Preto . . . .* (Rio, 1879); *Lista . . . Freguezia de Ipiabas . . . .* (Rio, 1879).

62 Guerreiro Ramos, *A crise do poder no Brasil (problemas da revolução nacional brasileira)* (Rio, 1961), p. 32; Faoro, *Os donos do poder,* 1:323, which states that "only between 1% and 3% of the people participated in the formation of the said national election."

63 Souza, *Ensaio,* p. 234; Tobias Monteiro, *Historia do imperio,* 2 vols. (Rio, 1938–39), 1:35–37.

64 J. M. Pereira da Silva, *Historia da fundação do imperio brazileiro,* 7 vols. (Rio, 1864–68), 7:241–42.

65 Ibid., 7:243:44.

66 Monteiro, *Historia do imperio*, 1:37; Souza, *Ensaio*, p. 153. Article 32 of the Ato Adicional suppressed the Council of State. An unabbreviated version of the 1834 constitutional amendment is in João Camillo de Oliveira Torres, *A democracia coroada: teoria política do império do Brasil*, 2nd ed. (Petrópolis, 1964), pp. 497–501.

67 C. H. Haring, *Empire in Brazil: A New World Experiment with Monarchy* (Cambridge, 1958), Chap. 3; Burns, *A History of Brazil*, pp. 170–76. A good history on the Regency period is still J. M. Pereira da Silva, *Historia do Brazil durante a menoridade de d. Pedro II (1831 a 1840)*, 2nd ed. (Rio, 1888).

68 Bastos, *A província*, p. 63.

69 Ibid., p. 80. Article 3 of the Ato Adicional is in Oliveira Torres, *A democracia coroada*, p. 497. The parliament could create an upper house for any province. These five provinces, the center of the population, were obviously judged to be the prime candidates to have the second chamber.

70 *Falas do trono*, pp. 138–203, reviews the major internal disturbances between 1831 and 1840. A good analysis of the period is provided by Faoro, *Os donos do poder*, 1:316–21.

71 Luis da Camara Cascudo, *O Marquez de Olinda e seu tempo (1793–1870)* (São Paulo, 1938), pp. 148–49.

72 Ibid., pp. 165–69; Faoro, *Os donos do poder*, 1:322–24.

73 Aurelino Leal, *Do Acto Addicional a maioridade (historia constitucional e politica)* (Rio, 1915), pp. 127–34; Paulino Pinheiro Chagas, *Teófilo Ottoni: ministro do povo*, 2nd ed. (Rio, 1956), pp. 125–26.

74 Leal, *Do Acto Addicional*, pp. 133–34. Some people, like Antônio Rebouças, a senator from Bahia, thought that the Council of State "is not compatible with the Constitution." For such a view, see Antonio Pereira Rebouças, *Recordações da vida parlamentar do advogado Antonio Pereira Rebouças: moral, jurisprudencia, politica e liberdade constitucional*, 2 vols. (Rio, 1870), 2:59–88.

75 *Falas do trono*, pp. 217–18.

76 Pimenta Bueno, *Direito publico*, p. 206; Magali Sarfatti, *Spanish Bureaucratic-Patrimonialism in America* (Berkeley, 1966), pp. 5–20, esp. 12–17.

77 Souza, *Ensaio*, pp. 153–54; Faoro, *Os donos do poder*, 1:330–31.

78 The best description of the multiple role of the council is given by Pimenta Bueno, *Direito publico*, pp. 285–318. All the subsequent discussion on the role of the council in the present volume is based on this source.

79 A near-complete bibliography on the manuscripts and published documents of the Conselho de Estado is in José Honório Rodrigues, org., *Atas do Conselho de Estado*, 9 vols. (Brasília, 1973), 1:lxv–lxxv. One good example of the council's far-ranging activities is a collection of its resolutions, consultas, and pareceres. For the Justice Section, see José Prospero Jehova da Silva Caroatá, org., *Imperiaes resoluções tomadas sobre consultas da Secção de Justiça do Conselho de Estado, desde o anno de 1842, em que começou a funcionar o mesmo conselho até hoje colligidas em virtude de autorisação do Exmo. Sr. Conselheiro Manoel*

Pinto de Souza Dantas, ex-Ministro e Secretario de Estado dos Negocios da Justiça, 2 vols. (Rio, 1884).

80 *Organizações e programas*, p. 426.

81 Eul-Soo Pang, *O Engenho Central do Bom Jardim na economia baiana: alguns aspectos de sua história 1875–1891* (Rio, 1979), pp. 30, 36–37. On the modernization of one of his engenhos, see the Barão de Cotegipe, *Descripção do aparelho de fabricar assucar assentado no Engenho Jacarancanga propriedade do Barão de Cotegipe—Bahia apresentada pelo mesmo Exmo. Sr. ao Imperial Instituto Fluminense de Agricultura* (Rio, 1867). For Saraiva and Fábrica Central de Pojuca, see José Antônio Saraiva et al. to Presidente da Provincia da Bahia, Pojuca, April 3, 1882, Pasta 1882, Fabricas Centraes-1846–1887, PP/SH/AEB. For the Bahian experience in refinery modernization, see Eul-Soo Pang, "Modernization and Slavocracy in Nineteenth-Century Brazil," *JIH* 9:4 (Spring 1979), pp. 667–88, and "Tecnologia e escravocracia no Brasil durante o século XIX: uma reinterpretação," *AMP* 30 (1980/1981), pp. 55–134.

82 *Manifesto do Centro Liberal*, pp. 66–67; Heitor Lyra, *História da queda do império*, 2 vols. (São Paulo, 1964), 2:77–81.

83 Faoro, *Os donos do poder*, 1:333.

84 Joaquim Nabuco, *Um estadista do império*, Volume único (Rio, 1975), pp. 594–95.

85 Oliveira Torres, *A democracia coroada*, p. 191; *Organizações e programas*, p. 99.

86 Brasil, Ministério do Império, *Relatorio do Imperio de 1845*, p. 6.

87 *Relatorio do Imperio de 1851*, pp. 6-7; *de 1857*, pp. 10–11.

88 *Relatorio do Imperio de 1886*, pp. 7–8.

89 Maria Thereza Schorer Petrone, "As crises da monarquia e o movimento republicano," *RIEB* 16 (1975), pp. 31–41. She cites seven factors, or "crises," that beset the empire by the end of the 1860s and that eventually contributed to the demise of the monarchy.

90 *Relatorio do Imperio de 1869*, p. 2. It is fitting that the minister of the empire who redefined the mandarin ideology was Paulino José Soares de Sousa, a Conservative monarchist and son of the Visconde do Uruguai, the mandarin par excellence.

91 *Relatorio do Imperio de 1860*, pp. 10–11.

92 Joaquim Candido de Azevedo Marques, *Legislação geral: Índice alphabetico explicativo das disposições dos annos de 1850 a 1884*, 5 vols. (Rio, 1874–80; São Paulo, 1886). The citations in Notes 93 through 115, immediately following, are based on these volumes.

93 Aviso-Imperio, No. 228 (1871), p. 26; Aviso-Imperio, No. 289 (1871), p. 54.

94 Aviso-Imperio, No. 170 (1859), pp. 55.

95 Aviso-Justiça, No. 175 (1859), p. 55; Aviso-Fazenda, No. 245 (1853), p. 75.

96 Aviso-Agricultura, No. 97 (1871), p. 26. On the rebellion, see Geraldo Ireneo Joffily, *O Quebra Quilo: A revolta dos matutos contra os doutores—1874* (Brasília, 1977); and Hamilton de Mattos Monteiro, *A crise agrária e luta de classes (o*

nordeste brasileiro entre 1850 a 1889) (Brasília, 1980), pp. 129–51. Monteiro reports that a total of seventy-eight rebellions occurred in four provinces: Alagoas seven, Paraíba thirty-five, Pernambuco twenty-three, and Rio Grande do Norte thirteen. These were the only instances known to the imperial authorities in Rio.

97   Ordem-Fazenda, 26 November 1862, p. 380; Aviso-Fazenda, 20 November 1866, p. 382.

98   Aviso-Fazenda, No. 377 (1871), p. 243.

99   Aviso-Agricultura, No. 215 (1872), and Circular-Guerra, No. 252 (1873), pp. 243–44.

100 Aviso-Imperio, No. 411 (1874), and Aviso-Justiça, No. 459 (1878), pp. 356–57.

101 A. C. Tavares Bastos, *A província: estudo sobre a descentralização no Brasil*, 3rd ed. (São Paulo, 1975), p. 87.

102 For an interesting study on the evolution of the Brazilian judicial system, see Thomas Flory, *Judge and Jury in Imperial Brazil, 1808–1871: Social Control and Political Stability in the New State* (Austin, 1981).

103 *Relatorio do Imperio de 1854*, pp. 5–6. The minister of the empire complained that the lack of uniformity in the organization and administration procedures of the municipal corporations impeded the efficient collection of taxes and the enforcement of imperial laws.

104 Aviso-Fazenda, No. 344 (1858), p. 88; Aviso-Imperio, 24 March 1865, p. 76; Aviso-Fazenda, No. 110 (1873), p. 47.

105 2ª Sessão ordinaria, Livro de Actas da Camara Municipal de Itu, 1882–1886, 8 October 1882, APCI/SP.

106 Aviso-Justiça, No. 6 (1856), p. 86; Aviso-Imperio, No. 24 (1851), p. 354; Aviso-Imperio, 12 April 1854, p. 356; Aviso-Justiça, No. 53 (1856), p. 356; Aviso-Justiça, No. 123 (1859), p. 356; Aviso-Imperio, No. 287 (1856), p. 359; Aviso-Imperio, No. 587 (1860), p. 360; Aviso-Justiça, 16 January 1861, p. 254; Aviso-Justiça, 5 November 1862, p. 256; Aviso-Imperio, 2 March 1865, p. 258; Aviso-Justiça, No. 215 (1877), p. 67; Aviso-Justiça, No. 379 (1877), p. 68; Aviso-Imperio, No. 28 (1882), p. 91.

107 Ordem-Imperio, No. 64 (1850), p. 354; Aviso-Justiça, No. 123 (1859), p. 356; Aviso-Imperio, No. 587, p. 360; Aviso-Imperio, 23 April 1861, p. 255; Aviso-Imperio, 17 April 1862, p. 256.

108 Aviso-Justiça, 23 October 1850, p. 354; Aviso-Imperio, 24 March 1854, p. 356; Aviso-Fazenda, 2 April 1855, p. 356; Aviso-Imperio, No. 235 (1856), p. 356; Aviso-Imperio, No. 291 (1860), p. 359; Aviso-Justiça, 7 February 1861, p. 254; Aviso-Justiça, 13 June 1861, p. 255; Aviso-Justiça, 3 June 1863, p. 256; Aviso-Justiça, 2 December 1864, p. 257; Aviso-Justiça, No. 199 (1878), p. 233.

109 Aviso-Imperio, No. 287 (1860), p. 359; Aviso-Imperio, No. 28 (1882), p. 91.

110 Aviso-Imperio, No. 25 (1850), p. 354; Aviso-Imperio, No. 24 (1851), p. 354.

111 Aviso-Fazenda, 2 April 1855, p. 356; Aviso-Justiça, 13 January 1861, p. 255; Aviso-Justiça, 5 November 1862, p. 256.

112 Aviso-Imperio, No. 164/219 (1858), p. 87.

113 Aviso-Imperio, No. 587 (1860), p. 360; Aviso-Justiça, No. 33 (1873), p. 46; Aviso-Justiça, No. 71 (1878), p. 68.

114 Aviso-Justiça, No. 215 (1877), p. 67; Aviso-Imperio, 7 November 1862, p. 256.

115 Aviso-Justiça, No. 263 (1859), p. 359, Aviso-Justiça, 30 October 1861, p. 254; Aviso-Justiça, No. 17 (1882), p. 91.

116 Sinimbu has been cited as a landowner earlier in this volume. The Alagoan sugar planter and prime minister (1878–80) was a councillor of state. He was just one of a few landowners in the council.

117 José Murilo de Carvalho, "Elite and State-Building in Imperial Brazil," Ph.D. Dissertation, Stanford University (1975), p. 143. The Visconde de Araxá (Domiciano Leite Ribeiro) was appointed to the council in 1866, serving on it until his death in 1886. Araxá, an important landowner in the Paraíba Valley of Rio, was minister of war in 1864. On a different level, Martinho Campos, the Visconde do Uruguai, and his son Paulino José Soares de Sousa should be included in this category. Several other cases could be cited.

118 Ibid., p. 144.

119 Frances V. Moulder, *Japan, China, and the Modern World Economy: Toward a Reinterpretation of East Asian Development, ca. 1600 to ca. 1918* (Cambridge, Eng., 1977), pp. 17–18. For the absence of political parties in China, see Uricoechea, *The Patrimonial Foundations*, pp. 21–22; Karl A. Wittfogel, *Oriental Despotism* (New Haven, 1957), passim; Cho-Yun Hsu, "The Changing Relationship between Society and the Central Political Power in Former Han: 206 B.C.–8 A.D.," *CSSH* 7:3 (July 1965), pp. 358–70; and Robert M. Marsh, *The Mandarins: The Circulation of Elites in China, 1600–1900* (New York, 1961), esp. pp. 14–20.

9 Vagaries of Rich Nobles, Poor Nobles

1 Joseph L. Love, *São Paulo in the Brazilian Federation, 1889–1937* (Stanford, 1980), p. 84.

2 June Hahner, "Women and Work in Brazil, 1850–1920: A Preliminary Investigation," in *Essays Concerning the Socioeconomic History of Brazil and Portuguese India*, ed. Dauril Alden and Warren Dean (Gainesville, 1977), pp. 87–117; Francisco Gomes de Oliveira Neto, "Rendas, bicos de almofadas e tecidos usados pela mulher bahiana," *Anais do Primeiro Congresso de Historia da Bahia* 5 (Salvador, 1951), pp. 156–66.

3 Inventário do Barão de Guanabara (Baronesa de Guanabara, widow/inventariante)-1875, Cx 2625/No. 625, SPJ/ANRJ.

4 Inventário de Pedro Ferreira de Vianna Bandeira (Anna Francisca Vianna Bandeira, widow/inventariante)-1831, Capital, Maço 775, Vol. 9, and Inventário de Custódio Ferreira de Vianna Bandeira (Baronesa de Alenquer, widow/inventariante)-1872, 1º Ofício, Forum do Município de Santo Amaro, Bahia.

5 Partilha amigavel entre os herdeiros dos finados Barão e Baronesa de São João da Barra-1863, Cx 2765/No. 8384, SPJ/ANRJ.

6 Inventário do Barão de Saubara (Torquato José Barreto, son/inventariante)-1867, 2° Ofício, Forum do Município de Santo Amaro, Bahia.

7 Inventário do Visconde de Ipiabas (Barão de Ipiabas, son/inventariante)-1892, Maço 83/No. 2, 1° Ofício, Forum do Município de Valença, RJ.

8 Inventário do 2° Visconde de Jaguary (Viscondessa de Jaguary, wife/inventariante)-1883, Cx 2758/No. 1, SPJ/ANRJ.

9 Inventário da Baronesa de Lorena (Barão de Lorena, widower/inventariante)-1864, Cx 2641/No. 634, SPJ/ANRJ.

10 Inventário do Barão do Rio Preto (Baronesa do Rio Preto, widow/inventariante)-1876, Maço 32/Doc. 10-B, 2° Ofício, Forum do Município de Valença.

11 Inventário da 1ª Baronesa do Rio Bonito (2° Barão do Rio Bonito, son/inventariante)-1854, Cx 2641/No. 107, SPJ/ANRJ.

12 Inventário do Visconde do Rio Bonito (João Pereira Darrigue Faro, son/inventariante)-1859, Cx 2759/No. 964, SPJ/ANRJ. For Rio Bonito's role in the Rio-São Paulo Railroad, see Jornal do Brasil, 4 July 1977.

13 Inventário da Condessa da Piedade (Manuel Marques de Sá, son/inventariante)-1863, Cx 2767/No. 45, SPJ/ANRJ. For biographical information on Piedade, see "Titulares do imperio (ampliações e retificações)," AGB 7 (1945), pp. 225–33. Piedade's first husband was Manuel José Ribeiro de Oliviera. Daughter Maria Custodia married Eusébio de Queirós in 1835. The condessa wedded José Clemente that same year, and the couple had no children.

14 Inventário do Marquês de Paraná (the Marquesa de Paraná, widow/inventariante)-1856, Cx 2762/No. 3001, SPJ/ANRJ; José Wanderley de Araújo Pinho, Salões e damas do segundo reinado, 4th ed. (São Paulo, 1970), pp. 15–23, 117–27; Adolfo Morales de los Ríos, O Rio de Janeiro imperial (Rio, 1946), pp. 298–99.

15 Affonso de E. Taunay, "Um grande estadista—grande fazendeiro," MJC 3:1 (July 1938), pp. 71–75; C. F. van Delden Laerne, Brazil and Java: Report on Coffee-Culture in America, Asia, and Africa, to H.E. the Minister of the Colonies (London, 1885), p. 364.

16 Inventário do Marquês de Barbacena (Conde de Iguassu, son/inventariante)-1842, Cx 2619/No. 6075, SPJ/ANRJ.

17 Inventário do Visconde de Bom Retiro (João Pedreira do Couto Ferraz, brother/inventariante)-1886, Cx 2619/No. 8096, SPJ/ANRJ.

18 Inventário do Barão de Pindaré (Franklin Antônio da Costa Ferreira, son-inventariante)-1860, Cx 2764/No. 5964, SPJ/ANRJ. Pindaré was a senator from 1834 until his death in 1860.

19 Inventário do Barão de Uruguaiana (Baronesa de Uruguaiana, widow/inventariante)-1868, Cx 2756/No. 624, SPJ/ANRJ.

20 Certidão passada a requerimento verbal do Engenheiro Antonio Bittencourt Mariani (on the inventário of Cotegipe's father, who died in Barra, Bahia, in 1841), Lata 91/Pasta 43, ABC.

21 Inventário da Baronesa de Cotegipe (Barão de Cotegipe, widower/inventariante)-1867, Lata 92/Pasta 4, ABC; Inventário do Barão de Cotegipe (Antônia Thereza Wanderley, daughter/inventariante)-1889, Cx 3692/No. 8158, SPJ/ANRJ.

22 Inventário do Marquês de Monte Alegre (José Joaquim Rodrigues Lopes, nephew-in-law/inventariante)-1877, Cx 2762/No. 367, SPJ/ANRJ.

23 Inventário da Viscondessa de Nictheroy (Visconde de Nictheroy, widower/inventariante)-1880, Cx 2759/No. 246, SPJ/ANRJ.

24 For information on Sapucai's political career, see Brasil, Ministério da Justiça, Arquivo Nacional, *Organizações e programas ministeriais: regime parlamentar no império*, 2nd ed. (Rio, 1962), pp. 140–64; and Documentos Biográficos, I-12, 2, 29, SM/BNRJ. Inventário do Marquês de Sapucahy (Marquesa de Sapucahy, widow/inventariante)-1875, Cx 2762/No. 5284 and Inventário da Marquesa de Sapucahy (Manoel de Araújo da Cunha, son-in-law/inventariante)-1876, Cx 2768/No. 5287, SPJ/ANRJ.

25 Maria Laura Ribeiro, "O testamento do Conselheiro João Alfredo Correa de Oliveira," *AMHN* 19 (1968), pp. 140–64.

26 Documentos Biográficos, C1046, 68, SM/BNRJ.

27 On the marquês, see Documentos Biográficos, C1046, 68, SM/BNRJ. On the Conde de Mesquita, see "Relação dos baronatos," *AMI* (1945), p. 57; 1° Barão Smith de Vasconcellos (Rodolpho Smith de Vasconcellos) and 2° Barão Smith de Vasconcellos (Jayme Luiz Smith de Vasconcellos), *Archivo nobiliarchico brasileiro* (Lausanne, Switzerland, 1918), p. 286; and Documentos Biográficos, C25, 10, C1017, 54, C1010, 95, C1011, 37, SM/BNRJ. On the Barão de Mesquita, see Smith de Vasconcellos and Smith de Vasconcellos, p. 286. On the Barão de Bomfim, see ibid., pp. 84–85. Sentença cível de formal de partilha—Conde de Mesquita-1886, Cx 2760/No. 1754, SPJ/ANRJ.

28 Inventário da Viscondessa de Figueiredo (Conde de Figueiredo, widower/inventariante)-1887, Cx 2758/No. 350 1881[?], SPJ/ANRJ.

29 Inventário do Barão de Alegrete (José Francisco Bernardes, son-in-law/inventariante)-1871, Cx 10666, SPJ/ANRJ.

30 Testamento do Conde de Pereira Marinho (Condessa de Pereira Marinho, wife/testamenteira)-1884, Capital, Maço 130/Doc. 1, SJ/AEB.

31 Inventário da Condessa de Pereira Marinho (Visconde de Guahy, son/inventariante)-1889–1919, Capital, Maço 130A–130B/Doc. 2, SJ/AEB.

32 Inventário do Visconde dos Fiais (Pedro Ferreira de Vianna Bandeira, son-in-law/inventariante)-1863–1864, Capital, Maço 128/Doc. 1, SJ/AEB.

33 Cassiano Ricardo, *Marcha para oeste (a influência da "bandeira" na formação social e política do Brasil*, 2 vols. (Rio, 1959), 1:146–47.

34 Affonso de E. Taunay, "Faustos fazendeiros," *MJC* 4:1 (October 1938), p. 82. The planter who spent this sum was the Barão de Campo Belo. Taunay argued that the coffee planters in Rio ostentatiously showed off their wealth.

35 Inventário do Barão de Rezende (Severino Ribeiro de Souza Resende, brother/inventariante)-1901, Maço 40/No. 14, 2° Ofício, Forum do Município de Valença.

36 Inventário do Barão de Itapororoca (Baronesa de Itapororoca, widow/inventariante)-1836, Vila de São Francisco, Pasta 38/Doc. 18, AIGHBa.

37 Livro de Registro de Testamentos, 1879–1918, ff 6v-7 (Sergimirim), ASCMSA.

38 Ibid., ff. 30v-31, ASCMSA.

39 Ibid., ff. 44v-45, ASCMSA. Alenquer was a daughter of the First Barão do Rio das Contas. She had three children. The first son became the Visconde de Ferreira Bandeira, who married a German. The second and third sons married their cousins, daughters of the Second Barão do Rio das Contas and the Third Barão do Rio das Contas, respectively. "Titulares do imperio: parte genealogica," *AGB* 2 (1940), p. 85.

40 Visconde da Pedra Branca to Itapagipe, London, 27 May 1829, I-6, 13, 50; Pedro Affonso de Carvalho to Itapagipe, Copenhagen, 9 January 1833, I-6, 13, 51; Pedra Branca to Itapagipe, Paris, 12 September 1830, I-6, 13, 55; and Barão de Saude (son-in-law) to Itapagipe, Porto, 29 October 1838, I-6, 13, 40, ANG.

41 Inventário da Condessa de Itapagipe (General Francisco Xavier Calmon de Sá Cabral, son/inventariante)-1865, Cx 2767/No. 271, SPJ/ANRJ. For her Bahian ties, see Afonso Costa, "Monizes da Bahia," *RIHGB* 210 (January–March 1951), p. 151.

42 Testamento do Conde de Carapebus (Braz Carneiro Nogueira da Gama, brother-in-law/inventariante)-1896, Cx 2760/No. 6; Testamento da Condessa de Carapebus (Braz Carneiro Nogueira da Gama, brother/inventariante)-1896, Livro de testamentos de 1899, f. 9, SPJ/ANRJ. For biographical data on Carapebus, see Vasconcellos and Vasconcellos, *Archivo nobiliarchico*, pp. 110–13; and *Almanak Laemert 1861*, pp. 214–33 (Campos).

43 Inventário da Baronesa de Sorocaba (Boaventura Delfim Pereira, son-inventariante)-1857, Cx 2655/No. 3345, SPJ/ANRJ.

44 Inventário da Marquesa de Santos (Felício Pinto Coelho de Mendonça e Castro, son/inventariante)-1867, Cx 1811/No. 3764, 5 vols., SPJ/ANRJ.

45 Inventário do Visconde de Santa Teresa (João Rodrigues da Fonseca Jordão, son/inventariante)-1879, Cx 2757/No. 959; Inventário da Marquesa de Santo Amaro (Visconde de Santo Amaro, son/inventariante)-1851, Cx 2762/No. 173; Inventário da Viscondessa de Uberaba (Constança Lima Duarte, sister/inventariante)-1882, Cx 2759/No. 5061, SPJ/ANRJ. On the luxurious life-style that Santo Amaro once used to lead at the court, see Pinho, *Salões e damas*, pp. 22–23.

46 For debt settlement in court, see Dez Dias—Barão de S. Luiz contra José Gonçalves Portugal-1865, Maço 12/No. 14, 1° Ofício; Execução Hypotheca—Barão do Val Formoso, antes Leocardio Gomes Franklin contra Messiano Francisco da Matta e sua mulher—1888, Maço 28/No. 15, 2° Ofício; and Dez Dias—Barão de Val Formoso contra Miguel Affonso Coimbra—1888, Maço 28/No. 11, 2° Ofício, Forum do Município de Valença. These are only a few examples.

47 Brasil, Bahia State, *Anais do Arquivo Público da Bahia*, Vol. 37: *Livros de tutelas e inventários da Vila de São Francisco do Conde* (Bahia, 1962), pp. 9–11, 13, 16, 23–24, 26, 33–34.

48 Carvalho Moura, *Ensaios economicos* (Rio, 1885), cited in Vicente Licinio Cardoso, *A margem da historia do Brasil (livro postumo)* (São Paulo, 1933), pp. 144–45.

49 Taunay, "Faustos fazendeiros," p. 83; A. C. D'Araujo Guimarães, *A corte no Brasil* (Porto Alegre, 1936), p. 219.

50 Francisco Antônio de Paula was said to have been the first Nogueira da Gama to

settle in Valença. Leoni Iorio, *Valença de ontem e de hoje (subsídios a história do Município de Marquês de Valença, 1789–1952)* (Valença, 1952), pp. 17, 170.

51 Conde de Baependy, *Apontamentos biographicos da familia Braz Carneiro Leão do Rio de Janeiro*, separata da *Biographias de brasileiros ilustres por armas, letras, virtudes, etc.* (n.p., n.d.), pp. 380–84. See also "Titulares do imperio (retificações e ampliações)," *AGB* 4 (1942), pp. 38–39.

52 Inventário do Marquês de Baependy (Marquesa de Baependy, widow/inventariante)-1847, Maço 6/No. 11, 2° Ofício, Forum do Município de Valença.

53 Partilha amigavel—Marquesa de Baependy (Conde de Baependy e outros)-1869, Maço 25/No. 24, 1° Ofício, Forum do Município de Valença.

54 Inventário do Barão de Juparana (Francisco Nicolau Carneiro Nogueira da Gama, brother/inventariante)-1876, Maço 133/No. 3, 1° Ofício, Forum do Município de Valença.

55 José da Rocha de Azevedo (procurador) to ERM, Rio, 10 September 1853, Documentos Biográficos, C990, 38, SM/BNRJ.

56 Precatoria de contas—Barão de Santa Mônica—1884, Maço 40/No. 9, 1° Ofício, Forum do Município de Valença.

57 Inventário do Barão de Santa Mônica (Baronesa de Santa Mônica, widow/inventariante)-1887, Maço 89/No. 14, 1° Ofício, Forum do Município de Valença.

58 Iorio, *Valença*, p. 190.

59 Inscripção de verba testamentaria, Livro No. 47, f. 125, SPJ/ANRJ.

60 Reclamação Conde de Baependy—supplicante vs. Evaristo e Honorio, escravos do mesmo—supplicados, 1876, Maço 36/No. 29, 2° Ofício, Forum do Município de Valença, RJ.

61 Iorio, *Valença*, p. 191

62 Livro da Mordomia da Casa Imperial, vol. 13, 1884–1885, Registro de Officios, Livro 13, SAP/ANRJ.

63 Medição—Barão e Baronesa de Santa Justa e Barão e Baronesa de Nogueira da Gama-1880, Maço 62/No. 37, 1° Ofício, Forum do Município de Valença.

64 Inventário dos Viscondes de Nogueira da Gama (Baronesa de Moniz de Aragão, daughter/inventariante)-1898, Cx 2619/No. 1190, SPJ/ANRJ.

65 *O Porvir* (Valença, RJ), 13 August 1876.

66 Guimarães, *A corte no Brasil*, p. 141; Brasil, Senado do Império, *Annaes do Senado do Imperio do Brasil. Terceiro Anno da Decima Legislativa. Sessão de 1859 de 10 de Maio a 30 de Junho*, Vol. 1 (Rio, 1859), p. 180.

67 Bernardo Pereira de Vasconcellos, *Cartas aos senhores eleitores da provincia de Minas Gerais*, 2nd ed. (Rio, 1899), pp. 58–60; Carvalho Moura, *Ensaios economicos*, in Cardoso, *A margem da historia*, p. 144.

68 Rui Vieira da Cunha, *Figuras e fatos da nobreza brasileira* (Rio, 1975), pp. 81–171.

Glossary

Adelantado: Chief of a conquering expedition; chief administrator of a conquered province.

Agregado: Tenant; sharecropper.

Água Portável: Running water.

Alqueire: Volume measure in Brazil, 13.8 liters; measurement of land: 48,400 m² in Goiás, Minas Gerais, and Rio de Janeiro; 24,200 m² in São Paulo.

Amazona Bárbara: Huge woman; untamed amazon.

Arroba: Brazilian weight measuring 15 kilograms.

Bacharel: Law-school graduate.

Bandeira: Pathfinding expedition to the interior that originated in colonial São Paulo.

Bandeirante: Member of a *bandeira*; in modern usage, an inhabitant of the state of São Paulo.

Beija-Mão: Ritual in which subjects kiss the hand of their sovereign.

Brazão da Arma: Coat of arms reserved for nobles.

Cabotagem: Coastal navigation and trade.

Cachaça: Brazilian rum made of sugar.

Câmara do Senado: Municipal council in colonial times.

Capitania: Colonial captaincy, an administrative territory held or governed by a donatory or lord proprietor.

Carta de Nobreza: Patent of nobiliary title.

Cartório da Nobreza: Chancery for the registration of nobility titles and coats of arms.

Caudillo: Spanish-American regional or national warlord.

Charque: Jerked or dried beef.

Colono: Immigrant worker, usually European.

Com Honras de Grandeza: "With honors of grandee," an honor sometimes accompanying a title of nobility.

Comarca: Judicial district, often consisting of two or three municípios.

Comissário: Commission agent for sugar or coffee and also source of agricultural capital.

Concunhado: Husband of wife's sister.

Consulta: Consultation; report of consultation.

Coronelismo: Rule by a *coronel;* an institution dominated by one man in politics, society, and economy in Brazil between ca. 1850 and 1950.

Corpos Sociais: Social groups or social corporations.

Criollo (Creole in Spanish): New World-born of Spanish parents.

Crioulo: New World-born black, servile or free; any black man in a pejorative sense.

Cruzado: Portuguese colonial monetary unit.

Dama: Dame in the service of the imperial house; lady-in-waiting for empress.

Dedução: Deduction; amount of debt and expenses deducted from an inventory of wealth.

Delegado de Polícia: County police chief.

Deputado geral: Member of the lower chamber of the imperial parliament.

Desembargador: Judge serving on appeals or supreme court.

Dignitário: Rank in several honorific orders.

Donatário: Colonial lord proprietor; donatory of a captaincy.

Dotação: Gift by grant from parent or state; parliamentary grant of annuity for the imperial family; dowry.

Engenho: Sugar mill or sugar plantation.

Fábrica: Factory; sugar refinery.

Farinha de Mandioca: Manioc flour.

Fazenda: Ranch or plantation.

Fazendeiro: Rancher or planter.

Fidalgo: Gentleman or noble by birthright (in Portugal, the right to nobility by birth was for three lives).

Fidalguia: Status of gentleman or noble by birthright.

Fidei Commuissum: Entail; unalienable family or clan property.

Foro: Privilege granted by the Crown to corporate groups, such as fidalgos, the church, and the military.

Fuero: Privilege of a corporate group in Spain and Spanish America.

Graças Honoríficas: Honorific commendations.

Hidalgo: Gentleman or noble by birthright in Spain and Spanish America.

Hidalguia: Status of gentleman or noble by birthright.

Imperialismo: Imperialism; supremacy of Braganza rule in Brazilian politics.

Inventariante: Executor or executrix of a legacy.

Inventário: List of property inventoried by a probate court to be divided by legal heirs.

Juiz de Direito: District judge in charge of a *comarca.*

Legua: League: in Brazil, 6,000 to 6,600 meters, depending on region.

Letrado: A university-trained governmental official, usually a law-school or seminary graduate, in the colonial service as a royal administrator.

Líquido: Assets after debts, court expenses, and other claims are deducted from a legacy or property.

Maiorista: Supporter of Pedro II's "majority" claim in 1840.

Mayorazgo: Primogeniture in Spain and Spanish America; first-born male; heir to family wealth.

Mazombo: New World-born of Portuguese parents.

Meiação: Half of the property belonging to a surviving spouse or heir.

Moço Fidalgo: "Young gentleman," a title given to a noble offspring by the imperial house.

Monte Mor: Total wealth inventoried by a probate court.

Morgado: Primogeniture in Portugal and Brazil, first-born male child; heir to family wealth.

Município: Lowest administrative unit, the equivalent of a county.

Nobreza: Nobility.

Nobreza Civil: Nobility of civil or military service.

Nobreza Natural: Nobility by hereditary claim and distinguished lineage.

Nobreza Teológica: Nobility created and living by the grace of God.

Novos Ricos: New money; nouveaux riches.

Ordem Privada: Private order; status of private control over a territory or region where a landlord exercised absolute power.

Peninsular: Person from Iberia.

Poder Moderador: Moderating power granted to the emperor, one of the four constitutional powers in imperial Brazil.

Prevedor: Chief administrator of a religious charity house.

Primogenitor: First-born male heir entitled to inheriting the entailed family wealth.

Promotor Público: County prosecutor.

Quinhão: Share of inherited legacy or property.

Resolução Imperial: Imperial decision; decision recommended by the Council of State to the emperor.

Sem Honras de Grandeza: Without honors of grandee.

Senador do Império: Senator of the empire (once selected, served for life).

Senhor de Engenho: Sugar planter; sugar mill owner.

Señorío: Right to or jurisdiction over land in Spain and Spanish America.

Sentinela Vitalícia: Life-tenure guard; indirect reference to the imperial senate and Council of State, which served as sentinels for the emperor.

Senzala: Slave quarter.

Sertão: Backland or hinterland.

Sesmaria: Portuguese colonial land grant.

Sesmeiro: Holder of a *sesmaria.*

Sobrado: Urban mansion.

Terra Boa: Literally "good land"; an endearing name for Bahia.

Terras Maninhas: Barren lands.

Titular: Titleholder; any headman or chief.

Título: Title.

Travessas: Narrow streets that connect main avenues.

Tropeiro: Operator of a mule train (*tropa*).

Turma: Graduating class.

Veador: Chamberlain for the empress; also *viador.*

Vitalicidade: Life tenure.

Bibliography

I. Public and Private Archives

BRAZIL

Arquivo do Barão de Cotegipe. Rio de Janeiro. (ABC)

Arquivo do Conde de Subaé. Rio de Janeiro. (ACS)

Arquivo de Ernesto Aleixo Boulanger. Rio de Janeiro. (AFAB)

Arquivo do Estado da Bahia. Salvador, Bahia. (AEB)

Arquivo do Estado do Rio de Janeiro. Niterói. (AERJ)

Arquivo do Estado de São Paulo. São Paulo. (DAE/SP)

Arquivo Histórico de Goiás. Goiânia. (AHGO)

Arquivo do Instituto Histórico e Geográfico Brasileiro. Rio de Janeiro. (AIHGB)

Arquivo de João Ferreira de Araújo Pinho. Rio de Janeiro. (AJFAP)

Arquivo de José Wanderley de Araújo Pinho. Rio de Janeiro. (AJWAP)

Arquivo do Museu Imperial. Petrópolis. (AMI)

Arquivo do Museu Paulista. Universidade de São Paulo. (AMP/USP)

Arquivo Nacional, Rio de Janeiro. (ANRJ)

Arquivo de Nogueira da Gama. Rio de Janeiro. (ANG)

Arquivo do 1° Ofício, Forum do Município de Santo Amaro, Bahia.

Arquivo do 1° Ofício, Forum do Município de Valença. Rio de Janeiro.

Arquivo do 2° Ofício, Forum do Município de Valença. Rio de Janeiro.

Arquivo do Senado Federal. Brasília. (ASF)

Arquivo da Viscondessa de Cavalcante. Rio de Janeiro (AVC)

Arquivo do Visconde de Ourém. Rio de Janeiro. (AVO)

Cartório de Registro de Imóveis e Hipotecas, Comarca de Santo Amaro, Bahia.

GREAT BRITAIN

Public Record Office. Foreign Office. PRO/FO. General Correspondence. Brazil. 1825–28. Microfilm.

UNITED STATES

Genealogical Society of Utah. Salt Lake City. (GSU)

II. Almanacs and Newspapers

Almanak administrativo, mercantil e industrial da corte e provincia do Rio de Janeiro. 1850–90. Rio de Janeiro: Editores Eduardo e Henrique Laemmert, 1850–90.

Almanak da Provincia de São Paulo administrativo, commercial e industrial para 1873. São Paulo: n.p., 1873.

Almanach da Provincia de São Paulo administrativo, commercial e industrial para 1888. Jorge Seckler, org. São Paulo: Jorge Seckler e Cia. 1888.

Brasil. Assemblea Constituinte. *Diario da Assemblea Geral, Constituinte e Legislativa do Imperio do Brasil.* Rio de Janeiro, 1823.

Jornal do Brasil. Rio de Janeiro.

Mensario do Jornal do Commercio. Rio de Janeiro.

O Porvir. Valença, Rio de Janeiro.

A Republica. Rio de Janeiro.

Veja. São Paulo.

III. Books, Monographs, Articles, and Theses

Aguiar, Pinto de. *A abertura dos portos do Brasil: Cairu e os inglêses.* Salvador: Livraria Progresso Editora, 1960.

Aguiar, Pinto de. *Bancos no Brasil colonial.* Salvador: Livraria Progresso Editora, 1960.

Albuquerque, Ulysses Lins de. *Um sertanejo e o sertão: memórias.* Rio de Janeiro: Livraria José Olympio Editora, 1957.

Alden, Dauril. *Royal Government in Colonial Brazil with Special Reference to the Administration of the Marquis de Lavradio, Viceroy, 1769–1779.* Berkeley: University of California Press, 1968.

Almeida, Antônio da Rocha. *Vultos da pátria.* 4 vols. Rio de Janeiro and Porto Alegre: Editora Globo, 1965.

Almeida, Romulo. *Traços da história econômica da Bahia no último século e meio.* Salvador: Instituto de Economica e Finanças da Bahia, 1951.

Amaral Júnior, Rubem. "Os falsos títulos de nobreza do império do Brasil na Cisplatina." *Mensário do Arquivo Nacional* (March 1979): 11–17.

Andrade, Manuel Correia de. *A terra e o homem no nordeste.* 3rd ed. São Paulo: Brasiliense, 1973.

Andreoni, João Antônio (pseud. André João Antonil). *Cultura e opulência do Brasil*. Introduction by Alice Piffer Canabrava. São Paulo: Companhia Editora Nacional, 1967.

Araripe, Tristão de Alencar. "Pater-familias no Brasil nos tempos coloniaes: memoria lida em sessão do Instituto Historico e Geografico Brasilieiro de 4 de Setembro de 1880." *Revista do Instituto Historico e Geografico Brasileiro* 52:2 (1893): 15–23.

Azevedo, Aroldo de. *Arnolfo Azevedo: parlamentar da primeira república 1868–1942*. São Paulo: Companhia Editora Nacional, 1968.

_____. "O vale do Paraíba (trecho paulista)." *Anais: IX Congresso Brasileiro de Geographia 1940* (Rio, 1944): 5: 573–87.

Baependy, Conde de. *Apontamentos biographicos da familia Braz Carneiro Leão do Rio de Janeiro*, separata da *Biographias de brasileiros ilustres por armas, letras, virtudes, etc.* N.p., n.d.

Barman, Roderick James. "Brazil at Mid-Empire: Political Accommodation and the Pursuit of Progress under the Conciliation Ministry, 1853–1857." Ph.D. Dissertation. University of California, Berkeley, 1970.

_____. "A New-World Nobility: The Role of Titles in Imperial Brazil." In *University of British Columbia Hispanic Studies*. Edited by Harold Livermore. London: Tamesis Books Limited, 1974. pp. 39–50.

_____. "Uma nobreza no novo mundo: a função dos títulos do Brasil imperial." Translated by Stanley E. Hilton. *Mensário do Arquivo Nacional* 4 (June 1973): 4–21.

Barman, Roderick James, and Jean Barman. "The Role of the Law Graduates in the Political Elite of Imperial Brazil." *Journal of Inter-American Studies and World Affairs* 18:4 (November 1981): 423–49.

Barreto, Carlos Xavier Paes. *Os primitivos colonizadores nordestinos e seus descendentes*. Rio de Janeiro: A Noite, 1960.

Barreto Filho, João Paulo de Mello, and Hermeto Lima. *Historia da policia do Rio de Janeiro: Aspectos da cidade e vida carioca*. 3 vols. Rio de Janeiro: A Noite, 1939.

Bastos, Tavares A. C. *A província: estudo sobre a descentralização no Brasil*. 3rd ed. São Paulo: Companhia Editora Nacional, 1975.

Becorud, Jean. "Noblesse et representation parlamentaire: les députés de 1871 a 1968." *Revue Française de Science Politique* 23:5 (October 1973): 972–93.

Belchior, Elysio de Oliveira. *Visconde de Cairu: Sua vida e sua obra*. Rio de Janeiro: Confederação Nacional do Comércio, 1959.

Bendix, Reinhard. *Kings or People: Power and the Mandate to Rule*. Berkeley: University of California Press, 1978.

Bethell, Leslie. *The Abolition of the Brazilian Slave Trade: Britain, Brazil, and the Slave Trade Question, 1807–1869*. Cambridge, Eng.: At the University Press, 1970.

Blake, Augusto Victorino Alves Sacramento. *Diccionario bibliographico brazileiro*. 7 vols. Rio de Janeiro: Typographia Nacional, 1883–1902.

Bloch, Marc. *Feudal Society.* Translated by L. A. Manyon. 2 vols. Chicago: University of Chicago Press, 1964.

Blum, Jerome. *The End of the Old Order in Rural Europe.* Princeton: Princeton University Press, 1978.

_____. *Lord and Peasant in Russia from the Ninth to the Nineteenth Century.* Princeton: Princeton University Press, 1961.

Boxer, C. R. *Four Centuries of Portuguese Expansion, 1415–1825: A Succinct Survey.* Berkeley: University of California Press; Johannesburg: Witwatersrand University Press, 1969.

_____. *The Golden Age of Brazil, 1695–1750: Growing Pains of a Colonial Society.* Berkeley: University of California Press, 1962.

_____. *The Portuguese Seaborne Empire, 1415–1825.* New York: Alfred A. Knopf, 1969.

Brading, David A. *Miners and Merchants in Bourbon Mexico, 1763–1810.* Cambridge, Eng.: At the University Press, 1971.

Braudel, Fernand. *The Mediterranean and the Mediterranean World in the Age of Phillip II.* Translated by Sian Reynolds. 2 vols. New York: Harper & Row, Publishers, 1976.

Brazil. Bahia State. *Anais do Arquivo Público da Bahia.* Vol. 37. *Livros de tutelas e inventários da Vila de São Francisco do Conde.* Bahia: Arquivo Público do Estado da Bahia, 1962.

_____. Caroatá, José Prospero Jehova da Silva, org. *Imperiaes resoluções tomadas sobre consultas da Secção de Justiça do Conselho de Estado, desde o anno de 1842, em que começou a funcionar o mesmo conselho até hoje colligidas em virtude de autorisação do Exmo. Sr. Conselheiro Manoel Pinto de Souza Dantas, ex-Ministro e Secretario de Estado dos Negocios da Justiça.* 2 vols. Rio de Janeiro: B. L. Garnier, 1884.

_____. *Falas do trono desde o ano de 1823 ate o ano de 1889.* 2nd ed. São Paulo: Edições Melhoramentos, 1977.

_____. Departmento Nacional do Café. *O café no segundo centenário de sua introdução no Brasil.* 2 vols. Rio de Janeiro, 1934.

_____. Ministério do Império. *Relatorio do Imperio.* Various years.

_____. Ministério da Justiça. Arquivo Nacional. *As câmaras municipais e a independência.* 2 vols. Rio de Janeiro, 1972.

_____. Ministério da Justiça. Arquivo Nacional. *As juntas governativas e a independência.* 3 vols. Rio de Janeiro, 1975.

_____. Ministério da Justiça. Arquivo Nacional. *Organizações e programas ministeriais: regime parlamentar no império.* 2nd ed. Rio de Janeiro, 1962.

_____. Rio de Janeiro Province. Câmara Municipal de Valença. *Lista dos cidadãos qualificados da Freguezia de Ipiabas do municipio de Valença no anno de 1879.* Rio de Janeiro: Typo. do Apostolo, 1879.

_____. Rio de Janeiro Province. Câmara Municipal de Valença. *Lista dos cidadãos qualificados da Freguezia de N.S. da Gloria do municipio de Valença no anno de 1879.* Rio de Janeiro: Typo. do Apostolo, 1879.

_____. Rio de Janeiro Province. Câmara Municipal de Valença. *Lista dos ci-*

dadãos qualificados da Freguezia de Santo Antonio do Rio Bonito do muni-cipio de Valença no anno de 1879. Rio de Janeiro: Typo. do Apostolo, 1879.

Brito, João Rodrigues de. *Cartas economico-politicas sobre a agricultura, e commercio da Bahia.* Bahia: Imprensa do Estado, 1924.

Brotero, Frederico de Barros. *A familia Monteiro de Barros.* São Paulo: n.p., 1951.

Bueno, José Antonio Pimenta. *Direito publico brasileiro e analyse da constituição do imperio.* Rio de Janeiro: Imp. E Const. de J. Villeneuve e C., 1857.

Bulcão Sobrinho, Antônio de Araújo de Aragão. *Famílias bahianas: Bulcão.* 3 vols. Salvador: Instituto Genealógico Bahiano, 1961.

Burns, E. Bradford. *A History of Brazil.* 2nd ed. New York: Columbia University Press, 1980.

————, ed. *A Documentary History of Brazil.* New York: Alfred A. Knopf, 1966.

Caldas, José Antônio. *Noticia geral de toda esta capitania da Bahia desde o seu descobrimento ao prezte anno de 1750.* Facsimile ed. Bahia: Tipografia Beneditina, 1951.

Calmon, Pedro. *Historia da Casa da Torre.* Rio de Janeiro: Livraria José Olympio Editora, 1939.

————. *História de D. Pedro II.* 5 vols. Rio de Janeiro: Livraria José Olympio Editora, 1975.

Calogeras, João Pandiá. *A politica exterior do imperio.* 3 vols. Rio de Janeiro: Imprensa Nacional, 1927–33.

Cardoso, Ciro Flamarion S. *Agricultura, escravidão e capitalismo.* Petrópolis: Vozes, 1979.

————. *Economia e sociedade em áreas colonais e periféricas: Guiana Francesa e Pará (1750–1817).* Rio: Graal, 1984.

Cardoso, Vicente Licinio. *A margem da historia do Brasil (livro postumo).* São Paulo: Companhia Editoria Nacional, 1933.

Carvalho, Affonso de. *Caxias.* Rio de Janeiro: Biblioteca do Exército, 1976.

Carvalho, José Murilo de. *A construção da ordem: a elite politica imperial.* Brasilia: Editora Universidade de Brasília, 1980.

————. "Elite and State-Building in Imperial Brazil." Ph.D. Dissertation, Stanford University, 1975.

————. "Political Elites and State Building: The Case of Nineteenth-Century Brazil." *Comparative Studies of Society and History* 24:3 (July 1982): 378–99.

Cascudo, Luis da Camara. *O Marquez de Olinda e seu tempo (1793–1870).* São Paulo: Companhia Editora Nacional, 1938.

Castro, M. Vianna de. *A aristocracia rural fluminense.* Rio de Janeiro: Grafica Laemmert, 1961.

Cavalcante, Viscondessa de. "Pequeno Diccionario Biografico Brasileiro." Manuscript. N.d., n.p. In Seção de Manuscritos, Biblioteca Nacional, Rio de Janeiro.

Centro Liberal. *Manifesto do Centro Liberal.* Rio de Janeiro: Typ. Americana, 1869.

Chagas, Paulino Pinheiro. *Teófilo Ottoni: ministro do povo.* 2nd ed. Rio de Janeiro: Livraria São Jose, 1956.

Chandler, Charles Lydon. "Commercial Relations between the United States and Brazil." *Anais do Congresso Internacional de Historia da America* 1 (1922): 397–414.

Corrêa, Francisco António. *História económica de Portugal.* 2 vols. Lisboa: Empresa Nacional de Publicidade, 1929.

Costa, Affonso (Afonso). "Genealogia baiana." *Revista do Instituto Histórico e Geográfico Brasileiro* 191 (April–June 1963): 3–279.

_____. "Monizes da Bahia." *Revista do Instituto Histórico e Geográfico Brasileiro* 210 (January–March 1951): 114–56.

Costa, Craveiro. *O Visconde de Sinimbu: Sua vida e sua atuação na politica nacional (1840–1889).* São Paulo: Cia. Editora Nacional. 1937.

Costa, Emília Viotti da. *Da monarquia à república: momentos decisivos.* São Paulo: Editorial Grijalbo, 1977.

_____. *Da senzala à colônia.* São Paulo: DIFEL, 1966 .

Costa, Francisco Augusto Pereira da. *Diccionario biographico de pernambucanos celebres.* Recife: Typographia Universal, 1882.

Costa, Sergio Correa da. *Every Inch a King: A Biography of Dom Pedro I, First Emperor of Brazil.* Translated by Samuel Putnam. New York: The MacMillan Co., 1950.

Cotegipe, João Mauricio Wanderley, Barão de. *Descripção do aparelho de fabricar assucar assentado no Engenho Jacarancanga propriedade do Barão de Cotegipe—Bahia apresentada pelo mesmo Exmo. Sr. ao Imperial Instituto Fluminense de Agricultura.* Rio de Janeiro: n.p., 1867.

Cunha, Rui Vieira da. *Estudos da nobreza brasileira.* 2 vols. Rio de Janeiro: Arquivo Nacional, 1966–69.

_____. *Figuras e fatos da nobreza brasileira.* Rio de Janeiro: Arquivo Nacional, 1975.

Curtin, Philip D. *The Atlantic Slave Trade: A Census.* Madison: University of Wisconsin Press, 1969.

Davatz, Thomas. *Memórias de um colono no Brasil* (1850). Introduction by Sérgio Buarque de Holanda. São Paulo: USP, 1972.

Dean, Warren. *Rio Claro: A Brazilian Plantation System, 1820–1920.* Stanford: Stanford University Press, 1976.

Dé Carli, Gileno. *A evolução do problema canavieiro fluminense.* Rio de Janeiro: Irmãos Pongetti, 1942.

Diegues Junior, Manuel. *O banguê nas Alagoas: traços da influência do sistema econômico do engenho de açúcar na vida e na cultura regional.* Rio de Janeiro: Instituto de Açúcar e Álcool, 1949.

_____. "O engenho de açúcar no século XVI (produção intensiva. O panorama econômico do açúcar no mundo)." *Anais do IV Congresso de História Nacional* (1950): 5:531–52.

Dorn, Walter L. *Competition for Empire, 1740–1763.* New York: Harper & Row, Publishers, 1963.

Dunn, Richard S. *Sugar and Slaves: The Rise of the Planter Class in the English West Indies, 1624–1713.* New York: W. W. Norton, 1973.

Economia açucareira da Bahia em 1820. Cartas de Feliberto Caldeira Brant Pontes (Marquês de Barbacena). Rio de Janeiro: Arquivo Nacional, 1973.

Eisenberg, Peter L. *The Sugar Industry in Pernambuco, 1840–1910: Modernization without Change.* Berkeley: University of California Press, 1974.

Emmons, Terence. *The Russian Landed Gentry and the Peasant Emancipation of 1861.* Cambridge, Eng.: At the University Press, 1968.

"Familias reaes: familia imperial brasileira (reinante no Brasil, de 1822 a 1889)." *Annuario Genealogico Brasileiro* 1 (1939): 5–140.

Faoro, Raymundo. *Machado de Assis: a pirâmide e o trapézio.* São Paulo: Companhia Editora Nacional, 1976.

————. *Os donos do poder.* 2 vols. 2nd ed. Porto Alegre and São Paulo: Globo/ Universidade de São Paulo, 1975.

Fenoaltea, Stefano. "Slavery and Supervision in Comparative Perspective: A Model." *Journal of Economic History* 44:3 (September 1984): 635–68.

Filler, Victor Morris. "Liberalism in Imperial Brazil: The Regional Rebellions of 1842." Ph.D. Dissertation, Stanford University, 1976.

Fleiuss, Max. *Historia administrativa do Brasil.* 2nd ed. São Paulo: Cia. Melhoramento de São Paulo, 1922.

Fonseca, Antonio José Victoriano Borges da. *Nobiliarquia pernambucana.* 2 vols. Rio de Janeiro: Biblioteca Nacional, 1935.

Forster, Robert. *The Nobility of Toulouse in the Eighteenth Century: A Social and Economic Study.* Baltimore: Johns Hopkins University Press, 1960.

Fox, Robin. *Kinship and Marriage: An Anthropological Perspective.* Hammonsworth, Eng.: Pelican Books, 1967.

Fragoso, Tasso. *A batalha do Passo do Rosário.* Rio de Janeiro: Imprensa Militar, 1922.

Freyre, Gilberto. *The Mansions and Shanties (sobrados e mucambos): The Making of Modern Brazil.* Translated by Harriet de Onis. New York: Alfred A. Knopf, 1963.

Fried, Morton H. *The Evolution of Political Society: An Essay in Political Anthropology.* New York: Random House, 1967.

Furtado, Celso. *The Economic Growth of Brazil: A Survey from Colonial to Modern Times.* Translated by Ricardo W. de Aguiar and Eric Charles Drysdale. Berkeley: University of California Press, 1963; paperback 1968.

Galvão, Miguel Arcanjo. *Relação dos cidadãos que tomaram parte no govêrno do Brasil no período de março de 1808 a 15 de novembro de 1889.* 2nd ed. Rio de Janeiro: Arquivo Nacional, 1969.

Gama, José da Saldanha da. "Historia da Imperial Fazenda de Santa Cruz." *Revista do Instituto Histórico e Geográfico Brasileiro* 38 (1875): 165–230.

Genovese, Eugene D. *Roll, Jordan, Roll: The World the Slaves Made.* New York: Pantheon Books, 1972.

Gerschenkron, Alexander. *Economic Backwardness in Historical Perspective.* New York: Praeger Publishers, 1962.

Goodwin, Albert, ed. *The European Nobility in the Eighteenth Century: Studies of the Nobilities of the Major European States in the Pre-Reform Era.* New York: Harper & Row, Publishers, 1967.

Goody, Jack, ed. *The Character of Kinship.* Cambridge, Eng.: At the University Press, 1973.

Graham, Richard. "Slavery and Economic Development: Brazil and the United States South in the Nineteenth Century." *Comparative Studies in Society and History* 23:4 (October 1981): 620–55.

Great Britain. *The Parliamentary Debates: The Parliamentary History of England.* Vol. XVIII. London: T. C. Hansard, Publisher, 1828.

———. Foreign Office. *British and Foreign State Papers, 1827–1828.* London: James Ridgeway and Sons, 1829.

Guimarães, Alberto Carlos de Araujo (D'Araujo). "Acção cultural e politica no governo de D. João VI." *Anais do Terceiro Congresso de Historia Nacional* 3 (October 1938): 274–79.

———. *A corte no Brasil.* Porto Alegre: Livraria do Globo, 1936.

Gutman, Hubert G. *The Black Family in Slavery and Freedom, 1750–1925.* New York: Pantheon Books, 1976.

Haring, C. H. *Empire in Brazil: A New World Experiment with Monarchy.* Cambridge, Mass.: Harvard University Press, 1958.

Herrmann, Lucilla. "Evolução da estrutura social de Guaratinguetá num periodo de trezentos anos." *Revista de Administração* 2 (March–June 1948): 3–326.

Hexter, J. H. *Reappraisal in History: New Views on History and Society in Early Modern Europe.* New York: Harper & Row, Publishers, 1963 [1961].

Hobsbawm, E. J. *Industry and Empire from 1750 to the Present Day.* Harmondsworth, Eng.: Pelican Books, 1974 [1968].

Holanda, Sérgio Buarque de. *Raízes do Brasil.* 3rd ed. Rio de Janeiro: Livraria José Olympio Editora, 1956.

Holanda, Sérgio Buarque de, org. *História Geral da Civilização Brasileira.* 12 vols. São Paulo: DIFEL, 1960–85.

Hsu, Cho-Yun. "The Changing Relationship between Society and the Central Political Power in Former Han: 206 B.C.–8 A.D." *Comparative Studies in Society and History* 7:3 (July 1965): 358–70.

Hsu, F. L. K. *Clan, Caste, and Club.* Princeton: D. Van Nostrand, 1963.

Huizinga, Johan. *The Waning of the Middle Ages: A Study of the Form of Life, Thought, and Art in France and the Netherlands in the Dawn of the Renaissance in the XIVth and XVth Centuries.* Garden City, N.Y.: Anchor Books, 1954.

Iorio, Leoni. *Valença de ontem e de hoje (subsídios a história do Município de Marquês de Valença, 1789–1952.* Valença: Jornal de Valença, 1952.

Ipanema, Cybelle de, org. *D. Pedro I, proclamações, cartas e artigos de imprensa.* Rio de Janeiro: Imprensa Nacional, 1972.

Jansen, José. "Introdução ao nobiliário maranhense." *Anuário do Museu Histórico Nacional* 21 (1969): 165–69.

Jarnagin, Laura. "The Role and Structure of the Brazilian Imperial Nobility in Society and Politics." *Anais do Museu Paulista* 29 (1979): 99–157.

Keith, Henry H., and S. Fred Edwards, eds. *Conflict and Continuity in Brazilian Society.* Columbia, S.C.: University of South Carolina Press, 1969.

Ladd, Doris M. *The Mexican Nobility at Independence, 1780–1826.* Austin, Tex.: University of Texas Press, 1976.

Laerne, C. F. van Delden. *Brazil and Java: Report on Coffee-Culture in America, Asia, and Africa, to H.E. the Minister of the Colonies.* London: W. H. Allen & Co., 1885.

Lamego, Alberto Ribeiro. *A terra goyataca.* 4 vols. Rio de Janeiro: Livraria Garnier, 1941.

—————. *O homem e o brejo.* Rio de Janeiro: IBGE-Conselho Nacional de Geografia, 1945.

—————. *O homem e a guanabara.* 2nd ed. Rio de Janeiro: IBGE, 1964.

—————. *O homem e a serra,* 2nd ed. Rio de Janeiro: IBGE-Conselho Nacional de Geografia, 1963.

—————. "O tronco de Caxias." *Mensario do Jornal do Commercio* 4:1 (October 1938): 133–36.

Leal, Aureliano. *Historia constitucional do Brasil.* Rio de Janeiro: Imprensa Nacional, 1915.

Leal, Aurelino. *Do Acto Addicional a maioridade (historia constitucional e politica).* Rio de Janeiro: n.p., 1915.

Leithold, T. von, and L. von Rango. *O Rio de Janeiro visto por dois prussianos em 1819.* Translated by Joaquim de Sousa Leão Filho. São Paulo: Companhia Editora Nacional, 1966.

Leitman, Spencer. *Raízes sócio-econômicas da Guerra dos Farrapos.* Translated by Sarita Linhares Barsted. Rio de Janeiro: Graal, 1979.

Lenharo, Alcir. *As tropas da moderação (o abastecimento da corte na formação política do Brasil—1808–1842).* São Paulo: Edições Símbolos, 1979.

Leonzo, Nanci. "Um empresário nas milícias paulistas: o Brigadeiro Luís Antônio de Souza." *Anais do Museu Paulista* 30 (1980/1981): 241–54.

Lima, Manuel de Oliviera. *Dom João VI no Brasil, 1808–1821.* 3 vols. Rio de Janeiro: Livraria José Olympio, 1945.

Livermore, H.V. *A New History of Portugal.* 2nd ed. Cambridge, Eng.: At the University Press, 1976.

Lockhart, James. *Spanish Peru, 1532–1560: A Colonial Society.* Madison: University of Wisconsin Press, 1968.

Lynch, John. *The Spanish-American Revolutions, 1808–1826.* New York: W. W. Norton & Company, 1973.

Lyra, Augusto Tavares de. *Organização política e administração do Brasil (colonia, imperio, e republica).* São Paulo: Companhia Editora Nacional, 1941.

—————. "Os ministros de estado da independência à república." *Revista do Instituto Histórico e Geográfico Brasileiro* 193 (October–December 1946): 3–104.

Lyra, Heitor. *Historia do Dom Pedro II, 1825–1891.* 3 vols. São Paulo: Companhia Editora Nacional, 1938.

_____. *História da queda do império.* 2 vols. São Paulo: Companhia Editora Nacional, 1964.

Magalhães Junior, R. *O império em chinelos.* Rio de Janeiro: Editora Civilização Brasileira, 1957.

Maia, Manoel Augusto Velho da Motta. *O conde de Motta Maia, medico e amigo dedicado de d. Pedro Segundo.* Rio de Janeiro: Livraria Francisco Alves, 1937.

Maier, Joseph, and Richard W. Weatherhead, eds. *Politics of Change in Latin America.* New York: Frederick A. Praeger, Publishers, 1964.

Mannheim, Karl. *Ideology and Utopia: An Introduction to the Sociology of Knowledge.* New York: Harvest Books, 1955.

Marchant, Anyda. *Visconde Mauá and the Empire of Brazil.* Berkeley: University of California Press, 1965.

Marsh, Robert M. *The Mandarins: The Circulation of Elites in China, 1600–1900.* New York: The Free Press, 1961.

Martins, Roberto Borges. "Growing in Silence: The Slave Economy of Nineteenth-Century Minas Gerais, Brazil." Ph.D. Dissertation, Vanderbilt University, 1980.

Martins Filho, Amilcar, and Roberto B. Martins. "Slavery in a Nonexport Economy: Nineteenth-Century Minas Gerais Revisited." *Hispanic American Historical Review* 63:3 (August 1983): 537–68.

Martins Filho, Eneas. *O Conselho de Estado Português e a transformação da família real em 1807.* Rio de Janeiro: Arquivo Nacional, 1968.

Matos, Odilon Nogueira de. *Café e ferrovias: A evolução ferroviária de São Paulo e o desenvolvimento da cultura cafeeira.* São Paulo: Editora Alfa-Omega, 1974.

Mattos, Waldemar. *Panorama econômica da Bahia 1808–1960.* Salvador: Associação Comercial da Bahia, 1960.

Mattoso, Kátia M. de Queirós. *Bahia: a cidade do Salvador e seu mercado no século XIX.* São Paulo: Editora HUCITEC, 1978.

Maximiliano (Principe de Wied-Neuwied). *Viagem ao Brasil.* Translated by Edgard Sussekind de Mendonça and Flavio Poppe de Figueiredo. 2nd ed. São Paulo: Compania Editora Nacional, 1958.

Maxwell, Kenneth R. *Conflicts and Conspiracies: Brazil and Portugal, 1750–1808.* Cambridge, Eng.: At the University Press, 1973.

Mello, Evaldo Cabral de. *O norte agrário e o império.* Rio: Editora Nova Fronteira-Memoria Instituto Nacional do Livro, 1984.

Mello, Barão Homem de. "Conselheiro Paulino José Soares de Souza." *Revista do Instituto Historico e Geografico Brasileiro* 66 (1905): 71–79.

Melo, Jerônimo Martiniano Figueira de. *Crônica da rebelião praieira 1848–1849.* 2nd ed. Brasília: Editora Universidade de Brasília, 1978.

Memoria sobre a nobreza no Brasil, por hum brasileiro. Rio de Janeiro: Typ. da Associação do Despertador, 1841.

Menezes, Paulo Braga de. *As constituições outorgadas ao Império do Brasil e ao Reino de Portugal.* Rio de Janeiro: Arquivo Nacional, 1964.

Mont'Alegre, Omer. *Capital e capitalismo no Brasil.* Rio de Janeiro: Editora Expressão e Cultura, 1972.

_____. *Um século na história do açúcar: Brasil-Cuba 1760/1860,* separata de Brasil Açucareiro (June 1969). Rio de Janeiro: Instituto do Açúcar e Álcool, 1969.

Monteiro, Hamilton de Mattos. *A crise agrária e luta de classes (o nordeste brasileiro entre 1850 a 1889).* Brasília: Horizonte Editora, 1980.

Monteiro, Tobias. *Historia do imperio.* 2 vols. Rio de Janeiro: F. Briguiet e Cia., 1938–39.

Moore, Jr., Barrington. *Social Origins of Dictatorship and Democracy: Lord and Peasant in the Making of the Modern World.* Boston: Beacon Press, 1966.

Mota, Carlos G., org. *1822: dimensões.* São Paulo: Editora Perspectiva, 1972.

Moulder, Francis V. *Japan, China, and the Modern World Economy: Toward a Reinterpretation of East Asian Development, ca. 1600 to ca. 1918.* Cambridge, Eng.: At the University Press, 1977.

Moura, Carlos Eugênio Marcondes de. *O Visconde de Guaratinguetá: Um titular do café no vale do Paraíba.* São Paulo: SCCT, 1976.

Moura, Francisco Amyntas de Carvalho. *Ensaios economicos e apreciações praticas sobre o estado financeiro do Brazil.* Rio de Janeiro: Imprensa Nacional, 1885.

Nabuco, Carolina. *A vida de Joaquim Nabuco.* 3rd ed. Rio de Janeiro: Americedit., 1943.

Nabuco, Joaquim. *Um estadista do império.* Volume único. Rio de Janeiro: Editora Nova Aguilar, 1975.

Naro, Nancy Priscilla. "The 1848 Praieira Revolt in Brazil." Ph.D. Dissertation, University of Chicago, 1981.

Oliveira, Luiz da Silva Pereira. *Privilegios da nobreza, e fidalguia de Portugal.* Lisboa: Na Nova Officina de João Rodrigues Neves, 1806.

Palmer, Francis Beaufort. *Peerage Law in England.* New York: Garland Publishing, Inc., 1978.

Pang, Eul-Soo. *Bahia in the First Brazilian Republic: Coronelismo and Oligarchies, 1889–1934.* Gainesville: University Presses of Florida, 1979.

_____. *O Engenho Central do Bom Jardim na economia baiana: alguns aspectos de sua história 1875–1891.* Rio de Janeiro: Arquivo Nacional and Instituto Histórico e Geográfico Brasileiro, 1979.

_____. "Modernization and Slavocracy in Nineteenth-Century Brazil." *Journal of Interdisciplinary History* 9:4 (Spring 1979): 667–88.

_____. "Tecnologia e escravocracia no Brasil durante o século XIX: uma reinterpretação." *Anais do Museu Paulista* 30 (1980/1981): 55–134.

Pang, Eul-Soo, and Ron L. Seckinger. "The Mandarins of Imperial Brazil." *Comparative Studies in Society and History* 14:2 (March 1972): 215–44.

Dom Pedro II. *Diário da viagem ao norte do Brasil.* Annotated by Lourenço Luiz Lacombe. Salvador: Livraria Progresso Editora, 1959.

Peixoto, Manoel Rodrigues. *A lavoura em Campos e a baixa do assucar.* Campos: Typographia do Monitor Campista, 1874.

—————. *Colonisação.* Rio de Janeiro: Typographia da Gazeta da Noticias, 1880.

Petrone, Maria Thereza Schorer. *A lavoura canavieira em São Paulo: Expansão e declínio (1765–1851).* São Paulo: DIFEL, 1968.

—————. *O Barão de Iguape: Um empresário da época da independência.* São Paulo: Companhia Editora Nacional, 1976.

Pinho, (José) Wanderley (de Araújo). *Cotegipe e seu tempo: primeira phase 1815–1867.* São Paulo: Companhia Editora Nacional, 1937.

—————. *Historia de um engenho do Recôncavo, 1552–1944.* Rio de Janeiro: Livraria Editora Zelio Valverde, 1946.

—————. *Politica e politicos no imperio: Contribuições documentaes.* Rio de Janeiro: Imprensa Nacional, 1930.

—————. *Salões e damas do segundo reinado.* 4th ed. São Paulo: Livraria Martins Editora, 1970.

Pinto, Albano da Silveira. *Resenha das familias titulares e grandes de Portugal,* 2 vols. Lisboa: Empreza Editora de Francisco Arthur da Silva, 1885.

Pita, Sebastião da Rocha. *História da América Portuguesa.* 3rd ed. Bahia: Livraria Progresso Editora, 1950.

Poliano, Luis Marques. *Ordens honorificas no Brasil: historia, organização, padrões, legislação.* Rio de Janeiro: Imprensa Nacional, 1943.

Porto, Luis de Almeida Nogueira. "Bananal, muito passado e algum presente." *Revista do Instituto Histórico e Geográfico Brasileiro* 308 (June–September 1975): 115–22.

—————. "Revelações de antigos inventários (Bananal, 1822–1882)." *Revista do Instituto Histórico e Geográfico Brasileiro* 308 (June–September 1975): 123–32.

Prado, J. F. de Almeida. *D. João VI e o ínicio da classe dirigente do Brasil 1815–1889 (depoimento de um pintor austríaco no Rio de Janeiro).* São Paulo: Companhia Editora Nacional, 1968.

Prado Júnior, Caio. *Evolução política do Brasil e outros estudos.* 4th ed. São Paulo: Brasiliense, 1963.

Queiroz, Maria Isaura Pereira de. *O mandonismo local na vida política brasileira e outros ensaios.* São Paulo: Editora Alfa-Omega, 1976.

Ramos, Guerreiro. *A crise do poder no Brasil (problemas da revolução nacional brasileira).* Rio de Janeiro: Zahar, 1961.

Rangel, Alberto. *Marginados: anotações às cartas de D. Pedro I a D. Domitila.* Rio de Janeiro: Arquivo Nacional, 1974.

—————. *Dom Pedro I e a Marqueza de Santos à vista de cartas íntimas e de outros documentos públicos e particulares.* 3rd ed. São Paulo: Editora Brasiliense, 1969.

Rebouças, Antonio Pereira. *Recordações da vida parlamentar do advogado Antonio Pereira Rebouças: moral, jurisprudencia, politica e liberdade constitucional.* 2 vols. Rio de Janeiro: Typ. Universal Laemmert, 1870.

Reyes, Manuel Martins do Couto. "Memoria de Santa Cruz: Seu estabelecimento e economia primitiva, seus sucessos mais notaveis, continuados do tempo da extinção dos denominados Jesuitas, seus fundadores, até o anno de 1804." *Revista do Instituto Historico e Geografico Brasileiro* 5 (1843): 143–86.

Rheingantz, Carlos G. *Titulares do império.* Rio de Janeiro: Arquivo Nacional, 1960.

———. "O título de Visconde com grandeza de Serro Azul: uma falsificação inqualificável." *Mensário do Arquivo Nacional* (February 1975): 3–8.

Ribeiro, Maria Laura. "O testamento do Conselheiro João Alfredo Correa de Oliveira." *Anais do Museu Histórico Nacional* 19 (1968): 140–64.

Ribeynolles, Charles. *Brasil pitoresco.* 3 in 2 vols. 2nd ed. São Paulo: Biblioteca Histórica Brasileira, 1976.

Ricardo, Cassiano. *Marcha para oeste (a influência da "bandeira" na formação social e política do Brasil)* 2 vols. Rio de Janeiro: Livraria José Olympio Editora, 1959.

Roberts, Panfield. *The Quest for Security, 1715–1740.* New York. Harper & Row, Publishers, 1963.

Rodrigues, José Honório. *A Assembleia Constituinte de 1823.* Petrópolis: Editora A Voz, 1974.

———, org. *Atas do Conselho de Estado.* 9 vols. Brasília: Senado Federal, 1973.

Roure, Agenor de. "Politica economica de D. João VI." *Anais do Congresso Internacional de Historia da America* 6 (1922): 625–98.

Russell-Wood, A. J. R. *Fidalgos and Philanthropists: The Santa Casa da Misericordia of Bahia, 1550–1755.* Berkeley: University of California Press, 1968.

———, ed. *From Colony to Nation: Essays on the Independence of Brazil.* Baltimore: Johns Hopkins University Press, 1975.

Ruy Affonso. *A primeira revolução social brasileira (1798).* 2nd ed. São Paulo: Companhia Editora Nacional, 1978.

Saint Hilaire, Auguste de. *Segunda Viagem do Rio de Janeiro a Minas Gerais e a São Paulo (1822).* Translated by Affonso de Taunay. São Paulo: Companhia Editora Nacional, 1932.

———. *A segunda viagem a São Paulo e outro histórico da Província de São Paulo.* São Paulo: Companhia Editora Nacional, 1954.

Sarfatti, Magali. *Spanish Bureaucratic-Patrimonialism in America.* Berkeley: Institute of International Studies, University of California, 1966.

Sawyer, Frederic H. *Estudos sobre a industria assucareira no estado de S. Paulo comparada com a dos demais paizes.* São Paulo: Typographia Brazil de Carlos Gerke e Rothchid, 1905.

Schwartz, Stuart B. *Sovereignty and Society in Colonial Brazil: The High Court of Bahia and Its Judges, 1609–1751.* Berkeley: University of California Press, 1973.

Silva, Conselheiro Francisco Gomes da (O Chalaça). *Memórias.* 2nd ed. Rio de Janeiro: Editora Souza, 1959.

Silva, J. M. Pereira da. *Historia do Brazil durante a menoridade de d. Pedro II (1831–1840).* 2nd ed. Rio de Janeiro: B. L. Garnier, 1888.

—————. *Historia da fundação do imperio brazileiro*. 7 vols. Rio de Janeiro: B. L. Garnier, Editor, 1864–68.

Silva, José Carneiro da. *Memoria topographica e historica sobre os Campos dos Goitacazes, com huma noticia breve de suas producções, e commercio offerecida ao muito alto e muito poderoso Rey e Senhor Nosso D. João VI*. Rio de Janeiro: n.p., 1819.

Simonsen, Roberto C. *História econômica do Brasil (1500/1820)*, 4th ed. São Paulo: Editora Companhia Nacional, 1962.

Smith de Vasconcellos, Rodolpho Smith de Vasconcellos, 1° Barão, and Jayme Luiz Smith de Vasconcellos, 2° Barão Smith de Vasconcellos. *Archivo nobiliarchico brasileiro*. Lausanne, Switzerland: La Concorde, 1918.

Sousa, Octavio Tarquínio de. *História dos fundadores do império*. 10 vols. 3rd ed. Rio de Janeiro: Livraria José Olympio Editora, 1957–58.

Souza, Alvaro Paulino Soares de. *Três brasileiros ilustres*. Rio de Janeiro: Typographia Leuzinger, 1923.

Souza, José Antônio Soares de. *A vida do Visconde do Uruguay (1807–1866) (Paulino José Soares de Souza)*. São Paulo: Companhia Editora Nacional, 1944.

—————. "O Barão de Vila Bela e a história de uma família." *Revista do Instituto Histórico e Geográfico Brasileiro* 294 (1972): 179–89.

Spalding, Walter. *A revolução farroupilha*. 2nd ed. São Paulo: Companhia Editora Nacional, 1980.

Spix, J. B. von, and C. F. P. von Martius. *Através da Bahia*, excerptos da obra *Reise in Brasilien*. Translated by Manuel A. Pirajá da Silva and Paulo Wolf. Bahia: Imprensa Official do Estado, 1916.

Spring, David, ed. *European Landed Elites in the Nineteenth Century*. Baltimore: Johns Hopkins University Press, 1977.

Stein, Stanley J. *Vassouras: A Brazilian Coffee County, 1850–1900*. Cambridge, Mass.: Harvard University Press, 1957.

Stone, Lawrence. *The Crisis of the Aristocracy, 1558–1641*. Abridged ed. New York: Oxford University Press, 1967.

—————. *The Family, Sex, and Marriage in England, 1500–1800*. Abridged ed. New York: Harper & Row, Publishers, 1979.

Sweigart, Joseph Earl. "Financing and Marketing Brazilian Export Agriculture: The Coffee Factors of Rio de Janeiro, 1850–1888." Ph.D. Dissertation, University of Texas, Austin, 1980.

Taunay, Affonso (Afonso) de E. *A câmara dos deputados sob o império*. São Paulo: Imprensa Oficial do Estado, 1950.

—————. "Faustos fazendeiros." *Mensario do Jornal do Commercio* 4:1 (October 1938): 81–84.

—————. *Historia do café no Brasil*, 15 vols. Rio de Janeiro: Departamento Nacional do Café, 1939–43.

—————. "O nobiliario do primeiro imperio." *Mensario do Jornal do Commercio* 1:3 (March 1938): 1–5.

—————. "Representantes do centro." *Mensario do Jornal do Commercio* 1:2 (August 1940): 399–403.

_____. "Vistia a Dom Pedro II (1886)." *Mensario do Jornal do Commercio* 27:3 (September 1944): 573–76.

"Titulares do imperio (ampliações e retificações). *Annuario Genealogico Brasileiro* 7 (1945): 225–33.

"Titulos usados no Brasil e concedidos no extrangeiro." *Annuario Genealogico Brasileiro* 1 (1939): 209–28.

Torres, Joáo Camillo de Oliveira. *A democracia coroada: teoria política do império do Brasil*. 2nd ed. Petrópolis: Editora A Voz, 1964.

Uricoechea, Fernando. *O minotauro imperial*. São Paulo: DIFEL, 1978.

_____. *The Patrimonial Foundations of the Brazilian Bureaucratic State*. Berkeley: University of California Press, 1980.

Uruguai, José Paulino Soares de Sousa, Visconde do. *Ensaio sobre o direito administrativo*. Rio de Janeiro: n.p., 1960.

Valle, Álvaro, org. *José Antônio Saraiva (Conselheiro Saraiva): Discursos parlamentares*. Brasília: Senado Federal, 1978.

Vasconcellos, Bernardo Pereira de. *Cartas aos senhores eleitores da provincia de Minas Gerais*. 2nd ed. Rio de Janeiro: F. Rodrigues de Paiva, 1899.

Verger, Pierre. *Flux et reflux de la traite de nègres entre le Golfe de Benin et Bahia de Todos os Santos du dix-septième au dix-neuvième siècle*. Paris: Mouton, 1968.

Vianna, Francisco José de Oliveira. *Instituições políticas brasileiras*. 2 vols. Rio de Janeiro: Livraria José Olympio Editora, 1949.

Vianna, Marfa Barbosa. "Antiga Fazenda Real de Santa Cruz—um pouco de história e lendas." *Anais do Museu Histórico Nacional* 15 (1965): 267–75.

Vilhena, Luís dos Santos. *A Bahia no século XVIII*. 3 vols. Bahia: Editora Itapuã, 1969.

Wallerstein, Immanuel. *The Capitalist World-Economy*. New York: Cambridge University Press, 1979.

_____. *The Modern World-System. Capitalist Agriculture and the Origins of the European World-Economy in the Sixteenth Century*. New York: Academic Press, 1974.

_____. *The Modern World System II: Mercantilism and the Consolidation of the European World-Economy, 1600–1750*. New York: Academic Press, 1980.

Wanderley, Maria de Nazareth Baudel. *Capital e propriedade fundiária*. Rio: Paz e Terra, 1978.

Weber, Max. *Economy and Society*. Edited by Guenther Roth and Claus Wittich. 2 vols. Berkeley: University of California Press, 1978.

_____. *The Theory of Social and Economic Organization*. Translated by H. M. Henderson and Talcott Parsons. New York: A Free Press Paperback, 1964.

Werneck, Francisco Klors. *Historia e genealogia fluminense*. Rio de Janeiro: Edição do Autor, 1947.

Wiarda, Howard J. *Corporatism and Development: The Portuguese Experiment*. Amherst: University of Massachusetts Press, 1977.

Wiederspahn, Oscar. *Companha de Ituzaingo*. Rio de Janeiro: Biblioteca do Exército, 1961.

Williams, Mary Wilhelmine. *Dom Pedro the Magnanimous: Second Emperor of Brazil.* 2nd ed. New York: Octagon Books, 1966 [1937].

Winkler, J. T. "Corporatism." *Archives Européennes de Sociologie* 17:1 (1976): 100–136.

Wittfogel, Karl A. *Oriental Despotism.* New Haven: Yale University Press, 1957.

Zaluar, Augusto Emílio. *Peregrinação pela Província de São Paulo (1860–1861).* São Paulo: Editora Itatiaia, 1975.

Index